Bishops, Clerks, and Diocesan Governance in Thirteenth-Century England

This book investigates how bishops wielded reward and punishment to control their administrative subordinates in thirteenth-century England. Bishops had few effective avenues available to them for disciplining their clerks, and they rarely pursued the ones they had, preferring to secure their clerks' service and loyalty through rewards. The chief reward was the benefice, often granted for life. Episcopal administrators' security of tenure in these benefices, however, made them free agents, allowing them to transfer from diocese to diocese or even leave administration altogether; these clerks did not constitute a standing episcopal civil service. This tenuous bureaucratic relationship made the personal relationship between bishop and clerk more important. Ultimately, many bishops communicated in terms of friendship with their administrators, who responded with expressions of devotion. Michael Burger's study brings together ecclesiastical, social, legal, and cultural history, producing the first synoptic study of thirteenth-century English diocesan administration in decades. His research provides an ecclesiastical counterpoint to numerous studies of bastard feudalism in secular contexts.

Michael Burger is Professor of History and Dean of the School of Liberal Arts at Auburn University at Montgomery. He is the author of *The Shaping of the West: From Antiquity to the Enlightenment* (2008) and the editor of the two-volume *Sources for the History of Western Civilization* (2003). His articles have appeared in *Historical Research* and *Mediaeval Studies*, among other journals.

Bishops, Clerks, and Diocesan Governance in Thirteenth-Century England

Reward and Punishment

MICHAEL BURGER
Auburn University at Montgomery

CAMBRIDGE UNIVERSITY PRESS
Cambridge, New York, Melbourne, Madrid, Cape Town,
Singapore, São Paulo, Delhi, Mexico City

Cambridge University Press
32 Avenue of the Americas, New York, NY 10013-2473, USA

www.cambridge.org
Information on this title: www.cambridge.org/9781107022140

© Michael Burger 2012

This publication is in copyright. Subject to statutory exception
and to the provisions of relevant collective licensing agreements,
no reproduction of any part may take place without the written
permission of Cambridge University Press.

First published 2012

Printed in the United States of America

A catalog record for this publication is available from the British Library.

Library of Congress Cataloging in Publication data
Burger, Michael, 1962–
Bishops, clerks, and diocesan governance in thirteenth-century
England : reward and punishment / Michael Burger.
p. cm.
Includes bibliographical references and index.
ISBN 978-1-107-02214-0 (hardback)
1. England – Church history – 1066–1485. 2. Benefices, Ecclesiastical –
England – History. 3. Church polity. 4. Church discipline. I. Title.
BR750.B87 2012
282'.4209022–dc23   2012012498

ISBN 978-1-107-02214-0 Hardback

Cambridge University Press has no responsibility for the persistence or accuracy of URLS
for external or third-party Internet Web sites referred to in this publication and does not
guarantee that any content on such Web sites is, or will remain, accurate or appropriate.

For Miriam, with infinite love and gratitude

Contents

Acknowledgments	page ix
List of Abbreviations	xi
Note on Citations	xvii

PART I   THE PROBLEM

1.	Introduction	3
2.	Dangers of Service	13

PART II   REWARDS AND PUNISHMENTS

3.	The Benefice for Service and as Benefit	23
	Benefices and Service	23
	The Benefits of Benefices	30
4.	Benefices and Security of Tenure	40
	Law and Sentiment	43
	Testing the Limits of Security of Tenure	52
	Bishops, Archbishops, Popes, and Benefices: Appeals	64
	Getting around Security of Tenure: Sequestration	70
	Archdeacons	72
	Getting around Security of Tenure: Commendation	74
	Incapacity	78
5.	Pensions	80
	Pensions de Camera *in General*	90
	Simple Pensions versus Pensions in Lieu of Benefices, and Pensions versus Benefices	95
6.	Other Rewards	110
	Uses of Episcopal Authority	110

Uses of Papal Authority   116
Enhancing Benefices   120
Secular Lands and Favors   124
Simple Gifts   126
Fees, Bribes, and Extortion   127

7. Punishment   136
Material Penalties: Bonds   136
Spiritual Penalties: Excommunication   141
Humiliation   146
Prison   147
Oaths   148
Social Exile   158

PART III   CONSEQUENCES

8. Patronage Hunger   169
Acquiring Advowsons   170
Collation by Lapse   173
Episcopal Pressure and Control of Process   175
Creating Benefices and a Move for Reform   182

9. Continuity and Discontinuity of Service   186
Continuity and Discontinuity in the Diocese of Lincoln   190
Other Dioceses   200
Some Observations   208

10. Affection and Devotion   210
Expressions of Affection and Devotion   211
Affection and Devotion in Action   224

11. Conclusions: Culture and Context   239

Appendix 1: Handlist of Pensions Granted
  by Thirteenth-Century Bishops   251
Appendix 2: Lay Servants Named as Legatees
  in Episcopal Wills   260
Sources Cited   265
Index   289

Acknowledgments

I had set out to write a book on bishops' attempts to exercise power over distance in thirteenth-century England. A necessary preliminary was an assessment of how those bishops rewarded and punished their clerks: a chapter or two, I thought. But that assessment demanded more attention; the result is this book. This circumstance helps explain why it has taken such a long time to write. How long the book took to write in turn helps explain why so many debts have been incurred in the writing. It is good at last to be able to offer thanks.

All historians depend on archivists and librarians. I am grateful for the cooperation of staff at the Bodleian Library, the British Library, the archives of Christ Church, Canterbury, the archives of the dean and chapter of Hereford Cathedral, the library and archives at Lambeth Palace, the Herefordshire Archive Service, the Lincolnshire Archives Office, the United Kingdom's National Archives, the West Sussex Record Office, and the Worcestershire Record Office. Most of this book was written at Mississippi University for Women, whose indefatigable interlibrary loan librarian, Gail Gunter, was indispensable. I would also like to thank the interlibrary loan staff at my new academic home, Auburn University at Montgomery, for their invariable cooperation with my requests. Professor Thomas Richardson, of Mississippi University for Women, also kindly provided me access to scholarly resources. Nicholas Vincent generously made available to me Jeanne Stones's preliminary transcripts of Ralph Neville's hard-to-read correspondence. David Smith, then director of the University of York's Borthwick Institute, gave me access to the Institute's collection of microfilms of manuscripts and a comfortable place to work as I labored on my dissertation, some of which ultimately found its way into this book.

Three institutions generously supported the research necessary to write this book. Mississippi University for Women made several small grants and also provided a sabbatical leave during which I made progress in reading sources. A summer stipend from the National Endowment for the Humanities provided critical help. Finally, I am grateful to Auburn University at Montgomery for support at the end.

Various scholars have also helped me with different parts of this book over the years, probably more than I will recall now. The late Jeffrey Denton gave me information concerning the *taxatio* of Nicholas IV and concerning archdeacons of the diocese of Coventry and Lichfield. Marie Lovatt helped me navigate part of the career of Archbishop Geoffrey Plantagenet of York. Sue Ridyard advised me regarding one of Thomas Cantilupe's clerks. David Smith offered guidance on abbatial registers and more. Nicholas Vincent rendered me one of the biggest favors one historian can do another by directing me to a new source.

I have also received helpful criticism. Marty Claussen, Sharon Farmer, Richard Helmholz, Warren Hollister, Paul Hyams, Sears McGee, David Smith, Richard Southern, Emily Tabuteau, and Scott Waugh commented years ago on a dissertation chapter in which I first laid out some of the ideas that appear in this book. Much more recently, David Smith and Nicholas Vincent took time to read and comment on the book in draft. Anonymous readers from the Cambridge University Press generously undertook that work too. Various papers presented at the Annual Congress on Medieval Studies at Western Michigan University and the Southern Conference on British Studies also led to this book; I am grateful to those audiences and commentators, in particular Robert Berkhofer, who offered comments and asked questions that moved the work along. This assemblage of critics has saved me from numerous mistakes, large and small. I am solely responsible for those that remain.

Emily Spangler, my first editor at Cambridge University Press, took an interest in the book, and Eric Crahan kindly took on the project at a later point. Patterson Lamb saved me from various errors at the copyediting stage, while two enthusiastic students, Antonio Byrd and Lacy Young, helped with page proofs, for which I hope readers will be as thankful as I am.

Finally, I am grateful to my wife, who has patiently watched for many years as this book took shape and who offered last-minute encouragement on a point of detail. I dedicate it to her with gratitude, and not just for her tolerance of my obsession with dead bishops and their dead clerks.

Abbreviations

Acta of Hugh of Wells	*The Acta of Hugh of Wells, Bishop of Lincoln 1209–1235*. Ed. David M. Smith. Lincoln Record Society 88. Woodbridge. 2000.
Acta Stephani Langton	*Acta Stephani Langton Cantuariensis Archiepiscopi A.D. 1207–1128*. Ed. Kathleen Major. Canterbury and York Society 50. Oxford. 1950.
Annales Monastici	*Annales Monastici*. Ed. Henry Richards Luard. Rolls Series. London. 1864–9.
BL	British Library.
Calendar of the Manuscripts of the Dean and Chapter of Wells	*Calendar of the Manuscripts of the Dean and Chapter of Wells*. Ed. W. H. B. Bird and W. P. Baildon. Royal Commission on Historical Manuscripts. London. 1907–14.
Councils and Synods	*Councils and Synods with Other Documents Relating to the English Church, II, A.D. 1205–1313*. Ed. F. M. Powicke and C. R. Cheney. Oxford. 1964.
CPL	*Calendar of Entries in the Papal Registers Relating to Great Britain and Ireland*. Ed. W. H. Bliss et al. London. 1893–.
EEA I: Lincoln	*English Episcopal Acta I: Lincoln 1067–1185*. Ed. David M. Smith. Oxford. 1980.
EEA II: Canterbury	*English Episcopal Acta II: Canterbury 1162–1190*. Ed. C. R. Cheney and B. E. A. Jones. Corrected edition. Oxford. 1991.

EEA III: Canterbury	*English Episcopal Acta III: Canterbury 1193–1205.* Ed. C. R. Cheney and Eric John. Corrected edition. Oxford. 1991.
EEA IV: Lincoln	*English Episcopal Acta IV: Lincoln 1186–1206.* Ed. David M. Smith. Oxford. 1986.
EEA VI: Norwich	*English Episcopal Acta VI: Norwich 1070–1214.* Ed. Christopher Harper-Bill. Oxford. 1990.
EEA VII: Hereford	*English Episcopal Acta VII: Hereford 1079–1234.* Ed. Julia Barrow. Oxford. 1993.
EEA IX: Winchester	*English Episcopal Acta IX: Winchester 1205–1238.* Ed. Nicholas Vincent. Oxford. 1994.
EEA X: Bath and Wells	*English Episcopal Acta X: Bath and Wells 1061–1205.* Ed. Frances M. R. Ramesey. Oxford. 1995.
EEA XI: Exeter	*English Episcopal Acta XI: Exeter 1046–1184.* Ed. Frank Barlow. Oxford. 1996.
EEA XII: Exeter	*English Episcopal Acta XII: Exeter 1186–1257.* Ed. Frank Barlow. Oxford. 1996.
EEA 13: Worcester	*English Episcopal Acta 13: Worcester 1218–1268.* Ed. Philippa M. Hoskin. Oxford. 1997.
EEA 17: Coventry and Lichfield	*English and Episcopal Acta 17: Coventry and Lichfield 1183–1208.* Ed. M. J. Franklin. Oxford. 1998.
EEA 18: Salisbury	*English Episcopal Acta 18: Salisbury 1078–1217.* Ed. B. R. Kemp. Oxford. 1999.
EEA 19: Salisbury	*English Episcopal Acta 19: Salisbury 1217–1228.* Ed. B. R. Kemp. Oxford. 2000.
EEA 21: Norwich	*English Episcopal Acta 21: Norwich 1215–1243.* Ed. Christopher Harper-Bill. Oxford. 2000.
EEA 22: Chichester	*English Episcopal Acta 22: Chichester 1215–1253.* Ed. Philippa M. Hoskin. Oxford. 2001.
EEA 23: Chichester	*English Episcopal Acta 23: Chichester 1254–1305.* Ed. Philippa M. Hoskin. Oxford. 2001.
EEA 24: Durham	*English Episcopal Acta 24: Durham 1153–1195.* Ed. M. G. Snape. Oxford. 2002.
EEA 25: Durham	*English Episcopal Acta 25: Durham 1196–1237.* Ed. M. G. Snape. Oxford. 2002.
EEA 27: York	*English Episcopal Acta 27: York 1189–1212.* Ed. Marie Lovatt. Oxford. 2004.

EEA 29: Durham	*English Episcopal Acta 29: Durham 1241–1283*. Ed. Philippa M. Hoskin. Oxford. 2005.
EEA 30: Carlisle	*English Episcopal Acta 30: Carlisle 1133–1292*. Ed. David M. Smith. Oxford. 2005.
EEA 32: Norwich	*English Episcopal Acta 32: Norwich 1244–1266*. Ed. Christopher Harper-Bill. Oxford. 2007.
EEA 34: Worcester	*English Episcopal Acta 34: Worcester 1186–1218*. Ed. Mary G. Cheney, David Smith, Christopher Brooke, and Philippa Hoskin. Oxford. 2008.
EEA 35: Hereford	*English Episcopal Acta 35: Hereford 1234–1275*. Ed. Julia Barrow. Oxford. 2009.
Grosseteste, *Epistolae*	*Roberti Grosseteste Episcopi Quondam Lincolniensis Epistolae*. Ed. H. R. Luard. RS. London. 1861.
LAO	Lincolnshire Archives Office.
LN Bath and Wells	John le Neve, *Fasti Ecclesiae Anglicanae 1066–1300 VII: Bath and Wells*. 3rd ed. Compiled by Diana Greenway. London. 2001.
LN Chichester	John le Neve, *Fasti Ecclesiae Anglicanae 1066–1300 V: Chichester*. 3rd ed. Compiled by Diana Greenway. London. 1996.
LN Exeter	John le Neve, *Fasti Ecclesiae Anglicanae 1066–1300 X: Exeter*. 3rd ed. Compiled by Diana Greenway. London. 2005.
LN Hereford	John le Neve, *Fasti Ecclesiae Anglicanae 1066–1300 VIII: Hereford*. 3rd ed. Compiled by Julia Barrow. London. 2002.
LN Lincoln	John le Neve, *Fasti Ecclesiae Anglicanae 1066–1300 III: Lincoln*. 3rd ed. Compiled by Diana Greenway. London. 1977.
LN London	John le Neve, *Fasti Ecclesiae Anglicanae 1066–1300 I: St. Paul's, London*. 3rd ed. Compiled by Diana Greenway. London. 1968.
LN Monastic Cathedrals	John le Neve, *Fasti Ecclesiae Anglicanae 1066–1300 II: Monastic Cathedrals*. 3rd ed. Compiled by Diana E. Greenway. London. 1971.
LN Salisbury	John le Neve, *Fasti Ecclesiae Anglicanae 1066–1300 IV: Salisbury*. 3rd ed. Compiled by Diana Greenway. London. 1991.

LN York	John le Neve, *Fasti Ecclesiae Anglicanae 1066–1300 VI: York*. 3rd ed. Compiled by Diana E. Greenway. London. 1999.
Pecham, *Epistolae*.	*Registrum Epistolarum Fratris Johannis Peckham, Archiepiscopi Cantuariensis*. Ed. C. T. Martin. Rolls Series. London. 1882–5.
Reg. Bronscombe	*The Register of Walter Bronscombe, Bishop of Exeter, 1258–1280*. Ed. O. F. Robinson. Canterbury and York Society 82, 87, 94. Woodbridge. 1995–2003.
Reg. Burghersh	*The Registers of Bishop Henry Burghersh 1320–1342*. Ed. Nicholas Bennett. Lincoln Record Society. 87, 90. Woodbridge. 1999–.
Reg. Cantilupe	*The Register of Thomas de Cantilupe, Bishop of Hereford (A.D. 1275–1282)*. Ed. R. G. Griffiths with an introduction by W. W. Capes. Canterbury and York Society 2. London. 1907.
Reg. Gainsborough	*The Register of William de Geynesburgh, Bishop of Worcester, 1302–1307*. Ed. J. W. Willis Bund with an introduction by R. A. Wilson. Worcestershire Historical Society 22. Oxford. 1907–22.
Reg. Gandavo	*Registrum Simonis de Gandavo, Diocesis Sarisberiensis, A.D. 1297–1315*. Ed. C. T. Flower and M. C. B. Dawes. Canterbury and York Society 40–41. Oxford. 1934.
Reg. Giffard of Worcester	*Episcopal Registers, Diocese of Worcester: Register of Bishop Godfrey Giffard, September 23rd 1268 to August 15th 1301*. Ed. J. W. Bund. Worcestershire Historical Society 15. Oxford. 1898–1902.
Reg. Giffard of York	*The Register of Walter Giffard, Lord Archbishop of York, 1266–1279*. Ed. W. Brown. Surtees Society 109. Durham. 1904.
Reg. Halton	*The Register of John de Halton, Bishop of Carlisle A.D. 1292–1324*. Ed. W. N. Thompson. Canterbury and York Society 12–13. London. 1913.

Reg. Langton	*The Register of Walter Langton, Bishop of Coventry and Lichfield, 1296–1321.* Ed. J. B. Hughes. Canterbury and York Society 91, 97. Woodbridge. 2001–7.
Reg. Martival	*The Registers of Roger Martival, Bishop of Salisbury, 1315–1330.* Ed. K. Edwards, C. R. Elrington, S. Reynolds, and D. Owen. Canterbury and York Society 55–59, 68. Oxford and Torquay. 1959–75.
Reg. Pecham	*The Register of John Pecham, Archbishop of Canterbury, 1279–1292.* Ed. F. N. Davis, D. L. Douie, et al. Canterbury and York Society 64–65. Torquay. 1908–69.
Reg. Pontissara	*Registrum Johannis de Pontissara, Episcopi Wintoniensis, A.D. MCCLXXXI–MCCCIV.* Ed. C. Deedes. Canterbury and York Society 19, 30. London. 1915–24.
Reg. Quivil	*The Registers of Walter Bronscombe (A.D. 1257–1280), and Peter Quivil (A.D. 1280–1291), Bishops of Exeter, With Some Records of the Episcopate of Bishop Thomas de Bytton (A.D. 1292–1307); also the Taxation of Pope Nicholas IV, A.D. 1291.* Ed. F. C. Hingeston-Randolph. London and Exeter. 1889.
Reg. Reynolds of Worcester	*The Register of Walter Reynolds, Bishop of Worcester, 1308–1313.* Ed. R. A. Wilson. Worcestershire Historical Society 39. London. 1927.
Reg. Romeyn	*The Register of John Le Romeyn, Lord Archbishop of York, 1286–1296.* Ed. W. Brown. Surtees Society 123, 128. Durham. 1913–17.
Reg. Swinfield	*Registrum Ricardi de Swinfield, Episcopi Herefordensis, A.D. MCCLXXXIII–MCCCXVIII.* Ed. W. W. Capes. Canterbury and York Society 6. London. 1909.
Reg. Wickwane	*The Register of William Wickwane, Lord Archbishop of York, 1279–1285.* Ed. W. Brown. Surtees Society 114. Durham. 1907.

Reg. Winchelsey	*Registrum Roberti Winchelsey Cantuariensis Archiepiscopi.* Ed. Rose Graham. Canterbury and York Society 51, 52. Oxford. 1952–6.
Rolls and Reg. Sutton	*The Rolls and Register of Bishop Oliver Sutton, 1280–1299.* Ed. R. M. T. Hill. Lincoln Record Society 39, 43, 48, 52, 60, 64, 69, 76. Hereford, Lincoln, Woodbridge. 1948–86.
Rot. Gravesend	*Rotuli Ricardi Gravesend, Diocesis Lincolniensis.* Ed. F. N. Davis, with additions by C. W. Foster and Alexander Hamilton Thompson. Canterbury and York Society 31. Oxford. 1925.
Rot. Gray	*The Register, or Rolls, of Walter Gray, Lord Archbishop of York: With Appendices of Illustrative Documents.* Ed. J. Raine. Surtees Society 56. Durham. 1872.
Rot. Grosseteste	*Rotuli Roberti Grosseteste, Episcopi Lincolniensis, A.D. MCCXXXV-MCCLIII.* Ed. F. N. Davis. Lincoln Record Society 11. Horncastle. 1914.
Rot. Welles	*Rotuli Hugonis de Welles, Episcopi Lincolniensis, A.D. MCCIX–MCCXXXV.* Ed. W. P. W. Phillimore, F. N. Davis, et al. Canterbury and York Society 1, 3–4. London. 1907–9.
RS	Rolls Series.
Swinfield Roll	*A Roll of the Household Expenses of Richard de Swinfield, Bishop of Hereford, during Part of the Years 1289 and 1290.* Ed. John Webb. Camden Society. First Series 59. London. 1854–5. I.
TNA	The National Archives (London).
WRO	Worcestershire Record Office.

Note on Citations

The historian of thirteenth-century English bishops is fortunate in that the bishops' registers of the thirteenth century have been edited, at least in calendar form. In some cases, however, evidence – appearing as additional information or occasionally as correction – has to come from the manuscript instead. I have cited manuscript in such cases only.

The manuscript of the register of Godfrey Giffard, bishop of Worcester (WRO, Rf.x716.093 BA 2648/1(i)) presents a difficulty in citation. Its foliation is marked in Roman numbers and by a later hand in Arabic numbers. Unfortunately, these numerations are not always consistent. Moreover, some of the folios are out of order, which probably explains why a third hand consecutively paginated the manuscript throughout in its current order. Where the manuscript is cited, I have given the Arabic folio number followed by the page number.

PART I

THE PROBLEM

I

Introduction

"You've always been such a sweet, innocent-looking creature, Jane, and all the time underneath nothing has ever surprised you, you always believe the worst."
"The worst is so often true," murmured Miss Marple.
– Agatha Christie, *They Do It with Mirrors*

On reading *Crime and Punishment*, my wife remarked that a better title would have been *Crime and Not Enough Punishment*. Some readers of this book about thirteenth-century English diocesan governance may have a similar response: that its subtitle should have been *Too Much Reward and Not Enough Punishment*. I prefer to avoid normative judgments in history, but such an observation would not be too off point. This book argues that the rewards bishops gave their administrators overshadowed the punishments they meted out to those men. That circumstance arguably made diocesan administration less effective than it could have been. It also pushed bishops to rely on the culture of their age when managing their relationships with subordinates.

There are several ways to understand this situation, but the benefice, I will argue, is key to most of them. A benefice, typically a church, was an ecclesiastical endowment that produced a regular revenue. Traditionally, most benefices came with cure of souls, that is, pastoral responsibilities to parishioners, although many benefices – often the ones of concern in this book – were quite literally sinecures.

Clerks obtained benefices in one of two ways. By the thirteenth century, the most usual was by "institution." The holder of an advowson – that is, the right to nominate a clerk to hold the benefice – presented the lucky candidate to the bishop. The bishop investigated the clerk and the advowson-holder's right and, if all went well, instituted the clerk to the benefice. Less usual, but important to this book, was collation. Where the bishop himself held the advowson, or for some other reason had the right to exercise it, he did not present the candidate to himself, but simply "collated" the benefice to the clerk. In terms of the clerk's rights, however, institution and collation were the same. In either case, the clerk became the incumbent, with all the rights that brought.

The law and courts of appeal conspired to protect episcopal servants in their benefices for their lifetimes, giving them independence, even from their bishops. The expectation that a benefice, and so a secure income for life, was the appropriate reward for diocesan service pushed bishops to provide such benefices, even though doing so reduced bishops' ability to discipline their men. Thus, demand from below for benefices was significant in driving patrons to give their men benefices. *Pace* the implications of some modern discussions, this demand appears to have been not less powerful than a desire among patrons, including bishops, to cut their out-of-pocket expenses by giving ecclesiastical endowments rather than paying their clerks cash. Although pensions (also known as annuities) offered bishops (and other patrons) a revocable reward for their clerks, bishops exploited such pensions to that end in only a limited way; pensions were often instead used simply as placeholders for an eventual gift of a benefice. Moreover, a culture that stressed reward over discipline led bishops and their men to do the same; it is hard to tell, however, to what extent the security of tenure offered by benefices was created by that culture, and to what extent it fostered or at least supported that culture. But the attempts of a couple of ornery bishops, angry enough to violate the cultural norms of their age, to expel their own clerks from those clerks' benefices will show these legal protections at work. Other gifts bestowed by bishops were also often irrevocable, for example, augmentations of a benefice already given. Diocesan service did, it is true, afford a bishop's clerks some additional continuing revenue streams – fees, the reception of bribes, and the profits of extortion – but these were either limited or not enough to bind a bureaucrat to one particular bishop.

Indeed, the culture of diocesan administration tended to decouple rewards from the work for which it was in fact given. Both bishops and episcopal clerks could act as though benefices were not given for service. After all, to give a benefice in return for service was simony, a sin. In addition, bishops regulated the fees for clerical work so fees would cover expenses and no more, thus prohibiting doing such work for profit. And bishops and their men made use of a by-then venerable culture of affection and devotion to describe their relations. To judge from what they said, bishops loved their clerks and clerks were devoted to their bishops: that, rather than the profits of administration, is why episcopal bureaucrats labored. It is easy to be cynical about such expressions, and this cynicism is often justified. Yet not always. Episcopal clerks often showed their bishops true devotion, and bishops did sometimes demonstrate, not just assert, their affection for their clerks. Affection and devotion, no matter how conventional, helped hold diocesan administration together.

Insofar as it did hold together. The near absence of punishment meant that while bishops relied on their clerks, that reliance had its limits. Episcopal clerks could easily leave their bishop's service, enriched with gifts that did not have to be returned. In this sense, a beneficed episcopal clerk was more an independent operator than an episcopal dependent, always able to jump ship to labor for some other bishop, to devote himself to pastoral or intellectual concerns, or simply cease to labor at all. The material security enjoyed by episcopal clerks made the culture of affection and devotion all the more important for bishops, even if that culture was not fully effective.

Many of these conclusions rely on certain methodological approaches, some general, some more technical. Broadly speaking, I have taken special interest in situations in which commonplace arrangements were under pressure. These occasions put in relief the forces that supported those arrangements, the contours of normalcy. That concern lies behind my investigation of attempts by bishops and other patrons to deprive clerks of benefices in their gift. Beginnings and endings are also good times to see situations under stress, as when one bishop succeeded another, or when incapable rectors and vicars entered the thirteenth-century ecclesiastical version of retirement.

By the early thirteenth century, the English Church, itself only a part of the Church Universal, had built up a complex administrative structure. Including Wales, the English Church included twenty-two dioceses, each ruled by its bishop. Most of these bishops were in the ecclesiastical province of Canterbury, and so subject to the archbishop of Canterbury, although they often resisted that subordination; the bishops of Durham and Carlisle had the same relationship with the archbishop of York. The dioceses themselves were made up of one or more archdeaconries, with archdeacons appointed by the bishop but not, except under special circumstances, removable by him. Indeed, an archdeaconry was an unusual benefice in that it included by definition administrative responsibilities, such as visiting and correcting the archdeaconry's parishes. Archdeacons could in turn look to at least two administrative subordinates. The "archdeacon's official" – early in the century called the "vice-archdeacon" – appears to have enjoyed jurisdiction throughout the archdeaconry as the archdeacon's lieutenant. Archdeaconries were in turn divided into deaneries, each headed by a rural dean. Rural deans are shadowy figures whose activities, and even identities, leave little trace in the sources.

Bishops also relied on other administrative officers. Originally, a bishop looked to his cathedral chapter for administrative help. But by the thirteenth century, many such chapters in England were monastic, their inmates not suited to prolonged activity outside the cloister. Even secular chapters had become corporations largely – although not entirely – beyond the bishop's control; the relationship between bishop and cathedral chapter was often tense, although bishops typically appointed most cathedral canons. While bishops often rewarded their administrators with cathedral canonries, being a canon no longer meant that one was ex officio an administrative officer of the bishop.

By the end of the century, under both the press of business and with uncertain support from archdeacon and chapter, bishops were appointing other officers instead. The sequestrator, sometimes called a sequestrator-general, took custody of vacant benefices and carried out duties regarding probate. Bishops also relied on an officer called an *officialis*. For most of the first half of the century, the bishop's *officialis* appears to have been a general alter ego of the bishop, someone who managed the diocese in his master's absence, a figure whom the later Middle Ages would call a vicar-general. From ca. 1250 or so, however, the term *officialis episcopi* came to reflect its use in the larger church: to designate the judge who headed the bishop's court consistory, which so embodied the bishop's judicial authority that no appeal from it to the bishop was possible.[1] In either case, the bishop's *officialis* was a major episcopal servant. The sources occasionally reveal some lesser officers: the bishop's registrar, charged with maintaining his archives, in particular his register; his chancellor, who administered the use of his seal; his proctors, who carried on his legal and diplomatic business; and his notaries, whose imprimatur was increasingly demanded late in the century. The bishop's chaplains often

---

[1] On this change, see David M. Smith, "The 'Officialis' of the Bishop in Twelfth- and Thirteenth-Century England: Problems of Terminology," in *Medieval Ecclesiastical Studies in Honour of Dorothy M. Owen*, ed. M. J. Franklin and Christopher Harper-Bill (Woodbridge, 1995), 201–20.

served as his secretariat as well as carrying out liturgical responsibilities in his chapel. Then there were clergy who carried out aspects of estate administration, and so less clearly diocesan business, such as his stewards and seneschal. The clearly domestic chamberlain was also often, perhaps usually, a clerk.

A very large amount of the work of diocesan administration – not quantifiable but nonetheless considerable – was carried out by clergy who held no definable office, but who were simply known as the "bishop's clerks." These men did what the bishop needed and looked to him for reward. They were the men on whom the bishop drew in appointing the officers discussed earlier, and remained *clerici episcopi* even as they served in the most exalted offices, such as that of *officialis*. Sometimes such men are designated by a term that suggests a closer attachment to the bishop, as the bishop's *familiaris*, that is, a member of his household. In relying on his *clerici* and *familiares*, bishops behaved like the kings and nobles of their time. When I discuss diocesan administrators in this book, I am discussing such men.

Much of this book is prosopographical. Reconstructing the minutiae of the lives of episcopal clerks makes for some unavoidably unpleasant piling up of detail. It also raises the more technical matter of identifying diocesan administrators. How does one determine whether a man was a bishop's clerk? Sometimes, thankfully, the sources simply say so, informing the historian that a man was a "bishop's clerk" (*clericus episcopi*) or perhaps a "member of the bishop's household" (*familiaris episcopi*). But often such clerks are not so described. At times those men can be found holding a particular administrative office (e.g., the bishop's *officialis*) and identified that way. As will be seen more than once in this book, other indications are less certain, sometimes much less certain. Men who can be shown to have received one or more ad hoc commands from a bishop (e.g., to administer the probate of a will) are candidates for identification as *clerici episcopi*. The more such commands a clerk received, the longer the period of time over which they were received, and the weightier the commission, the stronger the case that the clerk should be considered the bishop's clerk. I have also noted when such commissions were received jointly, as presumably that indicates less reliance by the bishop on any individual recipient – perhaps my one departure from the criteria implicit in most historians' discussions. Because bishops commonly collated benefices to their clerks, evidence that a clerk received a benefice by collation – particularly an archdeaconry – also points to his standing as a bishop's clerk. Sometimes the evidence for collation is conclusive: the record of the collation is in a bishop's register or less commonly in some other source. Sometimes the evidence is less direct: the clerk appears holding a benefice normally in the bishop's gift, but no record of collation survives. Decisions as to whether a man was a bishop's clerk often require weighing the evidence case by case. So I have laid out the evidence for identifying a man as a bishop's clerk, allowing readers to decide case by case whether that identification is credible.

Lists of witnesses are another source of evidence. Often a bishop's deeds were witnessed, and the names of the witnesses survive. Historians have long used those names to identify a bishop's clerks; if a clerk was often in the bishop's presence, the argument goes, he is likely to have been the bishop's clerk. Historians have also expressed reservations about this practice, in particular objecting that several deeds produced on the same day and in the same place could produce the appearance of a man very often in the bishop's company who in fact happened to be visiting the bishop for only a day.[2] Where I have relied on witness lists for this purpose, I have noted on how many different days and at how many different places a witness appears in the bishop's company; readers can thus more easily judge how strong or weak this evidence is.

I should also explain a terminological matter: the terms bishop's *act* and bishop's *actum* as used in this book. For most historians, a bishop's *acta* are his formally issued documents, such as charters or letters notifying the world of some administrative action (e.g., that so and so has been instituted to such and such a benefice). I have used *actum* in this sense here. The episcopal *acta* that have been most intensively studied have been those of the twelfth century, and so the witness lists to *acta* from that period have drawn the most attention when it comes to identifying a bishop's clerks. To that kind of episcopal witness the thirteenth century added a new one: witnesses recorded in *memoranda*, that is, records produced by bishops for in-house use, usually in a bishop's register.[3] The lists of such witnesses may well have often reflected a formal *actum* drawn up at the same time, but given how historians use the term *actum*, such a witnessed *memorandum*

---

[2] Hence the warning of David M. Smith in EEA I: Lincoln, xl. For a vigorous reply to such caveats, focusing on royal charters, see Thomas K. Keefe, "Counting Those Who Count: A Computer-Assisted Analysis of Charter Witness-Lists and the Itinerant Court in the First Year of the Reign of King Richard I," *Haskins Society Journal* 1 (1989), 135–45. I have taken the side of caution, especially because I have far fewer witness lists than does a student of late-twelfth-century royal government.

[3] E.g., Rot. Gravesend, 178 (regarding Adbury).

should probably not be called an *actum*. So I have used the word *act* to refer indifferently to a bishop's *actum* or the record of witnesses in a *memorandum*.

Before ca. 1214, such *acta* are the chief documents preserving a bishop's governance of his diocese. All students of the subject are indebted to the British Academy's English Episcopal Acta project, which has been publishing the *acta* collected from scattered archives.[4] From ca. 1214, however, English bishops began to keep registers, first at Lincoln, and then elsewhere.[5] Such registers, highly miscellaneous in their content, preserve the vast bulk of surviving episcopal memoranda and many *acta* too.[6]

My use of "the thirteenth century" also needs some explanation. In this book, the century is somewhat flexible. I have sometimes drawn on evidence from a decade or two before 1200 (thus still staying within C. R. Cheney's period "from Becket to Langton"[7] as a time characterized by close diocesan governance). I have also sometimes strayed a decade or two into the fourteenth century. Most of the latter instances regard bishops whose episcopates straddle the year 1300, like Richard Swinfield, consecrated bishop of Hereford in 1283, who lasted until 1317. When I have drawn on evidence concerning fourteenth-century bishops who cannot also be called thirteenth-century bishops in at least this extended sense, I have explicitly noted the date of the evidence.

I have also similarly cast the net widely when examining some of the rewards bishops gave their clerks. Other lords were also rewarding their clerks, with benefices and also with pensions. In these matters in particular, I have sometimes filled out thinner evidence regarding bishops and their clerks by looking at evidence regarding other lords, in particular monasteries, and their clerks. Both sorts of relationships were under similar pressures, and so the distinction seems, within limits, to have been without a difference. Readers will be able to judge for themselves the specific instances discussed. I have also noted where the distinction does

---

[4] The first volume of the project was published as EEA I: Lincoln in 1980. The series is still running strong.
[5] For the date 1214, that of the first surviving English bishop's register – strictly speaking, a set of rolls – see David Smith, "The Rolls of Hugh of Wells, Bishop of Lincoln, 1209–35," *Bulletin of the Institute of Historical Research* 45 (1972), 155–95. For a looser determination, see A. Daniel Frankforter, "The Origin of Episcopal Registration Procedures in Medieval England," *Manuscripta* 26 (1982), 67.
[6] For more on this, see Chapter 5.
[7] C. R. Cheney, *From Becket to Langton, English Church Government 1170–1213* (Manchester, 1956).

seem to have made a difference.⁸ So, too, I have sometimes examined how bishops punished clergy at large in their dioceses in order to provide context for how they punished, or did not punish, their own clerks. This practice of embracing the clergy beyond episcopal clerks may sometimes give this book the feel of a broader study of the clergy as a whole. But my quarry is, in the end, one aspect of diocesan governance, rather than a general survey of the thirteenth-century English Church like that of J. R. H. Moorman.⁹

Books about diocesan administration are naturally bishop-centered, especially when they, as they so often do, take the form of a bishop's biography. This book, however, is about bishops and their clerks. In writing it, I have worked to understand the relationships between these parties from each side's point of view. Hence, readers will, I hope, find the discussion bishop-centered and clerk-centered by turns. The focus on reward and punishment, especially in their material aspects, in understanding clerks, and to some extent bishops, may seem cynical. It threatens to reduce these men from spiritually-minded clergy to rational calculators of advantage. At the same time, such a reduction also flattens the differences between past and present, between, say, the medieval church and the modern corporation. Such a reduction is not, however, always incorrect. Medieval people could be rational calculators. Even medieval clergy could be – that, at least, they have in common with modern administrators. Miss Marple's observation applies then as now. But I have tried to leave room for other, less modern, considerations, such as honor; the evidence, I think, justifies doing so. The question of religious concerns – such as spirituality or the pastoral care, which clearly did distinguish the church, then and now, from other modern institutions – is largely postponed until the concluding chapter. I have also tried to have an eye out for individual personality. Indeed, I am grateful to those long-dead bishops whose passions led them to violate the norms of their day and, by doing so, illuminate them. Contemporaries, of course, felt differently.

Despite the weaknesses identified here, bishops and their men – with a healthy amount of stimulation by pope, king, and people – built an administrative edifice in the High Middle Ages. Classically, the later twelfth to earlier thirteenth centuries was the period of the great expansion of

---

⁸ E.g., papal provisions of benefices probably added to bishops' hunger for patronage of benefices, a pressure not experienced much by lay patrons.
⁹ J. R. H. Moorman, *Church Life in England in the Thirteenth Century* (Cambridge, 1955).

bishops' supervision of their dioceses, from control over benefices, to maintenance of clerical – and pastoral – standards, to the resolution of disputes.[10] The institutions thus created, further refined in the thirteenth century, would endure more or less to the end of the Middle Ages and beyond. That bureaucratic growth was, however, part and parcel of general, and so secular as well as ecclesiastical, developments in the High Middle Ages. Thus, the conclusions drawn here invite comparison with non-ecclesiastical administration.

There is another secular comparison. For more than a century, historians have held that English lords used means to reward followers, both military and administrative, besides the fief on which discussions of feudalism concentrate. Traditionally this kind of "bastard feudalism," as it has been called, centered on lords' grants of contractual annuities. The period in which annuities were at first considered relevant was the fourteenth and fifteenth centuries. But like feudalism itself, bastard feudalism has been defined differently by different historians: the various means of material reward other than the fief offered by lords to free followers of any description; such rewards and the relationships that went with them; the use by lords of influence in government to benefit their followers and inhibit their opponents. Moreover, the existence of bastard feudalism, seen either as the granting of annuities or the capture of royal authority by lords, has been pushed earlier, into the early thirteenth century at least.[11] Because lords often used ecclesiastical benefices – to which this book will devote a great deal of attention – to cultivate advisors and administrators as well as annuities, the giving of benefices has sometimes found its way into discussions of bastard feudalism, as a kind of ancillary practice.[12] One way to describe this book would be as an examination of bastard feudalism, under any of the above definitions, ecclesiastical style – or even more specifically, episcopal style.

---

[10] Hence Cheney, *From Becket to Langton*, especially 175–7. For a very rough confirmation from the perspective of a historian of the Anglo-Saxon period, with some late eleventh-century developments, see John Blair, *The Church in Anglo-Saxon Society* (Oxford, 2005), 507 and also 490–6. Claims can be put forward in some respects for earlier periods, a phenomenon not unknown to historians of secular developments. Hence, see Martin Brett, *The English Church under Henry* I (Oxford, 1975); Mary Frances Giandrea, *Episcopal Culture in Late Anglo-Saxon England* (Woodbridge, 2007), chap. 4.

[11] Michael Hicks, *Bastard Feudalism* (London, 1995), chap. 1, summarizes the historiography.

[12] Hence, the glancing reference ibid., 55–6. For a more extended discussion, see Scott Waugh, "Tenure to Contract: Lordship and Clientage in Thirteenth-Century England," *English Historical Review* 101 (1986), 821–2.

But these comparisons will have to wait. The problem itself among ecclesiastics could first use some highlighting. My goals are to show what rewards and punishments bishops used, how bishops kept the loyalties of episcopal bureaucrats, and how those discussions illuminate diocesan governance in thirteenth-century England. But before doing so, it is first worth establishing that clerks' loyalties to their bishops were indeed tested.

2

Dangers of Service

It seems likely that in 1301 Archbishop Winchelsey of Canterbury was annoyed with Robert de Lacy, canon of Lincoln. The bishop and the prior of Durham Cathedral Priory were engaged in one of those furious disputes that sometimes divided a bishop from his cathedral. Winchelsey had commanded Robert to summon the parties to appear before the pope, but Robert had refused to move. Indeed, Winchelsey now hoped that Robert's own lord could succeed where Winchelsey had failed, and wrote the bishop of Lincoln, asking him also to order Robert to carry out the summons.[1] In another letter, this one to the bishop of Durham, Winchelsey offers a clue to Robert's reluctance. The archbishop – who had himself done his best to support the bishop of Durham in his conflict with the priory – asks the bishop not to get angry with Robert when he delivers the summons, noting that Robert was the brother of the bishop's own clerk, John de Lacy, a point that may explain Robert's selection for this particular delicate mission.[2] Why was Robert so reluctant? He may have been afraid. Citing parties to court was risky business. Passions on such occasions could run high, as the archbishop of York's man discovered when he, with a sword to his chest, was forced to eat a written

---

[1] Reg. Winchelsey, 735. The episode involving Robert de Lacy is recounted by C. M. Fraser, *A History of Antony Bek Bishop of Durham 1283–1311* (Oxford, 1957), 154. Robert received several collations from the bishop of Lincoln (John Le Neve, *Fasti Ecclesiae Anglicanae 1300–1541 I: Lincoln Diocese*, compiled by H. P. King [London, 1962], 21, 52, 96).

[2] Reg. Winchelsey, 736. For Winchelsey's support of Bishop Bek in this instance, see ibid. and for their generally friendly relations, J. H. Denton, *Robert Winchelsey and the Crown 1294–1313: A Study in the Defence of Ecclesiastical Liberty* (Cambridge, 1980), 43–4.

summons he tried to deliver.³ The dean of Ospringe, on a mission from Archbishop Winchelsey to cite men to court, found himself thrown into the mud, led with song and dance backward on his horse into the middle of town. His horse was then mutilated and the dean thrown into the mud again. He did not deliver his citations.⁴

Getting people to court always had its dangers: to deliver a summons was, after all, to put oneself at that electric point of contact between the exercise of authority on the one hand and those that authority sought to coerce on the other. But working for a bishop posed dangers to episcopal servants far beyond the problem of summoning the irate to court. Diocesan governance could be hazardous in various respects. That fact in turn has implications for the bond between bishops and their men, for it meant that it was a bond liable to be tested. Being a bishop's clerk did not entail just pushing parchment or even just hard work. It could entail danger: physical, fiscal, even spiritual.

Certainly delivering other kinds of messages posed risks. Two rectors sent by the archbishop of Canterbury to cite people in Dover to be present when the archbishop visited the neighborhood, to make inquiries preliminary to the visitation, and to excommunicate those who did not attend were violently assaulted for their efforts; the archbishop complained that the community were degenerate sons attacking the holy mother church that nursed them.⁵ Delivering a warning could also be dangerous; the bishop of Exeter complained that his clerks, sent to warn the earl of Cornwall's men not to attack the liberties of the church, were themselves attacked by the earl's men, "atrociously wounded, flogged, and hurled to the ground."⁶ (Bishops, for that matter, themselves could engage in similar behavior. Grosseteste stamped in anger on a letter brought from the prior and convent of Christ Church, Canterbury, and had its carrier "thrown out of his presence"; he imprisoned the next clerk who dared bring a letter on this matter.)⁷

---

3 Reg. Romeyn II, 243–4. The charge was adultery.
4 James Buchanan Given, *Society and Homicide in Thirteenth-Century England* (Stanford, 1977), 89.
5 Reg. Winchelsey, 222–3 (and 240, and see 225–9). One of these men, William le Archer, held a rectory in the archbishop's gift, although its collation to him is unrecorded (Reg. Pecham, II, 114; Reg. Winchelsey, 1197). The other rector has no traceable connection to Winchelsey other than this episode.
6 Reg. Bronscombe, no. 1429 (editor's translation).
7 At least, according to the prior and convent's complaint: M. M. Morgan, "The Excommunication of Grosseteste in 1243," *English Historical Review* 57 (1942), 245–9.

Worse could happen. According to representatives sent by the archbishop of Canterbury to investigate a dispute between the bishop of Llandaff and certain clergy of the diocese, the bishop had had one of their messengers beaten to death.[8] Other activities also entailed risk. People got angry when summoned to court but also lost their tempers in court itself. An examiner in the Court of Canterbury was insulted by a litigant's friends in court, one of whom then moved to poke out the examiner's eye with his thumb.[9] Ecclesiastics were not immune from the endemic violence of the Middle Ages.

Service in a bishop's household could bring physical danger because bishops might do unpopular things or simply because bishops' households made big targets. As late as 1279, when the dispute about such matters was quite old, the men carrying the archbishop of York's crosses before him as he progressed though the province of Canterbury met violence.[10] At the close of the thirteenth century Archbishop Winchelsey, himself about to engage in the same offense against his northern neighbor, took precautions when venturing into the province of York, including a special escort.[11] But avoiding enemy territory was no protection. The sense of ambient danger is evident in a papal indult of 1253: the archbishop of Canterbury was empowered to enforce satisfaction from any who injured him or his household as he traveled through his province or stayed in any of his manors.[12] Rising tensions could lead to special precautions, as when the bishop of Winchester, perhaps concerned about hostility from the monks of his cathedral, posted guards at the city gates.[13] Royal displeasure always brought dangers. Archbishop Winchelsey's household was attacked in the rectory of Maidstone while Winchelsey was at odds with Edward I over *Clericis laicos*.[14]

---

[8] EEA III: Canterbury, no. 634 n.
[9] *Select Cases from the Ecclesiastical Courts of the Province of Canterbury c. 1200–1301*, ed. Norma Adams and Charles Donahue Jr. (Selden Society 95) (London, 1981 for 1978–9), 20, and 293–4.
[10] *Annales Monastici*, IV, 281. For the history of the dispute, see Roy Martin Haines, "Canterbury versus York: Fluctuating Fortunes in a Perennial Conflict," in Haines, *Ecclesia Anglicana: Studies in the English Church of the Later Middle Ages* (Toronto, 1989), 69–105, and for this episode, 88–9.
[11] Fraser, *History of Antony Bek*, 146–7.
[12] CPL, I, 287.
[13] Nicholas Vincent, "The Politics of Church and State as Reflected in the Winchester Pipe Rolls, 1208–80," in *The Winchester Pipe Rolls and English Society*, ed. Richard Britnell (Woodbridge, 2003), 172.
[14] Reg. Winchelsey, 217; Denton, *Robert Winchelsey and the Crown*, 119.

Being a bishop's clerk also entailed taking up the causes of one's master, which might turn violent. It is not clear why Prior Bernard of Champagne, the *officialis* of Bishop Peter de Aquablanca of Hereford, was murdered and his grange burned down, while another of the bishop's clerks was assaulted. But the archdeacon of Hereford was banished from the kingdom as a result, and so tension between archdeacon and bishop may well have been at the root of the affair; Prior Bernard and his colleague thus were quite likely targeted as episcopal servants.[15] Other conflicts, and their consequences for episcopal clerks, are more explicit in the sources. Gerald of Wales, a hostile witness to be sure, has Archbishop Hubert Walter complain not only that he lost 11,000 marks in his dispute with Gerald over the bishopric of Saint David's, but also the lives of several clerks.[16] Gerald also recounts how, when going to meet a neighboring bishop regarding rival claims to territory, Gerald raised an armed force (although the actual confrontation turned out to be rather comic).[17] A long-running dispute between Archbishop Pecham and Bishop Thomas Cantilupe of Hereford provides the setting of the continuing travails of one of Cantilupe's clerks, Robert de Wyse. A witness – one of Pecham's men – recalled the scene when Robert tried to read Cantilupe's appeal against Canterbury before the archbishop. Pecham, stirred up, ordered Robert removed – he was flung into a watery ditch.[18] Robert later tried again in the Court of Arches, where the dean had him grabbed by the arms to be thrown out when Robert refused to do his work in some out-of-the-way corner.[19] Pecham himself later had Robert manhandled to expel him

---

[15] For these incidents, EEA 35: Hereford, lii–liii, lxxv.

[16] Gerald of Wales, "De Jure et Statu Menevensis Ecclesiae," in *Giraldi Cambrensis Opera*, ed. J. S. Brewer (RS) (London, 1861–3), III, 264. Gerald makes a similar remark in relation to Walter concerning the archbishop's dispute with the monks of Christ Church, Canterbury: some of the archbishop's clerks feared to go to Rome to present their archbishop's case against the monks there, knowing that many men (Gerald names four) had already lost their lives at Rome in the archbishop's cause (Gerald of Wales, *De Invectionibus*, ed. W. S. Davies, *Y Cymmrodor: The Magazine of the Honourable Society of Cymmrodorion* 30 [1920], 95).

[17] Gerald of Wales, "De Rebus a Se Gestis," in *Giraldi Cambrensis Opera*, I, 33–7.

[18] R. C. Finucane, "The Cantilupe-Pecham Controversy," in *St. Thomas of Hereford Essays in His Honour*, ed. Meryl Jancey (Hereford, 1982), 109. This seems merely humiliating but may have also been more dangerous than it sounds; drowning in a ditch was a not uncommon death in late-medieval England (Barbara A. Hanawalt, *The Ties that Bound: Peasant Families in Medieval England* [Oxford, 1986], 27, 145). Robert's own testimony was milder, noting simply that the archbishop prevented him from reading his appeal (Finucane, "Cantilupe-Pecham Controversy," 109 n 34).

[19] Finucane, "Cantilupe-Pecham Controversy," 112; Finucane, "Two Notaries and Their Records in England, 1282–1307," *Journal of Medieval History* 13 (1987), 5–6.

from Exeter cathedral when Robert tried to read out Cantilupe's appeal there before the archbishop.[20]

Indeed, accompanying a bishop on visitation, often a time of high tension – particularly when the right to visit was itself contested – was perilous. When Boniface of Savoy, archbishop of Canterbury, exercised his right of visitation over St. Paul's, London, the canons resisted. And so the archbishop entered by force; several members of his household were killed, and others wounded.[21] Walter of Guisborough wrote that when the archbishop of York attempted to visit Durham Priory in 1282, the gates of the city were barred against him. He managed to enter and preach to the people, at the cost, Walter said, of some of his clerks' lives.[22]

Then there was imprisonment. In the course of his duties, the bishop of Exeter's *officialis* and chancellor found himself imprisoned on (what the bishop termed a false) charge of felony.[23] The king himself consigned to the Tower of London an archdeacon's official who had dared cite a woman to court within the royal verge.[24] Another move was kidnapping. The *officialis* of the bishop of Carlisle complained that as he traveled from Carlisle and Thorpenhow, he was beaten, robbed, and detained at the lord of Thorpenhow's residence; the jury that heard the case largely agreed.[25] And it was not only boisterous laity who engaged in such behavior; bishops could do this to each other's servants. The bishop

---

[20] Finucane, "Cantilupe-Pecham Controversy," 114; Finucane, "Two Notaries and Their Records," 6–7.
[21] *Annales Monastici*, IV, 102. The story that the archbishop wore armor under his vestments when he visited the priory of St. Bartholomew's and repeatedly punched the subprior in the chest (Matthew Paris, *Chronica Majora*, ed. H. R. Luard [RS] [London, 1872–83], V, 121–2) is probably false (Leland Edward Wilshire, "Boniface of Savoy, Carthusian and Archbishop of Canterbury 1207–1270," *Analecta Cartusiana* 31 [1977], 42–3). In any case, the detail about the armor was unusual among English bishops, hence Matthew Paris's horror at it (Robert Brentano, *Two Churches: England and Italy in the Thirteenth Century* [Princeton, 1968], 202–3).
[22] *The Chronicle of Walter of Guisborough*, ed. Harry Rothwell, Camden Society (third series) 89 (1957 for 1955–6, 1956–7), 350, and see Robert Brentano, *York Metropolitan Jurisdiction and Papal Judges Delegate (1279–1296)* (Berkeley and Los Angeles, 1959), 133–4; *Historiae Dunelmensis Scriptores Tres*, ed. James Raines, Surtees Society 9 (London, 1839), 60.
[23] Reg. Bronscombe, no. 1024 et al.
[24] *Select Cases in the Court of King's Bench under Edward II*, ed. G. O. Sayles, Selden Society 45, 47–8, 74, 76, 82, 88 (London, 1936–71), IV, 64–8. The archbishop of York's clerks were punished for excommunicating, on the archbishop's command, a person within the royal verge (Fraser, *History of Antony Bek*, 94–5).
[25] Henry Summerson, "Fearing God, Honouring the King: The Episcopate of Robert de Chaury, Bishop of Carlisle, 1258–1278," *Thirteenth Century England X: Proceedings of the Durham Conference 2003*, ed. Michael Prestwich, Richard Britnell, and Robin Frame (Woodbridge, 2005), 150.

of Durham, embroiled with Archbishop Romeyn of York over York's metropolitical claims, imprisoned two of the archbishop's clerks.[26] The bishop of Winchester asked his brother to carry off his own metropolitan's clerks, including the archbishop's *officialis*, and imprison them over a dispute regarding the hospital of St. Thomas, Southwark; some of the bishop's own clerks took part.[27]

Other dangers were less violent. Episcopal clerks could find themselves sued because of their involvement in their masters' affairs. A couple of the bishop of Durham's clerks were dragged into secular court, one of them thrown into prison and fined a princely £100, in relation to the bishop's visitation of his priory and subsequent deposition of the prior. (This was the dispute that prompted Archbishop Winchelsey's letter to Robert de Lacy. The visitation met strong resistance; the bishop's clerks wound up barring the doors of the priory church in order to prevent food from being taken there, and then imprisoned the prior.)[28] Robert de Wyse, the *officialis* of Bishop Cantilupe of Hereford, also faced financial hardship for his role in support of his bishop against Archbishop Pecham. Once the struggle was over, he had to offer a £100 surety to the archbishop to guarantee his obedience.[29] Even after Archbishop Baldwin of Canterbury was in his grave, his clerks were answering in court to the monks of Christ Church, Canterbury, regarding Baldwin's plans to erect a college of secular canons.[30] It was presumably to ward off just such retaliation or worse that a later archbishop wrote a letter of protection for his *capellanus* in relation to the chaplain's support for the archbishop's case against the Canterbury monks; to be safe, the chaplain, particularly vulnerable as a Canterbury monk himself, obtained an *inspeximus*, or confirmation, of this letter from several other bishops.[31] These sorts of legal problems were common enough for the bishop of Norwich to

---

[26] Reg. Romeyn II, xxvi–xxvii, 100–101. For discussion of this episode and the tense relations between the bishop and Archbishop Romeyn, see Fraser, *History of Antony Bek*, 94–6, 113–14.

[27] Vincent, "The Politics of Church and State," 172; H. W. Ridgeway, "The Ecclesiastical Career of Aymer de Lusignan, Bishop Elect of Winchester, 1250–1260," in *The Cloister and the World: Essays in Honour of Barbara Harvey*, ed. John Blair and Brian Golding (Oxford, 1996), 166.

[28] *Records of Antony Bek*, 115, 207, and Fraser, *History of Antony Bek*, 135, 171. The settlement between bishop and priory also provided exemption of the bishop's clerks from any claims by the priory (ibid., 152).

[29] Finucane, "The Cantilupe-Pecham Controversy," 120.

[30] EEA 10: Bath and Wells, no. 107, and see nos. 102–6 and no. 102 n.

[31] EEA 12: Exeter, no. 286B and see n.

take the special step of obtaining a papal privilege: that neither he nor his officers in his name were to be summoned by papal letters to a court more than two days' journey away, a limit that was in theory, but not in practice, guaranteed by the law.[32]

Naturally, in the church, where there were lawsuits there was spiritual danger. Excommunications took wing easily in court. In 1293, some of the bishop of Worcester's men were excommunicated by the *officialis* of Canterbury for their contumacy regarding the *officialis*'s jurisdiction during the bishop's dispute with his erstwhile servant, Peter de Leicester.[33] When Bishop Cantilupe of Hereford appealed a case against Archbishop Pecham, he took the precaution of seeking papal tuition not only for himself, but for his people, from excommunication, interdict, and suspension.[34] Later, the bishop of Durham's clerks would incur excommunication as part of their bishop's long-running dispute with the prior and monks of Durham.[35]

Then there were threats to dignity and public reputation. Violence, of course, was one instance of this; consider the rough treatment of Robert de Wyse, discussed earlier. But violence was not the end of it. When the bishop of Exeter's men were attacked by those of the earl of Cornwall, the earl's men not only drew blood but also cut the cowls of the bishop's men to mock their tonsures.[36] The Robert de Wyse who was forced to offer up a £100 bond after backing his bishop against Archbishop Pecham also had to make a pilgrimage to the Holy Land in atonement, make offerings at Becket's tomb, and on his return through London publicly acknowledge his guilt.[37] Even when the archbishop of York tried to smooth things over between the bishop of Durham and his priory, the bishop of Durham's men found themselves castigated by the archbishop as "satellites of Satan who claim to be your [i.e., the bishop's] officers" for their troubles in enforcing the blockade of the cathedral.[38]

---

[32] Unless, of course, the summons mentioned this privilege: CPL, I, 191. For law and practice on this point, Jane Sayers, *Papal Judges Delegate in the Provincial Court of Canterbury 1198–1254: A Study in Ecclesiastical Jurisdiction and Administration* (Oxford, 1971), 60–4.

[33] Reg. Giffard of Worcester, 429. For the larger dispute, see Michael Burger, "Peter of Leicester, Bishop Godfrey Giffard of Worcester, and the Problem of Benefices in Thirteenth-Century England," *Catholic Historical Review* 95 (2009), 453–73.

[34] Finucane, "The Cantilupe-Pecham Controversy," 107.

[35] Fraser, *History of Antony Bek*, 160.

[36] Reg. Bronscombe, no. 1429.

[37] Finucane, "The Cantlilupe-Pecham Controversy," 120.

[38] Fraser, *History of Antony Bek*, 144.

More mundanely, favors could become harder to obtain. One smaller move of Archbishop Romeyn of York in his battle with the bishop of Durham was to order his bailiff of Beverley to deny Walter le Boteler, one of the bishop's agents, a corrody from the provost of Beverley; Romeyn pointed out explicitly that Walter served the bishop of Durham, "opposed to us in all things as much as possible."[39]

Legal trouble cost money as well as time. But serving a bishop could also incur more direct expense. John de Merston, Bishop Merton of Rochester's clerk, lost several horses while traveling on his bishop's business: a bay at Charminster; a piebald at Aberford; a sorrel while in northern parts; a morel at York.[40] John may have had especially bad luck – or may have been especially hard on horses – but Merton's servant Ralph de Riplingham also lost a morel in the bishop's service.[41] Although these men did seek reimbursement from Merton's estate after the bishop's death (hence the evidence of these losses), it is notable that Merton had not compensated them while he lived. Moreover, even if they could have been confident that a future claim against the bishop's estate would be successful, they could hardly have been confident that they themselves would live to make such a claim.

The police-blotter approach of this chapter risks overstating the perils of diocesan administration. Still, the smooth institutional histories of medieval church administration may lead the unwary to forget what the men who ran those administrations were not in a position to forget: that ecclesiastical administration could always be dangerous, even if unpredictably so. Yet men did it. Even Robert de Lacy, reluctant to summon the bishop of Durham to the curia, acted. He did not do so in response to the command of Archbishop Winchelsey, though Winchelsey was the most powerful ecclesiastical figure in the realm and was himself acting on papal orders. Instead, Robert acted only after the archbishop asked Robert's own lord, the bishop of Lincoln, to exert pressure.[42] Across England, other administrators risked similar hazards on the orders of their bishops. Why? To answer that question requires an examination of the rewards and punishments available to bishops when dealing with their servants, of what rewards and punishments they in fact used, and of how those rewards and punishments shaped the relations between bishop and bureaucrat.

---

[39] Reg. Romeyn II, 69: "nobis, quantum potest, adversatur in omnibus."
[40] *The Early Rolls of Merton College Oxford*, ed. J. R. L. Highfield (Oxford, 1964), 125.
[41] Ibid., 126.
[42] Robert did deliver the summons in the end (Reg. Winchelsey, 599).

PART II

REWARDS AND PUNISHMENTS

3

The Benefice for Service and as Benefit

Since those who faithfully serve the Apostolic See, as the head of the universal Church, are held to give useful service as it were to all the members, it is right that they should be honored with suitable benefices, lest otherwise, if they had to serve at their own cost and were defrauded of special revenues, they might be slower to serve. Whence it is the practice that clerks who reside at the Apostolic See (not without many labors and expenses), have received for the time being ecclesiastical benefices in England and other parts of the world....

– Pope Honorius III to Walter Gray, Archbishop of York[1]

Benefices and Service

Like lay Christians, beneficed clerks had various responsibilities. God and his church set a minimum standard of moral behavior regarding matters such as drunkenness and fornication for the laity and an even higher standard for clergy. They also expected orthodoxy. Failures in these respects could be punished by loss of one's benefice, just as the church at least hoped that lay people would be punished by loss of their property. A holder of a benefice also had to respect the rights of his church. He was

---

[1] "Cum hi qui sedi Apostolicae, tanquam capiti ecclesiae generalis, fideliter famulantur, singulis quasi membris utiliter servire praebentur, dignum est congruis beneficiis honorari, ne, si tantum propriis stipendiis militantes separati fructus fraudarentur solatiis, redderentur ad obsequia tardiores; unde factum est quod clerici apud sedem Apostolicam, ne sine multis laboribus et sumptibus residentes, in Anglia et aliis partibus mundi ecclesiastica beneficia pro tempore sunt adepti" (Rot. Gray, 137–8). The translation is essentially from W. A. Pantin, who used it in his discussion of benefices in his *The English Church in the Fourteenth Century* (Cambridge, 1955), 41.

not to alienate property from it to lay people – especially his relatives – and was to maintain the church and its lands in good condition. (If it was discovered after his death that he had not done so, his estate could be compelled to make good the damage.)[2] Failure in any of these matters could result in suspension and, if necessary, deprivation: permanent loss of one's benefice. Unless dispensed by their superiors,[3] the canon law demanded these obligations.

Many benefices, moreover, also came with cure of souls and so carried the supreme duty of guiding Christians to eternal life. In concrete terms, the cure of souls meant first and foremost celebrating the mass and confessing one's flock. It also required minimum residence in the benefice because, in theory, an incumbent had to be present in order to tend his parishioners. Nonresidence, then, could also serve as grounds for suspension or deprivation. Moreover, benefices with cure of souls required incumbents who were priests or who, if in lower orders, would proceed to ordination to the priesthood within a year of receiving the benefice.

But a benefice came with more than just obligations. With cure of souls or without, it was also income-generating property. That income took various forms. Benefices came in the guise of an endowment of pensions; of land bringing in income from rents or produce to be sold; of tithes paid by parishioners; of a myriad of other money-generating rights; of some combination of these.[4]

Regarding benefices with cure of souls, the canon law distinguished between the benefice as an office (hence the obligations) and the benefice as a collection of revenues and rights, or *beneficium*, from which "benefice" derives.[5] And, as medieval people and modern historians have noted, in this dual nature of the benefice lay trouble.[6] The prospect of a

---

[2] On dilapidations, see Richard Helmholz, *The Oxford History of the Laws of England I: The Canon Law and Ecclesiastical Jurisdiction from 597 to the 1640s* (Oxford, 2004), 500–501.

[3] More on this in Chap. 6, at nn 31–50.

[4] For a report to a prebendary on the management of the prebend's produce: *Royal and Other Historical Letters Illustrative of the Reign of Henry III*, ed. W.W. Shirley (RS) (London, 1862–6), I, no. 167. It is hard to reconstruct the exact nature of most parochial revenues (R. N. Swanson, "Standards of Livings: Parochial Revenues in Pre-Reformation England," in *Religious Belief and Ecclesiastical Careers in Late Medieval England: Proceedings of the Conference Held at Strawberry Hill Easter 1989*, ed. Christopher Harper-Bill [Woodbridge, 1991], 151–96).

[5] Geoffrey Barraclough, *Papal Provisions: Aspects of Church Constitutional, Legal and Administrative History in the Later Middle Ages* (Oxford, 1935), 71–89.

[6] E.g., J. R. H. Moorman, *Church Life in England in the Thirteenth Century* (Cambridge, 1955), 6–8; J. C. Dickinson, *An Ecclesiastical History of England: The Later Middle*

beneficium drew men to the clergy like flies to honey; many such men, however, were unsuitable for the office. Much of the legislation of the medieval church tried to prevent this result. Bishops, for example, were to examine those nominated to benefices to determine their character and literacy (and so capacity to perform the mass, or even do some preaching); the unworthy were to be rejected. The focus on the abuse of office for the sake of property meant that the limits on the property aspect of the benefice centered on the office attached to it. Suspension for failure to observe the requirements of the office meant curtailment of one's property right in the benefice. Deprivation meant the extinction of one's property right. In either case, the canon law, true to its Christian calling, recognized the primacy of the office that came with a benefice.[7]

The requirement of residency, however, inconvenienced too many important people, and not just episcopal clerks, to endure unmodified. First among them were pluralists, that is, clerks who acquired two or more benefices, enjoying the income from each. Because it is hard to be in two places at the same time, pluralists had trouble being resident. Even those enjoying a single benefice with cure of souls could find residence difficult, for, crucially, benefices were often given for purposes having nothing to do with office. University scholars received benefices to support them in their studies. The sons of the great received benefices simply to supply them with an income. And, of chief interest in this book, the unsalaried bureaucrats of the new and busy high-medieval diocesan administrations – and of other administration too – received them. Indeed, benefices were seen as necessary to support bureaucrats. Benefices without cure of souls were naturally especially desirable. In 1284, the bishop of Durham founded a college with prebends – that is, with benefices to be held by its members – because "there were lacking in the diocese lawyers and councilors to aid the bishop in the arduous affairs of his church."[8] One commentator has suggested that England's relative wealth of benefices free from residence requirements explains why England developed a more bureaucratic secular administration

---

Ages, from the Norman Conquest to the Eve of the Reformation (London, 1979), 266–8. Robert E. Rodes Jr., as on other occasions, gives an original twist to an old line of analysis (*Ecclesiastical Administration in Medieval England: The Anglo-Saxons to the Reformation* [Notre Dame, 1977], 163).

[7] Glenn Olsen, "The Definition of the Ecclesiastical Benefice in the Twelfth Century: The Canonists' Discussion of Spiritualia," *Studia Gratiana* 11 (1967), 432–46.

[8] *Records of Antony Bek, Bishop and Patriarch: 1283–1311*, ed. C. M. Fraser, Surtees Society 162 (London, 1953), no. 3 (p. 3).

than Germany.[9] The fact that such bureaucrats were often pluralists as well only exacerbated the problem of nonresidence.

A solution was needed and it was found. Incumbents were permitted to appoint vicars, resident clergy who would carry out the spiritual office of the benefice while the holder drew the income, paying a usually small stipend to the vicar. Such nonresidence was to be licensed by the local bishop. But by the thirteenth century, the arrangement was increasingly to appoint perpetual vicars to the prebendal churches often held by cathedral canons. These vicars received a fixed portion of the benefice's income as a benefice of their own, with cure of souls.[10] In such cases, what one can call the mother benefice lost the duty of cure of souls entirely and its incumbent any requirement to be resident altogether. The liturgical duties of canons in the cathedral itself devolved onto another kind of vicar, the vicar choral. One way or another, vicars allowed the holders of benefices to be nonresident. Such sinecures were the usual reward of diocesan administrators, although certainly they sometimes held churches with cure.[11] Also helping attempts to evade residency requirements was the failure of the medieval English church to formulate a specific definition of residency: did residence mean being in the benefice three days out of seven? turning up in nine months out of twelve? The rules gave no answer.[12]

The papacy itself furnished another solution: dispensations for pluralism, which began to fill papal registers from the thirteenth century. Indeed, the problem in even some reformers' eyes came to be unlicensed pluralism rather than pluralism itself.[13] The attitude was evident in the case of Nicholas de Romsey, who held two benefices with cure of souls without dispensation. The pope determined that Nicholas had to resign them and do penance, whereupon he was to receive the two benefices back, along with a dispensation to hold them along with a third with cure of souls.[14] Here the other critical distinction in thinking through

---

[9] Julia Barrow, "Cathedrals, Provosts and Prebends: A Comparison of Twelfth-Century German and English Practice," *Journal of Ecclesiastical History* 37 (1986), 564.

[10] These vicars were usually "perpetual vicars," although the most common perpetual vicarages were those established when a monastery appropriated a vicarage.

[11] E.g., see Chapter 6.

[12] On this failure, see Robert C. Palmer, *Selling the Church: The English Parish Church in Law, Commerce, and Religion, 1350–1550* (Chapel Hill, 2002), 100–101.

[13] See the remarks of David M. Smith, "Thomas Cantilupe's Register: The Administration of the Diocese of Hereford 1275–1282," in *Saint Thomas Cantilupe of Hereford: Essays in His Honour*, ed. Meryl Jancey (Leominster, 1982), 92–3.

[14] CPL, I, 364–5. And see the case of Peter de Thoresby: CPL, I, 389; *Les Registres d'Urbain IV (1261–1264)*, ed. J. Guiraud and S. Clémencet, Bibliothèque des Ecoles françaises d'Athènes et de Rome (second series) 13 (Paris, 1892–1958), I, no. 276.

pluralism came to be that between compatible benefices (i.e., two or more benefices where only one had cure of souls) and incompatible benefices (two or more benefices each with cure of souls).[15]

The tension between the benefice as office and the benefice as property mirrored another tension: between the theoretical reasons for giving and receiving benefices and the actual reasons many people gave and received them. Benefices were, or seemed to be, a necessary reward for administrative service. Yet, the Gregorian Reform of the eleventh century had started a campaign to stamp out simony, the selling of salvation. In the eleventh century, this concern regarding simony focused on the sale of churches.[16] But the Gregorians refined the definition of selling a church further. A strong suspicion came to run in ecclesiastical circles regarding the giving of benefices for any nonpastoral reason.[17] To give a benefice in expectation of service, including administrative service, was in effect to sell it. Giving a benefice in return for service already smelled the same. Such transactions had come to be defined by reformers as simony, a sin, by the end of the eleventh century. Gerald of Wales complained in the early thirteenth century about a bishop who, he claimed, tried to screen his simoniacal behavior by saying that "I do not sell the church, but my favor." Gerald said that the bishop privately explained that he rejected most presentees because he had not received services (*obsequia*) or gifts (*munera*) from them.[18] And this definition of simony was built into the canon law that governed the church for the remainder of the Middle Ages. As Alexander III ruled, a church promised in return for undertaking the patron's business (*negotium* or *obsequium*) was a church given in simony.[19] Stephen Langton's provincial council of 1222 insisted that bishops require presentees to benefices to swear that they had neither promised nor given anything to be presented, nor made a pact concerning the

---

[15] The distinction was effectively legislated by the Fourth Lateran Council's prohibition against holding two or more benefices with cure of souls at one time, and was repeated in English conciliar legislation, which by the end of the century was explicitly cast in terms of compatibility and incompatibility (Alexander Hamilton Thompson, "Pluralism in the Medieval Church, with Notes on Pluralists in the Diocese of Lincoln, 1366," Part 1, *Reports and Papers of the Architectural and Archaeological Societies of the Counties of Lincoln and Northampton* 33 (1915), 42–9.

[16] Lester K. Little, *Religious Poverty and the Profit Economy in Medieval Europe* (Ithaca, NY, 1978), 31.

[17] Indeed, it was the fact that benefices could not be bought or sold that signified their standing as offices (Olsen, "Definition of the Ecclesiastical Benefice," 442–3, 445).

[18] "Non vendo ecclesiam, sed gratiam meam": Gerald of Wales, "Gemma Ecclesiastica," in *Geraldi Cambrensis Opera* (RS) (London, 1862), II, 295.

[19] X.5.3.12.

presentation.[20] Later in the century, the bishop of Chichester denounced as simony the oaths of fidelity that religious were exacting from clerks they presented to benefices before their institution.[21] The legal commentator Lyndwood would much later echo the concern regarding benefices given for service or gifts, noting that presentees receiving benefices were to swear that they had given nothing to the patron, nor had made any pact with the patron for the benefice.[22] It was this concern that Innocent III recognized when he nullified certain pacts entered into by the abbot and convent of Evesham. Evesham had promised to bestow on Richard de Tirington and others for their fidelity to the abbey the first benefices in the abbey's gift to fall vacant. Innocent ruled these arrangements to be contrary to canon law.[23] Such pacts were expectatives and had been prohibited by the Third Lateran Council, legislation that was repeated in England.[24] Indeed, Archbishop Pecham held that even to resign a benefice on a condition was simony.[25] Mid-century, the pope had felt similarly, ordering the bishop of Winchester to deprive people who had importuned their relatives to resign benefices in order to obtain them.[26]

Yet, the value of benefices as property – property to be given to reward and cultivate service and loyalty – was irresistible. And so the law permitted the giving of benefices in return for past or future service so long as there was no actual promise or agreement (*pactum*) involved. A later gloss of Alexander III's ruling against promising benefices in return for service carefully notes that it is licit to serve someone (a bishop is the example used), *in hope* (*spe*) of a benefice, and the person served (such as a bishop) may give such a servant a benefice so long as he does not mean *directly* to provide it on account of that service ("directe pro hoc servitio ei prouidere in beneficio intendat").[27] This put the line between licit and

---

[20] *Councils and Synods*, 113.
[21] Ibid., 1088. And see the archbishop of York's condemnation of the practice in 1241–55 (*Councils and Synods*, 492).
[22] William Lyndwood, *Provinciale, (seu Constitutiones Angliae) continens constitutiones provinciales quatuordecim archiepiscoporum Cantuariensium* (Oxford, 1679), Book 2, Titulus 6, chap. 1.
[23] *The Letters of Pope Innocent III (1198–1216) Concerning England and Wales*, ed. C. R. Cheney and Mary G. Cheney (Oxford, 1967), no. 618.
[24] C. R. Cheney, *From Becket to Langton, English Church Government 1170–1213* (Manchester, 1956), 76–7.
[25] Pecham, *Epistolae*, II, no. 423.
[26] Reg. Pontissara, 753. The register preserves material earlier than Pontoise's episcopate.
[27] *Corpus juris canonici emendatum et notis illustratum, Gregorii XIII. Pont. Max. iussu editum* (Rome, 1582), gloss on X.5.3.12, consulted in the electronic edition: UCLA Digital Library Program: Corpus Juris Canonici, 1582, http://digital.library.ucla.edu/canonlaw.

simoniacal behavior perilously thin. That a bishop should be the example the glossator chose was natural, given the circles in which ecclesiastical lawyers moved; bishops' need for administrators – and their administrators' need for employment – demanded to be catered to as far as the church's intellectual commitment against simony would allow.

In practice, benefices were given for just the sort of service the canon law condemned. This reason for the conferral of benefices could be explicit. When Archbishop Winchelsey collated a benefice to his chancellor because of the *servicium* he had given the archbishop and his church, as well as the *servicium* Winchelsey hoped to receive in the future, he engaged in what a hard-nosed lawyer could have described as simony.[28] Later Winchelsey offered another servant the deanery of south Malling, in consideration of the recipient's past service (*obsequia*), laboriously and faithfully rendered.[29] There is no hint of furtiveness here. Other cases are less problematic but show clearly the practical consideration of service by bishops giving benefices. Bishop Pontoise of Winchester told his agents that he wished to confer a benefice on a papal chaplain because of the "use he could be to us in the future."[30] In 1313, Bishop Swinfield of Hereford explained to his colleague, the bishop of Worcester, that Swinfield could not provide Worcester's nominee with a prebend in Hereford cathedral, as Swinfield needed first to reward his own *officialis*, who had served him faithfully for years.[31] Indeed, the link between receiving a benefice and loyal service was strong enough that Richard, called "de Douai," wrote his lord the bishop of Chichester, to whom he gave his service with all reverence and subjection, that he hesitated to accept a benefice from a third party without the bishop's advice.[32]

The notion that benefice holders should be beholden to their patrons was hard to reject. In 1214, Innocent III ordered that those who held benefices in the gift of the prior and convent of Durham were to observe their oaths of fidelity to Durham.[33] In 1248, the bishop of Chichester announced that vicars of a church newly appropriated to Battle Abbey

---

[28] Reg. Winchelsey, 292–3.
[29] Ibid., 403.
[30] Reg. Pontissara, 792: "utilis nobis esse poterit in futurum."
[31] Reg. Swinfield, 483. For a nonepiscopal example, see the formula for a grant by the prior and convent of Durham to Master N., clerk, on account of N.'s services (*obsequia*) to the priory of the first, second, third, etc., suitable benefice which N. will accept in Howdenshire or Allertonshire, "even if it has cure of souls" (*Durham Annals and Documents of the Thirteenth Century*, ed. Frank Barlow, Surtees Society 155 [1945], 158).
[32] "obsequium ... cum omni reuerencia et subieccione": TNA, SC1/6/56.
[33] *Letters of Pope Innocent III (1198–1216) Concerning England and Wales*, no. 974.

were to swear fidelity to the abbey, saving of course certain rights of the bishop; the legislation was repeated at Chichester in 1289.[34] Yet such oaths could also seem tainted by simony. In 1241–5, the archbishop of York legislated that an incumbent who had, before his institution to a benefice, sworn fidelity to the holder of the advowson was to lose the benefice for simony.[35] Yet, a gloss on the *Liber Extra* compares a proctor who pleads in court against the prelate from whom he received a benefice to a vassal (*vassalus*) who fails when needed to defend the lord from whom he receives his fief (*feudum*).[36] For that matter, promises of benefices were not unusual, despite prohibitions against expectatives.[37] The principles of the Gregorian Reform were difficult to reconcile with the demands of an administrative church.

The Benefits of Benefices

What, more precisely, were the benefits benefices brought incumbents? The most obvious is income. How much varied greatly. In 1291–2, Pope Nicholas IV had the incomes of all English benefices surveyed in order to tax them. The resulting *Taxatio Nicolai IV* is incomplete, but it is the best of such thirteenth-century evaluations and records the large majority of the kingdom's benefices.[38] They ranged from an annual income of more than £230 (comparable to that of a lesser baron) to a pitiful one of 3s 4d (about the price of a simple tunic in 1313).[39] On the whole, the

---

[34] EEA 22: Chichester, no. 116.
[35] *Councils and Synods*, 492, 1088.
[36] *Corpus juris canonici emendatum et notis illustratum,* gloss on X.1.37.3, consulted in the electronic edition: UCLA Digital Library Program: Corpus Juris Canonici, 1582, http://digital.library.ucla.edu/canonlaw.
[37] Cheney, *From Becket to Langton*, 77–8. See also pensions in lieu of benefices, Chapter 5 of this book.
[38] The *Taxatio* appears to undervalue at a considerably lesser rate than earlier assessments (W. E. Lunt, *The Valuation of Norwich* [Oxford, 1926], 106–67; J. H. Denton, "The Valuation of Ecclesiastical Benefices of England and Wales," *Historical Research* 66 [1993], 241).
[39] Moorman, *Church Life*, 136. Moorman concludes that the average benefice in the *Taxatio* was worth about £10 a year (ibid., 136). But since the *Taxatio* excluded most, though not all, benefices worth less than £4 a year, that average is misleadingly high. On benefices included in and excluded from the *Taxatio*, see Sarah Davnall, Jeffrey Denton, Sheila Griffith, Dorothy Ross, and Beryl Taylor, "The *Taxatio* Database," *Bulletin of the Institute of Historical Research* 74 (1992), 95. For baronial incomes, see Christopher Dyer, *Standards of Living in the Later Middle Ages* (Cambridge, 1989), 29; Sidney Painter, *Studies in the History of the English Feudal Barony* (Baltimore, 1943), 173–4. For the tunic, see Dyer, *Standards of Living*, 175.

Taxatio suggests that benefice holders did rather well. Modern scholars believe the *Taxatio* often understates the values of benefices;[40] income taxes inevitably produce underreported incomes.[41] The church judged five marks per year to be the minimum necessary to support a parish priest,[42] so this amount tended to form the lower limit aimed at for those who held the poorest benefices, usually perpetual vicars.[43] Rectors and archdeacons, including the administrators who are the subject of this book, generally did better. In all, then, benefices supplied bureaucrats with a healthy income, one that sustained a respectable standard of living for such men. A modern study of medieval incomes concludes that in the late thirteenth century rectors and vicars ranked roughly with knights and lesser gentry.[44] A study of farmed parishes from the late fourteenth century and after suggests their values ranked with those of manors.[45] Contemporary culture drew the same rough and ready analogy. In the later twelfth century the author of the *Imago Ecclesie* devised a diagram

---

[40] Denton, "The Valuation of Ecclesiastical Benefices," 240–1; Rose Graham, "The Taxation of Pope Nicholas IV, in Graham, *English Ecclesiastical Studies* (London, 1929), 286–96; Lunt, *Valuation of Norwich*, 147–52.

[41] Hence the remarks of R. A. R. Hartridge, *A History of Vicarages in the Middle Ages* (New York, rpt. 1968), 82.

[42] In 1221, Stephen Langton's provincial synod laid down five marks as the minimum portion for a perpetual vicar (except in parts of Wales) (*Councils and Synods*, 112). Later bishops concurred in their legislation (ibid., 130, and ibid., pt. 2, 1025). In the early thirteenth century, the ordination of vicarages by Hugh of Wells, bishop of Lincoln, ran about 5–6 marks (Hartridge, *History of Vicarages*, 81).

[43] Not everyone, it should be noted, thought vicars were well supported. Robert Grosseteste inveighed against vicars' portions as being so small that they could "scarcely support [a vicar's] own life" ("unde possint propriam vitam sustentare") ("Robert Grosseteste at the Papal Curia, Lyons 1250: Edition of the Documents," ed. Servus Gieben, *Collecteana Franciscana* 41 [1971], 359). And, of course, the Fourth Lateran Council mandated that appropriations be made in a way to make sure vicars were well endowed (for these matters, see R. A. R. Hartridge, *A History of Vicarages in the Middle Ages*, 21; C. H. Lawrence, "The English Parish and Its Clergy," in *The Medieval World*, ed. Peter Linehan and Janet L. Nelson [New York, 2003], 651–3). Robert E. Rodes points out that over time, vicars were not well positioned to have their portions enlarged should the portion's real value shrink, although the canon law allowed for such revisions (*Ecclesiastical Administration in Medieval England*, 164–5). Although the law permitted bishops to undo appropriations altogether in order to ensure a properly supported parish priest, not many bishops did so. A vicar of the appropriated church of Andover remarked (with resignation?) that the priors of Andover were the rectors of Andover and always would be (*Select Cases from the Ecclesiastical Courts of the Province of Canterbury c. 1200–1301*, ed. Norma Adams and Charles Donahue Jr., Selden Society 95 [London, 1981 for 1978–9], 417–18). But bishops could threaten to reverse appropriations (EEA 37: Salisbury, no. 347).

[44] Christopher Dyer, *Standards of Living*, 20.

[45] Palmer, *Selling the Church*, 99.

that equates parish clergy with knights.⁴⁶ The author of *De Diversis Ordinibus Hominum* (ca. 1220–40), ordering social ranks hierarchically, put rectors just after earls and knights and just before clerks and townsmen such as merchants.⁴⁷ That approximate equivalency held up long after the thirteenth century, as when John Russel's fifteenth-century *Boke of Nurture* ranked holders of benefices with knights (archdeacons) and merchants (rectors and, it seems vicars ["residencers"]) at table.⁴⁸

The value of benefices is evident in the care taken by the bishops of Winchester that cases involving the deprivation of benefices be reserved from the archidiaconal courts to their own.⁴⁹ Certainly considerations of income were primary for those fierce and resolute youths of the nobility who, it was said, "would oppose themselves to the greatest dangers before they suffered deprivation of their benefices, retaining one only," and thus be reduced to what was, by noble standards, penury.⁵⁰ The noble Bogo de Clare, perhaps the greatest of thirteenth-century pluralists, known as that "invader of churches," died in possession of twenty-nine benefices. In 1290–1, the value of his (then smaller) collection stood at £1,269 6s 8d, although this sum may be overstated.⁵¹ Pluralists as successful as Bogo – and most were not that spectacularly successful – could be wealthy enough not to be tempted by a bishopric. Aymer de Lusignan, bishop-elect of Winchester, had perhaps 1,000 marks in

---

⁴⁶ Christopher Norton, "History, Wisdom and Illumination," in *Symeon of Durham: Historian of Durham and the North*, ed. David Rollason (Stamford, 1998), 79.

⁴⁷ "De Diversis Ordinibus Hominum" in *The Latin Poems Attributed to Walter Mapes*, ed. T. Wright, Camden Society (first series) 16 (London, 1841), 232–4. For its arrangement and date, see David Crouch, *The Birth of Nobility: Constructing Aristocracy in England and France 900–1300* (Harlow, 2005), 243. It should be noted, however, that this author was concerned with status as well as wealth, for he puts monks and friars before earls and knights.

⁴⁸ *Babee's Book*, ed. Frederick J. Furnival, Early English Text Society (old series) 32 (London, 1868), 187.

⁴⁹ Reg. Pontissara, 1, 215. One bishop of that see was careful generally to reserve collations when he had to leave the diocese (ibid., 87, 153, 329, 780). He seems to have thought better of this instruction on one occasion (ibid., 783). On another, he relented a little, enough to permit his vicars to collate one specified rectory (ibid., 155).

⁵⁰ Matthew Paris, *Chronica Majora*, ed. H. R. Luard (RS) (London, 1872–83), III, 418. The bishop of Worcester who Paris has make this threat (Walter de Cantilupe) is also recounted as saying that before he had become a bishop, he would just as soon have lost all his benefices under such a reform as was now proposed than lose all but one (ibid., 418).

⁵¹ Alexander Hamilton Thompson, "Pluralism in the Medieval Church, with Notes on Pluralists in the Diocese of Lincoln," part 1, *Reports and Papers of the Architectural Societies of the Counties of Lincoln and Nottingham* 33 (1915), 53–6.

The Benefice for Service and as Benefit   33

benefices; the prospect of losing them may have led him to avoid consecration as bishop.[52] Another index of a benefice's value was the value of advowsons to patrons. That value seems to have been on the rise in the thirteenth century.[53]

But medieval bureaucrats did not live by bread alone. Ordination as a clerk itself increased one's standing, especially after the Gregorian Reform. But benefices also brought status. You could trust a clerk with a benefice more than one without. This does not seem to have been a directive of the canon law, which did not distinguish between the testimony of the beneficed and unbeneficed, although it excluded from court the testimony of various classes of people, such as the insane.[54] In England, however, judges applied the law flexibly.[55] That flexibility applied to holders of benefices. It is not clear whether the word of beneficed clerks in court carried more weight because a benefice enhanced their status directly, through simple prejudice, or because they had something to lose – the benefice – should they lie and later be convicted of perjury. In either case, however, holding a benefice increased one's standing in court. Archbishop Walter Giffard of York was careful to note that a compurgator's oath was particularly credible because, among other reasons, the compurgator was beneficed.[56] When, in about the middle of the thirteenth century, the dean and chapter of Lincoln wanted to challenge the testimony of certain witnesses against them in court, they instructed their proctor to charge that "several [witnesses], since they have no ecclesiastical benefices, have had themselves written of [i.e., described as] 'rector,' or 'rectors,' or as 'vicar,'

---

[52] H. W. Ridgeway, "The Ecclesiastical Career of Aymer de Lusignan, Bishop Elect of Winchester, 1250–1260," in *The Cloister and the World: Essays in Honour of Barbara Harvey*, ed. John Blair and Brian Golding (Oxford, 1996), 152–3.

[53] Ulrich Rasche, "The Early Phase of Appropriation of Parish Churches in Medieval England," *Journal of Medieval History* 26 (2000), 230–1. Advowsons became the prize of rising families as well as of monasteries (J. E. Newman, "Greater and Lesser Landowners and Parochial Patronage: Yorkshire in the Thirteenth Century," *English Historical Review* 92 [1977], 280–308). Given lords' increasing reliance on administrators in the thirteenth century, and so their increasing need to reward them (Scott Waugh, "Tenure to Contract: Lordship and Clientage in Thirteenth-Century England," *English Historical Review* 401 [1986], 816–18), one would expect the value of advowsons to rise.

[54] For distinctions the law did make: Charles Donahue Jr., "Proof by Witnesses in the Church Courts of Medieval England: An Imperfect Reception of the Learned Law," in *On the Laws and Customs of England: Essays in Honor of Samuel E. Thorne*, ed. Morris S. Arnold et al. (Chapel Hill, 1981), 120. In the court of Canterbury, lawyers made exceptions against witnesses who were paupers, vagabonds, or of servile status (*Select Cases from the Ecclesiastical Courts*, 50).

[55] Charles Donahue Jr., "Proof by Witnesses," 127–58.

[56] Reg. Giffard of York, 4.

or 'vicars,' of churches, etc., in order to give what they say greater color."[57] Earlier, Gerald of Wales had attacked his opponent's proctor (Andrew) for not being a rector of any church.[58] Clergy who lacked benefices show the other side of the coin. At the end of the fourteenth century, bishops worried about the laziness and disorderly behavior of the unbeneficed of their dioceses.[59] That, of course, was in troubled times. In the early thirteenth century, however, Bishop Richard Poore of Salisbury had quietly hinted that less might be expected of the unbeneficed than of others when he laid down that ministers of churches in holy orders, whether "they are beneficed or not," were to live honestly and chastely.[60] James Given's analysis of eyre rolls from five counties and two cities led him to conclude that unbeneficed clerks committed the vast bulk of clerical murder.[61] And C. H. Lawrence has more recently collected evidence from the Wiltshire Eyre of 1249 that unbeneficed clergy, "an underpaid and unstable clerical proletariat," were a source of violent crime.[62] Shropshire yields similar results. The eyre of 1256 there turned up four beneficed clerks accused of violence, compared with seventeen unbeneficed clerks.[63]

[57] "Aliquis seu aliqui cum nullum haberet ecclesiasticum beneficium fecit seu fecerunt se scribi rectorem sive rectores vicarium sive vicarios ecclesie etc ut dicta sua magis colorarent" (LAO, Dii/62/1/7c). This could, perhaps, have been put more clearly. I should note that this document appears to have been a draft of a letter, not a finished product.

[58] "Personatum in ecclesia non habet" – and whatever *redditus* he enjoys is insignificant: Gerald of Wales, "De Invectionibus," ed. W. S. Davies, in *Y Cymmrodor: The Magazine of the Honourable Society of Cymmrodorion* 30 (1920), 94.

[59] A. K. McHardy, "The Churchmen of Chaucer's London: The Seculars," *Medieval Prosopography* 16 (1995), 85. Bishops saw chantry priests as a problem because many resisted the caps on payment imposed in the wake of the Black Death (A. K. McHardy, "Ecclesiastics and Economics: Poor Priests, Prosperous Laymen, and Proud Prelates in the Reign of Richard II," *Studies in Church History* 24 [1987], 136–7); this attitude may well have had a negative consequence for the reputation of the unbeneficed generally in the Late Middle Ages.

[60] "sive sint beneficiati sive non" (*Councils and Synods*, 62, and see 229). Some statutes attributed to Archbishop Winchelsey regulate nonbeneficed clergy. They demand stipendiary priests swear, among other things, not to cause conflicts between rectors and vicars on the one hand, and parishioners on the other (ibid., 1383).

[61] James Buchanan Given, *Society and Homicide in Thirteenth-Century England* (Stanford, 1977), 14, 83–5.

[62] "The English Parish and Its Clergy in the Thirteenth Century," 656. See, by contrast, Simon Townley's more optimistic assessment: "Unbeneficed Clergy in Two English Dioceses," in *Studies in Medieval Clergy and Ministry in Medieval England*, ed. David M. Smith (York, 1991), 60.

[63] *The Rolls of the Shropshire Eyre of 1256*, ed. Alan Harding, Selden Society 96 (London, 1981 for 1980), 199, 202, 212, 214, 221–2, 241–3, 252, 255, 275–6, 283, 289–90, 294–5, 299, 308. For monastics, not included in this count, see ibid., 237, 259–60, 272, 289. Cases that went to a jury usually resulted in a guilty finding (ibid., 228, 233–4, 263, 272–5).

For some, the standing that came with a benefice was tied to its monetary value. One plaintiff, offered a benefice to settle a suit in 1315, sniffed that it was too piddling a one for him, "especially as [he] ... is a Master of Arts and son of Roger of Noyers, knight."[64] But even a vicar could have some standing. In 1281, the vicar of Wootton Wawen, whose living was worth a mere £5 annually according to the *Taxatio*,[65] was summoned from his house to stop an outbreak of fisticuffs between the prior of Wootton and one of his monks; the vicar had been the person to whom many of the prior's household had already turned to complain about their superior.[66] The vicar could furnish his own chaplain, servant, and clerk to back his story.[67] Local vicars as well as rectors were suitable to reinforce the authority of a rural dean in pronouncing an excommunication.[68]

Indeed, because benefices were so often rewards for distinguished achievement in the world of scholarship or governance, they likely conferred status because of that association itself. After all, it is always easy to think that those who have prizes have them because they deserve them.[69] One bold fourteenth-century defender of pluralism argued that a competent bureaucrat with many benefices was better for his parishes than a single resident and incompetent rector was for his, even if the latter was on the spot.[70] In the thirteenth century, Bishop Giffard of Worcester suggested that the rigor of papal rules against pluralism did not suit England.[71]

This attitude toward the beneficed made some sense. After all, obtaining a benefice was supposed to entail the investigation of one's character and attainments. At the time of institution, when the bishop granted the presentee the equivalent of title to the benefice, the bishop was expected to examine the presentee. The fact that this examination tested one's learning is especially noteworthy; this was an age in which educational

---

[64] *Year Books of Edward II*, 18, ed. F. W. Maitland et al., Selden Society 17- (passim) (London, 1903–), 27, 135. And see the remarks of Lawrence, "The English Parish and Its Clergy in the Thirteenth Century," 657.
[65] Taxatio of Pope Nicholas IV, online edition, www.hrionline.ac.uk/db/taxatio, sub "Wootton Wawen."
[66] Reg. Giffard of Worcester, 129.
[67] Ibid., 130, 131 n 1.
[68] Ibid., 179, 188.
[69] And so the conclusion could be drawn regarding benefices: M. Harvey, "The Benefice as Property: An Aspect of Anglo-Papal Relations during the Pontificate of Martin V, 1417–31," *Studies in Church History* 24 (1987), 169, 172–3.
[70] C. J. Godfrey, "Pluralists in the Province of Canterbury in 1366," *Journal of Ecclesiastical History* 11 (1960) 24–5.
[71] Reg. Giffard of Worcester, 116.

accomplishment itself conferred status, at least in the educated circles in which diocesan administrators moved.[72] Moreover, only men of legitimate birth could hold a benefice unless properly dispensed. And the bishop's examination was the second of two, for the bishop would have already had the results of a previous inquiry carried out in the neighborhood of the benefice to glean any information the locals might have about the presentee.[73] Thus, a beneficed clerk was, in theory, a thoroughly vetted man. Indeed, proof that one had a benefice, in the form of a letter of institution, was enough to allow a man to bypass the usual scrutiny of qualifications for ordination to the clergy.[74]

Moreover, benefices often conferred the standing that comes with authority. The chief variety of benefice held by diocesan administrators was the parish church, often conjoined to the prebends of cathedrals and so with the cure entrusted to a vicar. That holders of parishes were known as *rectores* was a sign that they could be regarded not simply as ministers to souls, but as rulers of them.[75] In their parishes they were like secular lords, exacting obligations, addressed as *dominus* and *seigneur*.[76]

---

[72] Alexander Murray, *Reason and Society in the Middle Ages* (reprint with corrections) (Oxford, 1985).

[73] The local investigation sometimes concerned only the benefice, not the presentee (Brian Kemp, "The Acta of the English Rural Deans," in *The Foundations of English Ecclesiastical History: Studies Presented to David Smith*, ed. Phillipa Hoskin, Christopher Brooke, and Barrie Dobson [Woodbridge, 2005], 143). For a list of articles of local inquiry, including those regarding the presentee's legitimate birth, free condition, age, life and conversation, letters, and lack of notoriety, see J. W. Gray, "The Ius Praesentandi in England from the Constitutions of Clarendon to Bracton," *English Historical Review* 67 (1952), 509, and for a similar list, Reg. Halton, I, 5.

[74] William J. Dohar, "*Sufficienter Litteratus*: Clerical Examination and Instruction for the Cure of Souls," in *A Distinct Voice: Medieval Studies in Honor of Leonard E. Boyle, O.P.*, ed. Jacqueline Brown and William P. Stoneman (Toronto, 1997), 307–8; idem, "Medieval Ordination Lists: The Origins of a Medieval Record," *Archives* 20 (1992), 22. And, of course, ordination to holy orders was itself the usual prerequisite for institution; benefice holders could often have been expected to have received the double examination required at ordination. (On the *duplex scrutinium*, see ibid., 24–5.)

[75] G. W. O. Addleshaw, *Rectors, Vicars, and Patrons in Twelfth and Early Thirteenth Century Canon Law*, Saint Anthony's Hall Publications 9 (York, 1956), 7. Addleshaw says that "rector" came into general use only in the twelfth century. If the original sense of rector as ruler in this context died, it died hard. A late fourteenth-century composition refers to a man as "gubernatorem siue rectorem ecclesie de Wappenham" (BL, Harley 4714, f. 218v). The scribe thus worked to make this sense clear.

[76] The comparison is made on these grounds by John Van Engen, "Sacred Sanctions for Lordship," in *Cultures of Power*, ed. Thomas N. Bisson (Philadelphia, 1995), 208–9. And some had other powers, like the prebendaries and dignitaries of York Minster, who exercised ecclesiastical jurisdiction over the lands attached to their benefices (Sandra Brown, *Medieval Courts of York Minster Peculiar*, Borthwick Papers 66 [York, 1984], 4).

While Adam Marsh warned that rectors hungered too often for riches, he also said that they lusted after domination (*dominandi*).[77] Sometimes this attitude simply and easily slipped out of the mouths of bishops whose minds were on other issues.[78] Bishop Sutton of Lincoln complained about rectors who were supposed to rule their churches ("reguntur") farming them out instead.[79] Bishop Suffield of Norwich determined the tithes and revenues to be enjoyed by a rector who governed ("gubernabit") the church of Cavenham.[80] Archbishop Walter Giffard of York referred to a church that was not accustomed to being governed by two rectors.[81] The latter situation was the sort against which the legate Ottobuono reacted strongly: a church with more than one rector was like a monster with more than one head, he thought,[82] thus likening a rectory to the body of Christ or the body politic, each of course ruled by its head.

Moreover, this attitude applied to (perpetual) vicars too. Robert Grosseteste couched his complaint about measly vicars' portions by pointing out that such men could not rule and govern without the supports necessary for their office.[83] Bishop Maidstone of Hereford announced that a rector and vicar should both retain their portions in a certain church as long as they should rule ("rexerint") there; their deaths would open the way to the church's appropriation.[84] In the late twelfth century one of his predecessors at Hereford had referred to two perpetual vicars as "ruling souls."[85] Peter of Blois applied the old moral precept to a vicar and his parish: if he is to "rule and teach" others, he must rule and teach himself.[86]

---

[77] *The Letters of Adam Marsh*, ed. C. H. Lawrence (Oxford, 2006–10), II, no. 245, 30a.

[78] And, also, out of the mouths of popes: a benefice given to a minor should during his minority be ruled (*regere*) by clerks, not laypeople (X.1.14.2).

[79] Rolls and Reg. Sutton, VI, 63.

[80] EEA 32: Norwich, no. 129.

[81] "quae per duos consuerit gubernari rectores" (Ref. Giffard of York, 75). See also the legate Ottobuono on appropriations, referring to a church accustomed to being governed ("consuevit gubernari") by its own rector (*Councils and Synods*, 770) and churches split between portioners "regenda" by more than one rector (ibid., 111).

[82] Ibid., 761: "there ought to be one rector in a church, as one head for one body," discussed by Addleshaw, *Rectors, Vicars, and Patrons*, 11.

[83] "Robert Grosseteste at the Papal Curia," ed. Gieben, 359.

[84] EEA 35: Hereford, no. 28.

[85] "regendarum animarum": EEA VII: Hereford, no. 218 See also the bishop of Chichester making a similar general statement, calling on the diocese's archdeacons, deans, "and all parsons, vicars, and chaplains ruling parishes" ("et omnibus personis, vicariis et capellanis parochias regentibus") to get the laity to take part in processions in 1248 (EEA 22: Chichester, no. 131, and see no. 132).

[86] Peter of Blois, *The Later Letters of Peter of Blois*, ed. Elizabeth Revell (Oxford, 1993), no. 79 ("regere et docere").

Lesser lights also spoke in these terms, like the archdeacon of Huntingdon who in 1175–90 announced that he had received one Richard the clerk "ad regimen ecclesie de Morbourne."[87] A Pipewell Abbey scribe referred to the father and proctor of an underage rector of Braybrooke as ruling on the incumbent's behalf.[88] According to his biographer, St. Edmund of Abingdon once took on the *regimen* of a wealthy church (solely, of course, to effect repairs to the fabric).[89]

Given this combination of income and status,[90] benefices were important to the men who had them. One Peter, at least according to his own account, surrendered his prebend only after he had gone insane, seeking his own death by drowning or the noose.[91] One clerk, William de Plaiz, wept to lose his benefice, even when he managed to keep most of the income.[92]

Concerns about service and simony, and an awareness of benefices as channels of status, presumably lie behind a papal tendency to speak in terms of "honoring" clerks with benefices. Honorius III's words in the epigraph to this chapter serve as an example. The pope informs the archbishop of York that faithful servants should be honored with benefices, for they might not serve if they must do so at their own expense.[93] Honorius thus acknowledged the obvious – that he gave benefices in return for service – but implied that such rewards were simply to cover his servants' expenses rather than constitute some sort of payment that could be regarded as profit. The suggestion of simony was thus delicately avoided. At the same time, he highlighted the fact that with a benefice went honor, thus further diverting attention from the economic value of the benefice, the aspect that more easily pointed toward simony.[94] The

---

[87] *Twelfth-Century English Archidiaconal and Vice-Archidiaconal Acta*, ed. Brian Kemp, Canterbury and York Society 92 (Woodbridge, 2001), no. 121.

[88] "regebat" (BL, Cotton MS Caligula A. xii, f. 80r).

[89] C. H. Lawrence, *St. Edmund of Abingdon: A Study of Hagiography and History* (Oxford, 1960), 253. For a rector who resigned the *regimen* of his church, see Rolls and Reg. Sutton, III, 66.

[90] There is, however, an argument to be made that hierarchical status groups were only coming to be distinguished from groups defined by income or wealth in thirteenth-century England: Crouch, *Birth of Nobility*, 228–52. For what appears to be an instance, see the discussion of *De Diversis Ordinibus Hominum*, earlier, at n 47.

[91] *Die Register Innocenz' III*, eds. Othmar Hageneder et al. (Graz, 1964-), I, no. 297, calendared CPL, I, 2.

[92] *Select Cases from the Ecclesiastical Courts*, 14, and see 12.

[93] Rot. Gray, 137–8.

[94] For a twelfth-century bishop honoring his clerk (out of friendship, he says) with a benefice, see *The Letters and Charters of Gilbert Foliot*, ed. Adrian Morey and C. N. L. Brooke (Cambridge, 1967), no. 240.

Fourth Lateran Council had earlier spoken of benefices as honors, noting that the apostolic see might issue dispensations for pluralism in order to honor exalted and lettered persons with greater benefices.⁹⁵

This point about language is not confined to Rome. Adam Marsh wrote to dissuade the bishop of London from instituting one Geoffrey Gross to the church of Ockendon. In the course of making his case, Adam criticized those who (like Gross, presumably) "obstinately use the pastoral office of ecclesiastical government to arrogate the honor to themselves and in every way avoid the burden, and have no fear in procuring the pride of transitory power and the quest for wealth."⁹⁶ It was presumably the desire to accomplish something like this that led Archbishop Romeyn of York in 1287 to grant a royal justice a pension of 100s a year until the archbishop could "honor" the justice with a benefice; the archbishop hoped that the grantee would work to protect the archbishop and his churches.⁹⁷ Late in his career, Peter of Blois complained of being expelled from the honor of his archdeaconry.⁹⁸

Finally, another benefit flowed from a benefice. This benefit was security. The Peter who went out of his mind was, after all, to get his benefices back. So long as an incumbent was sure to fulfill the obligations of office, or ensure that someone else fulfilled them, law and sentiment protected him in his tenure. After the income itself, this aspect of the benefice as property was perhaps its greatest allure.

---

⁹⁵ Fourth Lateran Council, chap. 29: *Decrees of the Ecumenical Councils I: Nicaea to Lateran V*, ed. Norman P. Tanner (Washington, DC, 1990), 249. For this particular rationale for pluralism and similar honor language in a papal letter to an English bishop, see EEA 13: Worcester, no. 159.

⁹⁶ *Letters of Adam Marsh*, I, no. 74: "per regiminis ecclesiastici officium pastorale, et peruicacius arrogantes honorem et onus declinantes omnimodis, tam fastum caduce potestatis, quam questum mobilis affluentie ... procurare non formidant." I have produced Lawrence's translation.

⁹⁷ Reg. Romeyn, II, 160–1.

⁹⁸ John D. Cotts, *The Clerical Dilemma: Peter of Blois and Literate Culture in the Twelfth Century* (Washington, DC, 2009), 44.

4

Benefices and Security of Tenure

> What miserable drones and traitors have I nourished and promoted in my household, who let their lord be treated with such shameful contempt by a low-born clerk![1]

Did Henry II actually say this about Thomas Becket? One cannot know.[2] Henry's frustration with the archbishop does, however, echo loud in the sources. The king had made his right-hand man archbishop, only to find he had created a resourceful, determined opponent who made life miserable. Henry's *cri de coeur* famously prompted four of his knights to set off for Canterbury, where they solved Henry's problem by murdering the archbishop; whether Henry had meant for them to do it is hard to tell.[3]

---

[1] Frank Barlow, *Thomas Becket* (Berkeley and Los Angeles, 1986), 235.
[2] The chroniclers agree that the knights who murdered Becket sought the king's favor in leaving for Canterbury and that Henry also complained of the lack of support among his followers (Nicholas Vincent, "The Murderers of Thomas Becket," in *Bischofsmord im Mittelalter/The Murder of Bishops in the Middle Ages*, ed. Natalie Fryde and Dirk Reitz [Göttingen, 2003], 243). Henry's words were presumably consistent with the knights' interpretation.
[3] Whatever Henry's intentions, these men "acted within, or on the fringe of, an official mission" from the king which held potential for the same result (Barlow, *Thomas Becket*, 236–7). W. L. Warren points to the uncertain evidence regarding the knights' own initial intentions (*Henry II* [Berkeley and Los Angeles, 1973], 509). Becket's medieval biographers, interestingly, often assumed that the knights intended Becket's death (ibid., n 4), but this likely reflects the biographers' interest in Becket as martyr at least as much as an expectation that murder was the most effective way to solve Henry's problem, the aspect of the situation I stress. The recent tendency is to see Becket's death as an attempted arrest gone wrong: Anne Duggan, *Thomas Becket* (London, 2004), 204–13, who also stresses the incipient violence of the situation, as does Frank Barlow, who seems to give credence to talk about Becket's murder at Henry's court leading up to the deed (Barlow, *Thomas*

In an earlier age, English kings had sometimes simply removed bishops they found unsatisfactory.⁴ Times had changed by Henry's reign. The Gregorian reform had loosened lay control over church office and had sought to break it entirely. At the top of society, a strong king might still bully his men into bishoprics, but even he could not so easily bully them out again. Only the pope could depose Becket, and that the pope was unwilling to do. At least Henry was still king, and so well positioned to harass Becket, seizing his lands, confiscating his supporters' property, driving them into exile. But with the archbishop obdurate, the only permanent solution was his death. If Henry had intended Becket's murder, the fact that Henry was king, and so had subordinates to do any dirty work, gave him plausible deniability.⁵ (Becket's martyrdom, however, forced Henry to compromise with a dead man.)

In outline, the conflict between Henry and Becket delineates those discussed in this chapter: conflicts between the patrons and recipients of benefices.⁶ Of course, Becket presented a problem that most incumbents did not. A simple rectory, for example, did not offer the platform from which to annoy one's patron that Canterbury gave its archbishop. But Becket's security of tenure in Canterbury was the same immovable object

---

Becket, 235). Duggan also points out that warnings that Henry might kill Becket had preceded the archbishop's flight from England (Duggan, *Thomas Becket*, 186). The editors of a recent collection of essays on the murder of medieval bishops note that "whether Henry II was actually responsible for giving the order to murder Becket will probably never be established. Such assassinations were often on the orders of rulers" ("Introduction," in *Bischofsmord im Mittelalter/Murder of Bishops*, 9).

⁴ E.g., Robert of Jumièges et al. in 1052 (Frank Barlow, *The English Church 1000–1066*, 2nd ed. [London, 1979], 50). For Duke William's expulsion of the archbishop of Rouen in 1055, see C. N. L. Brooke, with Rosalind Brooke, "The Bishops of England and Normandy in the Eleventh Century: A Contrast," in C. N. L. Brooke, *Churches and Churchmen in Medieval Europe* (London, 1999), 109.

⁵ Henry's ambivalent treatment of the murders (on which, see Vincent, "Murderers of Thomas Becket," 248–62) is consistent both with, on the one hand, Henry's responsibility for their actions and a wish to deny it, and, on the other, with scenarios in which Henry was innocent of murderous intent.

⁶ Here it is also worth noting that Henry had probably expected Becket's continued service in the office of royal chancellor, and was surprised and angry when Becket resigned the post on becoming archbishop (D. J. A. Matthew, "The Letter Writing of Archbishop Becket," in *Belief and Culture in the Middle Ages: Studies Presented to Henry Mayr-Harting*, ed. Richard Gameson and Henrietta Leyser [Oxford, 2001], 302–3). Matthew also suggests that Henry's relations with Becket, as opposed to the issue of clerical liberties, was more important in the Becket controversy than sources produced after Becket's martyrdom suggest (ibid., 303–4). These points heighten the similarity between Henry's struggle with his archbishop and the struggles of patrons with incumbents discussed in this chapter.

a dissatisfied patron faced in any incumbent. In the thirteenth century, lesser patrons of lesser ecclesiastical benefices were sometimes tempted to imitate Henry as well as they could. By that time, however, the canon law and the courts that administered it had grown great in complexity and power. And that law protected the holders of benefices from those who would deprive them. Here the nature of the benefice as property as well as office was critical.[7] The law and the courts protected the benefice as property. So, I will argue, did sentiment in favor of lifetime tenure in benefices. For patrons who expected continued loyal service from beneficed clerks, this protection was a problem. From the patron's point of view, security of tenure meant that benefices provided little means by which to discipline the subordinates who received them. Like Henry, such patrons had some room for maneuver. In Henry's case, that room came from his power as king. Lesser patrons naturally lacked a king's resources. But, as will be seen, they sometimes tried other options, some of them provided by complications in the canon law itself. Yet patrons' need to resort to those options and their mixed success ultimately show the solidity of incumbents' security against their patrons. In the end, patrons as well as incumbents would have to regard benefices as irrevocable gifts, not as salary that could be cut off for failure to perform duties unrelated to the office of the benefice itself, duties for which in fact benefices were given. And that hard fact of life applied even when the bishop himself was the patron. I will discuss both the limits that applied to patrons in general (because bishops also suffered from them) and also instances of bishops specifically dealing with the security of tenure of their own clerks.

Three factors constrained bishops – indeed, all patrons – from expelling incumbents from benefices in their own patronage: the law itself, which provided a narrow range of grounds on which bishops could do so; a general sentiment that narrowed that range even further in favor of incumbents; and courts of appeal to enforce the law against bishops who might disregard it, and in particular to apply the law in light of sentiment so as to foreclose the most obvious ground a patron, even a bishop, might use to deprive a disloyal or simply an inconvenient incumbent. Of course, bishops, more liable to be impressed by ecclesiastical jurisdiction than lay patrons, were presumably more constrained by these forces than were lay lords.

[7] For which, see Chapter 3.

Law and Sentiment

In general, the canon law protected clerks' tenure in their benefices. Such security pertained even in the face of ecclesiastical judges, who could not remove incumbents except lawfully, that is, for the canonically valid reasons of an unjust title, failure to perform the office, or other lapses. "He who is despoiled by a judge, with the order of law overlooked, shall be restored to all," said the law.[8] For good measure, an incumbent's renunciation of a benefice following such despoliation was counted as null.[9] Moreover, if an advowson changed hands, the new holder could not evict the incumbent from the benefice.[10] In England, however, the canon law permitted the removal of an incumbent who had been instituted on the presentation of a party who had had false title to the advowson.[11]

The law focused on what might be broadly called morals, qualifications, and obedience lapses as legitimate causes to deprive an incumbent. Incumbents guilty of simony, pluralism, heresy, or incontinence might be expelled. Failure to obtain ordination or license for an irregularity, such as bastardy, was a kind of qualifications flaw that could have the same result. Refusal to heed properly constituted ecclesiastical authority – by violating an interdict, for example – could trigger deprivation.[12] Three exceptions, however, pertain to service to one's lord. In a significant though limited case, a patron could turn out a beneficed proctor for bad service. A clerk who obtained a benefice but then acted as proctor or advocate in a suit against his patron was an ingrate who could be deprived.[13] This point was picked up by the glossators.[14] Archbishop Winchelsey may have applied the principle in 1309, when he moved to deprive Thomas de Gentham, "the ingrate on whom we conferred a

---

[8] X.2.13.7.
[9] X.2.13.2.
[10] X.3.28.19.
[11] X.3.28.19. The Common Law regarded an incumbent as secure even in this case. See at nn. 51–3.
[12] For a kind of catalog of grounds for deprivation, see G. Mollat, "Bénéfices ecclésiastiques en Occident," in *Dictionnaire de droit canonique*, ed. R. Naz (Paris, 1937), II, cols. 431–3.
[13] X.1.37.3.
[14] James A. Brundage, "The Ethics of Advocacy: Confidentiality and Conflict of Interest in Medieval Canon Law," in *Grundlagen als Rechts: Festschrift für Peter Landau zum 65. Gerburtstag II*, ed. Richard H. Helmholz, Paul Mikrat, and Michael Stolleis (Paderborn, 2000), 460; James Brundage, *The Medieval Origins of the Legal Profession: Canonists, Civilians, and Courts* (Chicago, 2008), 321–2.

church of the same place [i.e., Gentham]." Thomas had impetrated complaints against the archbishop at Rome, complaints evidently rooted in the archbishop's accusation against him of misusing funds as executor of a will.[15] Although Winchelsey explicitly describes Thomas as an *ingratus*, thus linking him by implication to this provision of the law, there is no evidence that Thomas had indeed been the archbishop's proctor. The archdiocese of York presents another possibility. Robert de Scarborough received several benefices from successive archbishops of York, rising to the deanery of the cathedral in 1279 under Archbishop Wickwane. But Robert refused to help the next archbishop, John Romeyn, meet the costs of a suit in Rome, a suit which, had Romeyn lost it, would have had the effect of removing Robert from one of his benefices. Le Romeyn, was, at the least, miffed by Robert's ungracious behavior. The archbishop proceeded to try to expel Robert from his benefices, demanding that Robert show by what dispensation he held incompatible benefices in plurality.[16] Here, it should be noted, Romeyn had a case to make on the grounds of disloyalty – specifically failure to defend the church of York – but he made it on a charge of pluralism instead. Another possible instance is that of Bishop Giffard of Worcester's years'-long campaign to deprive Peter de Leicester, his one-time steward and, at least in one instance, ad hoc proctor, although the case is murky.[17] Giffard, it should be noted, did accuse Peter of ingratitude.[18] These are only possibilities, and there are few enough of them. It is not clear that this provision, specifically aimed at lawyers, found much application. Perhaps the tendency to reward proctors with pensions *de camera* over benefices (see Chapter 5) helps account for the paucity of incidents of enforcement.

A second case, less significant because narrow, applied specifically to the *ministri* of the Court of Arches, the archbishop's court of appeal for the province of Canterbury. Those who had benefices were to lose them should they violate the rules of the court.[19] It should be noted in this instance that a benefice from any patron seems to have been subject to deprivation; the loss of benefices here was not to be a tool of discipline wielded by a patron unless the archbishop himself happened to be the patron.

[15] Reg. Winchelsey, 1048, 1060. I have not been able to determine whether Winchelsey succeeded in this deprivation.
[16] Reg. Romeyn, nos. 148, 555.
[17] M. Burger, "Peter of Leicester, Bishop Godfrey Giffard of Worcester, and the Problem of Benefices," *Catholic Historical Review* 95 (2009), 464–5.
[18] Reg. Giffard, 306; WRO, Rf.x716.093 BA 2648/1(i), f. 265v (p. 522).
[19] *The Medieval Court of Arches*, ed. F. Donald Logan, Canterbury and York Society 95 (Woodbridge, 2005), 19–20.

A third provision of the law did not apply to patrons but should have held great potential as a disciplinary tool for the bishops who are the focus of this book. The law permitted deprivation of those who had violated their oaths of homage to their prelate as their lord; the case that had prompted the rescript embodying this principle was that of an archdeacon who had sued his bishop in a secular court over spiritual matters.[20] This oath of homage was glossed as being the more ecclesiastical *fidelitas et obedientia* the archdeacon had sworn the bishop by reason of his archdeaconry.[21] One might expect bishops to have deprived subordinates on the basis of such oaths whenever such subordinates gave enough trouble to make deprivation desirable. But I have found no sign that bishops (or others for that matter) made such use of these oaths in expelling their servants from benefices. Perhaps oaths of fidelity and obedience were understood in ways sufficiently circumscribed (fidelity and obedience in regard to what?) that their usefulness for the purpose of discipline was limited. Perhaps in practice courts preferred to set the bar for deprivation higher. After all, the case from which the canon derived was that of an archdeacon who actively harmed his lord. Perhaps "fidelity and obedience" did not require active service so far as the courts were concerned. Such a reading suggests that sentiment in favor of security of tenure in benefices effectively curbed patrons, even bishops, from using failure to render administrative or legal service against holders of benefices in their gift. Courts of appeal, rather than the letter of the law, in turn allowed such sentiment greater rein. In any case, bishops made little use of even the tools that the letter of the law gave them. Sentiment in favor of security of tenure, either felt by bishops themselves or by the courts of appeal that constrained them, accounts for that failure.[22]

Sentiment that tenure for life in a benefice should be normal is evident in other ways. An essential element of the Gregorian reform had been

---

[20] X.5.31.15.

[21] *Corpus juris canonici emendatum et notis illustratum, Gregorii XIII. Pont. Max. iussu editum* (Rome, 1582), gloss on X.5.31.15, consulted in the electronic edition: UCLA Digital Library Program: Corpus Juris Canonici, 1582 <http://digital.library.ucla.edu/canonlaw>. Indeed, X.1.37.3, concerning a proctor who sued a patron, received a similar gloss comparing the situation to that of a lord and his fief-holding man (Brundage, *Origins of the Legal Profession*, 322).

[22] Although I have compared in this chapter the security of tenure of bishops and those who enjoyed other kinds of benefices, the analogy is, of course, imperfect. Consider sentiment and law regarding resignation. No authorities insisted that clerks be prevented from resigning ordinary benefices. Bishoprics, however, were a different matter (on which, see C. R. Cheney, *Pope Innocent III and England* [Stuttgart, 1976], 78–9; Marylou Ruud, "Episcopal Reluctance: Lanfranc's Resignation Reconsidered," *Albion* 19 [1987], 171–2).

an effort to stamp out the inheritance of benefices, a drive that had fed the accompanying move to enforce the requirement of clerical celibacy. It was this impulse and the request of some English bishops that had led Pope Honorius III to declare that anyone holding a benefice whose father had preceded him in that benefice was subject to automatic deprivation.[23] Now Honorius confronted an actual case. A father had resigned his benefice, and the patron had presented the previous incumbent's son, who had been instituted. The law was the law, and so the pope ordered the archbishop of York to deprive the son, but only after the archbishop had provided the son another benefice in its stead.[24] Such attitudes lay behind attempts – of uncertain success – to extend a measure of security even to nonbeneficed clergy. Stephen Langton warned that rectors should not remove stipendiary priests serving churches without reasonable cause.[25] In 1229, the bishop of Worcester legislated that such priests should not be removed by rectors within a seven-year period, except for a just and reasonable cause.[26] From a different angle, the canons of the Fourth Lateran Council imply a similar orientation. They call for the punishment of bishops who institute unworthy candidates to benefices but remain silent regarding eviction of instituted candidates themselves. Indeed, a decision of the bishop of Norwich similarly implies sentiment in favor of security that extended beyond legal requirements. A bishop of Norwich had collated a vicarage – but wrongly, for he did not in fact have the patronage, but had mistakenly derived his right from his predecessor's collation of the vicarage. Now the rector petitioned the next bishop to consolidate the vicarage and rectory, with the consent of the rectory's patron. The bishop agreed that the consolidation was consonant with the law (*ius*), but judged that the vicar should continue on until his death or resignation, at which point the consolidation should take effect.[27]

---

[23] *Councils and Synods*, 98–9. The legate Otho was mandating deprivation in such cases in 1237 (ibid., 253).

[24] CPL, I, 113; *Regesta Honorii Papae III Iussu et Mvnificentia Leonis XIII Pontificis Maximi ex Vaticanis Archetypis aliisque Fontibvs*, ed. Petrus Presutti (Rome, 1888–1895; rpt., Hildesheim, 1978), no. 5891. Of course, one should not assume that the facts of the case as Honorius recounts them are correct. Papal letters frequently rehearsed facts as presented to the curia by one side of the dispute (C. R. Cheney, "The Letters of Pope Innocent III," in Cheney, *Medieval Texts and Studies* [Oxford, 1973], 25–6). I have tried to keep this point clear in using such evidence in this book.

[25] *Councils and Synods*, 30, and see 84.

[26] Ibid., 175. This provision was also made in some unknown diocese at about this time (ibid., 186).

[27] EEA 32: Norwich, 216–17. Of course, another factor in this decision may have been the contrary view taken by the Common Law (on which, see at nn. 51–3), and a calculation by the rector that a friendly resolution – as the bishop termed it – would be best.

That ecclesiastical courts – especially courts of appeal, not subject to a bishop's power – should have taken this attitude makes sense. The officers of those courts themselves had a stake in the security of benefice holders because they themselves were generally beneficed. Indeed, bishops too were products of the same system; they generally shared the same education (grammar, logic, and rhetoric, followed by law or theology, in the universities) and had, too, held benefices before their elevation to the episcopate. They would have well understood, even felt, the pressures to keep incumbents secure.[28] The tendency of bishops and other patrons to use moral lapses rather than accusations of disloyalty to deprive incumbents (discussed later) points to sentiment in favor of incumbency: the focus on moral lapses took attention away from the tie between patron and incumbent as the locus of complaint even where the law might allow it. The tendency for some patrons to ignore the law altogether points to the same conclusion.

The notion that recipients of benefices should expect to hold them for life seems, so far as I have been able to determine, to have been more of an unspoken assumption of the canon law than an explicitly spelled out principle.[29] But the assumption was powerful, molding how benefices were treated by the courts and in legislation. The most explicit statements pertain to legislation regarding vicarages. Perpetual vicarages joined rectories, prebends, and archdeaconries only in the later twelfth century as benefices. Because they were newcomers,[30] the legislation concerning vicarages was explicit about what had only been implicit concerning older sorts of benefices: that they were to be held for life. Here the greatest danger came from the appropriator of the church or rectory, who had earlier been able to treat vicars as dismissible servants rather than as holders of

---

[28] These were forces that reinforced sentiment in favor of perpetuity in the High Middle Ages. That does not mean, however, that such sentiment originated in this period. Life tenures were frequently arranged among holders of benefices in the ninth through eleventh centuries (see instances in Susan Wood, *The Proprietary Church in the Medieval West* [Oxford, 2006], 543–9, 554, 574, 612).

[29] Though the principle is noted by G. W. O. Addleshaw, *Rectors, Vicars and Patrons in Twelfth and Early Thirteenth Century Canon Law* (London, 1956), 10–11, and Robert C. Palmer, *Selling the Church: The English Parish Church in Law, Commerce, and Religion, 1350–1550* (Chapel Hill, 2002), 16. R. N. Swanson, *Church and Society in Late Medieval England* (Manchester, 1989), refers to benefices in passing as "freehold income" (43). Robert E. Rodes Jr. states without elaboration that once a presentee to a benefice "was put in, his tenure was fully protected: he could not be put out except for specific misconduct established in full judicial proceedings" (*Ecclesiastical Administration in Medieval England* [Notre Dame, 1977], 117).

[30] Ulrich Rasche, "The Early Phase of Appropriation of Parish Churches in Medieval England," *Journal of Medieval History* 26 (2000), 214–23.

benefices. In 1215, the Fourth Lateran Council decreed that vicars were to be perpetual,[31] hence the modern description of its canons as the parish priest's *magna carta*.[32] This attitude is evident on the ground in England as well. In the early thirteenth century, the bishops of Norwich ordained various vicarages. They did allow that a vicar could be removed by the bishop – not, one might note, by the patron – but the reasons specified for such removal concern delinquencies in the vicar's conduct of his office or his defrauding of the church of Norwich or the appropriator.[33] From the later twelfth century, the bishops of Hereford were sure to stress the security of tenure of vicars when ordaining vicarages.[34] When in 1191–1201 the archbishop of York instituted his own man to a vicarage in the presentation of a third party, the archbishop said emphatically that the recipient was to have it for "tota vita sua … in perpetuam vicariam."[35] The archbishop stressed another vicar's security ca. 1202, instituting him so as to possess "peacefully the free, pure, and perpetual vicarage for life," noting that benefice holders were often disturbed by the perversity of the wicked; the archbishop sought to act so that "contention may not find the place that peaceful possession ought to have."[36] The situation was rather different from that of the mid-twelfth century, when the bishop of Carlisle appropriated Wetheral to Wetheral Priory, laying down that the vicar was to be put in or removed at the priory's own choice.[37] One sign

[31] Chapter 32: *Decrees of the Ecumenical Councils I*, ed. Norman P. Tanner (Washington, DC, 1990), 250.
[32] R. A. R. Hartridge, *A History of Vicarages in the Middle Ages* (Cambridge, 1930), 21. (Addleshaw, *Rectors, Vicars, and Patrons*, 23, however, thinks the description more properly belongs to Gregory IX's mandates that holders of churches not be dispossessed without judgment.)
[33] EEA 21: Norwich, nos. 2, 5, 15.
[34] EEA VII: Hereford, xliii. See also the series of thirteenth-century appropriations carried out by the bishops of Durham, to take effect only when the incumbent rector dies or resigns the church (EEA 29: Durham, nos. 11. 61, 63, 66, 102, 143, 172–3).
[35] EEA 27: York, no. 27.
[36] EEA 27: York, no. 12: "liberam, puram et perpetuam vicariam in vita sua pacifice possidendam"; "ne locum inveniat contentio ubi pacifica debet esse possessio." See also ibid., no. 15.
[37] EEA 30: Carlisle, no. 7. Changing times, and perhaps a lag in Welsh acceptance of Anglo-Continental practice, are evident in episcopal pronouncements regarding the vicarage of Caldicot in the diocese of Llandaff. In 1186–91, Bishop William de Saltmarsh confirmed earlier charters granting the church to Llanthony Priory. He himself laid down that the canons could "constitute" ("constituant") a vicar, either annual or perpetual, although also assumed that the vicar was to be presented to the bishop for institution. In 1219–22, Bishop William II revisited the matter. He ordained a perpetual vicarage in Caldicot, with Llanthony to have the church – no talk of annual vicars or the canons constituting vicars now (*Llandaff Episcopal Acta 1140–1287*, ed. David Crouch [Cardiff, 1988], nos. 36, 63).

that perpetuity entailed greater risks for patrons was the oath that vicars of the cathedral of Wells, presumably vicars choral in this case, swore on becoming perpetual: "obedience to the dean and chapter in canonical and lawful commandments ... [and] to keep the secrets of the chapter," among other points.[38]

A dispute of the 1270s suggests how secure vicars could be against their patrons. A canon of Barnwell Priory recounts the determined opposition the priory received from Luke de Abingdon, instituted vicar of the church of Guilden Morden on the priory's presentation in 1269. Luke refused to pay the priory an annual pension of one mark and 4s due annually for the church, and so the prior obtained papal letters for a trial concerning payment before the prior of St. Peter's and St. Paul's, Ipswich, as papal judge delegate. Soon after, however, Luke appeared before Archbishop Kilwardby when the archbishop conducted his visitation of the diocese. Far from volunteering to pay the pension, Luke sought augmentation of his vicarage on the ground of its poverty. The archbishop ordered an investigation, which resulted in the augmentation. Barnwell, however, obtained papal letters stopping these moves and summoning Luke to appear (again) before the prior of St. Peter's and St. Paul's, Ipswich. After mediation, Luke dropped his claim, receiving forty marks from Barnwell to cover his expenses.[39] Seven years later, however, the feisty Luke was at it again. Archbishop Pecham was now on his visitation of the diocese, and Luke sought the augmentation Pecham's predecessor had awarded. "How many labors, difficulties, expenses and vexations!" the prior and canons undertook regarding Luke, exclaims the Barnwell writer, struggling to relay them briefly.[40] Papal and archiepiscopal jurisdictions became entangled and the king's courts were also drawn in. Several years later, Luke died, the lawsuits still in play. The canons at least had the satisfaction that Luke died excommunicate for failing to appear before the pope's judge delegate, and so they were able to prevent Luke's body from being brought into church or mass being said for his soul.[41] But he still died as vicar. Such security could be turned

---

[38] *Calendar of the Manuscripts of the Dean and Chapter of Wells*, I, 100–101. This entry in a Wells cartulary is undated but falls among a series of documents of the mid-thirteenth century.

[39] *Liber Memorandorum Ecclesie de Bernewelle*, ed. John Willis Clark (Cambridge, 1907), 173–4.

[40] Ibid., 174: "Quot labores, angustias, expensas, et uexationes, Prior et canonici exinde sustineuerent, non uerbis paucis explicari." For another instance of a vicar suing the house that had appropriated the rectory, see EEA 36: Salisbury, no. 26.

[41] Ibid., 174–176.

against even the ordinary of the diocese by whose authority vicarages were ordained, as Bishop Henry Marshal of Exeter found when he was sued at Rome by a clerk who claimed that Marshal was harassing him in his possession of his vicarage.[42]

While vicarages joined rectories as benefices, other ecclesiastical bundles of income and responsibility failed to hit the mark. Some chantries got defined as benefices, with incumbents instituted by the bishop and patrons losing control over incumbents once instituted.[43] Other chantries, however, remained "service" chantries, served by clergy at the patron's will.[44] (Perhaps the contrast with parishes here is a contrast in chronology. Rectories, founded before or during the Gregorian Reform, fell subject to that reform, curbing patrons' rights. Chantries were later arrivals, just missing the great wave of ecclesiastical reform that had swept up vicarages.[45] By then, while sentiment and expectation led some founders to erect chantries as benefices, other founders preferred greater control.)[46] Even in the late twelfth century, bishops could also appropriate a parish to a monastery but fall short of ordaining a perpetual vicarage. In 1187–90, the bishop of Exeter confirmed to Modbury Priory a nearby church, along with permission to appoint a *capellanus* to serve it; bishop and priory would together retain the right to admonish or remove this *capellanus*.[47] Although a few religious houses managed to appropriate churches and retain the cure of souls in the hands of members of their own communities,[48] perpetual vicarages were the usual arrangement in

---

[42] EEA XII: Exeter, no. 186.
[43] E.g., the chapel priests of St. Andrew in Hales in Lodden: EEA 32: Norwich, no. 43.
[44] Kathleen Wood-Legh, *Perpetual Chantries in Britain* (Cambridge, 1965), 11–26.
[45] The ordination of vicarages, at least in England, was widespread from the 1180s (Rasche, "Early Phase of Appropriation," 216–23).
[46] Indeed, founders of chantries often tried to set various conditions on what chantry-holders could do that went beyond the requirements of the canon law (Wood-Legh, *Perpetual Chantries*, 185–8). David Crouch identifies the earliest chantry "as the later middle ages understood it" as founded 1193–1221. Such chantries emerged out of much earlier prototypical arrangements toward the end of the twelfth, or even at the beginning of the thirteenth, centuries (David Crouch, "The Origin of Chantries: Some Further Anglo-Norman Evidence," *Journal of Medieval History* 27 [2001], 159–80, especially 177–8 and 178 n 68).
[47] EEA XII: Exeter, no. 172; no. 173, of about the same time, refers to a vicarage being created in this church.
[48] E.g., Littleborough, served by the Premonstratensian canons of Welbeck, whose order enjoyed the privilege of serving parochial cures and, at least in the thirteenth century, used it (Alexander Hamilton Thompson, *The Premonstratensian Abbey of Welbeck* [London, 1938], 44; David Knowles, *The Religious Orders in England* [Cambridge, 1957], II, 139–40). See, more generally, Alexander Hamilton Thompson, *The Organization of*

the thirteenth century. Indeed, the canon law prohibited appropriated churches from being served by monks.[49] When the bishop of Bath and Wells discovered that the vicar of St. Decuman's had taken vows to enter religion, he declared the vicarage vacant.[50]

The Common Law also recognized that benefice holders enjoyed security of tenure. This recognition applied even in circumstances that might have led royal justices to override such rights. Although the king's courts did not claim jurisdiction over title to benefices themselves, they did exercise jurisdiction over ownership of advowsons, that is, the right to present a candidate for a benefice to the bishop for institution. One might, therefore, expect the secular courts to have refused to recognize an institution to a benefice where the institution flowed from a presentation by someone with no right to the advowson, as, indeed, did the canon law.[51] But that is not what a law report of 1268 instructs lawyers or would-be lawyers of the Common Law courts. It teaches that if A sells an adowson to B, and then A successfully presents a candidate to the benefice despite the sale, and that candidate is instituted by the bishop, B will be out of luck until the next vacancy.[52] It does not matter that A had no right to

---

the English Clergy in the Later Middle Ages (Oxford, 1947), 119–21. The diocese of Winchester seems to have been particularly liable to such arrangements (Reg. Pontissara, 141, 161–2, 272, 543 – the last two also a Premonstratensian house). Episcopal statements from the diocese of Durham concerning churches appropriated by regular canons clarify some of the problems raised by such canons serving cures by laying down limitations and conditions on them (EEA 30: Carlisle, nos. 161, 172, 191, 201). For what appears to be a Cistercian case, see Reg. Giffard of Worcester, 287 (for "induction," read "admission": WRO, Rf.x716.093 BA 2648/1(i), f. 253 [p. 497]). See also EEA 32: Norwich, liii–liv.

[49] C. H. Lawrence, *Medieval Monasticism*, 3rd ed. (Harlow, 2001), 133.
[50] *Calendar of the Manuscripts of the Dean and Chapter of Wells*, I, 122. The bishop was not the vicarage's patron.
[51] Not that Archbishop Giffard of York was incapable of trying out a claim that the canon law held the reverse when trying to deflect the king's attempt to get his own man instituted to a church which had gone to another (Reg. Giffard of York, 222). For the law, J. W. Gray, "The Ius Praesentandi in England from the Constitutions of Clarendon to Bracton," *English Historical Review* 67 (1952), 484 and 488 and 488 n 4. Indeed, when the incumbent enjoying such faulty title was the king's clerk, and the king was in the mood to override ecclesiastical rights, institution could protect such a clerk by being enforced by royal authority: hence the case of ecclesiastical patrons forced to live with a king's clerk instituted against their right of presentation because, in part, King John was at war with the Church (EEA 30: Carlisle, no. 34).
[52] *The Earliest English Law Reports*, ed. Paul Brand, Selden Society 111, 112, 122, 123 (London, 1996–2007), I, 5–6. For the purpose of the manuscript of this report, see ibid., xcix. A later report (1310) advises that if a bishop collated by lapse (because the advowson holder had failed to present an appropriate candidate within six months of the start of the vacancy), the patron should still sue, not to oust the holder of the benefice, for it

the advowson; the incumbent, once instituted, is safe. Indeed, he will keep the church "for his lifetime."[53] A royal justice of 1309 made a similar assumption about the meaning of a benefice, pointing out that one cannot fulfil one's obligation to grant a benefice by granting the office of holy water carrier, for a holy water carrier can lose his office at the will of the parishioners, and so does not enjoy "an estate for life."[54]

An unusual letter reveals expectations. In the thirteenth century, bishops often granted the recipient of a benefice a letter recording his reception of legal title from the bishop.[55] The technical ecclesiastical term for such reception was "institution" by the bishop of the recipient to the benefice, which is why such letters are referred to generically as "letters of institution." In 1228, however, the bishop of Salisbury chose for some unknown reason to eschew such technical language (in what was technically a letter of collation) and spell matters out. The bishop collated St. Martin's, Salisbury, and other churches and the recipient was to have them "for his whole life, freely and quietly."[56]

Testing the Limits of Security of Tenure

One presumes that patrons and incumbents usually got along. After all, patrons had generally chosen incumbents. Most patrons would have

---

cannot be done, but in order to clarify the patron's right to the advowson at the next vacancy (*Year Books of Edward II*, ed. F.W. Maitland et al., Selden Society 17- [passim] [London, 1903–], III, 38). Indeed, the sense of entitlement of one recipient of a prebend, Walter Hervey, in such a situation is suggested in the bishop having him renounce the ecclesiastical equivalent of the *escambium* that the holder of a lay fee claimed from his lord when losing that fee in court; should the prebend be successfully claimed by a third party, the bishop was to be under no obligation to collate anything to Hervey (Reg. Gandavo, 817–18).

[53] *Earliest English Law Reports*, I, 6, and see Gray, "Ius Praesentandi," 489, 505–6. The fourteenth century, however, would see the king launch a pragmatic attack on the security of tenure in benefices where the king had an interest in putting his own man in despite other patrons (P. C. Saunders, "Royal Ecclesiastical Patronage from Winchelsey to Stratford," *Bulletin of the John Rylands Library* 83 [2001], 104–9; Frederic Cheyette, "Kings, Courts, Cures, and Sinecures: The Statute of Provisors and the Common Law," *Traditio* 19 [1963], 295–349). For a discussion that illustrates the strong position of an instituted incumbent (at least in the thirteenth century) in the face of actions in the Common Law courts, see Peter M. Smith, "The Advowson: The History and Development of a Most Peculiar Property," *Ecclesiastical Law Journal* 26 (2000), 334–5.

[54] *Year Books of Edward II*, II, 126.

[55] But certainly not always: David M. Smith, "The Rolls of Hugh of Wells, Bishop of Lincoln 1209–1235," *Bulletin of the Institute of Historical Research* 45 (1972), 187 and *Acta of Hugh of Wells*, li–lii.

[56] EEA 19: Salisbury, no. 299.

had little trouble living up to Innocent IV's pronouncement to them that incumbents were to keep their benefices peacefully until they resign or die.[57] Any relationship, however, can go wrong. Innocent's statement implies as much. Security of tenure was an issue because, among other reasons, patrons and incumbents could come into conflict. The evidence for such conflicts largely takes the form of attempts to resolve them in some way. The most extreme such resolution was, of course, the Becket option, one that still worried ecclesiastical authorities in the thirteenth century. The Fourth Lateran Council forbade patrons from killing or mutilating incumbents.[58] A few years later the bishop of Salisbury laid down that should the patron of a church presume "to kill by wicked enterprise" the rector or other clerk of his church, he and his will lose the advowson to the fourth generation.[59] This punishment appears to have been tailored to one of the motives for such a crime. Murdering an incumbent added to any personal satisfaction the advantage of freeing up the benefice for another presentation. The bishop of Salisbury's decree robbed malefactors of that benefit.

Other moves fell short of murder. Simple violence might do. Bishop Giffard appears to have had his men occupy the church of Bishop's Cleeve, from which he was trying to eject his former steward, Peter de Leicester.[60] A gang of Ranulph de Rye's servants at Ranulph's behest attacked in arms the church of Gosberton, then evidently occupied by the clerk Ranulph had presented.[61] Ranulph's motive is undeterminable, and so one cannot be sure that he was attempting to expel his former presentee. Bishop Peter de Aquablanca's men set fire to the barns of Giles de Avenbury, dean of Hereford. The root of the dispute is uncertain. On the one hand, the bishop was in conflict with the dean and chapter over three churches, and the arson was not confined to the dean's property. On the other, the bishop was also trying to persuade Giles to resign the deanery

---

[57] *Les Registres d'Innocent IV (1243–54)*, ed. E. Berger, Bibliothèque des Ecoles françaises d'Athènes et de Rome (second series) 1 (Paris, 1884–1921), III, no. 7072.

[58] Canon no. 45: *Decrees of the Ecumenical Councils I: Nicaea to Lateran V*, ed. Norman P. Tanner (Washington, DC, 1990). On reverberations of Becket's murder in later medieval centuries, see Nicholas Vincent, "The Strange Case of the Missing Biographies: The Lives of the Plantagenet Kings of England, 1154–1272," in *Writing Medieval Biography 750–1250: Essays in Honour of Frank Barlow*, ed. David Bates, Julia Crick, and Sarah Hamilton (Woodbridge, 2006), 252.

[59] "occidere ausu nefario": *Councils and Synods*, 95. The provision was repeated 1225–30 (ibid., 196).

[60] Burger, "Peter of Leicester," 466.

[61] Reg. and Rolls Sutton, I, 202–203, V, 132–33, 169–70.

in favor of the bishop's own man.⁶² In the end, Giles did resign, but Julia Barrow suggests the bishop used a couple of carrots – a promise to obtain for Giles a papal dispensation to hold an additional benefice with cure of souls, and the promise of the cathedral treasurership. Giles gained the dispensation and the treasurership. Giles had also been in conflict with the bishop's *officialis* at the time of the latter's murder, and this put an unusual stick in the bishop's hands. Barrow believes that the bishop used the conflict to pressure Giles into resigning. And, of course, the most powerful man in the country could successfully pressure lower clergy to resign.⁶³ To judge from a letter of Innocent III, Master Elias of Chieveley had given up his church of Chieveley because he feared the king; the pope ordered an inquiry as to whether the threat was so grave as to affect a man of courage, so that Elias could be said to have been forced out (in which case, he should be restored).⁶⁴

Patrons could simply lie. Religious houses forged charters from bishops confirming their right to remove clergy who held appropriated churches.⁶⁵ Or patrons could assert that a benefice was vacant and so attempt to intrude a clerk and thus expel the incumbent. In 1289, to judge from a complaint in Rome, the abbot and convent of Malmesbury had simply pretended that the incumbent of Norton was dead and presented another candidate, who was accepted by the bishop of Salisbury. The incumbent, very much alive, sued to the pope for relief.⁶⁶ This seems to have been a not uncommon problem. The legate Otho complained about people eyeing the benefices of absent incumbents and, claiming the incumbents to be dead, procuring their own intrusion into such benefices; should the dead man return, the intruder tells him "I do not know you," and shuts the door against him.⁶⁷ Otho says nothing about collusion by

---

⁶² EEA 35: Hereford, li.
⁶³ Ibid., li–lv and n 209, no. 154 n.
⁶⁴ *The Letters of Pope Innocent III (1198–1216) Concerning England and Wales*, ed. C. R. Cheney and Mary G. Cheney (Oxford, 1967), no. 184. For more on this case, see C. R. Cheney, *Pope Innocent III and England* (Stuttgart, 1976), 87–8.
⁶⁵ Julia Barrow, "Why Forge Episcopal Acta?" in *The Foundations of Medieval English Ecclesiastical History: Studies Presented to David Smith*, ed. Philippa Hoskin, Christopher Brooke, and Barrie Dobson (Woodbridge, 2005), 24.
⁶⁶ CPL, I, 501; *Les Registres de Nicholas IV (1288–1292)*, ed. F. Soehnée et al., Bibliothèque des Ecoles françaises d'Athènes et de Rome (second series) 5 (Paris, 1887–93), I, no. 1276 reproduces the text of most of the letter.
⁶⁷ *Councils and Synods*, 249–50. The general problem concerned the legate enough for him to lay out a procedure for determining whether an incumbent was dead (ibid., 759–60). Perhaps suspicion led the bishop of Winchester to order his *officialis* to institute William de Humfrayville, presented to a prebend by the abbess and convent of Wherwell, on condition that the prebend indeed turned out to be vacant (Reg. Pontissara, 41).

the patron here. When the legate Ottobuono repeated Otho's warning on this score in 1268, however, he added that no patron should dare present a candidate to a benefice unless he or she had "probabilem ... notitiam" of a vacancy.[68] It was perhaps this situation that led the prior and convent of Durham to get the archdeacon of Durham's seal along with their own appended to an incumbent's letter resigning Saint Mary's Binewerk in Stamford, to which the priory wished to present. The bishop of Lincoln had already rejected such a letter of resignation because he had not known the incumbent's seal.[69] The prior and convent appear to have thought their own seal alone – surely recognizable to a bishop of Lincoln – would not satisfy the bishop that the resignation was authentic.

Another maneuver was to charge an incumbent with violations of the canon law's moral strictures in order to oust him and so free up the benefice. The diocese of Winchester yields up useful evidence. In 1304, the bishop sided with one Stephen de Doene, who, presented to Wotton, had argued (correctly) that its incumbent had de facto vacated Wotton when he had been instituted elsewhere.[70] Had the patron not presented, one wonders whether this pluralism would have come to the bishop's attention. William de Cryk was similarly attacked when one Robert de

[68] *Councils and Synods*, 759. Although I suggest that patrons sometimes colluded with new presentees in pretending that incumbents were dead, patrons could sometimes have been genuinely mystified in such matters. Such a case seems to be that of Peterborough Abbey's presentation of Roger de Rothwell to Kettering, which rumor thereupon said may not be vacant. Roger gave the abbey a bond for £200 not to make trouble if such was the case (*Chronicon Petroburgense*, ed. Thomas Stapleton and John Bruce, Camden Society (first series) 47 [London, 1849], 99–100). Roger appears to have gotten Kettering in the end (Rolls and Reg. Sutton, II, 42). A statement of Innocent IV addressed to patrons of benefices in the province of Canterbury hints at the vulnerability of absentee incumbents in the face of aggressive patrons. The pope allows the limited right of entry of patrons into such benefices, but only when they have become vacant, and takes care that this pronouncement not be used as a pretext to disturb incumbents (Hereford Dean and Chapter archives, no. 1856, listed in *Original Papal Documents in England and Wales from the Accession of Pope Innocent III to the Death of Pope Benedict XI (1198–1304)*, ed. Jane E. Sayers, [Oxford, 1999], no. 441).

[69] *Durham Annals and Documents of the Thirteenth Century*, ed. Frank Barlow, Surtees Society 155 (Durham, 1945), 177. Other resigning incumbents took care to get a seal from a known and trustworthy party from the outset. The rector of Rodington obtained the seal of the bishop of Coventry and Lichfield's *officialis* for his letter of resignation, as did the rector of Colton (Reg. Langton, nos. 64, 687). C. R. Cheney comments on these kinds of problems in his *Notaries Public in England in the Thirteenth and Fourteenth Centuries* (Oxford, 1972), 40–1.

[70] Reg. Pontissara, 177–8, and see 146. A patron could also, of course, raise charges against an incumbent not to expel him but to pressure him about other matters, such as the case in C. H. Lawrence, "The English Parish and Its Clergy in the Thirteenth Century," in *The Medieval World*, ed. Peter Linehan and Janet L. Nelson (New York, 2001), 660.

Worcester was presented to William's rectory of Laverstoke; William was charged with having held Laverstoke for four years without proceeding to the priesthood.[71] As with Wotton, one cannot know how active a role Laverstoke's patrons, as opposed to the presentee, played in these moves, but they at least had to have gone so far as to have presented to Laverstoke anew.

In some cases, both the pretext for ejection and the respective roles of patron and presentee are unclear. Adam de York was presented to Southwell by the prior and convent of Saint Andrew's, Northampton, as though the church were vacant.[72] The man who claimed incumbency, Adam de Stratton, who had indeed been instituted to Southwell in 1271 on Saint Andrew's presentation, resisted, hence a suit.[73] Sometimes the patron's role becomes clearer. A mandate of Innocent III demanded that his judges hear a complaint lodged by a nephew of Hugh de Merton that his patron had tried to take back the church he had been given.[74] What transpired is unknown and, of course, one cannot be sure that the facts had been accurately represented at Rome.[75] Bishop Sutton of Lincoln's register preserves the suit brought in 1297 by John de Willingham, claiming presentation by Robert de Benningworth, against Osbert, incumbent of Ludford Parva.[76] Had the case gone no further, one would conclude, if anything, that this was a conflict between an incumbent and a new presentee. The following month, however, the patron (Robert) himself seems to have taken John's place in the suit against Osbert.[77] This may have been a case of a patron trying to oust his predecessor's presentee. Osbert had been instituted in 1285 on the presentation of one John de Sotebi, and a Sotebi had successfully presented the previous incumbent.[78]

[71] Reg. Pontissara, 348–50. Unlike the case of Wotton, the attempt to present to Laverstoke failed. One William "de Croy" was still in possession some six months later, the bishop granting custody of the church to another man as William was underage, a circumstance that explains his failure to be ordained (Reg. Pontissara, 58).
[72] Rolls and Reg. Sutton, V, 18 and LAO, Episcopal Register I, f. 105v; Rolls and Reg. Sutton, II, 117.
[73] Ibid., V, 18; Rot. Gravesend, 118.
[74] *Letters of Pope Innocent III (1198–1215) Concerning England and Wales*, no. 260.
[75] It may be worth noting, however, that when the patron sued Hugh de Merton for robbery, Hugh defended by arguing, among other things, that the patron had given the church to Hugh's nephew "unde post redipiscere voluit," so that Hugh's nephew had to impetrate letters from the pope (*Curia Regis Rolls*, ed. C. T. Flower et al. (London, 1922–), I, 255–6).
[76] Rolls and Reg. Sutton, VI, 39.
[77] Ibid., VI, 44.
[78] Ibid., I, 63; Reg. Gravesend, 50.

Sutton's register unfortunately gives no account of the grounds of John's and Robert's suit, except to say that Robert claimed that Osbert held Ludford Parva *illicite*.[79] These bare facts suggest, if anything, that Robert probably claimed that he had had the right to the advowson rather than John de Sotebi, which would also help explain this suit being made in court Christian, where the canon law gave true patrons greater rights facing incumbents duly instituted on the presentation of false patrons than did the Common Law. But the case continued, yielding new information about the dispute. Robert appealed to the metropolitan. In that court he made his case claiming that Osbert had gained Ludford Parva simoniacally.[80] That may have been his argument all along, now revealed by the archbishop's register. Or it may be that Robert had changed his argument. He also claimed in the archbishop's court that Sutton had refused to give judgment,[81] perhaps a discreet way both to avoid acknowledging a case that had gone poorly in the bishop of Lincoln's court and to change the grounds of his suit to something with a better chance of winning. Perhaps Robert had acquired the advowson after Osbert's institution and tried to claim that it had been his by right all the time, and now thought better of it. The whole sequence of events and these plausible speculations about them show how obscure the roles and arguments of these actors can be. But they also show that patrons had some part in using the courts to try to oust incumbents and the morals arguments they might use there.

Bishops could also play at this game regarding benefices in their gift. Bishop Pontoise had himself taken pains to find a benefice in his collation for William Segin de Got, canon of Agen and papal chaplain.[82] Three and a half years later (in 1299), the bishop charged de Got with unlicensed pluralism, demanding that he appear before him to show why Wonston should not be collated to the bishop's clerk, "ydoneo et bene merito."[83]

---

[79] LAO, Episcopal Register I, f. 171v.
[80] Reg. Winchelsey, 731.
[81] Ibid., 731.
[82] Reg. Pontissara, 792, 801–2, and see Joseph A. Kicklighter, "An Unknown Brother of Pope Clement V," *Mediaeval Studies* 38 (1976), 493–4. The move may have been calculated to curry further influence not only at the curia but also with the king, who had friendly ties with the family (Sophia Menache, *Clement V* [Cambridge, 1998], 8, and see 247–8).
[83] Reg. Pontissara, 86–7. Ultimately Wonston opened up for a clerk closer to the bishop, an event no doubt helped by Segin's death by the end of September 1299 (for the date, see Kicklighter, "An Unknown Brother of Pope Clement V," 495). In 1307, Master Thomas de Port, whose institution is unrecorded, was active as rector of Wonston (*Registrum Henrici Woodlock, diocesis Wintoniensis, A.D. 13–5–1316*, ed. A. W. Goodman, Canterbury and York Society 43–4 [Oxford, 1940–1], I, 163. This Master Thomas is, I

De Got had received a dispensation for pluralism in 1297, but not one that mentioned Wonston.⁸⁴ One suspects a similar manipulation of the law by a bishop in the case of Bishop Dalderby of Lincoln (1300–20). After fifteen years in office, Dalderby decided that he did not want "blood on his hands," and so began an inquiry regarding Thomas de Sutton, his predecessor's relative.⁸⁵ The charge was pluralism. Thomas held the archdeaconry of Northampton along with the churches of Walgrave, Edlesborough, and Churchill; all but the last had been conferred on him under the previous bishop, Oliver Sutton. Should Walgrave or Thomas's archdeaconry have fallen vacant, they would have been in Dalderby's gift.⁸⁶ It seems very unlikely that Thomas's pluralism was a new discovery on Dalderby's part.⁸⁷ Indeed, Thomas had resigned Edlesborough, which carried with it cure of souls, long before, in 1292; Edlesborough's inclusion looks like an attempt to stack the deck against an opponent.⁸⁸ But Thomas was either properly dispensed or simply fought well,⁸⁹ for he died in possession.⁹⁰

Bishop Giffard of Worcester attempted a similar move. In 1282, the bishop was trying to oust his clerk Nicholas de Chilbauton from the church of Mickleton; a letter of 1283 suggests that the charge was pluralism.⁹¹ In 1284, Giffard complained that Nicholas had left his benefices to go to Rome; perhaps Nicholas had gone to appeal? Presumably the odd "revocation" by the bishop of the collation of any church ("cuiuscunque ecclesie") if the bishop had made one ("si quam fecerit") to Nicholas

---

think, the same man Pontoise referred to as Thomas "de Porres de Maidestane" and "our clerk," controller of the bishop's wardrobe in 1299 (Reg. Pontissara, 85–6). The identification is strengthened by the Master Thomas "de Port of Maydenstan" who received the king's writ of protection to go with Pontoise overseas in 1299 (*Calendar of the Patent Rolls Preserved in the Public Record Office (1232–1509)* [London, 1891–1916], III, 415). A Thomas de Maydenstan, Pointoise's clerk, had received collation of Esher from the bishop in 1292 (Reg. Pontissara, 56).

⁸⁴ CPL, I, 572–3.
⁸⁵ "sanguinis de nostris manibus" (LAO, Episcopal Register III, f. 321v).
⁸⁶ Ibid., III, f. 321v; Rolls and Reg. Sutton II, 128, VIII, 138, 172–3.
⁸⁷ It may be that Dalderby's move against Thomas was related to troubles he was generally having with the archdeacons of the diocese. I hope to explore these relationships elsewhere.
⁸⁸ Rolls and Reg. Sutton, VIII, 138.
⁸⁹ He had received a papal dispensation in 1292 as archdeacon of Northampton and prebendary to hold an additional benefice with cure of souls (CPL, I, 548; Rolls and Reg. Sutton, II, 129, III 197–8), but no further dispensation is traceable.
⁹⁰ LAO, Episcopal Register II, f. 119r; Reg. Burghersh, II, no. 2214; LN Lincoln, 10.
⁹¹ Reg. Giffard of Worcester, 152, 273. The evidence for Nicholas as Giffard's man is a letter from Giffard to Nicholas, "suo quondam obsequali," admitting him to Giffard's grace in 1284 (ibid., 229 [WRO, Rf.x716.093 BA 2648/1(i), f. 204 (p. 400)]).

pertains to Mickleton.⁹² This case – with the attempt to undo a collation, the citation for pluralism as a means to that end, and Nicholas's presence at the curia suggesting an appeal to a higher jurisdiction – resonates with others discussed here. How far matters went is unclear. Giffard's relationship with Nicholas, whether still a source of trouble or pacified, was cut short by Nicholas's death in 1284.⁹³

But it should not be assumed that all such enforcement of the canon law was a matter of manipulation. The bishop of Norwich – and legate – Pandulph expelled one James, formerly Pandulph's clerk and scribe, from the vicarage of South Creake which Pandulph had conferred upon him. The explanation was (unfortunately unspecified) *culpa* and *excessi* of which he was convicted in Pandulph's presence.⁹⁴ James was also temporarily deprived of the dignity of papal scribe, presumably by the pope,⁹⁵ which suggests that Pandulph's proceedings were not simply about disciplining an incumbent for bad service or expelling him to get the presentation.

Considerations of patronage can, however, shed new light on a bishop's reformist activities. Consider Bishop Thomas Cantilupe, who arrived in his new diocese of Hereford to open a campaign against pluralism. David Smith has carefully noted that Cantilupe, himself a pluralist of note before his elevation, attacked unlicensed pluralism, not the practice itself, in line with other bishops of his time.⁹⁶ Other motives for Cantilupe's prosecution of pluralists have been alleged. Some defendants were foreigners, and Cantilupe on one occasion made clear his reluctance to cultivate "exotic or unfruitful trees" in his orchard.⁹⁷ Smith also

---

⁹² Reg. Giffard of Worcester, 151 (WRO, Rf.x716.093 BA 2648/1(i), f. 141 [p. 274]).

⁹³ Reg. Giffard of Worcester, 273.

⁹⁴ EEA 21 Norwich, no. 8 n. The episode is recounted by Christopher Harper-Bill, "The Diocese of Norwich and the Italian Connection, 1198–1261," in *England and the Continent in the Middle Ages: Studies in Memory of the Andrew Martindale, Proceedings of the 1996 Harlaxton Symposium*, ed. John Mitchell, assisted by Matthew Moran (Stamford, 2000), 81.

⁹⁵ Ibid.

⁹⁶ David Smith, "Thomas Cantilupe's Register: The Administration of the Diocese of Hereford 1275–1282," in *Saint Thomas Cantilupe, Bishop of Hereford: Essays in His Honour*, ed. Meryl Jancey (Leominster, 1982), 92–3. Hervey de Boreham, the dean of Saint Paul's, would soon be dead, by November 19, 1276 (LN Hereford, 16).

⁹⁷ See Smith's comment on Reg. Cantilupe, 249: "arborem enim peregrinam vel non fructificantem non … in orto nostro … plantaremus" ("Thomas Cantilupe's Register," in *St. Thomas Cantilupe Bishop of Hereford, Essays in his Honour*, ed. Meryl Jancey [Leominster, 1982], 91) and, more emphatically, W. Nigel Yates, "Bishop Peter de Aquablanca (1240–1268): A Reconsideration," *Journal of Ecclesiastical History* 22 (1971), 312–17. David Carpenter, however, is unconvinced ("St. Thomas: His Political Career," in *St. Thomas Cantilupe Bishop of Hereford*, 71 n 66).

notes that one of his targets, Peter de Langon, had been an earlier rival of Cantilupe's for a prebend at Hereford, while Canon Capes pointed out that another target, the dean of Saint Paul's, had been a competitor in the election to the see of Hereford.[98] Many defendants were of the family of an earlier bishop of Hereford, Peter de Aquablanca, including Peter de Langon, and so perhaps dislike of this family, rather than of foreigners in general, led Cantilupe to challenge their possession of benefices (as also suggested by Smith).[99] Contrary alignments concerning national politics have also been suggested as a root of the conflict.[100] But to these considerations one should, I think, add the benefices that would have been freed up by Cantilupe's pursuit of pluralists. Had he succeeded, more than half of these benefices would have been in his gift.[101] Cantilupe did not bring in the entire haul. Some defendants had important friends, and some simply had good defenses, such as the argument that their other benefices were held neither by institution nor collation.[102]

Sometimes expelling an incumbent on canonical grounds simply presented a bishop with an opportunity, even if the bishop lacked the advowson. In 1302, Archbishop Winchelsey informed the abbot and convent of Ramsey that his court had deprived the incumbent of Knapwell,

---

[98] Smith, "Thomas Cantilupe's Register," 91; Reg. Cantilupe, xxxvi.
[99] Smith, "Thomas Cantilupe's Register," 91.
[100] Yates, "Bishop Peter de Aquablanca," 341.
[101] In Cantilupe's gift: the precentorship of the cathedral (Reg. Cantilupe, 111); the prebend held by Hervey de Boreham (Reg. Cantilupe, 121); the archdeaconry of Shropshire (Reg. Cantilupe, 150); the prebend of Ledbury (Reg. Cantilupe, 63); the prebend of Preston (Reg. Cantilupe, 187); two portions of Bromyard (Reg. Cantilupe, 91, and Reg. Swinfield, 527 for the bishop's right); Whitbourne (Smith, "Thomas Cantilupe's Register," 91, and Reg. Cantilupe, 251 for the bishop's right); Ullingswick (Reg. Cantilupe, 126, 136, 138, 142, and 241 for the bishop's right); Ross (*Acta Sanctorum Quotquot Toto Urbe Coluntur vel a Catholicis Scriptoribus Celebrantur*, ed. J. Stiltingo et al. [Paris and Rome, 1866], October 1, 562b; Reg. Swinfield, 527–8 for the bishop's right); Morton (Reg. Cantilupe, 141, 186, and 225 for bishop's right). Not in Cantilupe's gift: Tretire (Reg. Cantilupe, 127, 131; Reg. Swinfield, 542 for advowson); portion of Holdgate Castle (Reg. Cantilupe, 136–7, 141–2; Reg. Swinfield, 524–5 for advowson); Hope Mansel (Reg. Cantilupe, 142, 188; Reg. Swinfield, 530, 532 for advowson); Worthen (Reg. Cantilupe, 145, 150; Reg. Swinfield, 542 for advowson); Westbury (Reg. Cantilupe, 145, and 628 for advowson); two (or three?) portions of Pontesbury (Reg. Cantilupe, 145, 150, 152–3, 159–60, 189–91, 193; Reg. Swinfield, 532 for advowson).
[102] See Smith, "Thomas Cantilupe's Register," 91–2 for intervention by third parties. David, portionist of Pontesbury, said that he held only the custody of another church (Reg. Cantilupe, 189–90). Since "David" was a fairly uncommon name, the David fitz Reginald who vacated a portion of Pontesbury in 1300 (Reg. Swinfield, 532 n 5) was probably the portioner of Cantilupe's time. Thus, the David of temp. Cantilupe appears to have retained Pontesbury.

Benefices and Security of Tenure 61

in Ramsey's presentation. The incumbent had failed to proceed to priest's orders within a year of being instituted.[103] Could, the archbishop asked, the abbey present John de Haddenham, the archbishop's chaplain, to this "little church"?[104]

Patrons could also simply harass incumbents for failing to perform their office rather than seek to expel them. The canons of Merton and Dunstable took their complaint about the vicars of Steppingley and other places to the pope on this ground.[105] The abbot and convent of Saint Peter's, Gloucester, sued the rector of Nympsfield, in their presentation, for failure to pay the annual pension of two marks due them from the church.[106] Another means of harassment was to interfere with the incumbent's reception of tithes. In 1294, the patron of the church of Checkendon was said to have maliciously interfered with the rector's collection of tithes.[107] This patron was John Marmiun, called here the lord of Checkendon. The institution of this rector of Checkendon is lost, and thus so is the identity of the patron who presented him, but Marmiuns exercised the advowson before and after this incident,[108] so presumably a Marmiun had presented the incumbent now under fire. In 1276, the bishop of Durham took aim at just this sort of conflict, ordaining that patrons of churches were not to detain the tithes of churches in their gift or interfere with rectors' attempts to collect them.[109]

Again, it is unfortunately often unclear whether a putative dispute *was* the real dispute or whether the proceedings preserved in the sources were attempts to harass incumbents over other issues. Certainly tithes could be a real bone of contention between incumbents and patrons. In 1261, the bishop of Durham's *officialis* was charged to hear such a dispute between the vicar of Gainford and its appropriator, Saint Mary's (York).[110]

---

[103] Reg, Winchelsey, 443–4.
[104] "ecclesiola" (ibid.).
[105] *Letters of Pope Innocent III (1198–1215) Concerning England and Wales*, no. 544. Julia Barrow comments that Twynham Priory worked to stamp out "hereditary succession of priests in its churches in order to secure its own rights of patronage" (Julia Barrow, "Why Forge Episcopal Acta?" 24–5).
[106] *Select Cases From the Ecclesiastical Courts of the Province of Canterbury c. 1200–1301*, ed. Norma Adams and Charles Donahue Jr., Selden Society 95 (London, 1981 for 1978–9), 524–6. It is not clear, however, whether the abbot and convent had presented this particular incumbent. The Worcester registers are silent on the matter.
[107] Rolls and Reg. Sutton, V, 24–5.
[108] Rot. Gravesend, 223; Reg. Burghersh, II, no. 1862.
[109] *Councils and Synods*, 818.
[110] EEA 29: Durham, no. 147. The terms of the appropriation do not survive, but the earliest surviving evidence (1307) indicates that Saint Mary's held the patronage, the usual

Consider also the case referred to earlier, in which the abbot and convent of Malmesbury pretended an incumbent was dead in order to present another man. Those events could represent either a genuine attempt to expel an incumbent, merely an attempt to trouble one, or simply constitute the sole conflict itself.[111] A similar case may have been that of 1179–81, in which an incumbent complained that he was falsely said to have died, it appears by the church's patron, in order that another man be presented and instituted to the church.[112] Root causes of these conflicts and the ultimate goals of patrons are harder to discern than the important fact of conflict itself. It could happen, however, that such harassment was explicitly linked to an attempt to expel an incumbent. In about the third quarter of the twelfth century, certainly before 1180, Bury St. Edmunds tried to expel a parson by threatening his patrimony, held of the abbey.[113]

Patrons, of course, died. This fact of life meant that new patrons had to face incumbents whom they had not chosen. Such an incumbent was not beholden to the new patron for his living. At the same time, the incumbent blocked the new patron from presenting someone who might be more to the patron's liking. The issue of a change of patrons was sensitive enough for the bishop of Hereford to lay down that, while he confirmed the grant of the advowson of Monnington on Wye by the prior and convent of St. Guthlac's to a knight, the church's incumbent

---

arrangement (Reg. Halton, I, 276). See also the tithe dispute between the rector and vicar of Lancing in 1227; this vicar had been instituted on this rector's presentation (*The Chartulary of the High Church of Chichester*, ed. W. D. Peckham, Sussex Record Society 46 [Lewes, 1946], no. 1120; EEA 22: Chichester, no. 28). Perhaps these tithes were especially hard to sort out. A couple of generations later the rector and vicar of Lancing were again in dispute over them (*Chartulary of the High Church of Chichester*, no. 1121).

[111] Pensions due a rector from a vicar can present the same difficulty. The rector of Brandon successfully sued his vicar for payment of a pension (*Select Cases from the Province of Canterbury*, 87–8). It is not possible to know whether this dispute was part of some larger one between these parties. The diocese of Norwich produces some settlements between vicars and their patrons that suggest the dispute over pensions or tithes really was the dispute: EEA 32: Norwich, 225, no. 23 (for the status of one of the parties as patron, ibid., no. 9).

[112] EEA II: Canterbury, no. 48A; Mary G. Cheney, *Roger of Worcester* (Oxford, 1980), Appendix II, no. 48.

[113] Cheney, *Roger of Worcester*, 317, no. 1, discussed by Christopher Harper-Bill, "The Struggle over Benefices in Twelfth-Century East Anglia," in *Anglo-Norman Studies XI: Proceedings of the Battle Conference 1988*, ed. R. Allen Brown (1989), 124. The signs could also be more subtle. A settlement of a dispute between Walter, vicar of Totnes, and the appropriating monastery that focuses on the terms of the vicarage also states that Walter is to be the vicar "just as before" ("sicut prius" – Reg. Bronscombe, no. 212): a hint at an attempted expulsion?

was to have possession "toto tempore vite sue."¹¹⁴ Not surprisingly, some new patrons tried to rectify the situation. Joseph de Whixley, parson of Whixley, was sued in 1202 by Henry son of John to show by what right he held his church. Joseph pointed out that he had been presented to Whixley by Henry's father, and instituted by the bishop (and, he noted, owed no pension to the son).¹¹⁵ Another instance stems from the recollection of the parishioners of Letheringsett when they were asked about the history of the church's incumbents. They said that Hamo the rector was instituted on the presentation of his brother, the patron, but that, on the brother's death, the new patron "propter quamdam discordiam" presented another man to the church.¹¹⁶ Reginald de Cusaunce faced a more radical change of patron. The absentee Reginald had been instituted rector of Eckington on the presentation of Edward I, who had taken the advowson into his hands because its owner, Robert de Stoteville, was an enemy alien.¹¹⁷ Under Edward's successor, John de Stoteville, Robert's heir, presented his own man to Eckington, even getting him instituted, only to see the institution voided when Reginald made it clear that he was still very much alive.¹¹⁸

Bishops also pursued incumbents put in by their predecessors, and indeed were more likely to trouble such men than those enjoying their own collation. Thomas Cantilupe's pursuit of pluralists in his new diocese has already been noted; all of the incumbents of benefices in his gift held from before Cantilupe became bishop. Archbishop Romeyn's move against Robert de Scarborough is another instance.¹¹⁹ Only royal intervention brought that dispute to a resolution: a compromise, by which Robert resigned his benefices in return for a large pension and some other concessions.¹²⁰ Perhaps Robert's death soon after this result¹²¹ signals the poor health that would encourage a man to make peace. Thomas de

---

¹¹⁴ EEA VII: Hereford, no. 371. See also the conflict over Threxton, discussed by Christopher Harper-Bill, "The Struggle over Benefices," 124.
¹¹⁵ *Curia Regis Rolls*, II, 100. I have not discovered the result of the suit.
¹¹⁶ Colin Morris, "Letheringsett: The Early History of a Parish Church," *Bulletin of the Institute of Historical Research* 44 (1971), 119. A similar case is evidently that of R. de Arundel c. Sir Henry de Tresgoz (*Select Cases from the Ecclesiastical Courts*, 32).
¹¹⁷ Reg. Langton, no. 252.
¹¹⁸ Ibid., nos. 558 and 1024. For John as Robert's heir, see *Calendar of Inquisitions Post Mortem* (London, 1904–88), IV, no. 369. Robert's widow held Ekington after his death along with the advowson, for her life (ibid., V, no. 237).
¹¹⁹ See also the cases of Thomas de Sutton (discussed earlier) and Maurice de Arundel and James de Aquablanca (later).
¹²⁰ Reg. Romeyn, II, xix–xxi. Robert had served as a royal clerk (ibid.).
¹²¹ Ibid., xxi.

Sutton, archdeacon of Northampton, is another instance of an episcopal clerk challenged by his patron's successor.[122]

A change of patrons, or the recovery of patronage, could also spur incumbents to misbehave, to judge from a complaint of the abbot and convent of Saint Peter's, Gloucester. The abbey charged that Master Thomas, called "Stede," was describing himself as the rector of Burnham and had been withholding for three and half years a £35 annual pension due the abbey. Master Thomas, the abbey noted, had been instituted, but not on Saint Peter's presentation. The abbey asked that papal judges-delegate remove Master Thomas.[123]

The availability of a superior jurisdiction, however, always meant that incumbents had a potential protector. An early fourteenth-century incumbent complained to a friend that the prior and convent of Worcester, his patrons, were conspiring to carry out an appalling act: to give his church to someone else. But, the incumbent said, the bishop would likely prevent it.[124]

The canon law and sentiment in favor of security of tenure were two forces that helped protect incumbents against their patrons. But when it came to patrons who were bishops, a critical third factor was the availability of courts of appeal, courts that could bring a patron-bishop to heel.

Bishops, Archbishops, Popes, and Benefices: Appeals

One potential hindrance to a bishop was the courts of higher authority to which his subjects might appeal. This check could limit any exercise of episcopal authority, including authority over the benefices of the diocese.

Under usual circumstances, the person in any diocese best positioned to control who possessed a benefice was the local diocesan. He, after all,

---

[122] See at nn 86–97.

[123] I am presuming a change of advowson here: Hereford Cathedral Archives, no. 1813, dated May 14, 1282. (I am grateful to the archive for supplying me a photograph of this document, calendared in typescript in *A Calendar of the Earlier Cathedral Archives*, ed. B. G. Charles and H. D. Emanuel [1955], II, 558.) Another case may have been that of Richard, vicar of Peterborough, who supported a local cult aimed against the abbot of Peterborough (LAO, Episcopal Register III, f. 289v). (On the cult, see Laura Wertheimer, "Clerical Dissent, Popular Piety, and Sanctity in Fourteenth-Century Peterborough: The Cult of Laurence of Oxford," *Journal of British Studies* 45 [2006], 21 and 3–22.) This Richard was presumably Richard de Wansford, instituted on the presentation of the abbot's predecessor (Rolls and Reg. Sutton, II, 87).

[124] *The Liber Epistolaris of Richard de Bury*, ed. Noel Denholm Young (Oxford, 1950), no. 433.

instituted presentees to benefices (or, if he felt they fell short of requirements, refused to do so). Moreover, he was charged with ensuring that benefice holders performed their office and their legal obligations. His court heard complaints about his clergy and was empowered to give sentence of deprivation. Events of 1224–6 suggest the power a headstrong bishop might wield when it came to benefices in his see. In 1224, Bishop Marsh of Durham was able to install one of his clerks into what was in fact a chapelry, not a benefice, in a church appropriated to Durham Priory. He did so by claiming that the chapelry was in fact a church, and one to which the priory had failed to present an acceptable candidate for more than six months, thus giving the bishop the right of patronage. The priory resisted to no avail, and the bishop's man was able to stay in for the remaining two years of life left to his lord the bishop. Only on the bishop's death did the priory succeed in expelling the unwelcome clerk.[125] Here the bishop had used his authority to declare a benefice to exist when it did not, and then to go ahead and fill it against the will of those who would normally have exercised the patronage. Thus, for two years this bishop was able to obtrude a man into a benefice (or pseudo-benefice). Moreover, like any other judge, a bishop might attempt what the canons forbade and despoil an incumbent of his benefice "with the order of law overlooked."[126] In doing so, however, he faced a problem. His court might have been the highest in the diocese, but dissatisfied litigants could appeal his decisions as high as Rome. Things might not have gotten very far at Durham because the bishop had so little time left to live.[127]

Another case is an exception that tests the rule. On September 24, 1301, the bishop of Winchester revoked a collation of the vicarage of Camberwell to Roger de Hertford, which vicarage the bishop had collated by right of devolution.[128] But this was clearly an arrangement to safeguard the rights of the true patron – the prior and convent of Bermondsey – rather than to expel an unwelcome incumbent. The bishop's revocation

---

[125] EEA 25: Durham, no. 250. Later in the century, Bishop Poore would attempt to reach peace and tranquility with the priory regarding disputes entered by his predecessors, "praecipue" Bishop Marsh. The settlement included the appropriation of this chapelry (Ancroft) (*Historiae Dunelmensis Scriptores Tres*, ed. James Raines, Surtees Society 9 [London, 1839], lxxi).

[126] For the law, see at n 8.

[127] Trouble between France and England also delayed matters in 1225, as the prior and convent found it difficult under those circumstances to send to Rome its privileges regarding their conflict with the bishop (CPL, I, 101). The priory's suit over advowsons was still on later in the year (CPL, I, 104).

[128] Reg. Pontissara, 116, and see 107, where for "Hereford" read "Hertford."

explicitly cites his desire not to prejudice Bermondsey's rights as his reason, and the terms of the arrangement become clear from the expelled Roger's institution to Camberwell on Bermondsey's presentation two days later.[129] In behaving thus, the bishop heeded the canon law.[130]

Indeed, even when a bishop held an advowson, he had to do what other patrons facing filled benefices had to do; he waited. Bishop St. Hugh of Lincoln, his biographer remarked, gave to his administrators benefices in the diocese "when they began to become vacant."[131] In the early thirteenth century, a less saintly bishop was said by Gerald of Wales to have thanked God for the death of one of his clerks, for now the bishop could sell the dead man's church.[132] Gerald may have colored this episode or even invented it; after all, he was a polemicist. But the assumptions built into this story calculated to display episcopal simony are clear: incumbents enjoyed benefices for life, and that fact blocked patrons, including bishops. When the bishop of Winchester endowed his chapel of Saint Elizabeth, he similarly had to wait; the rectory of Hursley, in his gift, could be appropriated to the chapel only on the rector's death or resignation.[133] The constraint of the law is also evident in Gerald of Wales's assertion that wicked bishops would reserve the right to dispossess incumbents by instituting them with a saving clause, "saving the right of anyone else," so as to have a pretext to put in someone else in the future.[134] It is not clear, however, that this subterfuge was common practice; Gerald may not have been the most reliable of reporters.[135] If this

---

[129] Reg. Pontissara, 116, 117.
[130] For the canon law's solicitude for the rights of patrons, see Gray, "Ius Praesentandi," 494.
[131] Adam of Eynsham, *Magna Vita Sancti Hugonis*, ed. D. L. Douie and D. H. Farmer, 2nd ed. (Oxford, 1985), I, 110: "cum uacare cepissent, prebendas seu et alia beneficia conferebat."
[132] Gerald of Wales, "Gemma Ecclesiastica," in Gerald of Wales, *Opera* (RS) (London, 1861–3), II, 293.
[133] Reg. Pontissara, 136–7. When the monks of Rochester complained about their bishop's oppressions, they accused him of obtruding his own men into churches in the convent's gift – but only after they had fallen vacant through the deaths of their incumbents (*Select Cases from the Ecclesiastical Courts*, 45, 46, and 48, and see Charles Young, *Hubert Walter, Lord of Canterbury and Lord of England* [Durham, N.C., 1968], 137).
[134] "Instituo te in hac ecclesia salvo jure cujuslibet": Gerald of Wales, "Gemma Ecclesiastica," 300.
[135] Richard Kay, "Gerald of Wales and the Fourth Lateran Council," *Viator* 29 (1998), 80. See, however, the institution saving all other claims in Reg. Bronscombe, no. 884. Although, regarding Gerald's reliability, one can note that his account of his struggle with Archbishop Walter does tally with independent documents, where it can be checked (Michael Richter, *Giraldus Cambrensis: The Growth of the Welsh Nation*, 2nd ed. [Aberystwyth, 1976], 95).

story is a bit of exaggeration, it is still suggestive. Sometimes, however, an incumbent's security of tenure in his benefice could protect bishops too. Bishop Bronscombe of Exeter replied to Edward I's request that a prebend of Bosham be given a royal clerk by pointing out that he had already conferred the prebend on his friend and clerk Master Osbert.[136] With Osbert in, the prebend was off the market.

The pope was the ultimate authority regarding title to benefices. Thus, on the one hand, unconstrained by higher jurisdiction, he could evict men willy-nilly from their benefices, if he chose. Richard de Mepham, dean of Lincoln, was deprived of all his benefices when he not only dared to present the pope with the complaints of the English Church against papal oppression, but refused to disown them even when the pope gently invited him to do so. His Holiness relented after three days.[137] Those who successfully importuned Celestine V for benefices discovered their vulnerability to papal power in 1295, when Boniface VIII ascended the throne of Saint Peter. The new pope promptly revoked the papal provisions of his saintly and incompetent predecessor;[138] the sword of the vicar of Christ cut both ways. Indeed, two years later Boniface deprived his new enemies, the Colonna cardinals, along with their relatives and clerks, of their benefices.[139] While the Colonna still flew high, however, the bishop of Winchester sadly informed his own *officialis*, Philip de Barton, it would be wise to let the man who claimed one of Philip's benefices have it, as the claimant was a powerful man at Rome, and the Colonna cardinals took his business to heart "beyond measure."[140] The bishop himself did not want to be opposed to such men; Philip, he advised, should give way if he loved the bishop's honor and his own.[141] Papal power, and those it favored, were hard to resist.

---

[136] TNA, SC1/15/120. Could Master Osbert have been a blind? There is no trace of his institution to a prebend of Bosham in Reg. Bronscombe. For a similar case in the diocese of Bangor, where the bishop also noted that he had to "observe the rights of his church," see *Calendar of Ancient Correspondence Concerning Wales*, ed. J. G. Edwards (Cardiff, 1935), 178 and see 175–6.

[137] *Chronicle of Walter of Guisborough*, ed. Harry S. Rothwell, Camden Society (third series) 89 (London, 1957), 214.

[138] Rolls and Reg. Sutton, VIII, 216: for discussion, see T. S. R. Boase, *Boniface VIII* (London, 1933), 55–6, 103–4.

[139] *Annales Monastici*, IV, 531–2, and for their hangers on, see *Les Registres de Boniface VIII*, ed. Antoine Thomas et al. (Paris, 1884–1934), I, no. 2389 [col. 971]). The episode, and the reasons for it, are discussed by Boase, 164–81. For good measure, the pope reserved the cardinals' benefices to dispose of at his pleasure (*Registres de Boniface VIII*, I, no. 2388 [col. 966]; Reg. Pontissara, 579–84).

[140] "ultra modum": Reg. Pontissara, 831–2.

[141] Ibid., 832 and see 804–21.

The pope's freedom to do as he liked highlights the role of more or less neutral courts of appeal in keeping bishops from acting with similar freedom. Papal authority ordinarily constrained the behavior of those further down, including bishops, when it came to benefices. Bishops who attempted to expel incumbents found their decisions could be appealed; recall the appeal to Rome by the man who claimed that the bishop of Salisbury had effectively expelled him from his benefice by instituting another man to it.[142] In 1263, John de Exeter, bishop of Winchester, tried to exploit some confusion over who held the archdeaconry of Surrey in order to confer it on his own man, setting aside the incumbent, Peter de Sancto Mauro, who had received the archdeaconry from a previous bishop, Aymer de Lusignan. The pope, however, rescued Peter on appeal, eliminating two other claimants.[143] It seems that when his political opponents sought to blacken the name of Bishop Aymer himself with the pope, they did so by accusing him of forcibly dispossessing an incumbent of the diocese in order to exercise the advowson for himself.[144] Indeed, Rome's availability to hear appeals was open to abuse. Popes themselves were aware of the issue, as Innocent III showed when he informed the bishop of Exeter that the sons of deceased holders of benefices were appealing to the pope against the bishop's authority in a bid to keep their fathers' benefices; the bishop was to ignore such appeals and deprive the incumbents.[145]

When it came to benefices, as to much else, bishops did not have the free hand the pope did. One sign of the limits bishops faced is their attempts to appropriate benefices not to the use of some religious house of the diocese, but to their own, appointing perpetual vicars to carry out the cure of souls. Bishops who wished to appropriate to their own benefit found themselves in the same position vis-à-vis the pope as appropriating monasteries were vis-à-vis their bishop. And so one finds bishops campaigning at Rome for permission to appropriate.[146] The

---

[142] See at n 66.
[143] LN Monastic Cathedrals, 94–5; CPL, I, 40; *Les Registres d'Urbain IV*, ed. S. Clémencet, L. Dorez, and J. Guiraud, Bibliothèque des Ecoles Françaises d'Athènes et de Rome (second series) 13 (Paris, 1892–1958), III, no. 1042 reproduces the whole letter.
[144] Susan Stewart, "What Happened at Shere?" *Southern History* 22 (2000), 3–6.
[145] *Letters of Pope Innocent III (1198–1215) Concerning England and Wales*, no. 426. Later bishops asked the pope for similar decrees as reinforcement (*Councils and Synods*, 98–9).
[146] Reg. Giffard of Worcester, 302; Reg. Thomas Cantilupe 126–7; Reg. Halton, I, 240, II, 172–4; *Historical Papers and Letters from the Northern Registers*, ed. James Raine (RS) (London, 1873), 282–4.

bishop of Carlisle tried to strike two birds with one stone, sweetly asking the rector of Horncastle, "his friend ... dearest," himself to advocate the appropriation of Horncastle to the bishop's estate, offering as compensation an appropriate pension, whatever the rector would fitly ordain.[147]

Rome was not the only hindrance to bishops trying to have their way regarding benefices in their dioceses. The intermediate jurisdictions enjoyed by the metropolitans of Canterbury and York were another. It did not help that the court of Canterbury operated under the assumption that, when an incumbent was involved in a dispute over a benefice, he was to remain in possession while the suit was fought out.[148] The archbishop of Canterbury also offered tuition to litigants who appealed to Rome, often thus also in the bargain providing a forum in which to resolve the dispute.[149] When Bishop Godfrey Giffard of Worcester embarked on his campaign to drive his former steward Peter de Leicester from his benefices – one collated by Giffard himself – Peter appealed to Rome and for tuition in the meantime to the Court of Canterbury; the *officialis* of Canterbury himself warned Giffard that his case was weak. Peter kept all his benefices save the one collated to him, concerning which he accepted a compromise arrangement after years of effort on Giffard's part.[150] In another case, the vicar of Exford faced expulsion by his rector. The bishop of Bath and Wells as diocesan sided with the rector, but the vicar in turn appealed to the pope, successfully obtaining a favorable judgment from papal judges delegate. When the bishop resisted, however, it was Archbishop Walter of Canterbury who stepped in to enforce the decision.[151]

---

[147] "amico suo ... karissime": Reg. Halton, I, 240. For examples of nonepiscopal patrons having to wait for the rectory to fall vacant in order to appropriate – or for the appropriation to take effect – see EEA 32: Norwich, nos. 69, 106, 193, 195. Would-be appropriators were advised to buy out incumbents, as Saint Mary's Abbey (York) did when the rector of Gainford agreed to an appropriation on condition that he receive part of the £100 income of the church – presumably as a pension from the benefice free from obligation to serve the cure (EEA 29: Durham, no. 45A). See also the case in *Durham Annals and Documents*, 210–11. For a case of an appropriation that failed to become effective, and the appropriating house having to live with the next incumbent until his cession or death, see EEA 30: Carlisle, nos. 34–5, 64.
[148] *Medieval Court of Arches*, xliv, citing ibid., 79.
[149] Cheney, *Pope Innocent III and England*, 118–19.
[150] Burger, "Peter of Leicester," 453–73.
[151] Cheney, *Pope Innocent III and England*, 115. Unfortunately, the ultimate outcome of the case is lost.

Getting around Security of Tenure: Sequestration

A move short of expulsion available to bishops was sequestration of a benefice's revenues. Sequestration was one of the tools a bishop had for bringing an incumbent to heel, driving him to perform the obligations of his office. Strikingly, however, bishops do not seem to have availed themselves of this means to discipline administrators for failure to perform as administrators. True, Archbishop Pecham did sequestrate in a case that touched him personally, ordering the seizure of the church of a rector who owed him money.[152] And Archbishop Romeyn sequestrated the benefice that Robert de Scarborough had refused to help the archbishop defend, an event that turned out to be just the first in Romeyn's campaign against Robert.[153] But this kind of use of sequestration seems to have been rare.

For what purposes did bishops sequestrate benefices? A survey of the memoranda register of Bishop Sutton of Lincoln, running from 1290 to 1299, provides a good sample of references to sequestrations carried out at the bishop's behest. That source produces sixty-seven sequestrations of benefices.[154] The largest category of such sequestrations was prompted by a clerk's death, stemming either from a concern with probate or intestacy, or to ensure that dilapidations to the clerk's benefice were made good. Such sequestrations were routine anyway, even when they were not explicitly recorded, given that the fruits of vacant benefices went to the bishop. To their number one can add a few sequestrations of a benefice following a clerk's resignation, either to ensure the right person (i.e., the resigning clerk or his successor) got the proceeds or, again, to cover dilapidations. These various categories come to twenty-seven sequestrations in all.[155] In four cases, benefices were sequestrated pending a dispute over the benefice.[156] In some other cases, the register gives no reason for the sequestration.[157] Other instances are hard to categorize. Was the sequestration of Edworth in 1292, pending an inquiry as to whether the rector

---

[152] Pecham, *Epistolae*, II, 611.
[153] Reg. Romeyn, no. 148 and see earlier discussion.
[154] It produces only a few instances of sequestration of the property of the laity, evidently related to probate or intestacy (Rolls and Reg. Sutton, IV, 77, 79–80, VI, 119, 138–9).
[155] Ibid., III, 46, 50, 70, 165, 172–4, 189, 197, IV, 1, 7, 42, 55, 65–6, 80, 98–9, 122, 190, V, 6, 20, 41, 64, 112, 135, 150–1, VI, 54, 124, 150. One can also add a couple sequestrations on a report that the incumbent had died where the report turned out to be false (ibid., V, 20–1, VI, 36–7).
[156] Ibid., III, 137–8, 140, V, 28, 73.
[157] Ibid., IV, 9, 49, 122, V, 9–10, 27, 83.

had a received a vicarage in the diocese of Salisbury, a disciplinary action (for pluralism) or a cautious sequestration of a benefice which might be thus legally vacant?[158]

The target narrows with the twenty-four occasions on which Sutton sequestrated benefices for clearly disciplinary reasons, or twenty-seven if one counts ambiguous reasons under this heading.[159] By and large, Sutton imposed such sequestrations for nonresidence[160] or failure to be ordained.[161] But although that bishop might have manipulated the procedure to discipline his own clerks for poor service, he did not avail himself of this opportunity. Out of so many sequestrations, there is only a bare possible case: the sequestration of a mediety of Leverton in 1293 for nonresidence by the incumbent, who is unfortunately not named.[162] One mediety of Leverton was held by one Walter de Norton, the other by John de Leake.[163] Walter has no traceable career in Sutton's service. John, however, had carried out a sequestration himself on Sutton's behalf the previous year;[164] he seems to have part of Sutton's army of ad hoc commissaries. But without knowing which mediety of Leverton was sequestrated, it is impossible even to be sure John rather than Walter was penalized.[165] Not even the few religious houses that suffered sequestration of their appropriated churches – for being led by a prior not recognized by Sutton, for example – were among the houses Sutton occasionally drew upon for services such as reconciling churches polluted by bloodshed.[166] And,

---

[158] Ibid., IV, 14, and see 39. For the other ambiguous cases, ibid., IV, 121 (and 150), 162–3, V, 31.
[159] Ibid., III, 10–11, 22, 53, 66, IV, 39, 58, 74, 80, 86, 122, 129 (and see 187), V, 15–16 (and see 18), 88–9, 110, 118, 155, VI, 2, 7–8, 79, 117, 120–1, 128.
[160] Ibid., III, 10–11.
[161] E.g., ibid., VI, 2. There were a few other reasons: failure to pay procurations (ibid., VI, 79); failure to be instituted on attaining canonical age (ibid., IV, 150); illicit farming of the benefice (ibid., V, 15–16, 118); pluralism (ibid., V, 110).
[162] Ibid., IV, 122.
[163] Ibid., I, 91, 188.
[164] Ibid., IV, 32.
[165] The only other men connected with Sutton to have property sequestrated were Clement de Leake (ibid., IV, 32) and Roger de Beaufoy (ibid., V, 112), but the notices of both sequestrations appear after their deaths, and so were presumably concerned with probate or dilapidations rather than discipline. Clement had taken charge of the vacant archdeaconry of Lincoln on Sutton's behalf (ibid., III, 161, and see 137), and his death had vacated a mediety of Leake (ibid., I, 169), although the order to sequestrate does not mention the benefice specifically. Roger had received an ad hoc commission from Sutton jointly to administer probate in 1294 (ibid., V, 41, and see 134).
[166] The houses with churches sequestrated for disciplinary reasons were Ogbourne (ibid., III, 66); Beadlow (ibid., VI, 7–8); Saint Andrew's Northampton (ibid., VI, 117); Weedon Pinkney (ibid., VI, 128).

of course, those whose benefices were sequestrated could sue. Indeed, ca. 1290, the author of a treatise on the Court of Arches doubted that an incumbent in de facto possession of a benefice could be removed by sequestration "sine causa cognitione," except regarding dilapidations.[167]

Archdeacons

If a bishop were tempted to deprive anyone from a benefice in his gift, one would expect that person to have been an archdeacon. After all, an archdeaconry was not only a benefice, it was an administrative office, one on which bishops relied. Even so, archdeacons had staying power. There were exceptions. Maurice de Arundel was deprived of his archdeaconry of Gloucester by his bishop for, according to the Worcester annalist, "culpis exegentibus," unfortunately unspecified. The deprivation was said to have been done judicially ("sententialiter"), but no more is recoverable. The fact that Maurice did not long survive his loss means that he did not have much opportunity to appeal.[168] Bishop Cantilupe of Hereford pursued James de Aquablanca, archdeacon of Salop, for nonresidence.[169] In this case, Cantilupe attained his goal. Whether this should count as a simple deprivation without a compromise is, however, unclear, for James's obit as archdeacon was still observed at Hereford.[170] But these are the only two archdeacons clearly to suffer deprivation by their bishop in the thirteenth century. Both, it should be noted, were deprived not by the bishop who appointed them, but by a successor – the sort of change in patronage that might spark a move to deprive. That circumstance also applies in the case of an archdeacon of Hereford, Henry Bustard. He lost his archdeaconry after being implicated in the murder of the bishop of Hereford's *officialis* and being banished from the realm.[171] Whether Bustard was deprived by papal or episcopal authority is, however, unclear.

Other archdeacons faced other foes. Matthew Paris, who always liked heroes to match his villains, says that William Lupus boldly spoke against the archbishop of Canterbury to his very face over *sede vacante* administration at Lincoln. The archbishop deprived William of his archdeaconry of Lincoln. According to Paris, Lupus died at Rome, carrying on his appeal.[172] No doubt he appealed his own deprivation too.

[167] *Medieval Court of Arches*, 168.
[168] *Annales Monastici*, IV, 436; LN Hereford, 108.
[169] See n 99.
[170] LN Hereford, 28.
[171] EEA 35: Hereford, liii, lv n 211, 192–3; LN Hereford, 24.
[172] Matthew Paris, *Chronica Majora*, ed. H. R. Luard (RS) (London, 1872–83), V, 412, 497.

Master Honorius, archdeacon of Richmond, long sustained the hostility of his archbishop only, it seems, to have fallen when he lost royal favor too, being incarcerated far from the archdiocese at Gloucester.[173] Unfortunately, the source for his loss says only that he was "bonis omnibus spoliatus" and imprisoned, which is only vague evidence of deprivation of the archdeaconry.[174] Peter, archdeacon of Lincoln, was an unusual case; the clergy of his own archdeaconry appealed to the pope against his disgraceful behavior, and the pope deprived him, recommending pious works to make up for his deficiencies.[175]

The pope was the most dangerous opponent. William fitzWalter appears to have lost his archdeaconry of Hereford by papal action.[176] The pope deprived Ralph de Blonvilla for pluralism; the fact that he was in conflict with a royally-backed rival for the benefice could not have helped.[177] Two archdeacons of Surrey lost their archdeaconries when the pope ruled they had obtruded themselves into the archdeaconry.[178] Ralph de Hengham, the bishop of Worcester's friend, lost his archdeaconry of Worcester, which the bishop had collated to him, when the pope determined that he had already provided that benefice to another man.[179] Ralph de Malling, archdeacon of Middlesex, was brought down when he fell on the wrong side of a dispute. The archbishop of Canterbury was on one side, but both king and pope were on the other. And so the bishop of London – who had collated the archdeaconry to Ralph – deprived him because, it was said, Ralph was in the possession of Pagham (whose commend Winchelsey had given him), a move connected to Winchelsey's attempt to take Pagham away from the noble Theobald de Bar. But Theobald had the backing of both Edward I and the pope.[180] John de Colonna, archdeacon of Huntingdon, fell victim to Boniface VIII's campaign against his family.[181]

On the whole, however, archdeacons had an impressive survival rate. The new, reliable compilation of archdiaconal *fasti* covering the thirteenth

---

[173] EEA 27: York, lxv n 197; LN York, 149.
[174] *Annales Monastici*, III, 31.
[175] CPL, I, 47; LN Lincoln, 25.
[176] Z. N. Brooke and C. N. L. Brooke, "Hereford Cathedral Dignitaries in the Twelfth Century," *Cambridge Historical Journal* 8 (1944), 16–17; LN Hereford, 24.
[177] CPL, I, 179; LN Monastic Cathedrals, 66.
[178] CPL, I, 405; LN Monastic Cathedrals, 95.
[179] CPL, I, 495; Reg. Giffard of Worcester, lxi, 334.
[180] For the collation, Reg. Winchelsey, 30; for Ralph and Pagham, see "Annales Londinienses" in *Chronicles of the Reigns of Edward I and Edward II*, ed. W. Stubbs (RS) (London, 1882–3), I, 103. For the rest, J. H. Denton, *Robert Winchelsey and the Crown 1294–1313: A Study in the Defence of Ecclesiastical Liberty* (Cambridge, 1980), 273.
[181] LN Lincoln 29, and see at n 139.

century is nearly complete; only the diocese of Coventry and Lichfield remains to be finished. The revised volumes list 430 thirteenth-century archdeacons who held on until death or resignation, compared with the dozen men who lost their archdeaconries in the same period.[182]

Getting around Security of Tenure: Commendation

A practice with large potential to get around security of tenure was that of commendation of benefices. To hold a benefice *in commendam* was to hold it temporarily without actual institution. Thus, the holder lacked any permanent legal title to the benefice and enjoyed the income only temporarily. In an attempt to prevent the abuse of commendation, the Second Council of Lyons limited the duration of commends to six months.[183] The temptation, of course, was to hold them longer; in the mid-thirteenth century (1257–68?) Bishop Bridport of Salisbury complained that some holders of commends acted as though they were perpetual ("quasi perpetuas"), and so revoked all commends in his diocese made by himself or his predecessors.[184] Indeed, in 1279 the bishops of the southern province petitioned the pope, or at least drafted a petition, to soften the rigor of the six-month limit on commends.[185] The bishop of Winchester was willing to commend benefices "by the perpetual tenor" of his letters, implying a lifetime grant.[186] Bishop Gravesend of Lincoln made a similar perpetual commendation in 1264.[187] In 1285, the bishop of Winchester confirmed a commendation that had been made in 1243.[188]

Bishops commended benefices with the consent of the patron. Thus, a bishop faced no obstacles in commending benefices to which he himself

---

[182] LN London, 10–20; LN Monastic Cathedrals, 14–15, 23–5, 38–42, 50–2, 64–7, 70–1, 81–5, 106–109; LN Lincoln, 25–47; LN Salisbury, 26–33, 36–7; LN Chichester, 21–5; LN York, 31–52; LN Bath and Wells, 28–35, 37–8; LN Hereford, 24–5, 27–9; LN Exeter, 22–4, 26–9, 31–5. I am grateful to the late Professor Jeffrey Denton, who informed me that no thirteenth-century deprivations of archdeacons turned up for the volume he was preparing for the diocese of Coventry and Lichfield.

[183] Chapter 14: *Decrees of the Ecumenical Councils*, ed. Norman P. Tanner (Washington, DC, 1990), I, 322; Rodes, *Ecclesiastical Administration*, 160; J. R. H. Moorman, *Church Life in England in the Thirteenth Century* (Cambridge, 1955), 32–3. Bishops could explicitly raise the six-month rule, as Dalderby of Lincoln commonly did (LAO, Episcopal Register II, fos. 330r–338r, Episcopal Register III, f. 29r), but this does not seem to have been the usual practice.

[184] *Councils and Synods*, 562.

[185] Ibid., 864.

[186] Reg. Pontissara, 12, 13.

[187] Rot. Gravesend, 16.

[188] Reg. Pontissara, 17–18.

held the advowson. One purpose of commendation was as a stopgap, allowing a church to be cared for until a suitable incumbent could be found.[189] Benefices were also commended to give an unqualified presentee the opportunity to become qualified.[190] A candidate lacking ordination as a priest thus gained a delay to get himself properly ordained, at which point he could be instituted.[191] Commendation allowed a presentee to have a benefice on condition that the recipient improve his learning or that the right of the supposed patron be clarified.[192] Or a benefice could be commended to a candidate in order to buy time to get a dispensation for a condition that otherwise prevented his institution.[193]

In theory, a bishop could have kept his bureaucrats on a short leash by exploiting this practice, commending benefices to them and renewing the commendation after six months for as long as the clerks gave good service. Commended benefices in this way could have come close to being revocable salary, with all the advantages to a bishop that paying revocable salaries could bring. The case of Thomas de Standon, although not a recipient of episcopal bounty, illustrates the potential by bringing home the vulnerability of holding a benefice by commendation. Thomas received a benefice *in commendam* for a year (despite the six-month limit laid down at Lyons and its requirement of priestly orders). This was done at the request of the custodian of the patron, the patron being underage; Thomas himself was not yet a priest. Before the year was up, however, the patron attained his majority and now insisted on presenting to the benefice, despite the commend.[194] Had Thomas been instituted, the now grown patron would have been as stymied as other patrons discussed earlier.

Commendation, however, was not institution, whatever commendatories might hope. (And they could hope otherwise; Henry de Symplingham insinuated for himself the status of rector when he styled himself "Rector seu commendatarius" of Saint Martin's, Ellisfield.)[195] In the early fourteenth century, Bishop Dalderby noted that he had earlier commended Sutton to Peter de Dalderby for six months according to the form of the Council of Lyons, and now instituted him to the same church as rector.[196]

[189] Rodes, *Ecclesiastical Administration in Medieval England*, 160.
[190] As pointed out by David Smith, "Thomas Cantilupe's Register," 96.
[191] This reason is given explicitly on Reg. Giffard of Worcester, 127.
[192] Rodes, *Ecclesiastical Administration in Medieval England*, 257 n 32.
[193] *Royal and Historical Letters Illustrative of the Reign of Henry III*, ed. Walter Waddington Shirley (RS) (London, 1862–6), I, no. 281.
[194] Reg. Giffard of Worcester, 127.
[195] Reg. Pontissara, 79.
[196] LAO, Episcopal Register III, f. 29r.

Why did bishops commend men to benefices in their own gift? The reasons were various. Bishop Sutton of Lincoln commended William de la Gare, archdeacon of Lincoln, and Simon de Luda, another episcopal agent, to benefices in order to hold them vacant until the intended recipients came of age.[197] The same bishop also commended Martin Creuker to a benefice in his gift for more traditional reasons, because Creuker had not yet been ordained; the bishop collated the benefice to Creuker when he proceeded to orders.[198] Commendation also gave a certain flexibility, which allowed a bishop to delegate the giving of his patronage in a way that could be amended later. The bishop of Carlisle, departing the diocese, left his vicar-general a list of three benefices in the bishop's gift and the three men who were to be instituted to them should they fall vacant while the bishop was away. Should any other benefices in his gift become vacant, the bishop instructed, they were to be commended to appropriate men of the vicar-general's choice.[199]

Commendation could also be used primarily to benefit some party other than the bishop or the recipient. The bishop of Exeter commended the church of Egloshayle to his *officialis* as a favor to that church itself; it was in a state of decay, but the *officialis*, the bishop thought, had the industry to restore its rights and possessions.[200] Archbishop Pecham once commended a benefice to his clerk, B. de Sunting', in order to hold it open while his other clerk, John de Gloucester, attempted to obtain another benefice, then under litigation, for himself. If John failed, he could have the benefice commended to B.[201] Sometimes the reasons for commendations remain mysterious. Bishop Dalderby of Lincoln commended Normanby, in Dalderby's gift, to Thomas de Luda, and then collated it to him a mere six days later.[202]

---

[197] Rolls and Reg. Sutton, I, 57–8, 140. Simon de Luda, sometimes described as "Simon, rector of Ailby," received ad hoc commissions from Sutton dealing with probate and other business (ibid., I, 199, III, 41–2, 93, IV, 112, V, 156–7, 163). For his identity as rector of Ailby, see Rot. Gravesend, 82; Rolls and Reg. Sutton, I, 19; IV, 112, 119. At ibid.,V, 64, for "William of Louth" read "Simoni de Luda" (LAO, Episcopal Register I, f. 118r).

[198] Rolls and Reg. Sutton, I, 117.

[199] Reg. Halton, II, 38–39.

[200] Reg. Bronscombe, no. 980 and see no. 926. The bishop of Coventry and Lichfield commended Worfield, in the bishop's gift, to Ralph de Salop, rector of Walton-on-Trent. The bishop laid out his concern that the cure of souls and Worfield's temporalities and spiritualities not suffer (Reg. Langton, no. 1279). Whether they were already in bad condition is unclear.

[201] Pecham, *Epistolae*, II, 579.

[202] LAO, Episcopal Register II, f. 338r. Another mysterious case, though not concerning a benefice in the bishop's own gift, is that of the institution of John de Standon to Cound only three days after his commendation, as a priest, to that church (Reg. Langton, nos. 959–60). For another case, ibid., no. 1167.

But there is little evidence that bishops commended benefices as a means of controlling their men. John de Schalby, Bishop Sutton of Lincoln's registrar, received Sutton-le-Marsh by collation in 1290, of which he had already held the commend (for how long is unclear).[203] The commendation had not been a move to get around a lack of holy orders, for John had been a priest since at least 1288.[204] Nor does John appear to have held other benefices at this point, so pluralism restrictions also were not a concern. Perhaps Sutton used this commendation as a trial run of John's reliability. If so, the experiment seems to have been unusual.

Rather than use commendation to bend rewards for subordinates in the bishop's interest, bishops on the whole used commendations as a concession to their subordinates, a means to add to the rewards they already enjoyed. For perhaps the most frequent use of commendation by bishops where their clerks were concerned was to allow those clerks to get around prohibitions against pluralism,[205] a point evident in a survey of commends to episcopal servants in the thirteenth-century diocese of Lincoln. Sometimes the sources explicitly note this intention. In 1264, Bishop Gravesend commended Conisholme to Alexander de Swineshead (alias "de Holland"), so that Alexander could hold in plurality.[206] Gravesend merely noted and permitted William de Newark's pluralism when he commended Pytchley to William.[207] Bishop Grosseteste commended a church to John de Riston, his archdeacon of Lincoln's clerk, noting John's possession of another church.[208] Bishop Sutton's register notes that he

---

[203] Rolls and Reg. Sutton, I, 137–8.
[204] Ibid., I, 104.
[205] J. R. H. Moorman stresses this use: *Church Life*, 32 (and see Alexander Hamilton Thompson, "Pluralism in the Mediaeval Church; with Notes on Pluralists in the Diocese of Lincoln, 1366," part 1, *Reports and Papers of the Architectural and Archaeological Societies of the Counties of Lincoln and Northampton* 33 [1915], 39–40). In 1268 the legate Ottobuono complained about commends being used to evade rules against pluralism (*Councils and Synods*, 777–8). As his complaint suggests, the practice was not universally approved. See also the thirteenth-century case of the man who had one benefice by institution and another by commendation. He was challenged on this, and replied that he had a document allowing it; alas, the parchment was at Rome, where his proctor died looking for it (*Medieval Court of Arches*, ed. Donald Logan, 169–71).
[206] Rot. Gravesend, 16. This may have been a favor to the archdeacon of Lincoln, whose official Alexander was (LAO, Rolls of Bishop Richard Gravesend I, mm 2, 11, and see Cambridge University Library, Peterborough Dean and Chapter MS 23, f. 48; Spalding Gentlemen's Society MS: The Crowland Cartulary, f. 110r-v).
[207] Rot. Gravesend, 43, 124, 301–2. He was Gravesend's archdeacon of Huntingdon and his *officialis* (LN Lincoln, 29; Rot. Gravesend, 228).
[208] Rot. Grosseteste, 118. For John, see Kathleen Major, "The *Familia* of Robert Grosseteste," in *Robert Grosseteste: Scholar and Bishop*, ed. D. A. Callus (Oxford, 1955), 235–6.

had commended Ellesborough to Oliver Sutton (the younger), which he now collated to him because the young Oliver had obtained a papal dispensation for pluralism.[209] Other cases are only implicit. Grosseteste instituted his servant Remigius de Pocklington to Ab Kettelby the same day he commended Medbourne to Remigius.[210] Grosseteste similarly commended Ab Kettleby to his agent Leonard de Dunwich when Leonard had already been in possession of Boothby Pagnell; Leonard's continuation in Boothby Pagnell is confirmed by papal dispensation of 1243 for Boothby Pagnell and Ab Kettelby.[211] These commendations by Grosseteste had these men covering a distance of between eleven and fifteen miles to serve both of their cures – a not impossible distance for a full-time pastor, but one that would have prevented their tending both churches on a daily basis, especially given the administrative demands on these men. One suspects that parish chaplains were expected to take up the slack. At the start of the fourteenth century, Bishop Dalderby also noted when commending benefices with cure of souls that recipients could hold another such benefice too.[212] Indeed, a series of papal indults for pluralism recognized that men held commends in order to hold in plurality; the indults allowed such men to be instituted to what they had held in commendation and still retain the other benefice.[213] And Archbishop Winchelsey complained that commends were being used to evade pluralism restrictions.[214] The archbishop had hauled up at least one clerk on charges of pluralism, only to have to let him go when the man showed that he had been instituted to one benefice but had received the other *in commendam* before the Council of Lyons had limited the length of commends.[215]

Incapacity

A final test of incumbents' security of tenure was their physical incapacity, usually a result of old age. Even when a benefice bore cure of souls,

---

[209] Rolls and Reg. Sutton, VIII, 138.
[210] Rot. Grosseteste, 395, and see Major, "*Familia* of Robert Grosseteste," 232–3.
[211] Rot. Grosseteste, 22, 26, 420; CPL, I, 204.
[212] LAO, Episcopal Register II, 330r–338r.
[213] CPL, I, 361, 381, 382, 388 (bis) and passim. For a couple of instances of commendation that mention that the recipient is otherwise beneficed, see Reg. Langton, nos. 676, 723.
[214] Reg. Pontissara, 202.
[215] Rose Graham, "The Metropolitical Visitation of the Diocese of Worcester," in Graham, *English Ecclesiastical Studies* (London, 1929), 349.

incumbents who simply lost the ability to carry out their duties needed have no fear of losing the benefice. Instead, bishops typically appointed coadjutors to do what an incumbent could not do himself. There was also another alternative short of simple deprivation. Bishops could pension off the superannuated, often drawing the pension from the old man's former benefice.[216] But in the thirteenth century, at least, coadjutors – and so maintenance of the incumbent in his benefice – appear to have been the preferred solution.[217] A benefice for life was indeed for life, until the very end. Sentiment in favor of secure tenure in benefices was strong.

---

[216] Nicholas Orme in fact argues that such pension arrangements came to displace the use of coadjutors in the fourteenth- and fifteenth-century diocese of Exeter ("Sufferings of the Clergy, Illness and Old Age in Exeter Diocese 1300–1540," in *Life, Death, and the Elderly in Historical Perspective*, ed. Margaret Pelling and Richard M. Smith [London, 1991], 66). Joel Rosenthal's treatment of retirement arrangements for English clergy in the same period focuses on pensions and corrodies (*Old Age in Late Medieval England* [Philadelphia, 1996], 108–12) and his earlier account of elderly beneficed clergy similarly concerns pensions, with no mention of coadjutors ("Retirement and the Lifecycle in Fifteenth-Century England," in *Aging and the Aged: Selected Papers from the Annual Conference of the Centre for Medieval Studies*, ed. M. M. Sheehan [Toronto, 1990], 180–3).

[217] Moorman, *Church Life*, 201–2. A study of an almshouse for infirm clerks, even in the two succeeding centuries, finds that the clergy served there were overwhelmingly men who lacked benefices and indeed had never had one (Nicholas Orme, "A Medieval Almshouse for the Clergy: Clyst Gabriel Hospital Near Exeter," *Journal of Ecclesiastical History* 39 [1988], 7). Those who had had benefices, had poor ones.

5

Pensions

Nowadays, most people work for wages, regular cash payments from an employer. Some thirteenth-century clergy did receive *stipendia* of this kind, such as those priests hired by incumbents of parishes to serve the cure of souls either as substitutes for the incumbent or as assistants to him. This kind of payment was not, however, customary among diocesan administrators.

The closest thing to a stipend used to reward clerical administrators was the grant of a pension. The term *pensiones* usually applied to such payments can cause confusion, for it covered different kinds of arrangements. Many *pensiones* constituted a diversion of the income generated by a benefice from the incumbent to some other party. Such arrangements were often, perhaps generally, products of compromise settlements between rival claimants to a benefice.[1] Each party got something. The man determined to be the incumbent got the benefice, but the loser got a pension, that is, an annual portion of the income from the benefice. A number of such situations are recorded as charters in Dover Priory's cartulary. The rubricator generally calls these charters *pensiones*, even when the actual charter does not, and he gave the title "pensiones" to this section of the cartulary.[2] *Pensio* was also often used for the annual dues

---

[1] R. H. Helmholz, *The Oxford History of the Laws of England I: The Canon Law and Ecclesiastical Jurisdiction from 597 to the 1640s* (Oxford, 2004), 369–71; R. N. Swanson, *Church and Society in Late Medieval England* (Manchester, 1989), 144; Peter McDonald, "Poor Clerks' Provisions: A Case for Reassessment?" *Archivum Historiae Pontificae* 30 (1992), 343. For a pension that blurs the line between a pension charged to a benefice and one paid *de camera*, see EEA 32: Norwich, no. 71.

[2] Lambeth Palace, MS 241, fos. 46r–51v.

sometimes owed by holders of churches to their monastic patrons, an arrangement that became less common as more and more houses appropriated such benefices.³ The pensions of concern in this chapter, by contrast, were paid out of the grantor's treasury. For this reason, they are often said to have been granted *de camera*.⁴ They were usually paid twice a year, on specified dates.

It is natural that pensions *de camera* draw the eye of historians.⁵ Historians of what used to be called "bastard feudalism" have given them much attention,⁶ ecclesiastical historians, less. In such secular discussions they are usually called "annuities." Why have pensions garnered this attention? Perhaps so much discussion has traditionally centered on gifts of endowments, especially landed endowments (either fiefs or benefices), that the cash payments represented by pensions have the allure of the new. It may also help that cash payments seem to move medieval administration closer to modern practice. There may also be a sense that, in the reconstruction of seigneurial and episcopal households, witness lists to charters have too long held pride of place when it comes to identifying administrative personnel, whereas financial accounts have been left in the shadows, underused. Since such accounts often record money payments to administrative personnel, it is tempting to extend the enthusiasm these sources excite regarding the identification of administrators to an account of how administrators were rewarded. All these points suggest the possibility that a hitherto ignored economy of cash payment binding administrator and principal waits to be revealed. Moreover, of course, medieval authorities, rightly or wrongly, saw livery and maintainance, based in part on the grant of pensions, as a source of violent disorder.⁷

---

³ Ulrich Rasche, "The Early Phase of Appropriation of Parish Churches in Medieval England," *Journal of Medieval History* 26 (2000), 214, 228. For an instance of lawyers distinguishing between this kind of pension and one that can be litigated in the king's courts, i.e., an "annuity," see *Year Books of the Reign of King Edward I*, ed. Alfred J. Horwood (RS) (London, 1866–79), V, 478.
⁴ Hence the many examples in Appendix 1.
⁵ Recently, Elizabeth Rutledge, "Lawyers and Administrators: The Clerks of Late-Thirteenth-Century Norwich," in *Medieval East Anglia*, ed. Christopher Harper-Bill (2005), 88–91, in a study of the clerks of the priory of Norwich based on priory accounts.
⁶ E.g., Michael Hicks, *Bastard Feudalism* (London, 1995); J. M. W. Bean, *From Lord to Patron: Lordship in Medieval England* (Philadelphia, 1989); Scott Waugh, "Tenure to Contract: Lordship and Clientage in Thirteenth-Century England," *English Historical Review* 101 (1986), 811–39; K. B. McFarlane, "Bastard Feudalism," in McFarlane, *England in the Fifteenth Century: Collected Essays of K. B. McFarlane*, ed. G. L. Harris (London, 1981), 23–43.
⁷ Hicks, *Bastard Feudalism*, 124–9.

I will deal with the matter of occasional cash payments from bishops to their administrative personnel in Chapter 6. Here, however, I hope to answer the question, Did pensions *de camera* overshadow benefices as a reward for clerical administrators – in particular, episcopal administrators? I think the answer is "no." Bishops, other ecclesiastics, and lay lords did grant pensions to clerks, pensions that recipients valued. But benefices remained the gold standard in English church governance, the chief material reward of episcopal clerks and their chief material goal. Moreover, most pensions granted by bishops characteristically suffered from what was, from a grantor's point of view, one of the chief legal drawbacks of benefices: once granted, they could not (legally) be revoked because of failure to provide the service for which they had in fact been given. Such pensions, at least in law, did not provide bishops a disciplinary device much more effective than benefices. Grantors, however, in practice often failed to pay pensions. That should have made them good disciplinary tools. Instead, however, such failures seem to highlight the comparative value (for the recipient) of benefices, in particular, their security.[8]

I am concerned with two basic types of pension *de camera* here and will discuss them when granted by bishops and other kinds of lords where this distinction does not appear to affect the conclusion I draw. The first is what I will term a "simple" pension: a grant of a pension to be paid to the recipient. The second is what I will call a pension "in lieu of a benefice": a pension in which the grantor promises to pay the recipient a pension until the recipient receives a benefice.[9] (I am not asserting that medieval people categorized pensions in this way, although I think it would have been reasonable for them to have done so, especially given the – albeit prohibited – practice of expectatives. I introduce this distinction for my own analytical purposes and use this terminology to ease the discussion.) As

---

[8] For what appears to be a rare comparison of the advantages and disadvantages of pensions and benefices, see C. R. Cheney, *Pope Innocent III and England* (Stuttgart, 1976), 96.

[9] The earliest reference to such a grant I have come across, from a bishop or from anyone else, dates from the 1160s: one master R. claimed that a deceased bishop of Wells had granted him 40s a year as a pension until a prebend in the cathedral should fall vacant (*Sacrorum Conciliorum Nova et Amplissima Collectio*, ed. Joannes Dominicus Mansi [Padua, 1767] XXI, col. 1090; *Regesta Pontificum romanorum ab condita ecclesia*, compiled by Philipp Jaffé, directed by W. Wattenbach et al., 2nd ed. [Leipzig, 1885–8], 14,3000, and see EEA X: Bath and Wells, xlv). Grants of both kinds survive in much greater plenitude from the thirteenth century, perhaps because of the production of bishops' registers, perhaps because of developments in the Common Law. This particular kind of grant has been briefly discussed by Scott L. Waugh, "Tenure to Contract," 821–2 and by W. A. Pantin, *The English Church in the Fourteenth Century* (1955), 33, but otherwise appears little in the literature.

in the chapter on benefices (and as noted in Chapter 1), I have examined pensions granted by those other than bishops, as well as those granted by bishops, for a better grasp of general characteristics of this kind of grant.

I have found some thirty-eight grants of simple pensions by thirteenth-century English bishops.[10] Numerically, these are outweighed by the fifty-three grants by bishops of pensions in lieu of benefices surviving from the same period.[11] Bishop Dalderby of Lincoln's early fourteenth-century episcopate produces analogous figures. In the years 1300–20, Dalderby granted four surviving simple pensions compared with eight surviving pensions in lieu of benefices.[12] Thus, brute numbers imply that bishops generally granted pensions in lieu of benefices rather than simple pensions, either because bishops preferred to do so or because pensions in lieu of benefices were what recipients preferred to have.[13]

Are these figures misleading? One should naturally assume that many grants have been lost. But are there reasons for grants of simple pensions to have perished at a higher rate than pensions in lieu of benefices? It is worth bearing in mind that grants of pensions of both kinds generally survive in the archives of the grantor. It was grantors, rather than grantees, who preserved them over the long term.

It is hard to see how a consideration of the need of evidence by grantors in case of disputes can solve the problem. On the one hand, one could argue that grantors of pensions in lieu of a benefice would have kept the grants so that, should a grantee sue for payment of a pension even after receiving his benefice, the grantor could show that the pension had in fact

---

[10] For these, see Appendix 1. The definition of "thirteenth-century bishops" from Chapter 1 should be in particular noted in this case. Hence, grants from the early fourteenth century by bishops whose episcopates, and so registers, began in the thirteenth century are counted here.

[11] For these, see Appendix 1.

[12] LAO, Episcopal Register III, fos. 26v, 81r, 86r, 98v, 125r, 142v, 143r, 162v, 221r, 345r, 362v, 374r.

[13] This finding may run counter to that of Nigel Ramsey, who asserts that "the retention of quite a few canon lawyers must be masked as a result of such forms of remuneration [i.e., the giving of benefices in lieu of pensions], although monetary fees [i.e., pensions], seem to have been much more common" (Nigel Ramsey, "Retained Legal Counsel, c. 1275–c. 1475," *Transactions of the Royal Historical Society* 25 [1985], 98 n 20). It should be noted that Ramsey's article concerns only pensions going to lawyers, and over a much longer period of time than the discussion here, although he does seem to be making this point about the thirteenth century specifically. He provides no numbers. Interestingly, Paul Brand concludes that while some sergeants at law received pensions under Henry III, they appear to have done so commonly only from the time of Edward I (Paul Brand, *The Origins of the English Legal Profession* [Oxford, 1992], 100. I do, however, suggest that lords may have preferred to award pensions over benefices to lawyers.

been extinguished by institution to the benefice.[14] Grants of simple pensions, therefore, were less likely to be kept. This argument is reasonable, but speculative. On the other hand, one can observe that simple pensions must have more often run longer than grants in lieu of benefices because simple grants generally (as will be seen) ran until the death of the grantor or grantee, whichever came first, without a benefice extinguishing the grant. Grantors had reason to hold on to such grants longer, until that point was reached, in case of a dispute over the pension. This, too, is a reasonable, but speculative, argument.

A better case can be made that it is the nature of the archive in which most of these grants are preserved that explains the large proportion of grants of pensions in lieu of benefices. All but six of these bishops' grants of pensions in lieu of benefices are preserved in their registers.[15] Although episcopal registers are a highly miscellaneous source, if there is any essence of the genre, it is the recording of institutions to benefices.[16] Perhaps this concern with benefices led bishops to include grants of pensions in lieu of benefices in their registers. But there are several considerations to set against that explanation. It is true that if bishops' registers concerned anything, they concerned benefices. But that is largely because, although these registers generally include other kinds of business, the nature of that business varied from diocese to diocese.[17] Indeed, bishops' registers

[14] The copy of such a grant in a register was perhaps less evidentiary than simply a signal that an original had existed (perhaps as a cyrograph), to be searched for elsewhere: see Robert Swanson, "*Universis Christi Fidelibu*s: The Church and Its Records," in *Pragmatic Literacy, East and West 1200–1300*, ed. Richard Britnell (Woodbridge, 1997), 158–9.

[15] See Appendix 1. Two exceptions are each preserved in an inspeximus issued by the Dean and Chapter of Wells, one in favor of the resigning precentor of Wells, the other promising a prebend in Wells cathedral specifically. Presumably the cathedral's involvement helps account for the issue of the inspeximus. Both are preserved in a cartulary of the cathedral (*Calendar of the Manuscripts of the Dean and Chapter of Wells*, I, 105, 141). The same source also preserves a simple pension, albeit one *tempore* Edward II (ibid., 173) and a further pension in lieu of a benefice of a similar date (ibid.). Both are episcopal grants, and neither comes in an inspeximus. Another clutch of pensions in lieu of benefices, three in number, is preserved in the cartulary of Bath Priory preserved at Lincoln's Inn (*Two Chartularies of the Priory of St. Peter at Bath*, ed. William Hunt, Somerset Record Society 9 [London, 1893], 49, 52, 54–5). The same source also includes a grant of a simple pension (ibid., 34–5). The last exception is preserved in the fourteenth-century *Liber Epistolaris of Richard de Bury*, ed. Noel Denholm-Young (Oxford, 1950), no. 417, sub no. 14, and so in a collection of model letters. Indeed, the *Liber* does not preserve the grantee's name except as "N. de B.," nor does it preserve the date, appropriately for a letter book concerned to provide epistolary models.

[16] Hence Alison McHardy's careful comment: "records of institutions to benefices could be described as the core material of episcopal registers" ("Some Patterns of Ecclesiastical Patronage in the Later Middle Ages," in *Studies in Clergy and Medieval Ministry in Medieval England*, ed. David M. Smith [York, 1991], 20).

[17] Hence David M. Smith, *Guide to Bishops' Registers of England and Wales: A Survey from the Middle Ages to the Abolition of Episcopacy in 1646* (London, 1981), ix.

often included secular business, even when defining "ecclesiastical" generously.[18] Moreover, all but one[19] of the surviving grants by bishops of simple pensions also survive in bishops' registers. In other words, a number of bishops were willing to record grants of simple pensions in their registers. There is no compelling reason to think that they would not have had more simple pensions entered in their registers had they in fact granted them in greater proportion to pensions in lieu of benefices.

One procedure to overcome this possible bias in favor of benefices in bishops' registers is to count pensions in lieu of benefices only from those registers that include simple pensions too: registers from the dioceses of Canterbury, Carlisle, Coventry and Lichfield, and Exeter. Doing so certainly eliminates the imbalance in favor of pensions in lieu of benefices. But it still leaves simple pensions at half the total. Twenty-four grants of simple pensions survive in registers from those dioceses.[20] Twenty-five grants of pensions in lieu of benefices survive from the registers of these same sees.[21] And, of course, some simple grants were made to men who were ineligible to receive benefices, such as the two recipients identified as knights in the grants preserved in Archbishop Winchelsey's register.[22] Or to take again the early fourteenth-century diocese of Lincoln, Bishop Dalderby's register preserves four grants of simple pensions compared with eight grants of pensions in lieu of benefices.[23] Moreover, it should be noted that, perhaps unexpectedly, all but one of the surviving grants of simple pensions I have found come from episcopal registers, compared with seven episcopal grants of pensions in lieu of benefices from a source that is not a bishop's register.[24]

Another approach is to examine a kind of source analogous to bishops' registers, but one without the complicating stress on benefices. Monastic registers fit the bill. Like episcopal registers, monastic registers were highly

---

[18] Most emphatically, Bishop Pontoise's register "in temporalibus" (Reg. Pontissara, 371–836), which itself included material of a not so temporal nature (e.g., regulation of the behavior of the nuns of Wherwell [ibid., 546]). David Smith observes that the earliest register from Hereford had been planned to divide secular from ecclesiastical business, but the plan was not followed ("Thomas Cantilupe's Register: The Administration of the Diocese of Hereford 1275–1282," in *St. Thomas Cantilupe Bishop of Hereford: Essays in His Honour*, ed. Meryl Jancey [Leominster, 1982], 84).

[19] The exception is EEA 29: Durham, no. 252.

[20] See Appendix 1. Seven of these came from the register of Walter Langton, bishop of Coventry and Lichfield, which preserves only one grant of a pension in lieu of a benefice.

[21] See Appendix 1. This total does not include a grant worded as a formula, a grant of a pension until the recipient became a bishop or a monk, and a grant marked as canceled.

[22] Reg. Winchelsey, 431.

[23] See n 12.

[24] See Appendix 1.

miscellaneous collections, primarily of outgoing documents.[25] Unlike bishops' registers, however, monastic registers were not so tightly bound to institutions to benefices, although many did keep track of the house's bestowal of ecclesiastical patronage.[26] Monastic registers can thus serve as a useful proxy for bishops' registers regarding the question at hand: Did traffic in pensions in lieu of benefices predominate over simple pensions among ecclesiastics, or is the impression that they did so merely an effect of the nature of bishops' registers?

Unfortunately, few of the remaining thirteenth-century monastic registers are much help, being very short, or formularies, or providing little information regarding pensions.[27] The great exception is the register of Prior Henry Eastry of Christ Church, Canterbury, which at least begins in the thirteenth century, even if Eastry's priorate, and so the register, runs into the fourteenth. Between 1286 and 1318, Eastry's register records grants of eight (or seven, if one discounts an entry marked "vacat") simple pensions.[28] They are outnumbered by fifteen pensions in lieu of benefices.[29] The earliest fourteenth-century register of Peterborough Abbey tells a similar story. In an abbacy extending from 1300 to 1321, Godfrey de Crowland granted three simple pensions compared with fourteen pensions in lieu of benefices.[30]

Such numbers provide a warning against stressing too heavily the importance of simple pensions on the basis of account rolls. In the first place, it may not always be clear whether a cash payment recorded on such rolls marks an irregular payment or a payment of a pension. The latter can be established only if the account explicitly states the payment is for a pension[31] or if the payment occurs regularly in a series of rolls over more than one year. Unfortunately, both situations are uncommon

[25] W. A. Pantin, "English Monastic Letter-Books," in *Historical Essays in Honour of James Tait*, ed. J. G. Edwards, V. H. Galbraith, and E. F. Jacob (Manchester, 1933), 201. Both Pantin (ibid.) and Sandra Raban (*The White Book of Peterborough: The Registers of Abbot William of Woodford, 1295–99 and Abbot Godfrey of Crowland, 1299–1321*, ed. Sandra Raban [Northampton, 2001], xiii) draw the comparison with bishops' registers.
[26] Pantin, "Monastic Letter-Books," 201–2.
[27] See the survey in Pantin, "English Monastic Letter-Books," 213–22.
[28] Cambridge University Library, MS Ee V 31, fos. 19v, 20r, 25v, 28r, 52v, 169r.
[29] Ibid., fos. 18v, 19v, 22v-23r, 24v (and see 25r), 30r, 67r, 72v-73r, 83r, 93v, 103r, 105r, 109r, 112r, 193r.
[30] *White Book of Peterborough*, nos. 148, 169, 253 vs. nos. 108, 116, 135–6, 171–2, 193, 198, 218, 256, 303. The previous abbot's register, running 1294–9, is suggestive, recording three pensions in lieu of benefices (ibid., nos. 2, 14, 102), but since it lacks any grants of simple pensions, drawing conclusions is vulnerable to the objection that this imbalance is simply an effect of some peculiar nature of the source.
[31] As in Swinfield Roll, 125–6.

in thirteenth-century ecclesiastical accounts. But it must also be said that, even if one can establish that a payment to a clerk recorded in such an account meets one or both criteria, it is still possible – given the figures here, even likely – that that pension was not meant to run for life, but only until the grantee received a benefice. The form of the grant can be as important as the record of payment in understanding pensions.

Finally, a rare, year-long episcopal household roll provides useful negative evidence as to the prominence of pensions in rewarding episcopal clerks. Bishop Richard Swinfield of Hereford's household roll records expenditures on pensions, called "foeda diversa" there. Four men are recorded under this heading: Garin de Boys, the bishop's attorney in London; Roger Caperon, another attorney there; John de Canterbury, his proctor in the Court of Arches; and a rougher adherent, Thomas de Brugg, the bishop's *pugilarius*.[32] These men are certainly outnumbered by the twelve men identifiable as episcopal clerks at the time who fail to appear as receiving pensions.[33] And although none of the four pensioners

---

[32] Ibid., 125–6.

[33] The twelve were

John de Kemesey: In 1309 Swinfield remarked that John had served Swinfield faithfully since the bishop's own consecration (Reg. Swinfield, 475–6). As early as 1286, he is explicitly described as Swinfield's clerk (ibid., 112). He received several benefices by collation from Swinfield: Colwall in 1283; Ross-on-Wye in 1295; the prebend of Moreton Parva in 1302; the prebend of Bartsonsham in 1303; the treasurership of the cathedral in 1308 (ibid., 524, 530, 534–5, 538).

John de Schelving: In 1287, while still a minor, he received the collation of Hampton Bishop, in Swinfield's gift, by commendation (ibid., 526). The following year the bishop collated Ross-on-Wye to him (ibid., 527). Other collations followed: Hinton in 1290 (which failed) (ibid., 248–9, 528), and Canon Pyon in the same year and the prebend of Nonnington in 1295 (both of which succeeded) (ibid., 528, 530). He appears in the household roll handling payments on Swinfield's behalf (Swinfield Roll, 117) and was compensated for travel (ibid., 118).

Master John de Swinfield: Not to be confused with the bishop's brother (*dominus* John de Swinfield), Master John de Swinfield began to receive collations from the first year of the pontificate: Hampton Bishop, followed by the prebend of Fownhope in 1287, the archdeaconry of Salop in 1289, the treasurership of the cathedral in 1293, and the precentorship and the prebend of Ledbury in 1294 (Reg. Swinfield, 525–6, 528–9). He appears as a witness to several of the bishop's acts between 1285 and 1289 in three places (ibid., 97, 115, 182, 223).

Nicholas de Reigate: Nicholas began to receive Swinfield's patronage in 1285, receiving the commend of Coreley, in Swinfield's gift (Reg. Swinfield 525). Collations of Coddington (1286), a prebend in Bromyard (1299), the prebend of Wellington (1303), and the treasurership of the cathedral (1304) followed (ibid., 526, 531, 534–5). He is noted in the household roll as having audited the accounts (Swinfield Roll, 161).

Richard de Hertford: Richard received the collation of the archdeaconry of Hereford in 1287 and became the bishop's *officialis* in the same year, also serving as Swinfield's joint proctor in the ecclesiastical council at London (Reg. Swinfield, 158, 527). The following year the bishop collated a prebend in the cathedral to him, collating another prebend in

is traceable in Swinfield's register as being beneficed, all but two of the dozen other clerks identifiable in the bishop's service at this time were so beneficed.[34] Of course, it is possible, indeed likely, that other men were

> 1293 (ibid., 527, 529). His death in 1303 vacated his benefices, which still included his archdeaconry (ibid., 535).
> Richard de Puddlestone: Swinfield first appointed Richard as his joint proctor at the Roman curia in 1286, who continued to serve as late as 1292 (ibid., 67, 69, 127, 219–22, 246–7, 256, 278). His reception of funds for the defense of the bishop's causes there is noted in the household roll (Swinfield Roll, 127). See also the discussion of him in Chapter 7 at n 82.
> Master Robert de Gloucester: Swinfield appointed Robert, already canon of Hereford, his joint proctor to the papal court in 1283 (Reg. Swinfield, 66). He continued in this capacity at least as late as 1286 (ibid., 99). Collations of the chancellorship of the cathedral (1299) and the prebend of Huntington followed (ibid., 531, 536).
> Roger de Sevenake: Roger was active as Swinfield's *officialis* from Swinfield's first year as bishop, and was still acting in that capacity in 1287, when the bishop sent him as his proctor to the consecration of the bishop of Salisbury (ibid., 15, 142). Swinfield, as a papal judge-delegate, commissioned him jointly to hear a suit on his behalf in 1286 (ibid., 111). In 1288, he represented the bishop at the council in London and did so at another council of bishops in 1295 (ibid., 192, 331). In 1289–90 the bishop was providing him fur for trimming his clothes (Swinfield Roll, 113). Roger received various collations: a prebend in Bromyard and the archdeaconry of Hereford in 1287, the cathedral treasurership in 1294 (Reg. Swinfield, 526–7, 328, 529).
> Stephen de Thanet: He first appears in Swinfield's service in the household roll of 1289–90, receiving a small gift and other payments (none related to a pension) (Swinfield Roll, 116–7, 158). He is first explicitly called Swinfield's clerk in 1296 (Reg. Swinfield, 338, and see 382). Although his collation is unrecorded, he was a canon of Bromyard by 1312, to which the bishop collated (ibid., 472, and see 542). He received Hinton by collation in 1313 (ibid., 542). For his work as Swinfield's financial agent, see *Roll of the Household Expenses of Richard de Swinfield*, ed. John Webb, Camden Society, first series, 59 (1854–5) II, cxcvii–cxcviii.
> Thomas de la Dane: He witnessed an act of the bishop in 1287 at Northfleet, and Swinfield collated Hampton Bishop to him in the following year (Reg. Swinfield, 182, 527). He witnessed another of the bishop's acts at Bosbury in 1292 (ibid., 282).
> William de Mortimer: He appears as Swinfield's seneschal in the first year of the episcopate, still holding the position in 1313 (ibid., 93, 112, 127, 216, 418, 486). In 1287, Swinfield collated Fownhope to him, with the prebend of Madley to follow in 1299 (ibid., 526, 531).
> William de Morton: He appears as Swinfield's clerk in 1286, in which year he also received the collation (by lapse) of Fownhope (ibid., 112, 526). He was serving as Swinfield's seneschal in 1288, and was described as being of Swinfield's *familia* in 1288 (ibid., 138, 178). He witnessed some of the bishop's acts in eight different locations in the years 1288–92 (ibid., 162, 175, 178, 182, 222, 226, 238, 240, 249, 252, 282).
> One may note that the dean and chapter of Hereford also kept a *pugilarius* on retainer, for 4 marks a year, which he called an *annuus feodum* (*Charters and Records of Hereford Cathedral*, ed. William W. Capes, Cantilupe Society for 1908 [Hereford, 1908], 171).

[34] The exceptions are Richard de Puddlestone, who would soon try to use his connections in Rome to force Swinfield to give him a benefice (for this episode: Robert Brentano, *Two Churches: England and Italy in the Thirteenth Century* [Princeton, 1968], 43; Reg. Swinfield, 254–6, 278), and Stephen de Thanet, who would obtain a benefice by 1298 (Reg. Swinfield, 358).

owed pensions but they were not paid that year, and so fail to appear sub "foeda diversa" in the roll.³⁵ Presumably, too, men may have been paid pensions charged to specified manors and so do not appear in household accounts. But there is no reason to suppose that such men would have been more likely to have been clerks. (Balancing these points, of course, is the fact that other beneficed clerks in Swinfield's service probably also fail to be identifiable via his register.) Swinfield's household roll also records the payments of numerous "stipendia," annual payments (paid summer and winter), presumably not according to the formal grants that characterized the *foeda diversa*. These *stipendia* went almost wholly to secular folk; the subheadings describing the recipients read "armigeri," "vadlet' de ministerio," "garciones" and "pagi."³⁶ A few clergy appear here (Robert, clerk of the chapel and Ralph the clerk among the valets at 4s 12d a year and, perhaps, Adam de Capella at 4s a year).³⁷ Most of the men, however, seem to be among the menials: John the carter, Harpin the falconer, and so on.³⁸

Indeed, it may be that the English favored benefices more than other nations as a reward for clerical service. Innocent III had prohibited men in holy orders from becoming notaries, a ruling that entered the canons.³⁹ But this rule was frequently violated in England, in part, at least, so as better to provide notaries to benefices.⁴⁰ Certainly notaries in England received pensions just as other ecclesiastical bureaucrats and functionaries did.⁴¹ But in the thirteenth century, at least, benefices were commonly, perhaps most commonly, the means by which bishops rewarded the

---

35 The likelihood of not getting paid one's pension is discussed later in the chapter. Richard de Puddleston had almost certainly been granted a pension as the bishop's proctor at Rome. It is possible that the money he receives in the roll for expenses was also meant to cover his pension (Swinfield Roll, 127).
36 Ibid., 155–72, 194–7. Compare the stipend received by a summoner for the common jurisdiction of the bishop and the dean and chapter of Wells: *Calendar of the Manuscripts of the Dean and Chapter of Wells*, I, 50. The same entry concerns the cutting of such a stipend as punishment. See also the similar stipends, paid to the prior of Worcester's *familia*, to *armigeri*, and to lesser folk: *Registrum sive Liber Irrotularius et Consuetudinarius Prioratus Beatae Mariae Wignorniensis*, ed. William H. Hale, Camden Society (first series) 91 (London, 1865), 5.
37 Swinfield Roll, 168, 170.
38 Ibid., 168.
39 C. R. Cheney, *Notaries Public in England in the Thirteenth and Fourteenth Centuries* (Oxford, 1972), 78–9.
40 Ibid., 80.
41 E.g., ibid., 34, 184–5, and see 66 n 5. It should also be noted that none of the thirteenth- (or earlier fourteenth-) century evidence collected by Cheney reveals the form of the grant. These could have been pensions in lieu of benefices.

notaries attached to them. C. R. Cheney identifies five notaries in the service of Archbishop Pecham, still in the early days of notarial activity in England. Three are known to have held at least one benefice.[42] Indeed, one of the earliest notaries active in England found by Cheney, John Ertruri de Cadomo (fl. 1268–1310), a king's man, "found his main recompense in church revenues."[43]

Pensions *de Camera* in General

Before pursuing differences between simple pensions and pensions in lieu of benefices, it is first worth examining some common characteristics. One is that bishops usually granted pensions *de camera* without specifying any services to be done in return.[44] There were exceptions.[45]

Sometimes service was implied, but the grant did not state that its performance was required. It is striking that when such explicit conditions were laid down, they generally concern bishops' legal representatives in the ecclesiastical courts. Bishop Ireton of Carlisle granted a pension of 40s a year in lieu of a benefice to his proctor at the Court of York, also conceding the proctor's expenses on the bishop's business.[46] Bishop Quivil of Exeter granted John de la Wade, his proctor at the Roman court, 10 marks a year in lieu of a benefice; John was to serve, on his oath, concerning the bishop's suits and other business there.[47] Quivil also granted simple pensions to two proctors at the Court of Canterbury on condition they continue to serve there.[48] Bishop Langton of Coventry and Lichfield granted a number of simple pensions to proctors, all these grants specifying that the pension was given in return for service in court, some indeed explicitly laying down that the grantee was to be paid as long as he served there.[49] In 1301, William de Otteringham came to a

[42] For these men: ibid., 27–8, 30–2.
[43] Ibid., 143–51, and 149 for the quotation.
[44] This has been observed regarding pensions granted to proctors in particular: Ramsey, "Retained Legal Counsel," 97.
[45] More than appears in the account of grants by monastic houses, ibid., 97.
[46] Reg. Halton, I, 31 and see 32.
[47] Reg. Quivil, 381.
[48] Ibid., 322, 374. Further instances: Bishop Swinfield of Hereford granting two pensions under the same condition, one to his proctor in the Court of Arches, the other to his advocate in London (Reg. Swinfield, 156–7); Bishop Godfrey Giffard of Worcester, more vaguely, granting, "pro obsequio suo," 40s per year to his proctor in Rome, until the bishop provided him a benefice (Reg. Giffard of Worcester, 291 [WRO, Rf.x716.093 BA 2648/1(i), f. 255v (p. 502)]).
[49] Reg. Langton, nos. 62, 363, 791. An analogous grant was that made by the prior of Bath (*Two Cartularies of the Priory of St. Peter at Bath*, ed. William Hunt, Somerset Record Society 9 [1893], 102).

bargain with Bishop Dalderby of Lincoln that William would continue as Dalderby's proctor at Rome for a pension of 10 marks a year in lieu of a benefice and 50 marks for expenses.[50] One can add Dalderby's 1305 grant to Ralph de Lacu, his joint proctor at the Roman court: 5 marks a year so long as Ralph served there.[51] Dalderby's suffragan is an exception to this dominance of proctors as recipients of pensions granted with explicit conditions; he was granted, among other things, 40 marks a year for his labors, perhaps implying that should his labors stop, so would the pension.[52]

Occasionally, bishops referred to the recipient's qualifications when making a grant. Bishop Quivil of Exeter granted James de Hyspania 100s a year in lieu of a benefice in consideration of James's knowledge of letters, noble birth, morals, and probity — a list which in this case in particular should be read as boilerplate.[53] Sometimes such statements, by expressing hope of benefits in the future, imply an expectation of service without, it seems, requiring it. The bishop of Winchester granted a relative of Edward I's justiciar 100s per year in lieu of a benefice, considering his probity and discretion, and with the bishop also attending to the good the grantee could do the bishop and his church in the future.[54] The

---

[50] LAO, Episcopal Register III, f. 374r.

[51] Ibid., f. 86r.

[52] Ibid., f. 345r. Indeed, in the fourteenth century, pensions would be the usual way to compensate suffragans (David M. Smith, "Suffragan Bishops in the Medieval Diocese of Lincoln," *Lincolnshire History and Archaeology* 17 [1982], 21). L. A. S. Butler also points to the collection of fees by (late-medieval) suffragans, pensions, and benefices in the archdiocese of York, with benefices gaining in prominence after ca. 1400 (L. A. S. Butler, "Suffragan Bishops in the Medieval Diocese of York," *Northern History* 37 [2000], 54–5). Such practices extended to suffragans who were members of the Franciscan order as well; Michael Robson also points to their income from granting indulgences ("Franciscan Bishops *in Partibus Infidelium* Ministering in Medieval England," *Antonianum* 78 [2003], 563–6). David Smith implies that payment of pensions was dependent on continued service in these fourteenth-century arrangements ("Suffragan Bishops," 22). Pensions granted by those other than bishops, however, do not clearly hold to a pattern of specifying what the grantee was to give the grantor when the grantee was a legal representative (e.g., grants by the prior of Christ Church, Canterbury, in return for the recipient's *consilium et auxilium*: Cambridge University Library, MS Ee V 31, fos. 18v, 25v, 72v–73r). Others are ambiguous. A Durham formulary has the prior and convent grant a pension in lieu of a benefice to their dear clerk N., who is to expedite their affairs on both sides of the sea (*Durham Annals and Documents of the Thirteenth Century*, ed. Frank Barlow, Surtees Society 155 [Durham, 1945], 86). The condition smells like one appropriate to a proctor in the church courts. The recipient is also not to reveal the prior and convent's counsel to their damage, and not to act to the prior and convent's loss.

[53] Reg. Quivil, 335. James was the queen's nephew, and young. Quivil had earlier opposed his promotion to benefices in general (ibid., 390–1).

[54] Reg. Pontissara, 353–4.

bishop issued *consimiles litterae*, with pensions of differing amounts, on behalf of two royal clerks the following year.⁵⁵ Archbishop Romeyn of York granted the royal justice William de Saham 100s a year in lieu of a benefice. The archbishop thus admitted William into his heart and confidence, hoping that the justice's industry would protect the archbishop and his churches.⁵⁶

A pension *de camera* could also be granted to help settle a dispute, a kind of grant that moves one from considerations of service.⁵⁷ Archbishop Giffard of York granted a pension in lieu of a benefice to help resolve the claim of Ancher, cardinal-priest of St. Praxedis, to the prebend of North Newbald.⁵⁸ Indeed, in a bargain to end a conflict over a benefice, one clerk who ultimately obtained the benefice promised a pension charged to it (thus, not *de camera*, but of the sort discussed earlier), to be paid until the recipient received another benefice of a certain value.⁵⁹ If Bishop William Bitton I of Wells's words are to be trusted, he granted Gilbert de St. Leofardo a pension until a prebend in Wells Cathedral could be bestowed because he wanted to bring Gilbert into the cathedral community.⁶⁰ And, of course, a bishop could make such a grant simply as a liberal gesture, as when Archbishop Giffard of York "gratiose" granted one of the queen's clerks a healthy 40s a year in lieu of a benefice, so Giffard said, as a reward for bringing him news of the birth of a son to the prince of Wales.⁶¹

Often bishops granted pensions not because they wanted to, but because it was prudent to do so when faced by a request from the powerful. The pension James de Hyspania received from an unenthusiastic Bishop Quivil of Exeter falls into that category, despite Quivil's praise for James's qualities. Pecham of Canterbury,⁶² Winchelsey of Canterbury,⁶³

---

⁵⁵ Ibid., 354, and see 150.
⁵⁶ Reg. Romeyn, no. 1475.
⁵⁷ Or at least generally did so. For an instance of a pension in lieu of a benefice granted for service but also as part of a legal settlement, see EEA 37: Salisbury, no. 266. The grantor was not the opponent of the grantee, but a third party to the suit, and it appears that the grantor had previously given a pension to the grantee.
⁵⁸ Reg. Giffard of York, 7.
⁵⁹ Reg. Giffard of Worcester, 441 (WRO, Rf.x716.093 BA 2648/1(i) f. 377v [p. 746]). The calendar can mislead on some of this. For the dispute, see M. Burger, "Peter of Leicester, Bishop Godfrey Giffard of Worcester, and the Problem of Benefices in Thirteenth-Century England," *Catholic Historical Review* 95 (2009), 453–73.
⁶⁰ *Calendar of the Manuscripts of the Dean and Chapter of Wells*, I, 141.
⁶¹ Reg. Giffard of York, 101.
⁶² Reg. Pecham, I, 14 (calendared Pecham, *Epistolae*, III, 1000).
⁶³ Reg. Winchelsey, I, 908.

Sutton of Lincoln,[64] Dalderby of Lincoln,[65] and Wickwane of York[66] all granted pensions (in lieu of benefices) at the behest of the king or queen. One would expect papal provisors to have benefited from pensions granted for similar reasons, but they are not clearly represented among grantees.

Sometimes bishops tried to fend off such attempts. Archbishop Winchelsey rather lamely told the queen in 1300 that he could not give to her priest William de Lorey the first *bon benefice* in his collation or a pension until there was such a vacancy for fear of offense to God and peril to his estate. He explained that only the pope, who enjoys sovereign authority, could do what the queen asked.[67] Presumably Winchelsey had in mind canonical prohibitions against expectatives.[68] But bishops (Winchelsey, it seems, among their number),[69] had, and would commonly make, just such arrangements.[70] Richard Swinfield, the new bishop of Hereford, replied to a royal request that he give a benefice to Nicholas de Geneville, a ten-year-old boy, by granting Nicholas a pension of 10 marks a year until he was older. The bishop's grant was vague regarding what Nicholas might obtain when more mature; he was to receive the pension "until we provide him better."[71] Swinfield's explanation of his resistance to such pressures was more pragmatic than Winchelsey's. Four

---

[64] Rolls and Reg. Sutton, IV, 183.
[65] LAO, Episcopal Register III, fos. 81r, 143r and see LAO, Dii/56/1/7, Dii/56/1/67; Reg. Gandavo, 173.
[66] Reg. Wickwane, 246, and see 270.
[67] Reg. Winchelsey, 706.
[68] Discussed in Chapter 3 at nn 23–4.
[69] Winchelsey granted Ralph de Watervile five marks a year in lieu of a benefice (Reg. Winchelsey, 45). Although the charter's date was left off by the copyist, it falls among documents of 1295 in a section of the register that is roughly chronological. Support for the 1295 dates also comes from Winchelsey's ordination of Ralph to the priesthood "at the title of the archbishop, at the instance of the king" (ibid., 908). In other words, in 1295 Ralph was claiming financial support from Winchelsey, support given because of a royal request. Such arrangements are especially striking given Winchelsey's attempt to stem the numbers of royal clerks holding benefices (Jeffrey H. Denton, *Robert Winchelsey and the Crown 1294–1313: A Study in the Defence of Ecclesiastical Liberty* [Cambridge, 1980], 269–96). The archbishop did not involve himself in such arrangements only under royal pressure. In 1311, he demanded of the bishop of Ely a benefice or a pension in the meantime for Gilbert de Middleton, dean of Arches and archiepiscopal clerk (Reg. Winchelsey, 1244–5).
[70] Appendix 1. An example of a bishop arranging an expectative not involving a pension is that of the bishop of Worcester, who in 1294 received by a grant from Pershore Abbey the right to institute one of his clerks – specified in the grant – to Saint Peter's, Worcester, on Pershore's presentation (EEA 13: Worcester, no. 141).
[71] Reg. Swinfield, 1, 14: "ulterius duxerimus providendum."

years later Swinfield used the promise of a now vacant prebend to this same Nicholas after Christmas to explain to the king and Giles his clerk why the bishop could not give Giles the prebend.[72] At least Swinfield got something out of his promise to the ten-year-old Nicholas.[73]

So bishops granted pensions for many reasons, only sometimes in order to gain the services of the grantee. In principle, there was indeed no reason a bishop could not grant a pension for the same sort of reason the dean and chapter of Chichester granted 10s annually to Beatrix de Lindefield, widow.[74] Moreover, even those pensions that seem to have been granted for service did not generally make payment contingent on performance of that service; the sole exceptions are the six pensions to proctors noted earlier. These exceptions are, I suspect, significant. Pensions granted for no specific terms of service should, according to their form, have been no more effective as a disciplinary tool than benefices. An early fourteenth-century yearbook compares them to a freehold.[75] Grantees could demand payment even from dissatisfied grantors who did not want to pay. Indeed, historians have noted that recipients of pensions sometimes sued for payment in the king's courts.[76] Interestingly, these studies are all of pensions sued for by legal counselors and representatives, the one category of recipient whose terms of service were specified in surviving grants. Bishop Swinfield's household roll confirms the impression left by these studies; all the recipients of his "foeda diversa" were his legal representatives, even Thomas de Brugg, *pugilarius*.[77] If bishops and others trusted such professional hired guns less than other servants, that distrust would explain greater explicitness regarding terms of service. And if experience justified that distrust, that might explain a greater willingness

---

[72] Ibid., 151, 153, and see 526.

[73] Such pressures did not, however, end. In 1308 the queen asked Swinfield for a benefice for one of her clerks (unnamed) and a "congruam pensionem" in the meantime. She later made the same request, naming Hugh de Leominster as the clerk. Swinfield declined both requests (ibid., 443–5).

[74] Historical Manuscripts Commission, *Reports on Manuscripts in Various Collections I* (London, 1901), 191; *The Chartulary of the High Church of Chichester*, ed. W. D. Peckham, Sussex Record Society 46 (Lewes, 1946 for 1942 and 1943), no. 35. Beatrix had donated a reliquary to be kept at the cathedral, as keeping such an object was inappropriate for her sex (ibid.).

[75] Ramsey, "Retained Legal Counsel," 102.

[76] Robert C. Palmer, "The Origins of the Legal Profession in England," *The Irish Jurist* (new series) 11 (1976), 128–33. They also sued in ecclesiastical courts, too: see further discussion and, for the end of the Middle Ages, R. H. Helmholz, "Ethical Standards for Advocates and Proctors in Theory and Practice," in his *Canon Law and the Law of England* (London, 1987), 47.

[77] See at n 32.

by bishops and other grantors to reward such men with payments that could be withheld, rather than with benefices.[78] The fact that lawyers operated under rules that could call upon them to refuse to serve a client for the sake of justice[79] may also have made lords reluctant to give them gifts over pensions. While some lords were perhaps unaware of such rules, bishops with a background in canon law would not have been among them.[80] The same hesitance to pay could have been fostered by a culture of complaint regarding lawyers, that they could not be trusted.[81] When lords refused to pay, they sparked suits by lawyer-grantees. In this regard, it is striking that the pension in lieu of benefices I have found most hedged about by conditions – for example, specifications of how much the benefice is to be worth according to what evaluation; that the benefice is not to be outside the diocese of Bath and Wells; that the grantee will have fifteen days to accept the benefice – was granted in settlement of a lawsuit, in other words, where confidence in the grantee was low.[82] Indeed, one of the complaints about lawyers – justified or not – was that they worked only as long as they were paid.[83] These parties, like parties settling a lawsuit, distrusted each other. In general, to reward a grantee with a pension may have been the flip side of the mutual trust that could go into the gift of a benefice.[84]

Simple Pensions versus Pensions in Lieu of Benefices, and Pensions versus Benefices

Why did grantors grant pensions in lieu of benefices rather than simple pensions? Clearly a significant advantage of pensions in lieu of benefices

---

[78] Writing about the fourteenth century, Alison McHardy suspects that abbots favored pensions over benefices in rewarding various kinds of lawyers as well as proctorial representation in parliament ("Some Patterns of Ecclesiastical Patronage," 24–5, and see 26–8).
[79] R. H. Helmholz, "Ethical Standards for Advocates," 44; James A. Brundage, *The Medieval Origins of the Legal Profession* (Chicago, 2008), 315–16.
[80] There is not much sign, however, that such ethical requirements received much enforcement (Brundage, *Medieval Origins of the Legal Profession*, 341–2).
[81] On the tradition of such complaints, see ibid., 477–87.
[82] *Historia et Cartularium Monasterii Sancti Petri Gloucestriae*, ed. William Henry Hart (RS) (London, 1863–7), I, 213–14, and see ibid., 214–18 for what appear to be details of the suit. Paul Hyams suggests that grants of pensions that do not spell out expectations "surely hid an expectation that something more affective was at least possible between lord and man" (Paul R. Hyams, *Rancor and Reconciliation in Medieval England* [Ithaca, 2003], 260).
[83] Brundage, *Medieval Origins of the Legal Profession*, 479.
[84] On which, see Chapter 7 at nn 20–1.

for grantors was that, should the pension culminate in the granting of a benefice, the fiscal burden imposed by the pension came to an end. Indeed, scholars have long held that the advantage of benefices for patrons was that they were a way to give hangers-on an income without paying money out of pocket, instead displacing the burden onto the church.[85] It is pertinent to note in this context that an ordinance of 1279 regulating the king's household held that only clerks who had not received a benefice from the king were to receive wages.[86] Indeed, in the later thirteenth century, the granting of pensions to royal judges by private persons grew as the judiciary ceased to be dominated by clerks. The rising generation of lay justices could not receive benefices and so got pensions instead.[87] Although historians have not pointed to pensions in lieu of benefices regarding such cost-cutting lords, such pensions can nicely illustrate this position.[88] Paying a pension was a burden, one that giving benefices could alleviate. In the 1270s and 1280s the chronicler of Dunstable Priory carefully (and perhaps systematically) noted when pensions in lieu of benefices were extinguished by presentation to a benefice.[89] One can sometimes sense relief, as when the chronicler states that the priory, paying a pension to Geoffrey de Buguleun of 2 marks a year in lieu of a benefice, was "quit of it" on presenting him to St. Cuthbert's.[90] A series of complaints to the papacy by English monasteries leaves a similar impression. Ramsey Abbey asserted that although the abbey and convent had presented men to suitable benefices, the presentees had refused them, preferring to keep their pensions. Evidently these clerks had received pensions in lieu of benefices. The pope absolved Ramsey of further payment.[91] Facing a similar

---

[85] E.g., R. N. Swanson, "Learning and Livings: University Study and Clerical Careers in Later Medieval England," *History of Universities* 6 (1987 for 1986–7), 88 (a discussion which in some other respects is very sensitive to the position of those seeking benefices); Frederic Cheyette, "Kings, Courts, Cures, and Sinecures: The Statute of Provisors and the Common Law," *Traditio* 19 (1963), 297; W. A. Pantin, *The English Church in the Fourteenth Century*, 41–2; C. R. Cheney, *English Bishops' Chanceries 1100–1250* (Manchester 1950), 9; Waugh, "Tenure to Contract," 822.

[86] T. F. Tout, *Chapters in the Administrative History of Mediaeval England* (Manchester, 1920–37), II, 28. For a similar regulation regarding the household of the king of France in the early fourteenth century, see ibid., n 3.

[87] J. R. Maddicott, *Law and Lordship: Royal Justices as Retainers in Thirteenth- and Fourteenth-Century England*, Past and Present Supplement 4 (1978), 18, 22.

[88] And an especially useful one, given that there does not seem to be surviving medieval comment making this comparison with money payments.

[89] E.g., *Annales Monastici*, III, 275, 283, 289, 391.

[90] "fuimus ... quieti": ibid., III, 289.

[91] CPL, I, 94; *Regesta Honorii Papae III Iussu et Mvnificentia Leonis XIII Pontificis Maximi ex Vaticanis Archetypis aliisque Fontibvs*, ed. Petrus Presutti (Rome, 1888–95)

situation (they said), the monks of Teweksbury procured a papal order that the clerks were to accept the benefices offered or, should they refuse them, accept the cancellation of their pensions anyway.[92] In all these cases the monasteries succeeded in representing their version of the facts in Rome, to judge from papal commands and the absence of subsequent correspondence on these matters.[93]

Indeed, patrons sometimes tried to extinguish pensions by presenting men to benefices of doubtful status. One prior, having granted a pension in lieu of a benefice, made an arrangement with the recipient that the presentation of the recipient's cousin would extinguish the pension. But the recipient of the pension sued in the secular forum when he discovered that the status of the benefice offered was uncertain; the local bishop had expelled the incumbent, who, after the cousin's institution, won the benefice back on appeal. The plaintiff appears to have won the legal point.[94] At least one grantee foresaw that this situation was something to guard against; a 1317 grant of a pension in lieu of a benefice noted that the benefice must not be under litigation.[95] In another case, a patron tried to extinguish a pension in lieu of a benefice by conferring

---

(rpt., Hildesheim, 1978), II, no. 4767. Durham Cathedral Priory made a similar complaint regarding papal clerks who refused parish churches offered them, and gained similar relief (CPL, I, 95; *Regesta Honorii Papae III*, II, no. 4854). When Glastonbury complained likewise about certain clerks, some in English dioceses, the pope simply canceled the pensions (*Les Registres de Grégoire IX*, ed. Lucien Auvray et al. [Paris, 1896–1955], III, no. 5378, calendared in CPL, I, 193).

[92] This entry is printed in calendar form in two places; the calendared entries together indicate these points: *Registres de Grégoire IX*, I, no. 2442; CPL, I, 144.

[93] It is possible that a domestic instance may be that of 1197–1208, when the bishop of Durham ruled that the prior and convent of Durham had issued charters in which they had promised certain clerks pensions until the monks assigned them a "redditum," and that the monks were quit of these pensions according to the form of their charters (EEA 25: Durham, no. 200). Could the *redditum* have been a clumsy or vague way to indicate an endowed income that could include a benefice? One of these grantees, John de London, is known to have received a benefice in the chapter's presentation (EEA 24: Durham, xlvi and n 62).

[94] The jury was asked whether the plaintiff's cousin held the benefice on the day he died: *Year Books of the Reign of Edward I*, ed. A. J. Horwood (RS) (London, 1863–79), II, 174–9. The see of Worcester offers another possible instance. It is not clear whether Bishop Giffard was deliberately attempting to extinguish his proctor John de Butterley's pension in lieu of a benefice (Reg. Giffard of Worcester, 291 [and see WRO, Rf.x716.093 BA 2648/1(i), f. 255v (p. 502)]) with a doubtful benefice. But the bishop did collate a benefice to John de Badminton by lapse, and John does seem to have lost Badminton quickly, apparently in a lawsuit (Reg. Giffard, 303, 314, 325). Interestingly, John also seems to have dropped from Giffard's service at this point.

[95] *Year Books of Edward II*, ed. F. W. Maitland et al., Selden Society 17- (London, 1903–), XXI, 17.

on the grantee the office of holy water carrier; the grantee complained that such an office was not a benefice, as it was not an estate for life. The king's court agreed.[96]

It could be that one of the reasons for the prominence of pensions in lieu of benefices over simple pensions as grants by bishops and monasteries was the greater patronage of benefices enjoyed by such grantors. A comparison with grants by the lay nobility, were it possible for the thirteenth century, would be interesting.

But a (traditional) account of lords' motives is not a complete explanation. For their part, grantees sometimes preferred to receive a pension over a benefice. The cases noted earlier where grantees appear to have refused benefices in favor of a continuing pension indicate that preference. Why? I suspect the chief reasons were pluralism and residency regulations, complications that did not apply to pensions which, with the exception of some of those granted to proctors, came with even less baggage regarding behavior than did benefices.[97] Clerks who turned down benefices from Glastonbury did so, said the monks, "because they can obtain benefices with cure of souls elsewhere."[98] So did the pensioned clerks who refused an offer of benefices from Tewkesbury.[99] Such considerations may also lie behind the specifications in some grants as to the kind of benefice to be offered in future: that the benefice be without cure of souls[100] or that it is to be a prebendal benefice.[101] It is possible that pluralism or residency

[96] Ibid., II, 125 and 126 n 1. In 1289, a clerk admitted that the abbot who had granted him a pension in lieu of a benefice had indeed presented him. The clerk had, by his own account, failed to gain institution through the "negligencia" of the abbot. But the clerk would not specify the nature of that negligence. Years later, the clerk sued for arrears of the pension. This clerk's failure to specify how the abbot failed to live up to his word does, however, look suspicious. The abbot maintained that he had presented the plaintiff in good faith and the failure lay with the plaintiff. Indeed, ultimately the bishop collated the church to the plaintiff by right of devolution (*The Earliest English Law Reports*, ed. Paul Brand, Selden Society 111, 112, 122, 123 [London, 1996–2007], IV, 405–6).

[97] Indeed, one benefit of an examination of grants of pensions in lieu of benefices is that the grants indicate the kind of dickering that probably went on regarding the reception of benefices in general, but which is not preserved in records of institutions and collations.

[98] "cum alibi beneficia cum animarum cura obtineant": *Registres de Grégoire IX*, III, no. 5378, calendared in CPL, I, 193.

[99] *Registres de Grégoire IX*, I, no. 2442. This point does appear in W. H. Bliss's calendar (CPL, I, 144).

[100] Reg. Bronscombe, nos. 574, 1312.

[101] Reg. Quivil, 328, 366. The latter grantee was Adam de "Pilebey" (*recte* "Fileby"), archdeacon of Salop. He was already an important man and a significant pluralist (A. B. Emden, *A Biographical Register of the University of Oxford to A.D. 1500* [Oxford, 1957], sub nom.), and so probably did not need the trouble of another benefice with

rules lay behind one arrangement by which the bishop of Exeter granted Thomas de Windsor a pension of 10 marks a year until the bishop or his successors provided a benefice to Thomas or any appropriate clerk of Thomas's choice.[102]

At times recipients of grants in lieu of benefices expected a benefice worth more than the pension, suggesting that some recipients indeed preferred pensions to benefices, and had to be bought off with comparatively lucrative benefices. This kind of arrangement makes some financial sense because holders of benefices had to pay out some of their income in royal or papal taxes, procurations, payments to clerks exercising the cure, and so on.[103] It is impossible to tell whether the values given for benefices were values at farm, although they sometimes may well have been. The disparities between benefice and pension could be large. The prior and convent of Worcester promised their representative at Rome a half-mark a year until they gave him a benefice worth 10.[104] In 1317, an annuity of 20 marks a year until the grantor provided a benefice worth 45 marks a year wound up the subject of a suit in the king's courts.[105] Other such instances appear to have been part of a settlement and so may not reflect the free bargaining of grantor and grantee, but still indicate that some presumably thought a pension preferable to a benefice producing the same nominal sum. Thus, for example, the abbey of St. Albans was supposed to have given John de Camezan, papal chaplain, a better benefice but had failed to do so when one opened up. John sued, and St. Albans was sentenced to pay John 25 marks a year until the monks gave him a benefice worth 80 marks a year.[106] In another instance, the pope ordered the archdeacon of Canterbury to provide Peter, papal

cure of souls. See also the request of Edward II's queen to Bishop Swinfield of Hereford of a prebend or a pension in the meantime (Reg. Swinfield, 443). For more grants specifying the benefice was to be a prebend, see LAO, Episcopal Register III, fos. 125r, 142v and *Calendar of the Manuscripts of the Dean and Chapter of Wells*, I, 141. One grantee was to receive 20s a year until he received a benefice, excepting any kind of vicarage (*The Cartulary of the Abbey of Eynsham*, ed. H. E. Salter, Oxford Historical Society 49, 51 [Oxford, 1907–8], I, no. 328).

[102] Reg. Bronscombe, no. 56.
[103] On payments by incumbents to clergy serving or at least assisting in the cure, see Simon Townley, "Unbeneficed Clergy in the Thirteenth Century: Two Dioceses," in *Studies in Clergy and Ministry*, 49–52.
[104] *Annales Monastici*, IV, 416.
[105] *Year Books of Edward II*, XXI, 17. This case addresses a point little other evidence does: how the values of benefices were determined for these purposes. The grant said that the benefice was to be worth 45 marks annually or more according the assessments for the last tenth granted for the recovery of the Holy Land (ibid.).
[106] CPL, I, 333–4. See a similar arrangement for John regarding St. Augustine's (ibid., 290, 334).

subdeacon, a parish worth 60 marks in certain dioceses and, in the meantime, procure him a pension of 20 marks from a couple of abbots.[107] A case from 1314 is harder to read. William de Noyers sued the prior of St. Frideswide's, Oxford, in annuity, having rejected a benefice that William said was worth something less than 40s as replacement for a pension worth 2 marks. It is hard to tell whether William was simply making an argument for the sake of the suit or really would have refused such a benefice. (The prior countered by maintaining the benefice had been worth £10 a year.)[108] A simple pension offered by the monks of Durham is similarly ambiguous. The prior and convent instructed their agent to offer Peter de Montecute up to 50 marks *de camera* a year, or more if Peter's voracity demanded, to resign the church of Bishop Middleham, to which Durham held the advowson.[109] Bishop Middleham – later appropriated to Durham – would be valued at £36 13s 4d along with a vicarage worth £6 in the *Taxatio* of 1291.[110]

Sometimes the terms of pensions in lieu of benefices were vaguer about how much more a benefice should be worth compared with a pension: they state that the benefice should simply be richer, without specifying by how much. In 1229, Ramsey Abbey was ordered by Gregory IX to pay a clerk 5 marks a year until they found him a richer benefice.[111] Bishop Bronscombe of Exeter similarly granted several pensions in lieu of richer benefices.[112] And a pension of 40s until a benefice of greater value could be provided was the subject of litigation in the royal courts in 1317.[113]

On other occasions, however, the bargain was a pension until the recipient received a benefice of equal value, suggesting an equivalence of the two forms of income. Bishop Bronscombe also granted his archdeacon of Cornwall a pension of 40s in lieu of a benefice of the same value (without cure of souls).[114] Bishop William Bitton II of Wells granted Thomas de Bitton, who had resigned Wells's chancellorship, £20 a year until he received a benefice of the same value.[115] In 1237, the pope thanked the archbishop of Canterbury for giving two churches in his

[107] CPL, I, 195.
[108] *Year Books of Edward II*, XVIII, 133–5.
[109] *Durham Annals and Documents*, 151–3, and commentary on 210–11.
[110] Online Taxatio of Pope Nicholas IV, www.hrionline.ac.uk/taxatio/index.html, sub Bishop Middleham.
[111] CPL, I, 120.
[112] Reg. Bronscombe, nos. 727, 1115, 1312.
[113] *Year Books of Edward II*, XXI, 20.
[114] Reg. Bronscombe, no. 56.
[115] *Calendar of the Manuscripts of the Dean and Chapter of Wells*, I, 104.

gift worth together a total of 50 marks to the proctor of the monastery of St. Mary de Gloria, Anagni, to replace a pension of 50 marks previously paid.[116] Another settlement implies a similar equivalency. John de St. Ebulo, papal subdeacon, had failed to obtain a promised place in the chapter of London. So he was to receive another canonry and prebend in the same chapter, or if that was not yet possible, a pension of 40 marks. When a prebend fell open, if that prebend fell short of 40 marks a year, he was to have the prebend and whatever portion of the pension would make up the difference.[117]

Unfortunately, perhaps the most common description of a benefice in the grants is also the vaguest: that the benefice be "suitable" or "fit" (*competens*). The term turns up in seven grants of pensions in lieu of a benefice made by bishops in the thirteenth century, and in a number of early fourteenth-century ones as well.[118] What did "competens" mean in practice? It is hard to tell. As noted earlier, William de Noyers sued the prior of St. Frideswide's over a pension of 40s in lieu of a benefice, having turned down a benefice that, he said, was worth 2 marks (26s 8d). This suit regarded a grant that offered a *competens* benefice. The prior replied not by arguing that the benefice was indeed *competens*, but that the benefice had in fact been worth £10.[119] William had not explicitly said the benefice was not *competens*, nor did the defendant explicitly claim it was. It may be that the whole range of criteria by which a benefice might be judged went into determining its standing as *competens*: its value, of course, but also other concerns. Was it secure or under litigation? Would it raise issues regarding pluralism? Residency? Stating that a benefice was to be *competens* may have been a way of delaying negotiation over such considerations until an actual benefice materialized.[120]

---

[116] CPL, I, 164-5.

[117] Ibid., I, 417.

[118] Thirteenth century: Reg. Halton, I, 31; Reg. Bronscombe, no. 56; Reg. Quivil, 315, 319, 325-6; Reg. Pontissara, 195. Later instances: LAO, Episcopal Register III, fos. 26v, 98v, 362v; Reg. Gandavo, I, 152, 173. See also *Liber Epistolaris of Richard de Bury*, ed. Noel Denholm-Young (Oxford, 1950), no. 417, sub 14; *Cartulary of the Abbey of Eynsham*, no. 303.

[119] *Year Books of Edward II*, XVIII, 133-5.

[120] Evidently a judge could decide that a benefice was *competens* that a pensioner did not in fact want. When the pope canceled the pensions paid by Glastonbury Abbey in lieu of benefices, the pensioners having turned down benefices offered them, it seems that the terms of the grant stated that the benefices were to be *competentes* ("donec eis provideant in beneficio competenti"): *Registres de Grégoire IX*, III, no. 5378, calendared in CPL, I, 193. I am not sure what to make of a case in the Northamptonshire eyre of 1285. A clerk sued for payment of a pension, described in the plea rolls as a pension in lieu of a

One significant characteristic that distinguished benefices from most pensions, at least those granted by bishops, is that the latter were generally limited to the life of the grantor as well as the grantee. If X received a benefice, he had it for life, regardless of when the patron died. Most pensions granted by bishops, however, ran no longer than the life of the bishop himself. There were a few exceptions. Bishop Dalderby of Lincoln (1300–20) granted a simple pension to Hugh Gerald, a friend at the curia, "for as long as he [Gerald] shall live."[121] Two bishops of Carlisle granted pensions in lieu of benefices on behalf of themselves and their successors, as did two successive bishops of Exeter.[122] A later bishop of Carlisle also granted a simple pension on these terms.[123] Bishop Thomas Cantilupe of Hereford was presented with a claim to such a pension granted by his predecessor, who had also taken the precaution of obtaining the confirmation of the dean and chapter.[124] Bishops could also similarly protect grantees by making the cathedral chapter a co-grantor, as chapters never die.[125] This could be done not voluntarily, but in order to settle a dispute with the recipient.[126] But these were exceptions. For grantees, this aspect of the legal terms governing benefices could render benefices more attractive than pensions.

Indeed, if there is evidence that some men preferred a pension to a benefice, and that there were reasons for them to do so, there is also plenty to suggest that the opposite was also true. Requests for pensions in lieu of benefices point to pensions used as stopgaps until benefices could be gotten. Archbishop Winchelsey demanded that the bishop of Ely quickly give the dean of Arches ("nostrum clericum et vestrum devotum," Winchelsey assured the bishop) a benefice. Winchelsey added that the dean was to have a pension from the bishop in the meantime, promising

competens benefice. But the law report concerning the case says the pension was in lieu of a benefice of the same value as the pension (*Earliest English Law Reports*, III, 296–7). This is not, however, the only discrepancy between the report and the record regarding the case. The report has the clerk suing for £25, the plea rolls for £20. The fact that the pension was in lieu of a benefice was not a point of legal significance in the case.

[121] "quam diu vixerit" (LAO, Episcopal Register III, f. 221r).
[122] Reg. Halton, I, 31, 56; Reg. Bronscombe, no. 56; Reg. Quivil, 325. A notary public claimed to have a pension for his lifetime from the bishop-elect of Ely, but it is not clear that the bishop had indeed granted it on these terms (Reg. Winchelsey, 750).
[123] Reg. Halton, I, 138. So did the abbot of Westminster: *Documents of the Rule of Walter de Wenlock, Abbot of Westminster, 1283–1307*, ed. Barbara F. Harvey, Camden Society (fourth series) 2 (1965), 9.
[124] Reg. Cantilupe, 21.
[125] Hence the grant of Bishop Quivil of Exeter and the dean and chapter of Exeter to Peter *dictus* Haverwell (Reg. Quivil, 389).
[126] Reg. Giffard of York, 7.

that this would render the recipient attentive to the bishop's needs.[127] The future Edward II similarly expressed the need for haste when informing the bishop of Bangor that he was to give the prince's clerk Thomas de Cantebrigg a competent benefice as soon as possible, and that the clerk was to have a pension in the meantime.[128] And Edward later followed up, complaining that Thomas had not received a certain vacant prebend.[129] The desire of recipients that a benefice quickly follow a pension presumably lies behind the abbot and convent of Eynhsam's grant of a pension to a clerk of the bishop of Lincoln until they provide him a benefice, reassuring the grantee that "as soon as we are able to do so fittingly, we shall do it."[130] In another instance the abbey gave the grantee a loophole in case the first benefice available was not good enough; he was to have the first benefice available in Eynsham's gift that would suit him ("ei competens fuerit").[131] For these recipients, the benefice, not the pension, was the real quarry. Another pensioner, apparently promised a benefice in the grant, preferred the benefice. A papal *nepos* and canon of York, he asked Henry III's chancellor for help in getting his pension "commuted" into a benefice as contained in the grant.[132] One suspects that the Luke, son of Peter, who had procured two papal provisions for a benefice in the gift of the prior and convent of Lewes and had also obtained from the priory a pension of 6 marks until receiving an "ecclesiastical rent" of 20 marks, indeed sought the benefice. That he then may have tried to retain the pension anyway – he renounced it before the archbishop of Canterbury, the abbot of St. Augustine's, Canterbury, and the prior of Christ Church, Canterbury – merely indicates that 6 marks was 6 marks.[133]

Another royal follow-up reveals the desirability of benefices over pensions from a grantee's point of view, and the opposite attitude of the grantor. A royal request led Bishop Dalderby of Lincoln to grant a pension to a royal clerk "until," as the bishop vaguely put it, "we provide for him equivalently."[134] Two years later the king's successor demanded

---

[127] Reg. Winchelsey, 1244–5.
[128] *Calendar of Ancient Correspondence Concerning Wales*, ed. J. Goronwy Edwards (Cardiff, 1938), 175–6.
[129] Ibid., 178.
[130] "quod quamcitius commode poterimus, faciemus" (*Cartulary of the Abbey of Eynsham*, no. 299).
[131] Ibid., no. 589.
[132] "commutare": *Diplomatic Documents Preserved in the Public Record Office I: 1101–1272*, ed. Pierre Chaplais (London, 1964), no. 208.
[133] *Acta Stephani Langton*, no. 116.
[134] "Quousque ipsum congrue providimus" (LAO, Episcopal Register III, f. 81r).

a prebend for this grantee, stating that Dalderby had granted a pension until he provided a benefice.[135] A pension Dalderby had been willing to give, but not, however, a benefice. Dalderby rejoined that he was not bound to give benefices to those to whom he had granted pensions and that the grant did not mention a benefice.[136] (Dalderby presumably carried his point, as the clerk does not appear to have received a benefice from him.)

The examples discussed of grantees or their benefactors complaining that grantors were not diligent in replacing a pension with a benefice explain why a grantor might worry when he failed to give an influential pensioner the benefice the pensioner expected. Bishop Pontoise of Winchester feared the consequences when he failed to collate a benefice to the brother of the bishop of Albano to whom he had, at royal request, already granted a pension. But this collation had been delayed, he informed the king, and so now Pontoise had gone ahead and given the benefice to another royal clerk. Pontoise hoped that this fact would gain him the king's help in evading the wrath of the first candidate and his brother, the bishop of Albano, a powerful figure at the papal curia.[137]

While recipients, or those acting on their behalf, sought benefices and asked for pensions in the meantime, grantors of pensions might give a pension in lieu of a benefice as a sop to those who, sniffing a vacant church, asked for it. Archbishop Winchelsey deprecatingly asked the abbot of Ramsey for a certain "church or little church"[138] for a clerk of Winchelsey's chapel. Winchelsey (or his clerk) had the information – so he may have thought – to be first in line for this church, as it had fallen vacant when the incumbent was expelled by judgment of the archbishop's court. But the abbot replied softly that the church had already been filled, but, desiring that the archbishop's prayers not be without fruit, granted the clerk a pension with hope of something better.[139]

There were reasons for recipients to prefer benefices over pensions. In the first place, pensions did not carry the symbolic freight of benefices – the prestige discussed in Chapter 3. Moreover, as noted earlier, benefices could be held for life, whereas most pensions ran the life of the grantor at most, leaving the recipient high and dry on the grantor's death. Finally,

---

[135] LAO, Dii/56/1/67.
[136] TNA, SC1/33/119.
[137] Reg. Pontissara, 765.
[138] "ecclesiola": "Letter Book of John de Sautre, Abbot of Ramsey," in *Chronicon Abbatiae Rameseiensis*, ed. W. Dunn Macray (London, 1886) (RS), 377.
[139] Ibid., 377–8.

as discussed in Chapter 4, once institution or collation had taken place, benefices were held independently of the patron. Pensions, on the other hand, were not. True, the king's courts could enforce pension payments, and grantees did sue for payment. (The same Peter de Montecute who resigned Bishop Middleham in exchange for a pension *de camera* later found his pension in arrears and seems to have had to get a papal *curialis*, the bishop of Asti, gently to pressure the grantors to pay up.)[140] But getting periodic cash payments could be troublesome and worse. One man told Henry III that he blushed that his son had to go through the wearying (*tediosum*) process of showing up daily at the royal treasury for his *redditus* (presumably a pension). Could, the concerned father asked, the young man be assigned an ecclesiastical *redditus* (presumably some kind of benefice) instead?[141] Itinerating bishops and other lords did not even have stationary treasuries, creating the practical inconvenience of having to prearrange where one could receive payment; this was, after all, a world where small amounts could not be sent by check through the mail.[142] Another recipient of a pension in lieu of a benefice complained of the king that, although he served faithfully, his pension was not being paid. The cardinal who wrote the king on the grantee's behalf asked that the grantee be paid what was owed and be given the promised benefice, pointing out that this good treatment would be an example to others.[143] The more powerful the grantor, the harder collection was likely to prove.[144]

It is difficult to know how often grantors, in particular bishops, got away without paying pensions, or not paying them on time. Ideally, the historian would consult a long series of accounts. The historian who seeks to do so will be disappointed. The great pipe rolls of the bishops of

---

[140] *Durham Annals and Documents*, 153-4, 210-11.

[141] *Royal and Historical Letters Illustrative of the Reign of Henry III*, ed. Walter Waddington Shirley (RS) (London, 1862-6), I, no. 316.

[142] For a letter concerning arrangements for a transfer of funds, see *Liber Epistolaris of Richard de Bury*, no. 437 (p. 312).

[143] *Royal and Historical Letters of the Reign of Henry III*, II, no. 529. A modern account regarding the early fourteenth century suggests that cardinals, too, often had trouble collecting their royal pensions (J. Robert Wright, *The Church and the English Crown 1305-1334: A Study Based on the Register of Archbishop Walter Reynolds* [Toronto, 1980], 119).

[144] C. R. Cheney notes, in fact, that a disadvantage to the crown of giving its Italian clerks benefices over pensions was that the king could cut off the latter, whereas the former could not be taken back. He also notes that should a recipient of a benefice die at the papal court, the king was in the additional danger of finding the vacant benefice subject to papal provision (*Pope Innocent III and England* [Stuttgart, 1976], 96).

Winchester do not include pension payments *de camera*.[145] Other surviving thirteenth-century episcopal accounts may include pension payments but run no longer than a year, so finding failure to pay a pension by discovering inconsistencies from one year to the next is impossible.[146]

Once again, the priory of Christ Church, Canterbury, can provide a (rare) proxy for thirteenth-century episcopal documents. The priory accounts list pension payments over many years. The tenure as prior of Henry Eastry – whose register I discussed earlier – produces mixed results, although it was a financially stable period in the priory's history.[147] On the one hand, it is clear that most pensions were paid most of the time. It is equally clear, however, that grantees could not count on regular payments. Consider the years 1290–5.[148] It should be stressed that most of the priory's pensions were paid as they should be. Adam de Lymmyng, for example, received his 40s a year like clockwork.[149] Philip de Willoughby similarly received his annual 20 marks.[150] Others, however, were not so fortunate. In 1295–6, Thomas de Cobham received £10 in arrears on an annual pension of £3 6s 8d.[151] Although he was otherwise regularly paid, in 1293–4 John de Redingate was paid nothing.[152] John de Selvestone likewise missed his 10 marks in 1292–3,[153] a point that may help explain the £10 he received the following year as one of the priory's "privatis amicis."[154] Nicholas de St. Victor would wait until 1298–9 for payments due in 1295 and 1296, although a foreign grantee may have had trouble being paid in a time of war.[155] Well might one grantee have written the prior in 1290 to, among other things, thank him for payment of his pension.[156]

[145] Nicholas Vincent, "The Origins of the Winchester Pipe Rolls," *Archives* 21 (1994), 30–3.
[146] For a list, see *Household Accounts from Medieval England*, ed. C. M. Woolgar (Oxford, 1992–3), pt. 2, 691–726.
[147] R. A. L. Smith, *Canterbury Cathedral Priory* (Cambridge, 1943), 25, 53–4; Smith, "The Central Financial System of Christ Church, Canterbury, 1186–1512" in Smith, *Collected Papers* (London, 1947).
[148] Pensions were paid from the Altar of St. Thomas the Martyr accounts (Christ Church, Canterbury, Dc MA 1), which ran Michaelmas to Michaelmas.
[149] Christ Church, Canterbury, Dc MA 1, fos. 167r, 174r, 181r, 187r, 191r, 195v, 201v.
[150] Ibid., fos. 166v, 174v, 181r, 187r, 195r, 201v (for "dom. Wilebi" read "dom. Philipo de Wilebi").
[151] Ibid., f. 202v; Cambridge University Library, MS Ee V 31, f. 19v.
[152] Ibid., fos. 191r–192v. He was steward of the priory's liberty (Smith, *Canterbury Cathedral Priory*, 72).
[153] Christ Church, Canterbury, Dc MA 1, fos. 187r–188r.
[154] Ibid., f. 192v.
[155] Ibid., f. 223v. Nicholas would receive arrears for 1297, 1298, and 1299 in 1299–1300 (ibid., f. 228r).
[156] Historical Manuscripts Commission, *Reports on Manuscripts in Various Collections I* (London, 1901), 258.

Two early fourteenth-century sources suggest a similar conclusion from a different angle. Bishop Richard Gravesend of London died in 1303, his colleague Bishop Thomas Bitton of Exeter following him to the grave in 1310. The accounts of their executors both survive. And in both cases, those accounts reveal a third of the pensions in effect on the bishop's death to have been in arrears.[157] The accounts of another bishop's executors do not allow this kind of calculation, but they do support the conclusion that arrears could be significant. It is not clear whether a pension was included in the claim for "labor and expenses" in the service of Bishop Merton of Rochester made by Peter de Abingdon against Merton's estate. But Peter petitioned for payment of £100 for seventeen years "et amplius" of service.[158] William de St. Quentin, one of Merton's *officiales*, put in a claim of 20 marks for an annual pension of £10 owed him for two and a half years.[159] And William de la Leye, clerk, sought payment of 70 marks on arrears of a 5-mark annual pension over fourteen years; Merton had paid for two years.[160] William may have felt that a dead lord, or at least his executor, was more likely to pay than a live one. Perhaps that was so, but there is no evidence that William received payment.

The availability of the Common Law courts to enforce pensions *de camera* must have made them more attractive to grantees than they otherwise would have been; the king offered regular enforcement of such grants, and grantees sued in court Christian too.[161] The fact that grantees used the courts also confirms that they put some value on pensions.[162] Significantly, where the grantor was a bishop, such suits are found in the metropolitical jurisdiction, a situation reminiscent of the suits over benefices discussed in Chapter 4.[163] Without taking any position on whether plaintiffs deserved not to be paid, their experience suggests that, as J. M. W. Bean notes regarding pensioners in general, "in practice, it is more likely that, whatever their legal rights, many annuitants who proved

---

[157] Four out of twelve in each case: *Accounts of the Executors of Richard Bishop of London 1303 and of the Executors of Thomas Bishop of Exeter 1310*, ed. W. H. Hale and H. T. Ellacombe, Camden Society (second series) 10 (London, 1874), 26–7, 107.
[158] *Early Rolls of Merton College Oxford*, ed. J. R. L. Highfield (Oxford, 1964), 111.
[159] Ibid., 125. For him as *officialis*, see ibid., 39.
[160] Ibid., 115. And for similar cases, although not clearly over so long a period of time, see, e.g., John de Basing (ibid., 120); Richard de Turbevile (ibid., 121); William de Wlcherch (ibid., 121); and Andrew de Kilkenny, the bishop's *officialis* (ibid., 123).
[161] Waugh, "Tenure to Contract," 828–32 for the Common Law courts and see cases discussed earlier for both legal systems.
[162] As noted by R. H. Helmholz, "Ethical Standards for Advocates," 47.
[163] Reg. Halton, I, 59; Reg. Winchelsey, 465–6, 750, 780.

unfaithful found themselves deprived."[164] Indeed, lawyers' suits for payments of annuities due them could run for years.[165] Other suits indicate pensions *de camera* in arrears for some time, such as the ten years' arrears that the prior of Shrewsbury acknowledged in court that his house owed Robert de Littlebury, clerk, in the royal courts.[166] Another case may be presented by the bishop of Norwich, who was sued in 1301 by his notary public in the Court of Arches; the notary claimed payment of 20s – probably, but not certainly, a pension *de camera* or one charged to some endowment or a salary – and a robe annually. Presumably the notary had a reasonable case; the archbishop advised the bishop to settle.[167] The suit, however, was still going on two years later.[168] In 1285, Thomas de Blakesly sued the Hospitallers for £20 – arrears of twenty years of a pension *de camera* in lieu of a benefice. Both parties agreed that Thomas had never been paid.[169]

Although a lawsuit in the king's courts to enforce payment was always possible, soft words may still have been the better path. Reginald de Brandon, an experienced man of affairs, asked the prior and convent of Durham to pay arrears owing on two pensions – one of £10 for three years, the other of £5 for five years – which "you have taken away or you have not paid through an absence of mind."[170] Reginald begged with affectionate prayers ("supplico precibus affectuosis") that the monks pay up.[171] Another of the priory's grantees was able to effect an agreement with the priory to pay 17 marks on arrears of an annual pension of 5 marks (over how many years owed is unknown).[172] Even a grantee who was winning in court might find it safest to take a cash settlement smaller than the amount he was owed. Master Alan de Frestone, a proctor of the prior and convent of Barnwell, sued the priory for 27 marks in arrears of his pension of 40s

---

[164] Bean, *From Lord to Patron*, 33.
[165] For cases running seven and nine years, see Palmer, "Origins of the Legal Profession in England," 129, 131.
[166] TNA, CP 40/106, m 33d. The suit was over a pension in lieu of a benefice. For this and other suits, see Paul Brand, "Medieval Legal Bureaucracy: Clerks in the King's Courts in the Reign of Edward I," in his *The Making of the Common Law* (London, 1992), 184–5 and 185 n 97.
[167] Reg. Winchelsey, 750.
[168] Reg. Winchelsey, 465–6, and see 780.
[169] The dispute turned on what seisin was required for Thomas to make the claim. But because Thomas failed to prosecute his case, no answer was arrived at (*The Earliest English Law Reports*, III, 296–7).
[170] "subtraxistis sive per obliuionem non soluistis": *Durham Annals and Documents*, 89.
[171] Ibid.
[172] Ibid., 89.

a year (so nine years' arrears) plus 100s damages. The priory pleaded that Alan had frequently failed to serve the priory in disputes even when he had been called, whereas Alan countered that he had served faithfully when asked for thirty years. The issue went to the jury, which the priory's attorney saw would go against Barnwell, and so he sought a settlement. Alan accepted roughly half of what he had sought: £12.[173]

The problems grantees had in getting paid highlight what might have been an advantage, from the grantor's point of view, of granting pensions over giving benefices. A grantor of a pension could always refuse to pay. Even (or especially?) the king could be unreliable in this regard. Some cases have been mentioned. Although not exactly annuitants, royal judges after 1294 often counted arrears in their salaries in years.[174] True, from the point of view of recipients, the income from benefices was also potentially unreliable – tithes, for example, were always subject to dispute. But that unreliability was not under the control of the patron and so did not give the patron the disciplinary tool that pensions gave grantors. Of course, when the recipient was a member of the papal curia, grantors might have preferred pensions over benefices because of the pope's right to dispose of benefices of clerks who died or resigned at the curia.[175]

On the whole, one can say that various pressures, coming from both grantors and grantees, shaped the granting of pensions *de camera*; a pluralistic approach to these grants makes the most sense. But when it came to clerical grantees,[176] benefice hunger was surely one of these forces, shaping the grant of pensions as a stopgap, or even as a goad, until the prized benefice might be given. In 1301 the queen asked Ramsey Abbey to give one of her clerks a benefice and a pension in the meantime, "to make it more certain."[177] And, unlike pensions, no clerk is known to have blushed to collect the income from the benefice he ruled.

---

[173] *Liber Memorandorum Ecclesie de Bernwelle*, ed. John Willis Clark (Cambridge, 1907), 185–7.

[174] Maddicott, *Law and Lordship*, 18.

[175] For such "reservations," see Geoffrey Barraclough, *Papal Provisions: Aspects of Church Constitutional, Legal, and Administrative History in the Later Middle Ages* (Oxford, 1935), 9. For the impact of this rule, along with papal provisions, in England in the earlier thirteenth century, see *The Letters and Charters of Cardinal Guala Bicchieri, Papal Legate in England 1216–1218*, ed. Nicholas Vincent, Canterbury and York Society 83 (1996), lxxi–lxxiii.

[176] Laymen were, of course, differently positioned. Thus, as laity replaced clergy among royal justices, lords showered them with pensions rather than the benefices they had earlier given (Maddicott, *Law and Lordship*, 18).

[177] "Letter Book during the Abbacy of John de Sautre," 372. The clerk seems to have gotten the grant (ibid.).

6

Other Rewards

Use of Episcopal Authority

I have argued that the rise of an administrative church undermined bishops' ability to control their administrative subordinates. Insofar as courts of appeal made recipients of benefices more secure against the bishop who gave those benefices, that is true. At the same time, by making benefices more secure, courts of appeal made the benefices bishops gave even more valuable to recipients. This was not, however, the only way in which the rise of church government favored bishops as well as their men. An administrative church also created nodes of power exploitable by bishops at different levels of the hierarchy. Bishops' closer control over their dioceses better positioned them to dispense favors to their clerks. Bishops' influence higher up the hierarchy – in particular, at Rome – also positioned them to do the same.

More tightly administered bishoprics gave the bishops at their head more ways to reward their servants directly. Bishops could manipulate judicial and administrative procedure on behalf of their men. So the rector of Rudby found in 1275, when the archbishop of York ordered, "de gracia speciali," that attempts to get the rector to pay the clerical tenth should go slowly, as the rector was devoted to the archbishop and his church.[1] To judge from a charge levied by the archbishop of Canterbury – and one cannot be sure that the archbishop was not simply reproducing a plaintiff's biased or fraudulent accusation – the bishop of Exeter refused to admit a clerk accused of homicide to compurgation because,

---

[1] Reg. Giffard of York, 298.

scolded the archbishop, the bishop's *familiaris* and *domesticus* Richard de Merton opposed it.[2]

Authorities naturally frowned on these sorts of favors, and perhaps there were not so many of them. Other benefits of episcopal favoritism, however, appear canonical and so more common. Bishop Bronscombe of Exeter was so pleased by his *officialis*'s good service that Bronscombe released the *officialis* from responsibility for rendering accounts.[3] In doing so, Bronscombe exempted his *officialis* from normal expectations. John de Kemesey, the receiver and dispenser of Bishop Swinfield of Hereford's household income and expenses, also received such a privilege, the bishop desiring that John should be believed on his mere word, without judicial action.[4] Such benefits could also be spiritual. Bishop Sutton of Lincoln did what he could do for anyone by granting his archdeacon of Buckingham the right to keep a private chapel at Sherington and later at Bradwell; thus the archdeacon would not have to heed the normal demand that divine service be conducted at the parish church.[5] In 1308, the bishop of Worcester granted John de Redberrow, his *officialis*, John's request to choose his own confessor, even for sins normally reserved to the bishop, but was sure to reserve the right to revoke the gift.[6] Such licit favors were not always a matter of exemption. Sutton also favored Roger de Martival, whom he had made archdeacon of Huntingdon, with a twenty days' indulgence for those visiting his chapel at Noseley soon after Easter.[7]

Bishops could also put their weight behind transactions carried out by their servants. A simple way to do so was by issuing an *inspeximus*, rehearsing and then confirming a charter issued by some other authority.

---

[2] The archbishop ordered the bishop to receive the clerk for compurgation: Reg. Winchelsey, 777–8. Another possible instance: when Master Walter Hervy, the bishop of Salisbury's clerk and *familiaris* and the new rector of Wyke, petitioned the bishop to have the executors of the previous rector pay the clerical tenth owing on his church. The bishop sided with Hervy, ordering the executors to pay up (Reg. Gandavo, 76). For Hervy as the bishop's *clericus familiaris*, see ibid., 77. Hervy took the precaution of noting that he asked only for what was just, but such may well have been the case if this was indeed a simple dilapidations case (ibid., 76).

[3] Reg. Bronscombe, no. 431.

[4] Reg. Swinfield, 475–6.

[5] Rolls and Reg. Sutton, III, 71, V, 193. For examples of rights to private chapels granted by earlier bishops of Lincoln to parties who were not episcopal clerks, see Rot. Wells, II, 202–3, 259–69; Reg. Grosseteste, 25–6, 37–9, 188–9, 305, 350, 472–4, and for more such grants by Sutton: Rolls and Reg. Sutton, III, 47–8, 64–5, 123, IV, 68.

[6] Reg. Reynolds of Worcester, 6.

[7] Rolls and Reg. Sutton, IV, 7. For Roger as archdeacon, see LN Lincoln, 29.

A hint of an inspeximus's value comes from an inspeximus, one of letters of the prior and convent of Lewes, issued by the bishop of Chichester. The letters concerned the presentation of that bishop's clerk, Richard de Dale, to Tillington; the right of presentation was soon in dispute (a dispute that may have been brewing when Richard was presented, prompting him to obtain the inspeximus).[8] In 1293, Bishop Sutton of Lincoln issued an inspeximus for the exchange by Thomas de Birland, the bishop's *officialis*, of rights to certain tithes in return for an annual payment of one and a half marks from Barlings Abbey; the same year the bishop followed up with an inspeximus of the charter by which the abbot and convent of St. Nicholas, Angers, granted certain tithes to Walter de Wooton, Sutton's servant.[9] Bishop Swinfield of Hereford similarly confirmed an agreement between Nicholas de Reigate and Tewkesbury Abbey regarding Nicholas's prebend of Bromyard.[10] The fact that Sutton's and Swinfield's confirmations were preserved in the bishop's register further reinforced the original documents.[11] The bishop thus put his archive as well as his authority at the disposal of these men. Although episcopal archives were less secure than those of cathedrals and monasteries,[12] the security they did offer was evidently still worth having. Unlike most of the favors discussed here, inclusion of documents in episcopal archives was revocable.[13] Episcopal archives could also preserve other documents in favor of episcopal clerks.

---

[8] EEA 23: Chichester, nos. 287, 295, and n.

[9] Rolls and Reg. Sutton, IV, 114–15, 147. Thomas appears as Sutton's *officialis* in 1291 (ibid., 91). Walter had served Sutton as early as 1288, when the bishop ordered him to induct a candidate to a benefice. He was commissioned jointly to investigate certain misdeeds in 1290, and an election "viva voce" in 1297 (ibid., III, 8, VIII, 164). In 1291 Sutton commissioned him jointly to hear a suit (ibid., III, 104–5). Sutton collated the archdeaconry of Huntingdon to him in 1295 (LN Lincoln, 30). In the years 1290–7, he received numerous ad hoc commissions from the bishop as a collector of revenues, a visitor for the bishop, to hear legal cases, and to deal with other business (Rolls and Reg. Sutton, III, 52, 125, 93, 142, 177, 197, IV, 58, 104–5, 165, 182, 187, V, 12, 19, 89, 90, 94, 98, 107, 109, 208). He aided the bishop as an inspector of candidates for holy orders in the years 1290–8 (ibid., VII, 1, 4, 8, 14, 18, 22, 31, 39, 55, 81, 87, 103, 108, 115).

[10] Reg. Swinfield, 386–7. For the collation of the prebend to Nicholas, ibid., 531. Nicholas had at one point been auditor of Swinfield's household accounts: Swinfield Roll, 162 n.

[11] Not all such material was entered in episcopal registers. See Bishop Sutton's notice executing the testament of a late precentor of Lincoln, which was preserved in the cathedral archives but escaped Sutton's register, although it falls in the period when the register was kept (*The Registrum Antiquissimum of the Cathedral Church of Lincoln*, ed. C. W. Foster and K. Major, Lincoln Record Society 27–8, 32, 34, 41, 46, 51, 62, 67 [Hereford and Gateshead], 1931–1973, X, no. 2879).

[12] C. R. Cheney, *English Bishops' Chanceries 1100–1250* (Manchester, 1950), 134–6.

[13] One indication of their value to clerks is the fees clerks paid for the registration of their institutions to benefices (for which, Reg. Langton, xiv).

When, as rector of Ross-on-Wye, John de Kemesey, Bishop Swinfield's money man, negotiated changes in the rectory's relationship with Newent Priory, the agreement was preserved in the bishop's register.[14]

The recording, and even the production, of letters of institution was another benefit a bishop could offer his clerks. Not all recipients of benefices, at least in the diocese of Lincoln, received such letters, at least in the thirteenth century.[15] More important, no one could count on the bishop's registers including such letters. Kathleen Edwards has commented that the rights of Bishop Martival's clerks to their benefices are more extensively documented in his (early fourteenth-century) register than those of other incumbents.[16] And so institutions to benefices provided another opportunity for a bishop to favor his clerks. First, a bishop could issue a letter of institution, thus protecting both the clerk instituted and the advowson of the presenter. Second, the bishop could record the letter among his records of institution, thus adding a thin additional layer of security to the transaction. Bishop Grosseteste's rolls show many of his clerks receiving both favors.[17] The move from memory to written record could still favor the connected.[18]

One can only surmise that these confirmations were issued by bishops at the behest of their clerks. Third parties, however, could also have an interest in firming up such transactions. Consider, for example, that letters of institution protected the patron as well as the clerk. It is thus possible that third parties were responsible for drawing these bishops into the business. In one case, however, a source itself makes explicit what is

---

[14] Reg. Swinfield 358. For his financial administration of the household, see n 4.
[15] *Acta of Hugh of Wells*, li.
[16] Reg. Martival, IV, xxvii–xxviii.
[17] E.g., Thomas de Ashby (Rot. Grossesteste, 15; Major, "*Familia*," 219–20); John de Riston (Rot. Grosseteste, 24, 78, 118; Major, "*Familia*," 235); Leonard de Dunwich, (Rot. Grosseteste, 26, 420; Major, "*Familia*," 227); Remigius de Pocklington (Rot. Grosseteste, 56, 395; Major, "*Familia*," 232–3); Simon de Ardern (Rot. Grosseteste, 56, 57, 401; Major, "*Familia*," 219); Gerard de Wesenham (Rot. Grosseteste, 79; Major, "*Familia*," 239); Gilbert de Wycumb (Rot. Grosseteste, 142; Major, "*Familia*," 240); John de Crakehall (Rot. Grosseteste, 155; Major, "*Familia*," 225–6); Roger de Fretwell (Rot. Grosseteste, 191, 417; Major, "*Familia*," 228–9); John de Stokes (Rot. Grosseteste, 263, 267; Major, "*Familia*," 238); John de Dyham (Rot. Grosseteste, 267; Major, "*Familia*," 227–8); William de Southwell (Rot. Grosseteste, 338; Major, "*Familia*," 237–8); Simon Constable (Rot. Grosseteste, 410; Major, "*Familia*," 224–5).
[18] For the move "from memory to written record," see, of course, M. T. Clanchy, *From Memory to Written Record, England 1066–1307* 2nd ed. (Oxford, 1993). (Clanchy makes no claims one way or the other regarding what social groups benefited from the change at the time.)

usually merely implicit. In the third quarter of the twelfth century, the archbishop of Canterbury confirmed his clerk Gerard's grant of certain tithes belonging to his church of Teynham to the chapel of Doddington, at, the bishop notes, Gerard's instance (and not that of the holder of Doddington).[19] Perhaps Gerard also prompted the bishop to go the extra mile, calling on the wrath of God almighty, John the Baptist, Saint Peter, and Saint Paul, and all the saints against any who presumed to contravene his confirmation.[20]

Bishops also offered their followers protection, and not just in the form of confirmations and archives. Archbishop Pecham ordered that William de Sardinia, his clerk, not be harassed or injured in his possession of the tithes said to pertain to his church of Goodnestone while William was embroiled in a suit with two neighboring rectors, a declaration in line with the protection the law offered incumbents, but a favor done by the archbishop nonetheless.[21] Such protection in the fourteenth century would take the form of bishops stymieing royal demands to sequestrate benefices in order to force incumbents to come to the king's courts.[22] One bishop of Lincoln even blandly gave the king the studiously shameless reply that he could find no ecclesiastical property belonging to the archdeacon of Lincoln in the diocese.[23]

Having a place in a bishop's household was probably expected to afford one protection, including protection of one's dignity. In 1323–4, the bishop of Coventry and Lichfield complained that someone (probably the dean of Lichfield cathedral) dared to insult the bishop's seneschal, noting that the seneschal's connection with the bishop's household and *mensa* should have produced more moderate behavior.[24] Bishops also protected through deterrence, meting out punishment to those who might harm them and, more important here, harm theirs. Bishop Sutton of Lincoln sentenced John de Normanby to do public penance for laying violent hands, albeit without shedding blood, on Benedict de Ferriby, who soon becomes evident in Sutton's service.[25] It is true that Sutton

---

[19] EEA II: Canterbury, no. 65.
[20] Ibid. This anathema was not the standard one in this bishop's *acta* (ibid., lxix).
[21] Reg. Pecham, II, 209.
[22] R. H. Helmholz, *The Ius Commune in England: Four Studies* (Oxford, 2001), 232–7.
[23] Ibid., 233.
[24] *The Great Register of Lichfield Cathedral Known as Magnum Registrum Album*, ed. H. E. Savage (Kendal, 1926), no. 744.
[25] Rolls and Reg. Sutton, III, 20–1. This was in July 1290. The next year Sutton commissioned Benedict to discharge executors and later that year gave him charge of the archdeaconry of Stow, then vacant (ibid., III, 157, 169). In 1296 and 1297, Sutton commissioned

excommunicated many individuals at the behest of people who were strangers. Yet, Walter de Wooton's connection to the bishop likely gave Walter confidence that Sutton would excommunicate the culprits who cut down trees in Walter's custody.[26] The same bishop also punished Robert de Grendon, who had been unwise enough to give a servant of Nicholas de Appletree a bloody mouth over a game of dice; Nicholas was a proctor and hanger-on of the bishop's brother, Stephen de Sutton, archdeacon of Northampton. Robert was to undergo his penance by receiving two beatings in the presence of the archdeacon's *familia*.[27] It was perhaps a salutary reminder to the archdeacon's men of what their bishop, and so their archdeacon, could do for them.[28] Of course, bishops' efforts could fail. Archbishop Romeyn of York asked the prior of Durham to allow Thomas de Birland, according to the prior, the archbishop's *clericus specialis*, to be forgiven money he owed for the clerical tenth; the priory had covered the debt for Thomas. But the prior turned down the archbishop's request.[29]

---

him to grant probate (Rolls and Reg. Sutton, V, 157, VI, 43). On this last occasion he is noted as archidiaconal official of Stow.

[26] Ibid., V, 204–5. For Sutton's practice of excommunicating unknown malefactors on report of those they had injured, secular or lay, see ibid., xlvii.

[27] Ibid., III, 27. For Stephen de Sutton's dates as archdeacon and his relationship with Bishop Sutton, see LN Lincoln, 32. Nicholas was serving as Stephen de Sutton's proctor as early as 1286–7 (Reg. Romeyn, 257–8 and see *Select Cases from the Ecclesiastical Courts of the Province of Canterbury c. 1200–1301*, ed. Norma Adams and Charles Donahue Jr., Selden Society 95 [London, 1981 for 1978–9], 570 and n 13). This connection appears traceable earlier, to 1280 at least (Reg. Wickwane, 75). Nicholas eventually appears in Bishop Sutton's service. Sutton commissioned him jointly to settle a dispute in 1294 (Rolls and Reg. Sutton, V, 10) and to visit a hospital in 1297 (ibid., VI, 44). In 1298 Nicholas received ad hoc commissions to grant probate and absolution as well as a commission to administer the vacant archdeaconry of Buckingham (ibid., VI, 115, 143, 148, and see 161). Sutton commissioned him to grant probate in 1299 (ibid., VI, 186).

[28] Similarly, see Bishop Peter de Aquablanca's grant of land to a servant of one of his clerks (EEA 35: Hereford, nos. 110–12). Although they did not know it, the scene was an echo of the threat Anselm of Canterbury had made long before against all those who did violence to himself or his followers (William of Malmesbury, *De Gesta Pontificum Anglorum*, ed. N.E.S.A. Hamilton [RS] [London, 1870], 107 [1.56]). Perhaps a later reverberation is an anonymous letter, in which an unidentified writer accepts an unidentified correspondent's request to accept him as the writer's clerk. The writer promises that "vbicunque fueritis clericus noster sitis et beneficio favoris nostri sicut noster clericus gaudeatis" (*The Liber Epistolaris of Richard de Bury*, ed. Noel Denholm-Young [Oxford, 1950], 66). Does "vbicunque" suggest protection? The letter presumably antedates 1324–5, when the *Liber* was compiled (ibid., xii; Noel Denholm-Young, "Richard de Bury (1287–1345)," in Denholm-Young, *Collected Papers on Mediaeval Subjects* [Oxford, 1946], 6).

[29] *Durham Annals and Documents*, ed. Frank Barlow, Surtees Society 155 (Durham, 1945), 136.

Surely there were many more favors bishops could render those who served them relying on their own authority alone, favors that leave no parchment traces. Benefits of this type appear, however, to have been greatly outweighed in number by the many favors bestowed by bishops by virtue of papal authority, discussed in the next section. This could be a matter of sources. Most of the material in this section comes from bishops' registers and individual episcopal *acta* lodged in monastic cartularies. Most of the evidence of bishops providing favors by means of papal largesse derives from papally provided dispensations, preserved in the massive papal registers. Although they are not a complete record of documents issued by the popes, papal registers do survive in a more or less continuous series from the end of the twelfth century. I suspect, however, that the prominence of papally derived favors is not simply an accident of sources. After all, there are a lot of surviving episcopal registers. Rather, the role of the papacy here is both analogous to, and a foil for, the role of papal courts of appeal in fostering clerks' security of tenure in their benefices. On the one hand, in both situations papal authority rivaled, and so potentially checked, episcopal authority. In the case of benefices, courts of appeal resulted in that check being realized, making benefice holders secure even in the face of their bishops. On the other hand, the pope's authority to grant dispensations, and bishops' ability to reach Rome for favor more easily than their men, meant that bishops were able to channel papal powers of exemption through their own hands.

Use of Papal Authority

Bishops can easily appear to be losers in the High Middle Ages, clipped by the papacy's achievement of control over the Western church. Certainly bishops complained about litigants slipping through their jurisdiction to Rome.[30] Like any central authority, the papacy threatened to undermine local authorities. In other respects, however, papal authority reinforced episcopal authority back home.

Pertinent here was the pope's power to override the strictures of the canon law. The papacy exercised a dispensing power to exempt people from canonical requirements. By the beginning of the thirteenth century,

---

[30] Jane E. Sayers, *Papal Judges Delegate in the Province of Canterbury 1198–1254: A Study in Ecclesiastical Jurisdiction and Administration* (Oxford, 1971), 277. For a quiet complaint from an earlier time, see Avrom Saltman, *Theobald, Archbishop of Canterbury* (London, 1955), 151.

canonists largely held that only the pope could thus override the general laws of the church, although there was disagreement.³¹ One way to obtain papal help in overcoming the inconveniences of the law was to obtain direct representation at the curia. Doing so oneself, however, involved time and danger: a journey of weeks, the risk of robbery en route, and an often fatal climate at one's destination.³² The alternative still meant expense: the hiring of a proctor.

Episcopal servants, however, had an easier alternative. Their masters often, perhaps usually, maintained proctors at the papal court. On occasion, bishops met the pope personally, traveling to Rome for legal or diplomatic reasons, or taking part in one of the great papally sponsored councils. And so bishops' clerks often received papal dispensations at the behest of the bishops they served. In this way, papal authority became a source of gifts with which bishops rewarded their own followers.

By far the most frequently surviving kind of dispensation received by English bishops' clerks was for pluralism. The papal record of these dispensations often notes that they have been granted at the request of a bishop, and it is fair to suspect that at least some of these men received such favors because they were that bishop's clerks. In some cases the connection between beneficiary and bishop is demonstrable, for it was made explicit in the dispensation itself. Thus, in 1303, William de Ockham, the bishop of Durham's clerk, was dispensed to hold his rectory of Langton with cure of souls along with the normally incompatible archdeaconry of Stow at the bishop's request.³³ Pope Innocent IV permitted Robert Haget, whom the pope describes as the archbishop of York's clerk, to hold the rectory of Bilton along with the treasurership of the cathedral of York at the archbishop's request.³⁴ In 1250, the pope permitted Master Walter

---

³¹ Kenneth Pennington, *Pope and Bishops: The Papal Monarchy in the Twelfth and Thirteenth Centuries* (Philadelphia, 1984); Robert E. Rodes Jr., *Ecclesiastical Administration in Medieval England* (Notre Dame, 1977), 178. For some English authorities asserting the power of bishops to dispense for illegitimate birth to allow ordination to higher orders, despite papal claims to monopolize such dispensations, see Laura Wertheimer, "Illegitimate Birth and the English Clergy, 1198–1348," *Journal of Medieval History* 31 (2001), 214 and 224.

³² On travel and other dangers, see C. R. Cheney, *Pope Innocent III and England* (Stuttgart, 1976), 109.

³³ *Les Registres de Boniface VIII*, ed. A. Thomas et al., Bibliothèque des Ecoles françaises d'Athènes et de Rome (second series) IV (Paris, 1884–1938), III, no. 4753.

³⁴ Rot. Gray, 101. Another case is that of Robert de Sidesterne, the *medicus* who attended Archbishop Pecham on his deathbed. He can probably be described as the archbishop's clerk; the archbishop had collated two benefices to him as well as procuring him a papal dispensation for pluralism (CPL, I, 544). For his benefices and connection with

(de Vienne), the *officialis* of Bishop Walter Cantilupe of Worcester, to add another church with cure of souls to others, at the bishop's request.[35] In 1253, Thomas de Rumesi, the bishop of Bath and Wells's proctor, was dispensed to hold two benefices with cure of souls at his bishop's request.[36] In 1244, the pope, at the bishop of Winchester's instance, had permitted the archdeacon of Suffolk, Roger Pincerna, to hold additional benefices with cure of souls.[37] In 1245, the pope confirmed the bishop of Winchester's dispensation to the archdeacon of Surrey to hold three incompatible benefices.[38]

To judge from the papal registers – where most dispensations are preserved – dispensations to bishops' clerks were usually not simply distributed to this or that clerk at a bishop's request. Instead, the pope empowered bishops themselves to dispense their clerks for pluralism.[39] These faculties, as they were sometimes called, generally limited the bishop to dispensing only a certain number of clerks, limiting the pluralist to two benefices with cure of souls. One example can stand for many across the thirteenth century. In 1226, the pope empowered the bishop of Hereford to dispense two of his clerks to hold two benefices apiece with cure of souls.[40] Occasionally the pope added further conditions, in this case, that the clerks be of legitimate birth. But an important element of these dispensations was that their award was left to the bishop's disposal;

Pecham, see A. B. Emden, *A Biographical Register of the University of Oxford to A.D. 1500* (Oxford, 1957), III, 1700 and Reg. Pecham, I, 44, 72, 87. On other occasions the recipient of the dispensation is described as the clerk of some English bishop, but the pope says nothing as to whether the dispensation was granted to fulfill the bishop's request: dispensations to John de Crakehale, the bishop of Lincoln's clerk (CPL, I, 216); to Master Henry de Ho, the bishop of Ely's clerk (ibid., 217); to Walter de Merton, the archbishop of York's chancellor (ibid., 225). The fact that the pope knew that these recipients belonged to these bishops encourages one to think that these bishops had some role in procuring the dispensations.

[35] EEA 13: Worcester, no. 159.
[36] CPL, I, 285.
[37] Ibid., 210. This archdeacon had first appeared as such under this bishop when he had been bishop of Norwich, in which the archdeaconry lay; he had earlier appeared as archdeacon of Sudbury under this same bishop, and so presumably enjoyed both by this bishop's collation (LN Monastic Cathedrals, 69, 70).
[38] CPL, I, 219.
[39] In the twelfth century, bishops had dispensed their clerks for pluralism on their own authority. Thirteenth-century canonists disagreed about whether the bishops of their own time could do so; some argued that only the pope enjoyed this authority, a position with which the popes agreed (Pennington, *Pope and Bishops*, 135–48). It has been asserted that new bishops were routinely empowered, with restrictions, to dispense for bastardy (Wertheimer, "Illegitimate Birth and the English Clergy," 219).
[40] CPL, I, 113.

the men who were to be dispensed were left unnamed. Whoever received the gift of legal exemption from a bishop armed with such a document clearly received it from the bishop himself. Most English dioceses furnish examples in the thirteenth century, with bishops being permitted to exempt from two to six of their clerks.[41] In addition, some faculties issued to bishops to dispense for pluralism do not limit the dispensations to the bishop's clerks.[42] It does not strain the imagination, however, to suspect that such dispensations often went to the bishops' own men.

Rome was a font of other exemptions for bishops to scoop up and give to their own men. Had their clerks not yet proceeded to ordination? The bishop of Durham received a faculty to dispense four of his clerks to hold churches in such circumstances, although they were to proceed to orders.[43] Were a bishop's men too young to be ordained to the priesthood, a status required to hold a benefice? The bishop of Winchester was permitted to allow six of his clerks, underage, nevertheless each to hold a benefice with cure of souls.[44] Again, bishops also received such faculties that did not specify that the clerks receiving dispensation be in the bishop's service, but there was nothing to prevent bishops from deploying such faculties to benefit their own followers.[45]

Bishops also used Roman authority to waive residency requirements for their men.[46] The same letter that empowered the bishop of Winchester to allow six underage clerks to hold benefices without benefit of ordination also waived the requirement that they reside in their cures; the combination of youth and nonresidence suggests expectations that they study at the schools.[47] The bishop of Norwich obtained papal authority to dispense two of his clerks, the bishop's *familiares et domestici*, *even if perpetual vicars*, to be nonresident.[48] The bishop of Hereford did better,

---

[41] Norwich: ibid., 71, 192; Hereford: ibid., 101, 113; York: ibid., 108, 162 (printed Rot. Gray, 176); Lincoln: CPL, I, 158; 207; 223; Worcester: ibid., 162; Canterbury: ibid., 189, 214, and see Reg. Bronscombe, nos. 489–90; Durham: CPL, I, 224, 310; Coventry and Lichfield: ibid., 198; Bath and Wells: ibid., 206; Winchester: ibid., 220, 569; Ely: ibid., 268.

[42] Lincoln: ibid., 310; York: ibid., 587; Worcester: ibid., 26, 52; Carlisle: ibid., 141.

[43] Ibid., 616.

[44] Ibid., 570.

[45] Ibid., II, 52, 121, 142. See also Reg. Langton, nos. 797–8.

[46] Although bishops did not have to have Roman authority to do so: see Leonard Boyle's comments on X.3.4.4: "The Constitution 'Cum ex eo' of Pope Boniface VIII: Education of Parochial Clergy," *Mediaeval Studies* 24 (1962), 267.

[47] CPL, I, 570 and see ibid., II, 98.

[48] Ibid., II, 54; *Les Registres de Clément V*, ed. the Benedictines (Rome, 1884–94), III, no. 4072. Emphasis mine.

obtaining a papal faculty to dispense six beneficed clerks in his service to be nonresident.⁴⁹ (The pope also noted that this dispensation would not, however, entitle nonresidents to daily distributions, presumably the distributions that resident canons, often bishops' men, enjoyed from the cathedral common in addition to their prebends.)⁵⁰

Bishops used their standing at Rome to obtain other, more miscellaneous papal favors that they could in turn pass on to their clerks. In 1307, the pope ordered that the bishop of Worcester's officers be received and lodged wherever they went on the bishop's business, setting aside the archbishop of Canterbury's order to the contrary.⁵¹ In 1317, the pope authorized the bishop of Norwich to absolve any in his service who laid violent hands on others, an event all too possible when conducting episcopal business (see Chapter 2).⁵² The bishop also received a faculty to absolve ten of his subjects from penance normally reserved to the pope.

Enhancing Benefices

Bishops also found ways to enhance the attractions of the benefices in their gift. The most obvious way to do so was to increase their endowment. An example was the bishop of Hereford's grant of land at Gorwell, certain rents, and a meadow, to augment the cathedral prebend of Adam de Shrewsbury, his clerk.⁵³ Bishop Jocelin of Bath and Wells granted ten acres and pasture rights to the church and cathedral prebend of Compton Bishop, in the possession of his chaplain, Elias.⁵⁴ These, of course, were grants that any secular figure could also bestow. But bishops also used their more specifically episcopal powers in such efforts. In 1235, Bishop Poore of Durham diverted some of the tithes of the church of Haughton le Skerne, then vacant, to increase the endowment of the archdeaconry of Durham, perhaps thus cultivating an archdeacon apparently appointed by his predecessor.⁵⁵ (The patrons, the prioress, and convent of Neasham

---

⁴⁹ CPL, I, 300.
⁵⁰ Kathleen Edwards notes that at Hereford nonresident canons kept a share in these distributions anyway (*The English Secular Cathedrals in the Middle Ages: A Constitutional Study with Special Reference to the Fourteenth Century*, 2nd ed. [Manchester, 1967], 43).
⁵¹ CPL, II, 26.
⁵² Ibid., 142.
⁵³ EEA VII: Hereford, no. 341.
⁵⁴ *Calendar of the Manuscripts of the Dean and Chapter of Wells*, I, 27.
⁵⁵ EEA 25: Durham, no. 319. The archdeacon was William de Lanham, who first appears as archdeacon under Poore's predecessor (LN Monastic Cathedrals, 38).

were also favored with income from this church as part of the deal; essentially this was an appropriation in which the bishop ensured that his archdeacon received a cut.) The bishop of Coventry and Lichfield simply appropriated the rectory of Boulton to the archdeaconry of Chester, to take effect when the rectory fell vacant.[56] Or one could enrich a rectory by reversing the ordination of a vicarage. Bishop Swinfield of Hereford did this for his one-time proctor at Rome, John de Butterley, when he united John's rectory of Lindridge with the vicarage when it fell vacant.[57] Swinfield later did the same for his long-time servant John de Kemesey, uniting John's rectory of Ross-on-Wye with the newly vacant vicarage.[58] The bishop of Worcester, however, found material gifts for his church of Hillingdon that did not produce revenue: "a chasuble of red samite, a tunic and dalmatic of the same suit, one cloth of gold elaborately woven for a frontal, one mitre, sandals of silk, and a pillow likewise of silk" – tangible reminders, he pointed out, of the bishops of Worcester.[59]

---

[56] *Great Register of Lichfield Cathedral*, no. 486. The bishop also ordained a vicarage, freeing the archdeacon from the burden of the cure of souls. The archdeacon receiving the grant had also received the archdeaconry from the same bishop, Roger de Weseham. This archdeacon (in 1253) would have been Adam de Stanford (I am grateful regarding this information for a communication from the late Professor Jeffrey Denton regarding the volume of Le Neve's *Fasti* he was preparing for this see), not, pace Thomas Duffus Hardy, John Basing (John Le Neve, *Fasti Ecclesiae Anglicanae, or a Calendar of the Principal Ecclesiastical Dignitaries of England and Wales*, corrected and continued by T. Duffus Hardy [Oxford, 1844], I, 548, 565). The archbishop of York similarly gave the church of Acomb to the treasurer of York, William de Rotherfield, and his successors (someone in this case was able to effect the resignation of Acomb's incumbent) (Rot. Gray, 17; *The Cartulary of the Treasurer of York Minster and Related Documents*, ed. Janet E. Burton [York, 1978], nos. 29–30). The resignation may be somehow related to a dispute the incumbent was having with the dean and chapter regarding residence and the chapter's common fund (Rot. Gray, 154–6). William first appears as treasurer in 1220, and so presumably by collation by Archbishop Gray (LN York, 24). The name "Rotherfield" also probably itself indicates some relationship with this archbishop (ibid., xxxix). In 1281, Bishop Wickhampton of Salisbury appropriated Gussage All Saints to the archdeaconry of Dorset without even requiring a vicarage (EEA 37: Salisbury, no. 288 and, for what may be a similar instance in this diocese, ibid., no. 355).

[57] Reg. Swinfield, 97. Henry promised to reside as rector (ibid.). For Henry as the bishop's proctor, see ibid., 12–13.

[58] Ibid., 346. This time there was no mention of the rector having to be resident. Such residence would have been unlikely, given what seems to have been John's constant attendance on the bishop. (For instances of John's presence with the bishop, see ibid., 15, 93, 97, 112, 128, 182, 222, 226, 238, 240, 249, 252, 256, 276, 278–9, 282, 338, 377, 380, 382, 389, 395, 418–19, 423, 439, 443, 461, 471, 505, 512; Herefordshire Records Office, AL 19/2, f. 131v (witness list not printed in Reg. Swinfield).

[59] Reg. Giffard of Worcester, 208. The church appears to have been in the bishop's collation, for he would later appropriate it to himself (ibid., 468).

Augmenting a benefice's endowment did not, of course, overcome what was – at least from a modern managerial point of view – a basic problem of benefices as tools of discipline: their irrevocability. Such a grant merely increased a benefice's value. Indeed, gifts like the ones enumerated here presented the additional disadvantage of being permanent because they were made to a benefice, not to the person holding it. At least when an incumbent died, the holder of the advowson could present someone else to the living. A gift like that of the bishop of Hereford to Adam de Shrewsbury's prebend could not be given again, although the prebend could be on Adam's death or resignation. A later patron-bishop tried to get around the problem. Bishop Swinfield obtained the union of the (vacant) church of Credenhill to the archdeaconry of Salop so long as the current man, John Talbot, held the archdeaconry.[60] Bishop Jocelin of Bath and Wells similarly augmented the prebend of the archdeacon of Taunton so it would yield 22 marks a year; but once Master W. de St. Quentin ceased to hold the prebend, it was to drop to 10 marks annually.[61]

But augmentations of benefices tended to be permanent alienations, although a prebend's endowment could be subject to repeated horse trading.[62] Even when the conferral of extra – and lucrative – privileges stemmed from a personal connection, the grant was likely to be permanent. Archbishop Langton gave his brother Simon, archdeacon of Canterbury, the right to visit the churches in his jurisdiction that fell in the archbishop's and Christ Church, Canterbury's gift, as well as uniting two churches to the archdeaconry and giving the archdeacon sole power to appoint rural deans. All this was in perpetuity.[63]

---

[60] Reg. Swinfield, 379–80. The holder of the advowson of Credenhill was Robert Talbot, perhaps the archdeacon's relative. Robert Talbot was to present when John Talbot either died or resigned (ibid., 380).

[61] *Calendar of the Manuscripts of the Dean and Chapter of Wells*, I, 469.

[62] A survey of Diana Greenway's reconstruction of the prebends of Lincoln cathedral suggests that they generally did not lose endowment, except in the form of the ordination of vicarages (LN Lincoln, 47–109). For a less stable endowment, see Julia Barrow's account of the prebend of Gorwell and Overby in the time of Bishop Hugh Foliot of Hereford (LN Hereford, 38). The prebend was held by Foliot's clerk, Adam de Shrewsbury (ibid., 39). For another case, see the 1291 grant of the church of Stanton by the bishop of Bath and Wells to the archdeacon of Bath and his successors (*Two Chartularies of the Priory of St. Peter at Bath*, ed. William Hunt, Somerset Record Society 9 [London, 1893], 96).

[63] *Acta Stephani Langton*, nos. 111–13. The archbishop did remark it was absurd that someone other than the archdeacon – namely the bishop's own *officialis* – should appoint rural deans (ibid., no. 113 and on this episode, Daniel Baumann, *Stephen Langton: Erzbischof von Canterbury im England der Magna Carta (1207–1228)* [Leiden, 2009], 411–12; Kathleen Major, "The 'Familia' of Archbishop Stephen Langton," *English Historical Review* 48 [1933], 535). Simon had been exiled for some years until reunited

In the 1190s, the bishop of Coventry and Lichfield granted the archdeacon of Stafford the right of presentation to other prebends in the church of Gnosall, a right the archdeacon had often claimed by right of his own prebend in that church. The bishop, however, did insist that the grant was purely to the archdeacon himself, out of love for him, and would not pertain to the archdeacon's prebend; the bishop was making a fairly rare temporary grant.[64] Interestingly, the archdeacon (at roughly the same time?) promised the bishop the disposal of the three prebends when they should become vacant; this was probably a reciprocal arrangement.[65] Permanent gifts were, however, more usual. In 1315, Bishop Walter Langton of Coventry and Lichfield confirmed the annexation of the church of Compton Verney to the prebendary of Saint Mary's and All Saints', in the collegiate church of Warwick, given by his predecessor more than a century earlier.[66]

Another move was for bishops to apply their own power of granting exemptions to benefices held by their clerks. Thus, in the mid-thirteenth century, the bishop of Worcester confirmed that benefices in his collation would be exempt from archidiaconal procurations or even visitation, and, indeed, the archdeacon's court.[67] True, such exemptions tightened the bishop's grip on these benefices. But at the same time incumbents escaped some procurations and one potential source of interference while preserving access to help from higher jurisdiction. Exemptions of this kind could be applied in a way that implied irrevocability. Indeed, bishops in many dioceses with secular cathedrals had given the canons' prebends, lands, and other cathedral property general exemption from archidiaconal jurisdiction.[68] Since bishops' clerks in such dioceses might generally hope for a cathedral prebend from the bishop, this effectively meant an enhancement of the benefices held by many episcopal clerks.

---

with his brother when these grants were made (F. M. Powicke, *Stephen Langton* [Oxford, 1928], 136–7; Baumann, *Stephen Langton*, 411–12); perhaps the archbishop felt especially bound to help him.

[64] EEA 17: Coventry and Lichfield, no. 37. Here the bishop was presumably acting as Gnosall's dean, who had patronage of the prebends, as Gnosall was a royal free chapel that had been granted to the bishops of the see by the king (J. H. Denton, *English Royal Free Chapels 1100–1300: A Constitutional Study* [Manchester, 1970], 69–71).

[65] *The Great Register of Lichfield Cathedral*, no. 173.

[66] Ibid., no. 273; for the earlier annexation: EEA 14: Coventry and Lichfield, no. 76.

[67] *Councils and Synods*, 413 and see 718, as well as R. M. Haines, *The Administration of the Diocese of Worcester in the First Half of the Fourteenth Century* (London, 1963), 17–18. Haines sees this sort of exemption as a privilege of those who had it (ibid., 24).

[68] Edwards, *English Secular Cathedrals*, 245.

The bishop of Bath and Wells, aping papal language of legates *a latere*, similarly asserted that archdeacons might not take procurations from churches of "clerks adhering to our side, doing our work with us." He thus affirmed, or at least purported to affirm, ancient custom.[69] By explicitly attaching the exemption to service rather than to the benefice itself, the bishop implied a revocable privilege, a reason to remain in his service. Likewise, in the fourteenth century, in the archdeaconry of Surrey, in Winchester diocese, the wills of members of the bishop's *familia* were reserved to the bishop's own jurisdiction, cutting out lower authorities.[70] This move also had the added effect of strengthening discipline by making the execution of an episcopal servant's testament more subject to the bishop himself.

The techniques employed by bishops may be compared to the grants of revocable exceptions to the rigor of increasingly effective government by the Norman and Angevin kings, and to those rulers' distribution to their servants of revenues which a more effective administration gathered into the king's hand.[71] The comparison is useful in two ways. In the first place it is, I hope, apt. But in the second place, it returns attention to the benefice. For those kings the ultimate sanction – other than execution – for disobedience was dispossession of the fief. They could exercise that power, when they were indeed able to do so, because they had for most purposes no superior on earth. The same could not be said for a bishop. Enmeshed in a system of courts which led to Canterbury or York and then to Rome, he had to respect a law that protected the recipients of his greatest gifts.

Secular Lands and Favors

Bishops might also give the same kinds of gifts that secular lords gave their hangers-on, although bishops had to give them under the eyes of their cathedral chapters, vigilant to protect the long-term interests of the see. Thus Bishop Giffard of Worcester sold to his steward, already the

---

[69] "clericorum nostrorum lateribus nostris adherentium, honera nostra nobiscum portantium" (*Councils and Synods*, 614). See ibid., n 4 for a similar move by the bishop of Lincoln in 1311.
[70] R. M. Haines, *Archbishop John Stratford: Political Revolutionary and Champion of the Liberties of the English Church, ca. 1275/80–1348* (Toronto, 1986), 105 n 36.
[71] Judith Green, *The Government of England under Henry I* (Cambridge, 1986), 173; C. Warren Hollister, "Henry I and the Anglo-Norman Magnates," in Hollister, *Monarchy, Magnates, and Institutions in the Anglo-Norman World* (London, 1986), 177; W. L. Warren, *King John* (Berkeley and Los Angeles, 1961), 181–4.

rector of Fladbury, the wardship and marriage of an heir to one of the bishop's tenants.[72] The bishop later granted his clerk Henry de Hacton half a virgate "pro servicio suo."[73] The bishop of Hereford granted in fee to John de Kemesey a tenancy at Colwall, for John's homage and service.[74] (John also obtained grants of the freedom of two of the bishop's villeins and their families.[75]) Indeed, it has been suggested that secular grants of land held a special attraction for bishops whose dioceses had a monastic chapter, and so a shortage of benefices in the bishop's gift.[76] Such gifts could also, however, go to men who already held a benefice.[77] Or the gift could be less permanent. In 1278, the bishop of Durham granted one of his clerks custody of an episcopal manor, with the same two robes per year and 2d per day that custodians of the manor had customarily received from the bishop's predecessors.[78] Archbishop Pecham chose to support the project undertaken by John de Lewis, the archbishop's clerk and *familiaris*, of building a chapel dependent on John's rectory of Buxted in a remote part of his parish, so that parishioners would not be lost to a neighboring church; Pecham provided the two acres on which the chapel, along with a cemetery, would be set up.[79]

Two points should be made about such gifts. In the first place, they (again) seem to have been largely irrevocable, giving bishops little advantage over benefices. Second, such gifts were add-ons rather than attempts to give administrators a basic endowment that guaranteed them a livelihood. A twelfth-century exception may prove the rule. While the bishops of Norwich rewarded some of their ecclesiastical servants with revenues derived from episcopal estates, it should be noted that those bishops were rather short on advowsons; it also seems that benefices were in the end what those servants sought and got.[80]

---

[72] Reg. Giffard of Worcester, 54.
[73] Ibid., 456, and see ibid., 518 (and WRO, Rf.x716.093 BA 2648/1(i), f. 443 [p. 827]).
[74] Reg. Swinfield, 486. For John's service to the bishop, see n 7. For a grant of tenancy for life by the bishop of Carlisle to his clerk, see Reg. Halton, I, 84–5.
[75] Reg. Swinfield, 384, 392. See also the grant by the bishop of Durham of a lifetime tenancy in two manors to one of his clerks (EEA 25: Durham, no. 315).
[76] EEA 29: Durham, xlii, and see l and no. 101.
[77] E.g., ibid., no. 166.
[78] Ibid., no. 223.
[79] Pecham, *Epistolae*, III, 987–8 and ibid., 984–7 for the circumstances leading to the chapel's foundation.
[80] EEA VI: Norwich, xlviii–xlix: hence the socage tenure that Ernald Lovel received from the bishop and later gave up; Lovel did find a benefice, although not at the bishop's hand.

Simple Gifts

Of course there were also the small, simple gifts that other lords gave. Bishop Swinfield of Hereford's household roll, unfortunately extant for only one year, indicates the scale of such gift-giving: many small, inexpensive gifts, some of which went to administrators, some to those attached to administrators. There were small cash presents. Stephen de Thanet, Swinfield's clerk, received 2s under "dona" in the roll.[81] A sort of negative gift was the debt of 2 marks Swinfield forgave the keeper of his accounts, John de Kemesey or the mark forgiven his seneschal.[82] Or the bishop gave in kind, such as the venison that went to Richard de Bello.[83] Swinfield also gave to his men's hangers-on. Richard de Bello's boy received 6d in the gift section of the roll.[84] John de Schelving was a recipient of benefices in Bishop Swinfield of Hereford's collation and his agent.[85] The bishop chose to give woolens to John's niece and what looks like some other female relatives.[86] Strikingly, however, most of Swinfield's greater men did not receive the sort of stocking stuffers – either cash or kind – that the roll records.[87]

Other gifts may be hidden by the paucity of pertinent sources. Bishops covered their clerks' business expenses, travel in particular. When Bartholomew de Gatesdene, Thomas de la Dane, and Simon de Schelving accompanied John de Swinfield, archdeacon of Salop and their bishop's brother, from London to Dover, they took with them six horses and five boys, incurring expenses preserved in the bishop's household roll of 30s 8d 1 ob.[88]

Bishops' wills provide another perspective on gifts.[89] Legacies to episcopal clerks could come as cash or as objects, such as silver cups. But the

---

[81] Swinfield Roll, 158. For explicit references to him as Swinfield's clerk, see Reg. Swinfield, 338, 382. The *dona* are listed in ibid., 143–59.

[82] Ibid., 161–2 and n, 187–8 n. William de Mortimer was the bishop's seneschal (Reg. Swinfield, 93, 418).

[83] Swinfield Roll, 20. Richard's connection with Swinfield becomes manifest only later, however: receiving the collation of a cathedral prebend in 1305 and commissioned by the bishop as a proctor to a council in London (Reg. Swinfield, 491, 536).

[84] Swinfield Roll, 151 and again, 158.

[85] For the benefices: Reg. Swinfield, 527–8, 530. For his expedition to Exeter on a mission, presumably on Swinfield's behalf, see Swinfield Roll, 133 (referred to only as the rector of Ross, to be identified as John from Reg. Swinfield, 527).

[86] Swinfield Roll, 122. The presumptive relatives are one Heloise de Schelvinge and her daughters (ibid.).

[87] For the men clearly in service at the time of this roll, see Chapter 5, n 33.

[88] Swinfield Roll, 119.

[89] For a more detailed analysis, see Chapter 10.

reception of a benefice from one's bishop in life could obviate a cash gift from one's bishop in death. Godfrey Giffard of Worcester laid down in his will that 40s should go to each of the clerks of his chapel who were not beneficed.[90] Archbishop Winchelsey bequeathed sums ranging from 10 marks to £20 to a number of clerks, on condition that he had not provided them with benefices by the time of his death.[91] Indeed, while in his will Bishop Merton of Rochester left his *officialis* Andrew de Kilkenny 40 marks and a silver cup with a stand, the payment of 40 marks was disallowed on the grounds that Andrew had been provided with a benefice before Merton's death.[92] Andrew was to receive the cup, laden with sentiment, but not the cash.

Once again, benefices appear to have been the big gifts.

Fees, Bribes, and Extortion

Benefices and pensions were two material rewards of serving a bishop. There were others, more vulnerable to episcopal displeasure even though they flowed not from the bishop, but from those who would benefit from administrative or judicial action. Consider fees. Those who needed the performance of administrative process might pay fees to episcopal agents. So did litigants appearing in episcopal courts. As benefits accruing to administrators for their work, fees bore a resemblance to gifts, bribes, and payments gained through extortion. True, for the people involved there were important distinctions, although those distinctions could be somewhat fuzzy. Bribes and extortion were illicit; gifts and fees were legitimate. Bribes and gifts were voluntary; extorted payments and fees were not. For the recipients – and for the administrative historian – they all, however, had some things in common. First, fees, bribes, gifts, and the proceeds of extortion were continuing revenue streams that flowed from continuing activity in diocesan governance. Second, although the bishop did not supply these revenues, he did make them possible. It was he who put the recipients in the position to collect. Moreover, he could also (with exceptions to be discussed later) take away those opportunities by taking away the administrative positions from which they derived. Thus, more

---

[90] Reg. Gainsborough, 53.
[91] Reg. Winchelsey, 1342.
[92] *Early Rolls of Merton College Oxford*, ed. J. R. L. Highfield (Oxford, 1964), 81, 156. This decision appears to have been rooted in a rather gross interpretation of a clause in the will – an authority disallowing the legacy refers explicitly to some clause in the will – stating that legacies given over by the bishop while he was alive are not to be paid (ibid., 83).

than benefices and even more than pensions, such payments held potential as disciplinary tools for bishops. In the end, however, fees and the profits of corruption do not seem to have been up to the job.

Reception of gifts and bribes ran up and down the hierarchy. "Radix Omnium Malorum Avaritia" had been a byword for the papal court since the twelfth century. Bishop Cantilupe of Hereford could spare only the still very substantial sum of £100 for gifts to officials at Rome to promote the bishop's business there.[93] The situation was little different at home. Works in praise or blame of prelates are revealing. Gerald of Wales, that hammer of bishops, complained that a Welsh bishop publicly took a silver mark in return for a benefice.[94] A rather different source has members of Edmund of Abingdon's household praising Edmund as archbishop of Canterbury for not accepting *munera* – a term that could mean either bribes or gifts[95] – pointing up the blurriness of these categories. The same claim was made to the same end by the hagiographer of Bishop Richard de Wyche of Chichester, addressing specifically Richard's unwillingness to accept gifts from litigants in his court.[96] But saints were special; more mundane bishops, as Gerald knew, might behave differently.[97] Sometimes such gifts took more discreet forms, as when the prior of Daventry promised to pay the vicars choral of Lincoln cathedral £10 a year, explicitly noting that he did so having received the bishop's (favorable) ordinance on certain churches.[98] The same principles applied to lesser folk. Richard

---

[93] Reg. Cantilupe, 273–4. See also the list of gifts made by the bishop of Worcester at Rome (Reg. Giffard of Worcester, 292 and see 301).

[94] Gerald of Wales, *Speculum Duorum or a Mirror of Two Men*, ed. Yves Lefèvre and R. B. C. Hughes, trans. Brian Dawson (Cardiff, 1974), 264.

[95] C. H. Lawrence, *Saint Edmund of Abingdon: A Study of Hagiography and History* (Oxford, 1960), 191, 197. Matthew Paris repeated praise on this score (ibid., 244). On the ambiguity of the term *munera*, see John T. Noonan, Jr., *Bribes: The Intellectual History of a Moral Idea* (Berkeley and Los Angeles, 1984), 140.

[96] *Saint Richard of Chichester: The Sources for His Life*, ed. David Jones, Sussex Record Society 79 (Lewes, 1995 for 1993), 116.

[97] See the rather negative assessment in *The Letters and Charters of Cardinal Guala Bicchieri, Papal Legate in England, 1216–1218*, ed. Nicholas Vincent, Canterbury and York Society 83 (Woodbridge, 1996), lx.

[98] BL, Cotton Claudius xii, f. 161r, entry calendared in *The Cartulary of Daventry Priory*, ed. M. J. Franklin, Northamptonshire Record Society 35 (Northampton, 1988 for 1987), no. 940. This entry is marked "vacat" (ibid.), but the arrangement was under litigation under a later prior (ibid., no. 941), so it is unlikely that this document was drawn up in sheer error. Such gifts can be compared with the proffers litigants gave for the king's justice. That does not mean that they could not be considered attempts to buy justice – i.e., as bribes. For complaints about the king's receipt of such proffers as selling justice, see J. C. Holt, *Magna Carta*, 2nd ed. (Oxford, 1992), Chapter 5, and for a discussion of canonical prohibitions, 285–6.

de Wyche was also commemorated for his sanctity when, still the archbishop of Canterbury's chancellor, he turned down *munera* offered by litigants before the archbishop's court.[99] (Indeed, such problems ran down to the lowest jurisdictions, that of the rural dean.)[100] In a less normatively centered document, Archbishop Pecham set in motion an inquiry as to whether any of his clerks, on the pretext of an archiepiscopal visitation of Yarmouth, received money or *munera* against the archbishop's will.[101] These problems had deep roots. Archbishop Theobald of Canterbury (1139–61) and his two successors had to work to purify their courts of what they saw as corruption, although others may have seen more benign gift-giving.[102] (To pursue matters even earlier runs beyond my purpose.)

As in contributions for modern electoral campaigns, the line between gifts freely offered from below and renders extorted from above was also probably fine. But extortion could be seen as just that – illicit forcing of payment in cash or kind – at least by some. Diocesan administrators were certainly capable of applying pressure. The bishop of Norwich received a report from the archbishop that the bishop's clerks were making the process of compurgation artificially difficult in order to extort large sums for relief.[103] Indeed, an earlier bishop of Norwich was so weighed down by the thought of those he himself had oppressed when he had served as *officialis* that he left 20 marks for their relief in his will.[104] Much later,

---

[99] *Saint Richard of Chichester: The Sources for His Life*, 92.

[100] Jean Scammell, "The Rural Chapter in England from the Eleventh to the Fourteenth Century," *English Historical Review* 86 (1971), 12–21; Paul R. Hyams, "Deans and Their Doings: The Norwich Inquiry of 1286," *Monumenta iuris canonici*, series C: Subsidia 7 (1985), 639–43. And, of course, such offerings were rife among secular officialdom too (e.g., the instances recounted by Noel Denholm-Young, *Seignorial Administration in England* [Oxford, 1937; reprint, New York, rpt. 1964], 109–16).

[101] Pecham, *Epistolae*, I, 176–7.

[102] C. R. Cheney, *From Becket to Langton: English Church Government 1170–1213* (Manchester, 1956), 67. Lester K. Little argues that what had been seen as (acceptable) gifts intended to establish relationships came to be seen as bribes in the eleventh and twelfth centuries (*Religious Poverty and the Profit Economy in Medieval Europe* [Ithaca, 1978], 3–41, 75). For an argument that such benign views of gifts still characterized English courts in the early fourteenth century, see Franklin J. Pegues, "A Monastic Society at Law in the Kent Eyre of 1313–1314," *English Historical Review* 87 (1972), 548–64.

[103] Pecham, *Epistolae*, I, 177–8.

[104] EEA 32: Norwich, no. 138. His conscience may, however, have been especially tender. Such clauses are rare in bishops' wills in the thirteenth century (although not in other wills – see M. M. Sheehan, *The Will in Medieval England: From the Conversion of the Anglo-Saxons to the End of the Thirteenth Century* [Toronto, 1963], 260), and he (also unusually) left 100 marks to be given to the poor in recompense to all those from whom he had received anything that ought to wound the conscience (EEA 32: Norwich,

Lyndwood complained about exactions demanded by episcopal clerks in return for drawing up letters of institution.[105]

In the course of their duties, ecclesiastical functionaries also received licit payments for work, in court and out. Unfortunately, details for the ecclesiastical courts of thirteenth-century England are scarce.[106] At the end of the century, Archbishop Winchelsey limited fees for documents that required sealing to 6d in his court of Canterbury.[107] These fees for judicial administration had analogies in secular justice, such as those paid to clerks of the common law courts.[108] The Canterbury Provincial Council of 1329 laid down that nothing was to be charged for probate of estates worth less than 100s, although this evidence is a bit late.[109] Other renders could easily be both customary and, increasingly, suspect as illicit, indeed, simoniacal payments. Innocent III ordered the archbishop of Canterbury to forbid the customs by which archdeacons and rural deans demanded, respectively, a silver mark or a white cow for inducting presentees to benefices.[110] In doing so, the pope was trying to execute the decree of the Third Lateran Council of 1179, which banned the reception of anything in return for, among other things, induction or installation to a benefice or installation of the head of a religious house; the Council had specifically noted that the plea that old custom justifies such payments would

---

no. 138). Michael Sheehan finds that thirteenth-century testators "very often [made] an attempt ... to make restitution" to those they had done wrong (*Will in Medieval England*, 260). Bishops, to judge from the evidence collected here, seem conspicuously uncommon among such testators (see Chapter 10).

[105] William Lyndwood, *Provinciale (seu Constitutiones Angliae) continens constitutiones provinciales quatuordecim archiepiscoporum cantuariensium* (Oxford, 1679), Book 3, Title 22, Chapter 4.

[106] Fuller documentation survives from the Late Middle Ages. For various fees related to probate administration, see David M. Smith, "The Exercise of the Probate Jurisdiction of the Medieval Archbishops of York," in *Life and Thought in the Northern Church, c. 1100–c. 1700*, ed. Diana Wood (Woodbridge, 1999), 125–6, 141, and in other matters, R. M. Haines, "The Appropriation of Longdon Church to Westminster Abbey," in Haines, *Ecclesia Anglicana: Studies in the English Church of the Later Middle Ages* (Toronto, 1989), 8–9.

[107] *The Medieval Court of Arches*, ed. F. Donald Logan, Canterbury and York Society 95 (Woodbridge, 2005), 7. For a more precise breakdown of costs in ecclesiastical courts, unfortunately available only for a later period, see Brian L. Woodcock, *Medieval Ecclesiastical Courts in the Diocese of Canterbury* (Oxford, 1952), 61–2.

[108] On which, see Paul Brand, "The Clerks of the King's Courts in the Reign of Edward I," in his *The Making of the Common Law* (London, 1992), 183–4.

[109] *Records of Convocation III: Canterbury 1317–1377*, ed. Gerald Bray (Woodbridge, 2005), 112.

[110] *The Letters of Pope Innocent III (1198–1216) Concerning England and Wales*, ed. C. R. Cheney and Mary G. Cheney (Oxford, 1967), no. 143.

Other Rewards 131

not stand.[111] Exhortation and even the availability of judicial appeals did not, however, stamp out such transactions. In 1280, the archdeacon of Bedford demanded a palfrey in return for installing the new prior of Dunstable, although he settled for a payment of 5 marks in order to make peace.[112] So long as the exactions were not too great, it probably made sense to pay even if one could win at law. After all, the priory might have found a friendly archdeacon of Bedford useful, his friendship well worth 5 marks or even a palfrey. Such considerations probably help explain why the line between involuntary payment and freely offered gift is, and perhaps was, hard to draw. They also may explain why such payments continued to be common; such charges would still be a concern in the next century.[113]

Fees, gifts, and extorted payments were all continuing revenue streams, albeit received on an ad hoc basis. Fees for documents, such as those issued in relation to judicial proceedings or reception of benefices, were perhaps the most effectively subject to episcopal oversight, and so regulation. Trying to extirpate venality, Innocent III fixed such fees for scribes and sealers of bulls at the curia.[114] Unfortunately, accounts for thirteenth-

---

[111] Third Lateran, Chapter 7: *Decrees of the Ecumenical Councils I: Nicaea I to Lateran V*, ed. Norman Tanner (Washington, DC, 1990), 214. The Council complains of charges for being "introduced" into a church ("introducendis") and then legislates against charges for "instituting" ("instituendis") priests. The complaints and the items of legislation are given in parallel, so presumably introducing into churches is what is meant by instituting priests here. It is unclear whether what would later be called institution or induction is meant by this canon; "institution" had not at this point, in England at any rate, become the technical term for receiving title to a benefice that it would later (B. R. Kemp, "Towards Admission and Institution: English Episcopal Formulae for the Appointment of Parochial Incumbents in the Twelfth Century," in *Anglo-Norman Studies XVI: Proceedings of the Battle Conference 1993*, ed. Marjorie Chibnall [Woodbridge, 1994], 155–76), and I have not seen reason to think so regarding papal usage. On the struggle in the late twelfth-century English church over attempts to impose the canon law and various kinds of payments among ecclesiastics (especially to archdeacons), sometimes dignified by description as customs, see Stanley Chodorow, "Custom, Roman Canon Law, and Economic Interests in Late Twelfth-Century England," in *Grundlagen des Rechts: Festschrift für Peter Landau zum 65. Geburtstag II*, ed. Richard H. Helmholz, Paul Mikat, Jörge Müller, and Michal Stolleis (Paderborn, 2000), 291–9. The development was an echo of earlier redefinitions of payments wrought by the Gregorian Reform and economic change (Little, *Religious Poverty*, 73).

[112] *Annales Monastici*, III, 284. Or a similar instance: the official of the archdeacon of Lincoln had demanded what was, according to Bishop Sutton, an immoderate sum for installing the new prior of Kyme (Rolls and Reg. Sutton, IV, 144–5).

[113] Michael Haren, *Sin and Society in Fourteenth-Century England: A Study of the Memoriale Presbiterorum* (Oxford, 2000), 98.

[114] "Gesta Innocentii PP. III.," in *Patrologiae Cursus Completus*, ed. J.-P., Migne (Paris, 1844–55), CCXIV, col. lxxx (Chapter 41); Brigide Schwarz, *Die Organisation kurialer*

century English church courts do not survive, although they appear to have been kept.[115] Moreover, bishops not only permitted court officials to charge fees, but also undertook to set them; Winchelsey's limit of 6d for documents requiring a seal has already been mentioned.[116]

What was the justification for these fees? The answer is obscure. One possibility is that such fees were a means of rewarding and supporting clerical personnel. Indeed, Irene Churchill suggests just this in her discussion of the Canterbury court.[117] Unfortunately, her evidence for this point comes from the time of Reformation. Evidence closer to the thirteenth century points to a different rationale. Unfortunately, it is still late, in legislation by the councils of the southern province of 1341 and of London of 1342. The 1341 council, protesting immoderate fees, limited the fee for letters certifying induction to a benefice to a half mark to cover labor and all expenses. No more than 12d was to be taken for letters of inquiry regarding institution to, or commissioning an induction to, a benefice and no more than 6d for letters concerning ordination or for letters dismissory. As for the rest, ordinaries were bound to give their ministers *stipendia* with which they should be content; nothing, for example, was to be received for sealing letters.[118] The 1342 convocation repeated these complaints about archdeacons and their officials demanding excessive sums to prepare letters of inquiry for benefices and for letters certifying induction to benefices. Archdeacons or their officials were, again, to have no more than 12d for letters of inquiry regarding benefices; regarding inductions to benefices, archdeacons or their officials were to have no more than 40d, and archidiaconal officials no more than 2s for sealing and their expenses "pro diaeta." For the rest, ordinaries were (again) bound to give their *ministri* "stipendia," which, said the council,

---

Schreiberkollegien von ihrer Entstehung bis zur Mitte des 15. Jahrhunderts (Tübingen, 1972), 25–6; Peter Herde, *Beiträge zum päpstlichen Kanzlei- und Urkundenwesen im dreizehnten Jahrhundert* (Munich, 1967), 50.

[115] It was from keeping such accounts that the bishop of Exeter absolved the *officialis* of his court in 1262 (the bishop was well pleased with his *officialis*'s exemplary service): see n 3.

[116] The same could said for royal government: *The Memoranda Roll for the Michaelmas Term of the First Year of the Reign of King John (1199–1200)*, ed. H. G. Richardson, Pipe Rolls Society (new series) 21 (London, 1943), xxxvi–li. For correction of some of Richardson's conclusions here, see Nicholas Vincent, "Why 1199? Bureaucracy and Enrolment under John and His Contemporaries," in *English Government in the Thirteenth Century*, ed. Adrian Jobson (Woodbridge, 2004), 36–8.

[117] Irene Josephine Churchill, *Canterbury Administration: The Administrative Machinery of the Archbishopric of Canterbury Illustrated from Original Records* (London, 1933), I, 543.

[118] *Records of Convocation III*, 176.

were to suffice. Letters, the council asserted, should not be sold, echoing the *corpus iuris canonici*.[119] Imposing such limits recognized the cost of performing administrative duties, but prohibited actual reward from the performance of administrative duties. Was this the thinking in the thirteenth century? Probably, for John of Salisbury was making such arguments in the 1150s, arguing that officials should not receive fees beyond the requirement of daily subsistence, preferring "fixed fees" instead, although John equivocated in allowing also gifts beyond that so long as they did not take on "the quality of offerings."[120] Winchelsey's limit of fees for sealed documents in his court to 6d also points in that direction. The scale is similar to the limit set in 1342, and so presumably left little for profit.[121] Indeed, the general principle was broadly applied, accounting for attempts to restrict the procurations bishops themselves received when visiting religious houses to in-kind, rather than cash, renders.[122] Discussions of benefices as rewards were also cast as compensation for expenses incurred in the course of service rather than as opportunities for profit (see Chapter 3).

It appears that bishops at their best tried to limit fees to a level that simply covered the cost of materials and travel (where pertinent),[123] and tried to eliminate other sorts of remuneration (i.e., bribes and, especially, renders via extortion) altogether, categorizing them as illicit. To the extent that bishops' attempts succeeded, these revenue streams were limited. Of course, bishops were not always at their best and would have not been wholly successful even had they been so.[124] It is reasonable to suppose

---

[119] Ibid., 189–90 and 190 n 619 for canon-law references.

[120] "munerum qualitatem": John of Salisbury, *Ioannis Saresberiensis Episcopi Carnotensis Policratici sive de Nvgis Cvrialivm et Vestigiis Philosophorvm Libri VIII*, ed. Clemens I. Webb (Oxford, 1909), 577a (5.15); Noonan, *Bribes*, 157. In the thirteenth century, Geoffrey of Trani would allow litigants to give judges supplies to be used to support themselves and their households; clerks were permitted smaller gifts (James Brundage, "Taxation Costs in Medieval Canonical Courts," in *Forschungen zur Reichs-, Papst-, und Landesgeschichte, Peter Herde zum 65. Geburtstag von Freunden, Schülern und Kollegen dargebracht I*, ed. Karl Borchardt and Enno Bünz [Stuttgart, 1998], 571).

[121] According to Richard Kay, the elimination of all profit derived from litigants at the papal curia was also the aim of a reform proposed by Honorius III, who would, however, still have permitted litigants to reimburse the expense of materials such as parchment (*The Council of Bourges 1225: A Documentary History* [Aldershot, 2002], 195–6).

[122] For such attempts, see C. R. Cheney, *Episcopal Visitations of Monasteries in the Thirteenth Century*, 2nd ed. (Manchester, 1983), 107–10.

[123] For a discussion of limits on procurations in the thirteenth and fourteenth centuries: Haren, *Sin and Society*, 91–3.

[124] For illicit fees exacted by examiners of the bishop of Exeter's court consistory in 1323, see Mark Buck, *Politics, Finance and the Church in the Reign of Edward II: Walter Stapeldon, Treasurer of England* (Cambridge, 1983), 57.

that fees, gifts, and bribes were a significant element in the income of diocesan administrators. But it is also reasonable to be wary of overstating the case. Certainly there were institutional imperatives set to block or limit these revenues. Moreover, although it has been observed that fees would have been largely the concern of "humbler clerical staff," there is reason to think that fees did not always go to the men who collected them.[125] The charge at Exeter for registering institutions to benefices was referred to as the "bishop's fee,"[126] while beneficed clergy who applied for a license to be nonresident in order to study in the schools paid a fee that the bishop devoted to alms.[127] Among the charges an angry prior and convent of Worcester leveled against Bishop Giffard of Worcester was that he received a fee of 2s 6d for sealing letters testifying to the ordination of clergy.[128] Such practices were analogous to fees for sealing in the king's chancery, which went to the chancellor rather than his clerks.[129] In the end, fees probably should be seen as adjuncts, helpful adjuncts, to clerks' other material support, in particular from that of benefices.

Indeed, contemporaries expected that benefices were, or at least should be, a form of income that would make the profits of corruption unnecessary. The emperor Henry VI proposed abolishing bribery at the papal court by putting at the pope's disposal certain benefices in every cathedral in Christendom. He evidently expected that beneficed clergy would not require gifts. The scheme was revived in an altered form, but unsuccessfully, by Innocent III in 1215 and Honorius III in 1225.[130]

So did such useful revenue streams offer bishops a disciplinary tool? Presumably they did. But there were limits, at least for beneficed clergy. After all, a benefice could provide a sound, basic, and secure income. Moreover, it is worth noting that the collection (or extortion) of bribes and gifts was, in a sense, a sort of entrepreneurial activity, whether people regarded it as licit or illicit. A dissatisfied clerk could choose to direct

---

[125] C. R. Cheney, *Hubert Walter* (London, 1967), 162.
[126] Reg. Langton, no. 317.
[127] "A 1301 Sequestrator-General's Account Roll for the Diocese of Coventry and Lichfield," ed. Jill B. Hughes, in *Chronology, Conquest and Conflict in Medieval England*, Camden Society Miscellany 34, Camden Society (fifth series) 10 (London, 1997), 113.
[128] Reg. Giffard of Worcester, 549. Giffard denied the charge (ibid.).
[129] H. C. Maxwell-Lyte, *Historical Notes on the Use of the Great Seal of England* (London, 1926), 328–9.
[130] Richard Kay, "Gerald of Wales and the Fourth Lateran Council," 79–80 and Kay, *The Council of Bourges*, 75–231. In 1235, it should be noted, critics not unreasonably pointed out that giving papal clerks a regular income would simply mean that clerks would continue to accept (and demand) gifts under the table (ibid., 212).

the energy devoted to milking the diocese to other revenue-enhancing activities instead. He might, for example, choose to engage in business activities of one kind or another.[131] He could go to work for some other bishop, or some other lord altogether (see Chapter 9). If his bishop had made him a member of the cathedral chapter, he could become a resident canon, which brought remuneration simply for residency.[132] Or he might engage in various combinations of these activities. Opportunities for graft – or the collection of gifts – had limits as a means of binding bishops and bureaucrat.

---

[131] Robert Palmer finds evidence of the English Reformation sharply reducing clergy's involvement in commerce (*Selling the Church: The English Parish in Law, Commerce, and Religion, 1350–1550* [Chapel Hill, 2002], 195–7, 252–3). A study of such engagement in earlier periods would be interesting.

[132] For payments to canons resident, see Edwards, *English Secular Cathedrals*, 39–49.

7

Punishment

Bishops had various means of punishing – that is, disciplining – their administrative subordinates. Some of these were negative versions of the material rewards of serving a bishop. As discussed in previous chapters, bishops gave their followers benefices, granted them pensions, and positioned them to collect bribes, receive presents, and practice extortion. Bishops sometimes gave their administrators various other gifts. Conversely, bishops could try to cut off their clerks' income by sequestrating benefices or even by taking them away entirely. They more often refused to pay the pensions granted to their men. If they dismissed a man from their service, they could hope at least to curb the flow of occasional gifts and bribes to him as well as his capacity to engage in extortion. They could always, of course, refuse to give of their own bounty to their clerks. As I have argued, with the exceptions of ceasing to give gifts and cutting off pensions, for various reasons bishops did not often undertake these measures. What about other penalties?

Material Penalties: Bonds

There was, potentially at least, another material penalty. In theory, bishops could require or request that their clerks grant them bonds to guarantee their good behavior. Were bishops in the habit of using bonds for the surety of anyone? Of clergy? Certainly bishops did sometimes make use of such bonds as disciplinary devices when dealing with the diocesan clergy at large. Such uses centered on incontinence. Bishop Bronscombe, worrying that the newly instituted rector of Yarnscombe had been accused of fornication, received (or perhaps demanded as a condition of his institution?) a bond from the rector that, should he in the future be convicted of fornication, the rector would ipso facto lose the benefice, without resistance or right of appeal.¹ The vicar of Orton gave a bond to the bishop of Carlisle, committing to a payment of 30 marks should the vicar be defamed, and convicted, of incontinence.² Archbishop Romeyn of York similarly received bonds from clergy regarding morals questions. An example was the rector of Pocklington, who had had carnal relations with one of his parishioners and had forcefully oppressed her (a case of rape?) as well. The archbishop sentenced him to pay the lady 20s. Romeyn also, however, ensured that this fiscal penalty would multiply in case of a relapse by receiving the rector's bond for 40 marks should the rector be defamed for incontinence or any other notable crime and fail to purge himself of the charge.³ When bonds from clergy appear in diocesan legislation, they are employed in the same way – and again, in particular, to discourage clerical incontinence.⁴ As Grosseteste set out to visit his diocese, he sent notice that he was to have bonds from all clergy who had undertaken to resign their benefices or suffer some other canonical penalty if they lapsed a second time into the vice of incontinence.⁵

Bishops also used bonds to other ends. The bishop of Norwich, settling a conflict between the archdeacon of Richmond and Battle Abbey, laid down that the parties were to observe the settlement on penalty of £300 to be levied on their benefices.⁶ Archbishop Pecham received a bond for £100 from one of Bishop Cantilupe of Hereford's clerks, guaranteeing that the clerk would undertake various penances that flowed from

---

[1] Reg. Bronscombe, no. 801. The rector notes that the bishop had put him in "ex gratia speciali." See also this bishop's reception of a bond that a rector would obey the church's commands after obtruding himself into another church (ibid., no. 477).

[2] Reg. Halton, I, 178 and ibid. for what appears to be a second bond from this vicar on the same issue.

[3] Reg. Romeyn, no. 249. For other cases of the archbishop using bonds to underwrite clerical good behavior, see ibid., nos. 250, 251, 269, 274. Romeyn also tried to use such bonds to regulate the behavior of laity. Thus John le Cupper de Nottingham, accused by his wife Agatha of multiple adultery – she wanted a legal separation – was reconciled to Agatha, but gave the bishop a bond to pay the bishop £10 and receive beatings on five days should he fail in his marital obligations (ibid., no. 279). In 1314, the bishop of Salisbury availed himself of similar bonds (Reg. Gandavo, 548 [incumbent of a chantry to resign his chantry, without appeal, if again convicted] and see 549–50 for similar bonds putting benefices in jeopardy).

[4] Thus *Councils and Synods*, 175 (apparently aimed at stipendiary priests rather than beneficed clergy), 320 (and see n 1) (against beneficed clergy).

[5] Ibid., 264. The order was striking enough for the Dunstable annalist to take note of it (ibid.).

[6] EEA 21: Norwich, no. 1.

the epic contest between Pecham and Cantilupe.[7] Bishop Giffard of Worcester's register preserves a number of bonds: for example, from a rector to whom the bishop had given a letter testifying to the excommunication of another party – the rector was to pay Giffard 20 marks if the excommunication turned out to be unjustified;[8] and from the rector of Martley to maintain residence.[9]

These instances largely concern attempts to discipline parochial clergy. They show that thirteenth- and early fourteenth-century bishops, like their Reformation successors, were acquainted with the use of bonds to underwrite the good conduct of subordinates.[10] And, strikingly, these bonds were used not only to impose financial penalties for bad behavior but even to make benefices revocable. The quarry of this book, however, is the bishop's own clerks. Did bishops use such bonds to ensure the good reliability and loyalty of their diocesan administrators? There is little evidence that they did, and even that evidence does not concern diocesan administrators as administrators.

In 1296, Bishop Swinfield of Hereford did take a bond from John de Ponte (alias de Bridgenorth), canon of Hereford, in which John promised to desist from impeding the holding of the bishop's consistory court in John's prebendal church of Wellington on penalty of £20, to be paid at the bishop's will.[11] Cathedral canons are often to be counted among a bishop's bureaucrats, as cathedral prebends were one of the chief rewards bishops had to offer. But John should probably not be counted among Swinfield's clerks.[12]

---

[7] R. C. Finucane, "The Cantilupe-Pecham Controversy," in *St. Thomas Cantilupe, Bishop of Hereford: Essays in His Honour*, ed. Meryl Jancey (Leominster, 1982), 120.

[8] Reg. Giffard of Worcester, 122.

[9] A bond on which Giffard moved to collect: Reg. Giffard of Worcester, 515. See also bonds ibid., 169, 246, 272, 287.

[10] Robert E. Rodes Jr. remarks that bonds issued by incumbents promising resignation on some contingency were "more prominent after the Reformation than at this time [i.e., the Middle Ages?, the late Middle Ages?]" (*Ecclesiastical Administration in Medieval England* [Notre Dame, 1977], 118).

[11] Reg. Swinfield, 337–8. Swinfield did end up requiring payment: ibid., 380.

[12] He appears to have received his canonry at Hereford from Bishop Peter de Aquablanca (LN Hereford, 60, 74). Moreover, Thomas Cantilupe, who was to be Swinfield's own patron and Aquablanca's successor, had been at odds with Aquablanca and his following (Nigel Yates, "Bishop Peter de Aquablanca (1240–1268): A Reconsideration," *Journal of Ecclesiastical History* 22 [1971], 303–17; David M. Smith, "Thomas Cantilupe's Register: The Administration of the Diocese of Hereford 1275–1282," in *St. Thomas Cantilupe, Bishop of Hereford: Essays in His Honour*, 91–2).

Three bishops received bonds from their clerks in order to protect themselves; they feared that instituting those clerks to benefices would draw fire on themselves. John de Pontoise, archdeacon of Exeter, promised Bishop Bronscombe of Exeter that he would defend his possession of the church of Tawstock, to which the bishop instituted him on the presentation of the prior and convent of Barnstaple, keeping the bishop immune in the matter, on penalty of 100 marks.[13] Evidently litigation over this church was brewing and is soon manifest in Bronscombe's register.[14] Bishop Giffard of Worcester took a similar precaution regarding Robert de Wiche, his clerk, receiving from Robert a pledge to resign Twyning, to which he had been presented by the abbot and convent of Winchcombe, if a man who had been previously presented made trouble.[15] Giffard also received a bond from his servant Peter de Leicester, who pledged to aid the bishop in any lawsuit sparked by Peter's institution to Budbrooke.[16] Bishop Swinfield, on instituting Adam de Herwyton to Aure, received a bond whereby Adam promised all his goods to indemnify the bishop for the collation in any court should it be challenged. The fact that this was a collation by lapse presumably helps explain the precaution.[17]

Did bishops receive bonds from their men to ensure administrative service or at least to ensure better service after bad conduct? The case that looks most like the target is that of John de Ardern's bond to his lord Bishop Swinfield of Hereford. John had evidently been in charge of Swinfield's prison at Ross, from which two priests had fled. John committed himself, his heirs, and his executors to pay the bishop or his successors £40 should the king prosecute the bishop on account of the escapees.[18] While this bond pertains to administrative failure, its purpose is to keep the bishop from being harmed by a failure that has already occurred; the bond did not attempt to put a servant in peril in order to discourage such failures in the future. Indeed, insofar as the bond was to protect the

---

[13] Reg. Bronscombe, nos. 1112, 1114. Bronscombe had collated the archdeaconry to John (ibid., no. 1033).

[14] Ibid., no. 1162.

[15] Reg. Giffard of Worcester, 171; WRO, Rf.x716.093 BA 2648/1(i) f. 153v (p. 298). Giffard, among other duties, commissioned Robert to assist his *officialis* in 1272 (Reg. Giffard of Worcester, 50) and to hear proofs of wills (ibid., 90).

[16] Ibid., 169; WRO, Rf.x716.093 BA 2648/1(i) f. 152 (p. 295).

[17] Reg. Swinfield, 381–2, and see 533. Besides this collation, in 1307 Adam assisted the bishop in his examination of the election of the prior of Wormsley, and in 1312 he served as this bishop's joint proctor to Parliament (ibid., 439, 468).

[18] Ibid., 85. It is not clear, however, whether John was a clerk.

bishop from harm rather than to ensure future service, this bond is analogous to the bonds offered by episcopal clerks to reassure a bishop that the reception of a benefice would not injure that bishop.

What is striking here is the conjunction of, on the one hand, the potential of bonds as a disciplinary tool from a bishop's point of view and, on the other hand, bishops' failure to exploit that potential. The absence of many bonds from administrators to bishops is not to be explained as an accident of evidence. As the foregoing account suggests, bonds issued to bishops were fair game for inclusion in episcopal registers. Moreover, the law reports, at least to 1327, give no indication of bishops suing to enforce bonds against their clerks. It appears that bishops simply did not avail themselves of this device in dealing with their administrative subordinates. Why not? One explanation may be that bonds were enforced in the Common Law courts. Perhaps bishops were reluctant to subject their relationships with their clerks to secular jurisdiction. This explanation, however, seems unlikely. Such considerations might also apply to bishops receiving bonds from parochial clergy as a disciplinary device, a practice that is certainly more prominent in the registers than reception of bonds from diocesan administrators, albeit one that still appears underused. Bishops may also have made little use of bonds because their society as a whole did not. That would change in the fourteenth century;[19] whether bishops followed that larger trend remains for some future investigation.

The relative absence of bonds offered to bishops by their clerks compared with those offered by the diocesan clergy at large indicates that bishops trusted their clerks more than the clergy at large. Indeed, trust was a necessary component of the relations between thirteenth-century bishops and their men. Bishops, like any superior, likely found it hard to monitor their subordinates; trust could help fill the gap. But trust is always a two-way street. Clerks had to trust their bishop too, or at least they sometimes had to.[20] Consider a simple instance: the many times

---

[19] Robert C. Palmer, *English Law in the Age of the Black Death 1348–1381: A Transformation of Governance and Law* (Chapel Hill, 1993), 59–91.

[20] An example, although rare of its kind, is Peter Caballus. Early in the thirteenth century, he verbally asked the bishop of Worcester, the prior of Little Malvern, and Luke de Cailly to dispose of his worldly goods on his death (EEA 34: Worcester, no. 134). Caballus should be identified as one of that bishop's clerks. The editors of this bishop's *acta* conclude that he was, presumably from Caballus's appearance as a witness to ten of the bishop's *acta* (EEA 34: Worcester, xlv, and see ibid., no. 134 n). Moreover, Caballus's church of Withington appears, toward the end of the century, to have been in the gift of the bishops of Worcester (WRO, Rf.x716.093 BA 2648/1(i), f. 290r [p. 717]); Online Taxatio

a bishop's clerk resigned one benefice in order to receive collation of another. Such moments required that a clerk be confident that that collation would come, that one's bishop would really confer what must have been promised after one resigned one's previous benefice. Such a leap of faith was short, but it was over a deep chasm.[21]

Spiritual Penalties: Excommunication

Bishops also had spiritual penalties at their disposal. Bishops could excommunicate their clerks, depriving them of the sacraments (minor excommunication) or doing both that and severing their social intercourse with the community of the faithful (major excommunication).[22] Although the canon law had constricted spontaneous, almost charismatic, excommunication by the thirteenth century, bishops could still undertake, or order subordinates to undertake, excommunication in its full, impressive ritual: the bells tolling, the candles snuffed out, the denunciation solemn and public.[23] A bishop's clerks would also thus be treated to a spectacle underlining their bishop's authority and the consequences of ignoring it.

Certainly bishops were capable of using excommunication as an instrument, not just to encourage people to repent of their sins but also for more mundane purposes. The Third Lateran Council specifically attempted to prevent bishops from excommunicating those whom they suspected were about to appeal a case from the bishop's jurisdiction.[24] Episcopal clerks in dispute with their bishop, not to mention other litigants, were thus

---

of Pope Nicholas IV, www.hrionline.ac.uk/taxatio/index.html, sub "Withington"). The bishop and his colleagues faithfully looked after Caballus's nieces (EEA 34: Worcester, no. 134).

[21] Some rather later evidence, not concerning benefices in a bishop's gift, illuminates the dilemma from a different angle: formal statements by incumbents that they are not resigning their current benefices until a new one is in hand. In two of these cases the future benefice was contested by another claimant (*John Lydford's Book*, ed. Dorothy M. Owen [London, 1974], nos. 143–4, 246). While the specific legislation these incumbents may have had in mind was the papal constitution *Execrabilis*, the issue of pluralism as understood through most or all of the thirteenth century would have applied.

[22] For the distinction, see Peter D. Clarke, *The Interdict in the Thirteenth Century: A Question of Collective Guilt* (Oxford, 2007), 75–6; Elisabeth Vodola, *Excommunication in the Middle Ages* (Berkeley and Los Angeles, 1986), 36.

[23] E.g., Reg. Pecham, II, 172; Reg. and Rolls Sutton, III, 21, 23, 27, 32, 78, 111, 141, 169, 173, 178, 188, 201; Reg. Bronscombe, nos. 1175, 1429. The procedure was still common enough to find its place in some episcopal letters in a thirteenth-century formulary (EEA 37: Salisbury, Appendix I, nos. 8–11).

[24] Third Lateran Council, Chapter 6: *Decrees of the Ecumenical Councils I: Nicaea I to Lateran V*, ed. Norman Tanner (Washington, DC, 1990), 214.

protected should their bishop try to use excommunication to cut them off from authorities that might restrain him. By the later thirteenth century, the king's judges also disallowed a bishop from refusing to answer plaintiffs in the Common Law courts by claiming the plaintiff was excommunicate – at the bishop's behest. As a plaintiff observed in a suit over the right to present to a benefice, were bishops allowed to make this defense, they could "deforce a hundred patrons from their advowsons."[25]

Like bonds, however, excommunication was an available but seldom used punishment for administrative subordinates.[26] That is not to say that bishops never resorted to excommunication regarding such men. A natural place to look for such excommunications is those (few) instances where bishops attempted to drive their clerks from benefices in their collation (discussed in Chapter 4). Such conflicts were hot. If any confrontation between a bishop and his clerk would lead a bishop to excommunicate his clerk, this would be it. In the course of Bishop Giffard of Worcester's attempt to oust his erstwhile steward and proctor Peter de Leicester from Peter's church of Bishop's Cleeve, Giffard excommunicated Peter – maliciously, according to the *officialis* of the court of Canterbury.[27] Indeed, in another case Giffard used excommunication itself as a pretext for depriving an opponent of his benefice.[28] Archbishop Romeyn excommunicated Robert de Scarborough – whom he was trying to deprive on the grounds of Robert's contumacy – for failing to appear at Romeyn's visitation of the college of Beverley and failing to reply to charges made against Robert on that occasion.[29] But this case is something of an exception that tests the rule, as it flows from an archbishop attempting to revoke collations made by an earlier bishop; Robert was not Romeyn's clerk but the clerk of his predecessors (see Chapter 4). Bishop Pontoise, in his attempt to oust William de Got from the benefice Pontoise had collated to him, stated that he had cited William on multiple occasions to appear in court to answer charges of pluralism, but he made

---

[25] *Year Books of the Reign of Edward I*, ed. A. F. Horwood (RS) (London, 1853–77), I, 204–5 and for the issue see also ibid., III, 268–73.
[26] In 1298, the precentor of Chichester cathedral did engage himself and his successors to pay the cathedral common fund 56s 8d annually, and to accept both excommunication and sequestration by the dean in case of default, without appeal (*The Chartulary of the High Church of Chichester*, ed. W. D. Peckham, Sussex Record Society 46 [Lewes, 1946 for 1942 and 1943], no. 701).
[27] Reg. Giffard of Worcester, 437 (WRO, Rf.x716.093 BA 2648/1(i) f. 373 [p. 737]). This entry in Giffard's register was, however, ultimately canceled.
[28] Reg. Giffard of Worcester, 297.
[29] Reg. Romeyn, no. 1026. For the larger conflict, see Chapter 4 at n 16.

no mention of having excommunicated William, although excommunication was a common penalty for failure to appear in court.[30]

In other cases where a conflict was great enough to lead a bishop to move toward expelling one of his men from a benefice, it is similarly unclear whether the bishop excommunicated the clerk. Bishop Pandulph of Norwich deprived James, his clerk, of his benefice; the source of this information does not reveal whether Pandulph also excommunicated James. But this *actum* concerns primarily the subsequent fate of the benefice and mentions James's deprivation only in passing.[31] One cannot read this absence as positive evidence that James did not suffer excommunication. Bishop Dalderby of Lincoln does not mention excommunication in his notice regarding Thomas de Sutton in the early fourteenth century,[32] but Dalderby's move against Thomas never got far enough for this absence to be significant. Another conflict, this one in which an attempted deprivation of a benefice did not figure, shows a bishop reaching for excommunication in a conflict with his clerk, but in fact his former clerk. John de Fotheringhay, formerly the clerk of audience in the Court of Arches, along with certain other clerks and laity of both sexes, was withholding "protocols, *acta*, and registers" belonging to the court. There is no evidence that Archbishop Winchelsey attempted to expel John from his rectory of Stone. But Winchelsey did order that John return what he was withholding, on pain of excommunication.[33] Had John simply walked away from his duties, including the documents, he might well have received no such threat.

This survey disappoints the historian in search of bishops active in excommunicating their own clerks. Looking further is no help. For example, Bishop Sutton certainly regarded excommunication as a usable tool in his armory of discipline; more than a hundred references to

---

[30] For Pontoise and William de Got, see Chapter 4 at nn 82–4. On excommunication to get people to court, see F. Donald Logan, *Excommunication and the Secular Arm in Medieval England* (Toronto, 1968), 46; Vodola, *Excommunication in the Middle Ages*, 36–7, Brian L. Woodcock, *Medieval Ecclesiastical Courts of the Diocese of Canterbury* (Oxford, 1952), 93–5.

[31] EEA 21: Norwich, no. 8. See also Chapter 4 at nn 94–5.

[32] LAO, Episcopal Register III, f. 321v. See also Chapter 4 at nn 85–90.

[33] Reg. Winchelsey, 1242: "prothocolla, acta et registra." John had also earlier been one of Winchelsey's examiners at ordinations and had himself been ordained deacon on the archbishop's title (ibid., 928, 942, 951). Earlier the archbishop had tried to procure for him, "dilecto clerico nostro," a benefice from Ramsey Abbey, only to be rebuffed (ibid., 805). For John's rectory of Stone, in the presentation of St. Augustine's, Canterbury, and likely received at Winchelsey's instigation, see ibid., 501, 657.

excommunications made or threatened by Sutton pour forth from his memoranda register for the years 1290–9.[34] A variety of issues triggered these instances, from a failure to return a lost letter to assault on a clerk.[35] Most of these instances do not name the malefactors but were aimed at a person or persons unknown who had acted wrongly, such as the excommunications levied at the request of laypeople who wanted action against whoever had taken their animals.[36]

But although Sutton's register and requests to the king show the bishop often unleashing excommunicates and asking the secular arm to bring the obdurate to heel, Sutton's clerks are rarely named as excommunicates.[37] His clerks also appear almost never to have been caught in the net of excommunications released against anonymous malefactors. An exception is John de Clipston, Sutton's notary and a member of his household. In 1299, Sutton ordered that an inquiry be made into an accusation of theft levied by a rector, and that, if the accusation proved true, the culprits be excommunicated. The result of the investigation is unrecorded, but a note by the order to investigate states that John "appealed" in person on his own behalf ("facta fuit appellatio per J. de Clipston' pro se"), suggesting that the investigation had turned up something, and that John was implicated.[38] Here it is worth noting that, whether John was an innocent party or not,[39] Sutton had not apparently intended to excommunicate

---

[34] Rolls and Reg. Sutton, III, 6–9, 11, 21–3, 26, 32, 36–7, 59–60, 77, 82 (aimed against whom is unclear because of damage to the ms), 85, 98, 101–2, 105, 107, 120, 125, 125–6, 127, 132–3, 137, 140–1, 149–50, 151, 154, 168–9, 172–5, 177–8, 188–90, 200–201, IV, 3–4, 8–9, 12–17, 21–2, 25, 33, 35–7, 40–1, 47, 75, 78–9, 88, 95, 99, 101, 110–12, 120–1, 128, 144, 148–49, 154–5, 158, 163, 165, 167, 172, 174, 178, 182–83, 187–8, V, 1–2, 4, 9, 15, 17, 19, 21–2, 24, 27, 30–2, 37, 44, 45, 47–50, 55, 58–63, 71, 81–2, 89–92, 94, 102–5, 111–14, 116–17, 126–8, 135, 137, 140–3, 146–9, 154, 156, 159–60, 163, 166–67, 175, 179–80, 183, 190, 197–8, 200, 204, 209, 216–17, VI, 1, 9, 23, 24–8, 33–5, 39, 49, 76, 78, 81–3, 85–6, 88, 90–1, 96, 98–9, 109–10, 113–114, 119–120, 124–7, 129–30, 132–33, 138–39, 145, 148–9, 158, 163–4, 169–71, 176, 180, 183–4, 189–92, 198–203.

[35] Ibid., IV, 3, V, 191–92.

[36] Discussed by Rosalind Hill (ibid., III, xlvii).

[37] For his significations to the Crown for caption of excommunicates, see TNA, C 85/100, 101.

[38] Rolls and Reg. Sutton, VI, 163–4 and 164 n 1. Sutton made John a notary public on papal authority in 1293 (ibid., IV, 130–1 and see 110). John drew up documents for the bishop in 1295, 1296, 1297, and 1299 (ibid., V, 110, VI, 13, 166, VIII, 218). He examined candidates for ordination on Sutton's behalf in 1297 and 1299 (ibid., VII, 99, 115, 119).

[39] Sutton's editor thinks he was probably not a malefactor here (ibid., VI, 164 n 1), but the ground for her conclusion seems to have been simply John's association with the bishop.

him specifically, for he was indeed snared in an excommunication aimed at unnamed persons. William de Rothwell, official of the archdeacon of Bedford, was a different matter. Admittedly, he was not, strictly speaking, Sutton's clerk, but the archdeacon's. Sutton excommunicated all those who had seized the house and borne away the goods of the rector of Oakley on the false story that he was dead. The bishop at the same time noted that William was said to be one of the principal authors of this presumption. He ordered that William be peremptorily cited to appear before him.[40] Another possible exception is Master Henry Sampson the younger. He appears in Sutton's service in 1298.[41] Was he in Sutton's service earlier, in 1287 (before Sutton's memoranda register commences), when the bishop asked for the king's help in bringing in an obdurate excommunicate? The man in question was Master Henry Sampson (no mention of the younger or the elder).[42] One cannot know, as one cannot be sure that this is the same Sampson, although the title *magister* and his presence in the same diocese suggests that he is. In any case, excommunication cannot be said to be a tool by which Sutton commonly disciplined his own men.

Nor does this appear to have been the case with other bishops. To judge from his register and his appeals to the king for help against stubborn excommunicates, Bishop Bronscombe of Exeter, for example, excommunicated various people, clerical and lay.[43] But none of his own clerks. Bishop Swinfield of Hereford's thirty-five-year pontificate does not turn up much more – two possible, but dubious, cases – although he sent some ninety-eight letters to the king requesting help against obdurate excommunicates.[44] It is possible that the Richard de Persouere de Ludlow whom the bishop excommunicated in 1306 is the same man as the Richard de Ludlow to whom the bishop collated a prebend in Westbury in 1308, but

---

[40] Ibid., V, 21–2.
[41] In 1298 Sutton commissioned him jointly to grant probate (ibid., VI, 111). For his status as "junior," see ibid., VIII, 68–9.
[42] TNA, C 85/100/66, 71. Unfortunately, his manifest offenses are, as often in such caption requests, unspecified. Sutton issued 147 significations of excommunication to the king (TNA, C 85/100, 101).
[43] From his register, Reg. Bronscombe, no. 417, and nos. 78, 82, 129–30, 266, 488, 733, 901, 1175–7, 1229, 1239, 1342 and for more than twice this number of caption requests, TNA, C 85/71.
[44] TNA, C 85/87, 88, 89. The bishop's register largely records excommunications against unknown miscreants, later identifiable from the record of their absolution. In any case, none of those identifiable in the register as excommunicates was among the bishop's known clerks (Reg. Swinfield, 377–8, 406–8, 510–13).

I have found no evidence besides what may be a coincidence of names to confirm the identification.[45] Master Stephen de Montgomery, rector of Dunre, appears to have been one of the bishop's clerks in 1288.[46] In 1316, the bishop requested the help of the secular arm against a Stephen de Montgomery. I suspect, however, that this Stephen de Montgomery is not Swinfield's clerk, but a relative. Although this obdurate excommunicate's crime is not stated, he is referred to as the executor of a rector of Dunre. Unfortunately, the name of the deceased rector is lost to a hole in the manuscript, but he was probably, like Swinfield's clerk, a Master of Arts, for Swinfield's letter has "ma[gister?]" before the hole.[47] The bishop may have in fact been pursuing a badly behaved executor, not designated as a Master, of his clerk, now deceased. It should be noted that this reluctance to employ excommunication did not clearly extend to the clerks of other bishops. Archbishop Pecham excommunicated Robert de Wyse, clerk of Bishop Cantilupe of Hereford, as well as Cantilupe's other adherents.[48] To the north, Archbishop Romeyn of York excommunicated his suffragan's *officialis* and then that bishop's other men when they imprisoned two of his clerks.[49]

Humiliation

Discipline in the Middle Ages often included a measure of public humiliation.[50] The damage to reputation was part of the point. Bishops, among other authorities, were ready and willing to inflict such punishments. This measure, however, was more likely to be used to defend episcopal clerks than to be applied to them. When John de Normanby assaulted one of Bishop Sutton of Lincoln's clerks, he failed to shed blood or produce any troublesome wound. His penance for the attack, however, was a public beating on the porch of the church of St. John in Newport.[51] The

---

[45] For the excommunication: TNA, C 85/89/19. For the collation: Reg. Swinfield, 538.
[46] He witnessed two of the bishop's acts in different places in 1288, and carried letters for the bishop in that year (ibid., 162, 182, 196, and see 19).
[47] TNA, C 85/89/34.
[48] R. C. Finucane, "The Cantilupe-Pecham Controversy," 105–9, 113.
[49] Robert Brentano, *York Metropolitan Jurisdiction and Papal Judges Delegate (1279–1296)* (Berkeley and Los Angeles, 1959), 166, 168.
[50] Dave Postles, "Penance and the Market Place: A Reformation Dialogue with the Medieval Church (*c.* 1250–*c.* 1600)," *Journal of Ecclesiastical History* 54 (2003), 443–7, and for parishes: 467–8; James Maesschaele, "The Public Space of the Marketplace in Medieval England," *Speculum* 77 (2002), 383–421.
[51] Rolls and Reg. Sutton, III, 20–1. John's victim was Master Benedict de Ferriby. For Benedict's standing as Sutton's clerk, see Chapter 6, n 25.

audience for such punishments could be finely calibrated, as when the man who struck the servant of Bishop Sutton's clerk, Master Nicholas de Appletree, was sentenced to do his penance before the household of the archdeacon of Northampton. Perhaps the game of dice that had produced the violence had taken place there.[52] And Sutton was capable of mitigating the humiliation of public penance in order to preserve the public standing of a knight who needed it.[53] Unfortunately, all of the many penances, public and private, that litter Sutton's register are penances following excommunication. Because Sutton did not excommunicate his own clerks, one cannot know whether he inflicted public humiliation on them short of excommunication. If he did, such occasions do not appear in his register.

But bishops appear rarely to have imposed public humiliation on their clerks. Michael de Leigh, the clerk of the deceased bishop of Exeter who had forged letters in that bishop's name, did penance for his crime, but the nature of that penance is unspecified.[54] Two other culprits confessed in chapter at Buckfast. One performed an unspecified penance. The other did undergo a further public action in relation to the case. This, however, was compurgation (presumably regarding those parts of the charges that he denied), a proclamation of innocence rather than guilt.[55] Indeed, episcopal clerks may have been largely protected from public penance because they were clerks rather than because of their special relationship with their bishop. In England, as in France, public penance was more for the laity than the clergy.[56]

Prison

Despite some modern claims, imprisonment was a punishment, not simply a way of detaining people, in the Middle Ages. That held for ecclesiastical

---

[52] Rolls and Reg. Sutton, III, 27. Sutton commissioned Nicholas jointly to settle a dispute in 1294 (ibid., V, 10) and to visit a hospital in 1297 (ibid., VI, 44). In 1298, Nicholas received ad hoc commissions to grant probate and absolution as well as a commission to administer the vacant archdeaconry of Buckingham (ibid., VI, 115, 143, 148 and see 161). Sutton commissioned him to grant probate in 1299 (ibid., VI, 186). Nicholas had other connections with the archdeacon, serving as his proctor in 1286–7 and receiving Warsop on the archdeacon's presentation (Reg. Romeyn, I, 257–8 and n; Reg. Wickwane, 75).

[53] Rosalind Hill, "Public Penance and the Problems of a Thirteenth-Century Bishop," *History* 36 (1951), 220–4.

[54] Reg. Bronscombe, no. 103. On the forgeries, see Chapter 9 at nn 1–2.

[55] Ibid., no. 83.

[56] Mary C. Mansfield, *The Humiliation of Sinners: Public Penance in Thirteenth-Century France* (Ithaca, 1995), 127.

authorities.⁵⁷ Bishops could certainly have tried to imprison unruly subordinates. Bishops were expected to keep prisons; the council of Lambeth of 1261 laid down that every bishop was to keep one or two prisons in his diocese.⁵⁸ These prisons were meant to house clergy. The king's courts turned over to their diocesan men accused of crimes who successfully claimed benefit of clergy. Bishops, in turn, did not always free such men.⁵⁹ And bishops felt able to imprison clergy for other offenses. The bishop of Durham imprisoned two of the archbishop of York's clerks in the course of the conflict between them.⁶⁰ For some unexplained rebellion and disobedience, the bishop of Exeter imprisoned a canon of Bodmin, leading the archdeacon and the prior of his house to plead for his release.⁶¹ Robert Brentano remarks on other cases.⁶² But I have found no signs of bishops imprisoning their own clerks, although it must be said that episcopal prisons generally lie in shadow for the thirteenth-century English Church.

Oaths

A bond was a kind of tripwire: fail to do or not do as the bond promised, and one became vulnerable to whatever penalty the bond indicated. In theory, the oath of obedience to a bishop could function as another such tripwire. Certainly other lords employed oaths in order to render their servants accountable, as argued by Robert F. Berkhofer regarding twelfth-century abbots in northern France and Flanders.⁶³

It is reasonable to think that bishops received oaths of obedience from their clerks; subordinates routinely swore obedience and loyalty

---

[57] Richard W. Ireland, "Theory and Practice in the Medieval English Prison," *American Journal of Legal History* 31 (1987), 63–4; Ralph B. Pugh, *Imprisonment in Medieval England* (Cambridge, 1968), 48 for the possibility of clerks serving for life.

[58] *Councils and Synods*, 684. References to bishops' prisons are plentiful in the thirteenth century (Leona C. Gabel, *Benefit of Clergy in the Later Middle Ages* [reprint with a new introduction] [New York, 1969], 111–12). For the suggestion that bishops' prisons became more common in the thirteenth century, see Pugh, *Imprisonment in Medieval England*, 135.

[59] Gabel, *Benefit of Clergy*, 109–110, and see C. R. Cheney, "The Punishment of Felonous Clerks," *English Historical Review* 51 (1936), 232.

[60] Reg. Romeyn, xxvi–xxvii, 100–101, and Brentano, *York Metropolitan Jurisdiction*, 165–68.

[61] Reg. Giffard of Worcester, 293. Unfortunately, the bishop of Exeter's own register appears to shed no light on this situation (Reg. Quivil).

[62] Brentano, *York Metropolitan Jurisdiction*, 169.

[63] *Day of Reckoning: Power and Accountability in Medieval France* (Philadelphia, 2004), 130–44.

to superiors. The forms of oaths of various papal functionaries survive, largely, however, in fourteenth-century form.⁶⁴ Like their predecessors, thirteenth-century archbishops of Canterbury received professions of obedience from their suffragans.⁶⁵ Such professions may have been an inheritance from a resurgent practice of the eleventh century, but the concern was still a live one in the thirteenth. After one bishop of Exeter managed to exploit circumstance to make a rather loosely worded profession, his successor was required to swear an especially carefully composed one.⁶⁶ Newly instituted clergy swore obedience to the instituting bishop.⁶⁷ Given that a bishop's clerks usually received benefices from their bishop, most would thus have also sworn obedience to him in that context if no other. And certainly a bishop might impose an oath on his subordinates for particular purposes as a matter of policy, as when Bishop Jocelin of Bath and Wells laid down that archdeacons would hold vacant churches in the gift of the dean and chapter of Wells after they swore to deliver two-thirds of the revenue to the dean and chapter, keeping the remainder.⁶⁸ Especially pertinent to this discussion, lords probably usually received their counselors' oaths as well as those of their local estate managers.⁶⁹ There is no reason to think that English bishops behaved any differently from other lords in this respect, although the earliest such instances Irene Churchill found at Canterbury date to the later thirteenth century, in the time of Archbishop Pecham.⁷⁰ Sworn councils were outgrowths of the household, and council and *familia* tended to be linked. Pecham referred on one occasion to those "qui de nostro consilio et familia iurati existunt."⁷¹ The fourteenth-century bishops of Worcester have been shown to have received an oath of fidelity from the clerks who gave them "domestic service," and Roy Martin Haines points to an early example of such an oath taken in 1300 by one of the bishop's notaries.⁷²

---

⁶⁴ *Die Päpstlichen Kanzleiordnungen von 1200–1500*, ed. Michael Tangl (Innsbruck, 1894), 33–50.
⁶⁵ See in particular *Canterbury Professions*, ed. Michael Richter, Canterbury and York Society 67 (Torquay, 1973).
⁶⁶ EEA XII: Exeter, no. 316 n.
⁶⁷ Rodes, *Ecclesiastical Administration in Medieval England*, 135.
⁶⁸ *Calendar of the Manuscripts of the Dean and Chapter of Wells*, I, 67.
⁶⁹ Noel Denholm-Young, *Seignorial Administration in England* (reprint, New York, 1964), 26, 30, 71, 147.
⁷⁰ Irene Churchill, *Canterbury Administration* (London, 1933), I, 11. For the text of such an oath in the early fourteenth century, see ibid., 13–14.
⁷¹ Reg. Pecham, II, 160.
⁷² R. M. Haines, *The Administration of the Diocese of Worcester in the First Half of the Fourteenth Century* (London, 1965), 90 and n 1.

It is not clear, however, how much bishops relied on such oaths, as opposed to administering them, although the canon law held oaths to be judicially enforceable, especially from the time of Innocent III on.[73] Oddly, no oaths of any description are invoked in the disputes between bishops and the recipients of their bounty discussed in Chapter 4. This absence – from what are admittedly very few cases – is especially striking given that the canon law did allow deprivation of disloyal clerks who violated their oaths of fidelity to their bishop (see Chapter 4). Certainly bishops were capable of raising the matter of oaths when subordinates proved difficult. In 1302, Bishop Ghent of Salisbury complained that Richard de Sottwell, archdeacon of Wiltshire, had failed to order a patron to present to a vacant church and report back, as though he had forgotten his oath.[74] When Winchelsey demanded that John de Fotheringhay, his former clerk of audience of the Court of Arches, return documents in his care, the archbishop invoked John's oath.[75] And no difficulty need have arisen to prompt a bishop to recall such an oath; Bishop Quivil of Exeter noted the oath his lawyer, John de la Wade, had taken to him when he granted John a pension of 10 marks and two robes a year, with hope of a prebendal benefice.[76]

Is there any way to confirm this apparent lack of reliance on oaths? I think there is. An important point of Berkhofer's case regarding the significance of oaths received by his French abbots is not simply that they had their administrative subordinates make such oaths, but that abbots took care to record that fact.[77] Indeed, in a different connection, Adam Davis has described bishops' registers as tools of accountability, recording clerical commitments for a bishop's later use.[78] How concerned were England's thirteenth-century bishops to do the same when it came to oaths?

A bishop's register is a good place to find out. To begin with, there are institutions to benefices. On receiving a benefice, clergy took an oath

---

[73] For the canonists, see Jan Hallebeek, "Actio ex Iuramento: The Legal Enforcement of Oaths," *Ius Commune: Veröffentlichungen des Max-Planck-Instituts für europäische Rechtsgeschichte, Frankfurt am Main* 17 (1990), 80–4, 89.
[74] Reg. Gandavo, I, 81. Richard was a holdover in the dioceses of Bishop Ghent's predecessor, although it is possible that he held the archdeaconry by collation from Bishop Ghent (LN Salisbury, 37).
[75] Reg. Winchelsey, 1242.
[76] Reg. Quivil, 381.
[77] Berkhofer, *Day of Reckoning*, 133, 139, 144.
[78] Adam J. Davis, *The Holy Bureaucrat: Eudes Rigaud and Religious Reform in Thirteenth-Century Normandy* (Ithaca, 2006), 4.

of canonical obedience to the bishop. When instituted, clerks also might have to swear other oaths: perhaps to be resident or to progress to higher orders within a year. What picture do bishops' registers give of bishops' interest in *recording* these oaths? And what oaths did they take care to record?

Before answering those questions, however, a point about the form of the documents. An episcopal register might record an institution to a benefice in one of two ways. The register might include a memorandum of an institution, that is, an account written in the third person, for internal use by the bishop's administration. Or the register might record an institution by rehearsing a copy of a letter of institution: a public document issued to the instituted clerk in which the bishop in his own voice announced that he had instituted the clerk to such and such benefice on so and so's presentation. Such letters of institution were issued to protect clerks or their patrons, as evidence of title to the benefice and of exercise of the advowson. But including a copy of the letter of institution in a bishop's register evidently served at times as an alternative to writing up a memorandum in the register.[79] How does this pertain to the matter of whether an oath was recorded? Memoranda sometimes mention an oath or oaths taken by the clerk receiving the benefice (more on this later in the chapter). The form of a letter of institution, however, evidently precluded mention of an oath – or so I conclude from the fact that I have not come across a letter of institution that mentions an oath. This failure makes sense, as such letters served the interests of incumbents (documenting title) and patron (documenting seisin of the advowson). Thus, where an institution to a benefice is recorded in a register by copying a letter of institution rather than by inserting a memorandum, it may be dangerous to conclude that the failure to mention an oath betrays a lack of concern regarding the oath; that failure could simply reflect the form of the record the bishop or his registrar chose. True, one might argue that the very fact the bishop or scribe chose to rehearse the letter rather than write a memorandum suggests a lack of interest in recording oaths. Moreover, bishops' clerks sometimes composed a sort of composite entry: a rehearsal of a letter of institution followed by a note concerning related matters, such as some enregistered letters of institution issued by Bishop Cantilupe of Hereford followed by notes as to who was ordered to induct, in one case also noting that the bishop collated by lapse.[80] Presumably a record of oaths

---

[79] Rehearsing the letter of institution could be the routine method (Reg. Langton, xiv).
[80] Reg. Cantilupe, 81–2. See also Reg. Langton, xiv.

could have been included in such entries had bishop or scribe wished to do so (although I have not found such notices). But the safest course is to consider only "pure" memoranda of institutions, in order to prevent an overstatement of any case that registers betray a lack of interest in oaths of obedience at the time of institution or, for that matter, induction.

Here I survey several registers with this issue in mind. In different ways, they suggest that recording oaths of obedience sworn when their clerks received benefices was not a high priority for bishops. Certainly bishops were capable of recording an oath following a crisis. Bishop Giffard of Worcester collated the archdeaconry of Gloucester to Walter Burdon, only to be later opposed by Burdon. On the occasion of Burdon's surrender, Giffard's register notes Burdon's (renewed) oath of obedience to his bishop.[81] At Hereford, Bishop Swinfield had to deal with his proctor, Richard de Puddlestone, who had returned from the curia with a papal provision to a prebend in Swinfield's gift, a provision to his own benefit – and not in accord with his master's wishes. Swinfield was able to secure Richard's resignation of the benefice, but took care also to receive, and record, a renewed oath of good faith and fidelity.[82]

Routine, however, was another matter. Consider, for example, Archbishop Pecham's register. Oaths were certainly fodder for the register, which includes a number of oaths of homage sworn to the bishop for tenancies held of him.[83] Setting aside collations to benefices for the moment, the register contains memoranda of 186 institutions to benefices;[84] 177 of these memoranda contain no mention of any oath of any kind. But this is not a case of memoranda in so cast-iron a form that information about oaths simply could not be included. In nine instances the memorandum records that the clerk swore to be resident.[85] And, most pertinent to the issue of concern here, in two further instances a memorandum records not only an oath to reside, but the fact that the clerk swore obedience.[86] Pecham's institutions show that oaths of obedience might be recorded, but generally were not.

Now for Pecham's memoranda of collations. These are the most pertinent to the issue here, because these are the entries in which the bishop himself most likely conferred benefices on his own clerks. Pecham's

[81] Reg. Giffard of Worcester, lxiv, 461, 513, 526.
[82] Reg. Swinfield, 256.
[83] Reg. Pecham, I, 2–22.
[84] Ibid., 45–55, 67–88, 90–6, 98, 102–3, 108, 110, 119–23, 125, 128–9, 133–9.
[85] Ibid., 48–50, 67, 70, 90, 121, 127. Strikingly, 67 of the institutions that record no oath to reside were to vicarages, where the canons specifically required such an oath (*Councils and Synods*, 249, 758).
[86] Reg. Pecham, I, 48, 67.

register contains ninety-four memoranda of collations to benefices.[87] In no case were his scribes moved to record an oath of obedience, or oaths of any other kind, for that matter.

From the Welsh border, the register of Pecham's nemesis, Thomas Cantilupe of Hereford, produces analogous, although more muted, results. Aside from notices of collations, his register yields forty-six memoranda of institutions to benefices.[88] (Institutions signified by the text of a letter of institution, or even of induction, are very common in Cantilupe's register.) Mentioning an oath to reside was a live option; one of these notices includes such an oath – but only one.[89] None of these memoranda mentions the oath of canonical obedience. Cantilupe's clerks did, however, record the oath of obedience to the bishop taken by the abbot-elect of Flaxley on his installation. Because the entry preserves the text of the oath, rather than the mere fact that the abbot swore it, the scribes may have included this item in order to have on hand in the future a formulaic model for abbatial oaths to their bishop.[90] Cantilupe's register also includes twenty-two memoranda of collations. Like this category of entry in Pecham's register, none includes a notice of an oath by the recipient of any sort. Yet, these scribes could include oaths in such memoranda, if they were important enough. Thus, the notice of a rather surreptitious collation of a cathedral prebend mentions that the men who witnessed the installation swore not to reveal publicly that they had received the bishop's command to install![91]

The rolls and register of the bishops of Lincoln stand in contrast to those of both Canterbury and Hereford. Yet, even the Lincoln material ultimately suggests that oaths of obedience were not high on the list of tools for disciplining *clerici episcopi*. From the start, memoranda of institutions in general at Lincoln routinely recorded oaths of obedience.[92] The practice continued to the end of the thirteenth century at least.[93] An

---

[87] Ibid., 44–5, 50, 52, 54–5, 66–70, 72, 74–9, 81–3, 85–7, 89, 91, 93, 102–5, 110, 113–14, 116, 118, 120, 122, 125–9, 131–7, 139.

[88] Reg. Cantilupe, 7, 116, 119–23, 138, 156, 192, 202–3, 227, 235, 240, 243, 250–1, 291–2.

[89] Ibid., 7.

[90] Ibid., 157.

[91] Ibid., 63. This entry was, however, later canceled (ibid., n 1).

[92] Rot. Wells, I, x.

[93] Bishop Sutton's editor includes the notice of the oath in her sample of typical entries when she discusses her principles for calendaring such entries (Rolls and Reg. Sutton, I, ix–x). A survey of the memoranda of institutions in the archdeaconry of Stow in Sutton's register confirms that indeed these oaths were systematically recorded; not one memorandum of institution lacks such a notice (LAO, Episcopal Register I, fos. 246r–254r).

unusual feature of the Lincoln rolls, however, is that collations to prebends, cathedral dignities, and archdeaconries were either not recorded, or, more likely, were recorded separately from other kinds of benefices in rolls that have been lost.[94] In 1290, however, Bishop Sutton replaced the rolls with a register. He thus earned the gratitude of historians, for from that point are preserved various memoranda of the kind that doubtless had been recorded on rolls now perished, including collations to prebends, cathedral dignities, and archdeaconries. Those collations are of particular interest here because such benefices were most likely to go to episcopal clerks; the record reads like a *Who's Who* of the upper reaches of Lincoln's diocesan administration in the late thirteenth century. The clerks who composed these memoranda were not, however, moved to record the oaths of obedience to the bishops taken by these men when they received their benefices,[95] in striking contrast with ordinary institutions. There are, however, two exceptions to this absence, exceptions that revealingly test the rule. Like other bishops, Sutton disliked papal provisions, writing to the pope himself that their recipients cared only for the income, farming their benefices.[96] But the pope was the pope, so the bishop had to accept the provision of the alien Boniface de Saluzzo as archdeacon of Buckingham.[97] Sutton, however, also had entered into the collation section of his register a notice that the new archdeacon swore canonical obedience, indeed listing the witnesses present for the event.[98] Sutton acted similarly regarding another import, William de Estiniaco, whom the pope provided to the archdeaconry of Lincoln and the prebend of Corringham.[99] A notice (again, with witnesses) that William had sworn obedience as archdeacon appears in the memoranda section of Sutton's register rather than among the collations.[100] Hence, when Sutton's suspicions were heightened, he recorded the fact that the recipients of collations, forced collations, had sworn him obedience. This evidence throws

---

[94] After all, some of the rolls of ordinary institutions in certain archdeaconries have also been lost; Sutton's rolls for the archdeaconries of Huntingdon and Oxford have perished (David M. Smith, *Guide to Bishops' Registers of England and Wales: A Survey from the Middle Ages to the Abolition of Episcopacy in 1646* [London, 1981], 109).

[95] LAO, Episcopal Register I, fos. 353r–62v, calendared in Rolls and Reg. Sutton, VIII, 203–21.

[96] Rolls and Reg. Sutton, VI, 63.

[97] Ibid., VIII, 221.

[98] Ibid., VIII, 222.

[99] Ibid., VIII, 204.

[100] Ibid., IV, 36. This was not done to preserve the oath's form, as the entry does not rehearse the oath itself (LAO, Episcopal Register I, f. 61). That the oath was not unusual is signaled by its description as being "in forma consueta" (ibid.).

into relief the willingness not to record such oaths taken by other recipients of his bounty.[101]

Another situation in which one might expect bishops' clerks to have sworn oaths to their bishops was when they received administrative office or a general commission from their bishop. Do the registers record such oaths, and if they do not, how significant is that failure? As with institutions and collations to benefices, it is best to distinguish rehearsals of letters of appointment from memoranda recording an appointment. Letters of appointment may have been copied into the register in order to record both the fact of the appointment and the exact powers delegated by the bishop to the recipient, as well as to provide a model for future letters. But such letters were themselves intended to be shown to third parties, a way for the recipient to prove that he indeed had the office or the authority from the bishop that he claimed to have. Given that purpose, letters of appointment were unlikely to mention an oath taken by the recipient to the bishop and, indeed, they did not.

Recording such appointments by enregistering the letters of appointment seems to have been the most common practice. Cantilupe's register generally records appointments of proctors by reproducing their letters of appointment, which, composed primarily as letters of credence, naturally did not mention any oath taken to the bishop.[102] In one case, however, the register marks such an appointment with a memorandum, but nonetheless still fails to mention an oath.[103] In another instance, the register presents a letter in which the bishop binds himself to pay his attorneys in King's Bench a pension "for their homage and service,"[104] implying an oath, but this seems aimed more at describing what the bishop got for his money than at raising the issue of an oath itself. Cantilupe's letters appointing vicars general[105] and his *officialis*[106] mention no oaths. More

---

[101] Although somewhat late for this study, Bishop Ghent of Salisbury's register sheds an interesting light on the preservation of oaths of obedience. On ascending to the see in 1315, the bishop commissioned men to receive on his behalf oaths of canonical obedience owed to him by any of his new subjects (Reg. Gandavo, II, 24). By contrast, however, his register can be said to record oaths of obedience by clergy when instituted to benefices only occasionally (ibid., I, 22, 59, 165-5, 261, 285-6, 356, 361, 391). For a couple of examples of oaths taken by new heads of religious houses, see ibid., I, 419, 427. The bishop did, however, take care to reserve oaths of obedience to himself as well as induction in cases of exchanges of benefices (ibid., I, 339, 391).
[102] Reg. Cantilupe, 12, 106-7, 210, 215, 222, 243.
[103] Ibid., 13-14.
[104] Ibid., 22.
[105] Ibid., 221-2.
[106] Ibid., 254-5.

remarkably, a memorandum recording the appointment of a bailiff mentions the bailiff's *fideiussores*, but not the bailiff's own oath.[107]

The register of Cantilupe's opponent, Archbishop Pecham, does not preserve the appointments of his *officiales* for the archdiocese. But his register does record a number of appointments of *officiales* in other sees during their vacancies. The form could certainly allow for references to an oath to the archbishop. Pecham referred to the oath taken by the archdeacon of Leicester when appointing the archdeacon as the *officialis* of Lincoln *sede vacante*, and did so also when appointing an *officialis* to the vacant see of London.[108] And Pecham certainly concerned himself enough about these oaths to require the man nominated to be the *officialis* of the vacant see of Salisbury to take the oath before assuming the office.[109] Yet letters appointing *officiales sede vacante* to Winchester, Hereford, and Rochester make no allusions to oaths.[110] A memorandum recording the appointment of the *officialis sede vacante* of Llandaff does not mention an oath to the archbishop, but simply states that the *officialis* has letters of appointment in common form.[111] Pecham's letter appointing a general commissary similarly fails to refer to an oath.[112] The archbishop's memoranda recording the appointments of his stewards ignore the oaths those men surely took.[113] By contrast, Pecham's memoranda regarding his tenants regularly record that they swore homage and fealty.[114]

The Lincoln registers are more revealing in the matter of oaths. Bishop Sutton recorded the appointment of penitentiaries,[115] proctors,[116] an

---

[107] Ibid., 20–1.
[108] Reg. Pecham, I, 98–9; Pecham, *Epistolae*, I, 97.
[109] Reg. Pecham, II, 225. It is not clear whether Pecham's letter of two years later (Pecham, *Epistolae*, II, 932–3) refers to this same man or not.
[110] Reg. Pecham, II, 43, 60, 90, and see 70.
[111] Ibid., 6–7.
[112] Churchill, *Canterbury Administration*, II, 13.
[113] Reg. Pecham, I, 1–4, 8, 11.
[114] Ibid., 2, 4, 7–22: some 71 tenancies in all.
[115] Rolls and Reg. Sutton, IV, 45–6, 159, 174–5, V 119 (LAO, Episcopal Register I, fos. 92r, 96v, 190r).
[116] Rolls and Reg. Sutton, III, 42, 48–9, 78–80, IV, 122, V, 201, VI, 111, 188 (LAO, Episcopal Register I, fos. 83v, 154r, 188v [recte ed.], 205r). I note here only general proctorial appointments, to represent the bishop before a certain court or all courts rather than an appointment for a specific suit or piece of business only; presumably only the former appointments would have included an oath, whereas the ad hoc ones were less likely to do so.

officialis,[117] an official of a vacant archdeaconry,[118] and sequestrators[119] by rehearsing their letters of appointment. Only in a few cases does Sutton's register record such appointments with a memorandum: the appointments of a bailiff,[120] a custodian of a vacant archdeaconry,[121] and a sequestrator.[122] In none of these cases did Sutton or his scribes find it necessary to record the recipient's swearing an oath.

Again, an exception tests the rule. Sutton's memoranda record that Benedict de Hallam (alias de Suwell) swore obedience to Sutton as the official of William de Estiniaco, archdeacon of Lincoln, the only such notice regarding an archdeacon's official in Sutton's register.[123] (The entry was to have included a list of witnesses too, but these were never listed.)[124] Indeed, it may be that Sutton's reservations about this alien archdeacon account for a certain reservation about the archdeacon's official too. But it is also the case that troubles blossomed between Sutton's successor Dalderby on the one hand, and archdeacons and their officials on the other.[125] And so Dalderby systematically recorded the oaths sworn him by archdeacons' officials on taking office, noting witnesses.[126] Here again, bishops recorded oaths of obedience when they distrusted the men who made them. The fact that such oaths in general were not recorded suggests a fairly easygoing attitude. Bishops were presumably not willing to forgo receiving oaths. But, unless there was trouble, oaths do not seem

---

[117] Rolls and Reg. Sutton, V, 41 (LAO, Episcopal Register I, f. 112r).
[118] Rolls and Reg. Sutton, V, 92 (LAO, Episcopal Register I, f. 125v).
[119] Rolls and Reg. Sutton, III, 3, V, 71 (LAO, Episcopal Register I, fos. 1v, 120v). Again, these are appointments of men to the office of sequestrator, where an oath might be expected, rather than the numerous ad hoc commissions to sequestrate that litter Sutton's memoranda register.
[120] Rolls and Reg. Sutton, VI, 161.
[121] Ibid., V, 55 (LAO, Episcopal Register I, f. 155v).
[122] Rolls and Reg. Sutton, V, 97 (LAO, Episcopal Register I, f. 127r). The entry also notes that the recipient received letters patent.
[123] Rolls and Reg. Sutton, III, 93. The entry does not preserve the form of the oath (LAO, Episcopal Register I, f. 22v), so the point must have been to record the fact that the oath was taken.
[124] Ibid. The entry reads "presentibus," but no names follow.
[125] LAO, Episcopal Register III, fos. 40v, 97v, 105r, 133v, 134r, 177v, 214r, 228r, and, for what seems to be a failure of an archdeacon or his *familiaris* to follow the bishop's command, BL, Add. MS 35296, f. 82v. I hope to discuss these episodes more fully elsewhere.
[126] LAO, Episcopal Register II, f. 134v; III, fos. 134v, 140r, 204v, 259v, 265v, 278, 289v, 304v, 325r, 398v, 402v, 411r. Dalderby also continued selectively to record oaths of obedience by archdeacons on their collation (ibid., fos. 286r, 300v).

to have been a high priority for them when it came to disciplining their administrative personnel. Or, I think, a better way to read the evidence is that disciplining their administrative personnel was not a high priority for bishops.

Social Exile

At the start of his struggle with his steward, Bishop Giffard of Worcester demanded of one of his clerks that he was to avoid counsel with Peter de Leicester, "our former *familiaris*," so as to avoid the vice of ingratitude, and was indeed to write back on the matter without delay.[127] The man thus warned off in 1284 was William Pikeril, who had been Giffard's *officialis* but had ceased to exercise that office by 1284.[128] Pikeril and Peter were part of the same social world. In 1279 Pikeril had granted Hanlegh to Hugh Burnel, knight, a grant which John Kirkby, apparently Peter's friend, witnessed.[129] Hugh Burnel was the brother of Robert Burnel,[130] who had earlier intervened on Peter's behalf in another matter.[131] The abbey of Tewkesbury was another connection. Pikeril had been instituted to Thornbury on Tewkesbury's presentation.[132] On Pikeril's death, the abbot and convent of Tewkesbury would present Peter to Thornbury.[133]

There is no direct evidence as to what choice Pikeril made when faced with Giffard's demand. But Pikeril is not to be found in Giffard's service

---

[127] Reg. Giffard of Worcester, 306 (WRO, Rf.x716.093 BA 2648/1(i) fos. 265v–266r [pp. 522–3]). On the conflict, see M. Burger, "Peter of Leicester, Bishop Giffard of Worcester, and the Problem of Benefices in Thirteenth-Century England," *Catholic Historical Review* 95 (2009), 453–73.

[128] Susan Jane Davies, "Studies in the Administration of the Diocese of Worcester in the Thirteenth Century," University of Wales PhD Thesis (1971), 273–4.

[129] *Calendar of the Close Rolls (1272–1485)*, ed. H. C. Maxwell Lyte et al. (London, 1892–1954), I, 579. When Giffard and Peter, himself a royal clerk, finally compromised, the transaction was witnessed by John Kirkby, bishop of Ely and Edward I's treasurer (Reg. Giffard of Worcester, 334 [WRO, Rf.x716.093 BA 2648/1(i) f. 291 (p. 573)]). Kirkby intervened on Peter's behalf with Bishop Giffard (ibid., fos. 291, 363v-64 [pp. 573, 718–19]).

[130] *Oxford Dictionary of National Biography*, ed. H. G. C. Matthew and Brian Howard Harrison (Oxford, 2004), sub "Robert Burnel."

[131] Ca. February, 1283, Robert Burnel, bishop of Bath and Wells and chancellor of the Exchequer, had written to an unknown person excusing Peter, as chamberlain of the Exchequer, from being present during a visitation of the diocese (TNA, SC1/29/5). This probably relates to the visitation of the diocese of Worcester conducted by the archbishop of Canterbury in spring 1283 (on which, see Decima L. Douie, *Archbishop Pecham* [Oxford, 1952], 162).

[132] Reg. Giffard of Worcester, 171.

[133] Ibid., 489.

after Giffard broke with Peter de Leicester.[134] And there are signs that Giffard's hostility to Peter came to extend to Pikeril. In 1297, Giffard cited five men for pluralism on his visitation of the diocese. Peter de Leicester was one of them;[135] but nothing ever came of it, and Peter lost nothing.[136] Another of these five was Pikeril. If Pikeril was on a list of people to harass in 1297, one can again say only that the attempt went nowhere, although Pikeril was soon dead.[137]

This episode points to a tool of discipline latent in the environment of diocesan administrators. Peter de Leicester and William Pikeril were socially connected. They illustrate what was true of many bishops' clerks: that they formed a community, or at least overlapping communities.[138] And for this reason, an angry bishop like Giffard could threaten to cut one off from that community. Displeasing a bishop risked a clerk's social relationships.

Unfortunately, the soft tissue of these relationships has generally perished. The sources, mostly legal or administrative, reveal little about what such men said to one another. Their recreations – did they dine together? walk together? – are similarly obscure.[139] Nonetheless, some important

---

[134] Following Peter's (and his own) break with Giffard, Pikeril appears as chancellor of Oxford (A. B. Emden, *A Biographical Register of the University of Oxford to A.D. 1500* [Oxford, 1957], sub nom.). Pikeril evidently kept some connection in the diocese, however. He was engaged there in a lawsuit for debt in 1286 against Clement, parson of Chaddesley Corbett. Giffard was attached as ordinary to get Clement to court; it is tempting to suspect that Giffard was less than cooperative with the court because of his bad relations with Pikeril (TNA, CP 40/69, m 101d, also available online in the digital archive assembled by Robert C. Palmer and Elspeth K. Palmer, The Anglo-American Legal Tradition, aalt.law.uh.edu/aalt.html: CP 40/69 AALT 5013: http://aalt.law.uh.edu/E1/CP40n069/bCP40n069dorses/IMG_5013.htm). But such episcopal failures were not unusual. I have found no evidence of a special connection between Clement and Giffard.

[135] Reg. Giffard of Worcester, 487.

[136] He would, however, eventually get caught on pluralism charges leveled by Archbishop Winchelsey (Rose Graham, "The Metropolitical Visitation of the Diocese of Worcester," in Graham, *English Ecclesiastical Studies* [London, 1929], 356–7). But he pretty well landed on his feet, passing one of his benefices to his own clerk and keeping the rest.

[137] Emden, *Biographical Register of the University of Oxford*, sub nom.

[138] I am not sure whether episcopal clerks enjoyed the sort of collective identity to be found among king's clerks in the fourteenth century (on which see W. M. Ormrod, "Accountability and Collegiality: The English Royal Secretariat in the Mid-Fourteenth Century," in *Ecrit et pouvoire dans les chancelleries medievales*, ed. Kouky Fianu and DeLloyd Guth [Louvain, 1997], 78–85). If they did, I suspect it was expressed in the form of the episcopal *familia*. I hope to explore this subject elsewhere.

[139] Episcopal vitae are richer sources for the ties between bishops and their men (e.g., that between Archbishop Edmund of Abingdon and his clerks, discussed in Chapter 9) than for ties among bishops' men.

aspects of their relationships are recoverable. Diocesan bureaucrats often entrusted their affairs to one another. This could take the form of service as a proctor or attorney. In death, such representation took the form of executorship.

A number of men in diocesan service acted as the executors of the wills of other men in diocesan service. The formality of such a relationship should not obscure the degree of trust between man and man such ties reveal. Professor Sheehan noted that the executor, who in the thirteenth century "tended more and more to become a legal projection after death of the legal personality of the deceased," exercised "a remarkable discretion" over movable property, sometimes even enjoying the right to choose beneficiaries or to revise the deceased's testament.[140] If a testator had not already endowed a chantry or given to the monks, he or she looked to executors to execute or even arrange for his or her spiritual welfare, and indeed it is in this context that most of the executors discussed here appear in the sources.[141] Moreover, those who acted as executors presumably knew that they thus took on a potentially onerous burden, although dishonest executors might make it a profitable one.[142] Challenges from discontented legatees and creditors were not uncommon.[143] Instructive in this regard are the trials of one of Bishop Sutton of Lincoln's most frequent ad hoc commissaries, William de Langworth, in executing the will of his colleague, Master Durand de Lincoln, the deceased archdeacon of Stow.[144] Soon after Master Durand's death, the bishop began proceedings

---

[140] M. M. Sheehan, *The Will in Medieval England, from the Conversion of the Anglo-Saxons to the End of the Thirteenth Century* (Toronto, 1963), 215–16, and see 153–61, 219.

[141] Executors might also arrange one's funeral (ibid., 216).

[142] For dishonest executors, ibid., 219. Sheehan concludes that medieval literature exaggerated the amount of abuse.

[143] Michael Sheehan, "English Wills and the Records of Ecclesiastical and Civil Jurisdiction," *Journal of Medieval History* 14 (1988), 8.

[144] Sutton commissioned William de Langworth once in 1290 jointly to try a case, and twice jointly to discharge executors (Rolls and Reg. Sutton, III, 48–9, 54). The following year he was commissioned jointly to hear three suits (ibid., 69, 147, 151) and received nine commissions to discharge executors (ibid., 94–6, 101, 108, 159 and see 150–1) and was to examine some executors (ibid., 145, 154). Sutton commissioned him four times jointly to discharge executors in 1292 (ibid., 197, IV, 4, 17, 49), once to inquire regarding certain executors' activities, and once to hear a case of usury (ibid., IV, 10, 14). The following year he received nine commissions jointly to discharge executors (ibid., IV, 57, 80, 82, 85–6, 103, 129, 138). He received numerous joint commissions, mostly to hear suits to deal with matters arising from wills, in 1294 (ibid., V, 3, 4, 18, 44), 1295 (ibid., 54, 56, 59, 67, 68, 71, 83, 90–1, 98, 102, 110–11), 1296 (ibid., 133, 155, 157, 165, 185–6, and see 10), 1297 (ibid., VI, 39–40, 43), 1298 (ibid., 67, 72, 83, 97, 116, 119 and

against all those who had hidden Durand's jewels and other property, preventing the execution of his will.[145] Some four years later William was still acting as Durand's executor, and in that capacity was embroiled in a lawsuit.[146] One would not choose an executor lightly, nor lightly undertake to be one.

Such evidence appears in other dioceses. Nicholas de Knovile, Bishop Cantilupe of Hereford's man for dealing with Archbishop Pecham and the clerk to whom Cantilupe collated a prebend in his cathedral, served as executor for Luke de Bré, Cantilupe's *officialis*.[147] In the diocese of Carlisle, Thomas de Kirkeswold worked to execute the testament of the late archdeacon of Carlisle.[148] Thomas himself enjoyed the bishop's patronage; his death would vacate the vicarage of Penrith, to which the bishop held the advowson.[149] Thomas's ties to the archdeacon began early; when he had been ordained subdeacon at least fifteen years earlier, the archdeacon had provided the bishop the required guarantee that Thomas would have an income necessary for holy orders.[150] (It is impossible to tell whether Thomas in the end suffered the distraint that the king ordered Thomas's bishop to impose upon him, but the bishop told the king that his writ arrived too late, and the place concerned was too far, for him to distrain.)[151] Death reveals the closer bond between William de Sardinia ("Cardene"), *officialis* of the court of Canterbury, and Walter de Thorp, dean of Arches. As William's executor, Walter traveled to the bishop of Hereford's manor at Bosbury to seek probate of William's will.[152]

---

see 69) and 1299 (ibid., 137–8, 165–7). Durand de Lincoln served as Sutton's archdeacon of Stow 1289–1291 (LN Lincoln, 47), but a "Master Durand," very likely the same man given the uncommon name, is to be found in this bishop's service as early as 1280 (Reg. Wickwane, 68 n5). A roll, apparently of his visitations as archdeacon, survives as LAO, Dii/64/2/7.

[145] Rolls and Reg. Sutton, III, 188.
[146] Ibid., V, 141–2.
[147] Reg. Swinfield, 334. For Nicholas's connections with Cantilupe, see Reg. Cantilupe, 259, 268, and for Luke's connections with that bishop, ibid., lxix. I am grateful to Susan Ridyard for advice regarding Nicholas.
[148] Reg. Halton, II, 100.
[149] Ibid., II, 170.
[150] Ibid., I, 132.
[151] Ibid., II, 100. The archdeacon had been a collector of taxes owed the king, and the king sought to make good deficiencies in the returns from the archdeacon's goods, or those of his executors.
[152] Reg. Swinfield, 395. For the identification of William de Sardinia, see *The Medieval Court of Arches*, ed. F. Donald Logan, Canterbury and York Society 95 (Woodbridge, 2005), 198.

The delicate ties recoverable between Bishop Giffard of Worcester's men, Peter de Leicester and William Pikeril, are partly preserved through their shared connection with Tewkesbury Abbey. Diocesan administrators often received benefices at the hand of lords other than their bishops; monastic houses in the diocese, which might often need a bishop's favor, were especially likely to steer their patronage in that direction (see Chapter 9). The benefices they thus gave, or better, the record of those benefices in the bishops' registers, are the hard bones that remain of once living social networks.

Such institutions to benefices shed additional light on William de Langworth, Sutton's clerk and the long-suffering executor of Sutton's archdeacon of Stow, Durand de Lincoln. William de Langworth was connected to Legbourne priory, as the prior and convent tried to present William to a mediety in Theddlethorpe, although the presentation was blocked when Legbourne was sued over the advowson.[153] The priory, it should be noted, also presented two of Sutton's lesser commissaries – William de Aysterby and Hervey de Threkeston – to benefices.[154] In 1296, William de Langworth also received a benefice on the presentation of Thornholm Priory. So did Benedict de Utterby and Walter, vicar of Appleby, a minor commissary of Bishop Sutton and an episcopal penitentiary, as well as Roger de Sixil, then (1285) soon to become a member of the bishop's household.[155] Thornholm's connections with the diocesan bureaucracy went even further. Walter de Malling, ad hoc commissary and canon of Lincoln, enjoyed the commend of one of the benefices to which Thornholm held the advowson, and the priory presented Thomas de Luda, evidently the brother of Walter de Luda, a minor episcopal commissary, to Bottesford.[156]

---

[153] Rolls and Reg. Sutton, I, 111.

[154] The vicar of Farlesthorpe, commissioned in the years 1290–8, was presumably William de Aysterby, instituted to the vicarage in 1267 on Legbourne's presentation (Rot. Gravesend, 24). Hervey de Threkeston had received what was apparently his first benefice under Gravesend in 1271 from Roger de Fuldon, archdeacon of Lincoln, but seems to have resigned this on receiving the vicarage of St. Mary's, North Sumercotes, in 1274 on Legbourne's presentation (ibid., 49, 60, 279).

[155] Rot. Gravesend, 82; Rolls and Reg. Sutton, VIII, 23, 26–8. The institution of Walter, vicar of Appleby, is not recorded. But Appleby was vacant in 1294 through the death of one Master Walter (ibid., VIII, 24). This would appear to be the Master Walter who, in a document of 1278?, 1279?, was listed as "magister Walterus vicarius [of Appleby], septuagenarius," having been presented by Thornholm (Rot. Gravesend, 351, and for the date, ibid., 347). Walter may have been old, but was certainly not impossibly so, to receive his episcopal commission in 1292 (Rolls and Reg. Sutton, IV, 46).

[156] Ibid., VIII, 27–8. Master Thomas de Luda, "dictus Malherb," was instituted to Bottesford in 1295, and had renounced the same in favor of William de Langworth the following

A consideration of William de Langworth's activities as an executor extends the network. As noted, William served as a co-executor of Durand de Lincoln, archdeacon of Stow.[157] He also served as the executor of the occasional episcopal commissary Adam de Brampton, in which work he had a co-executor, Henry de Camera, who himself received a collation from the bishop.[158] Ralph de Geyton, a citizen of Lincoln, similarly entrusted the final disposition of his goods to William de Langworth, and in his labors William had as a colleague Robert de Burton, Sutton's sequestrator.[159]

---

year (ibid., 21, 26). This may be the same Master Thomas de Luda who resigned Ingham in 1286, to which Bullington Priory thereupon presented Durand de Lincoln, archdeacon of Stow (ibid., 7). The relationship with Walter de Luda is suggested by documents of 1326 and 1327 in which Thomas de Luda, canon of Lincoln, made Walter de Luda, his brother, his representative to receive seisin of some property (LAO, A/1/8 nos. 875, 904 [fos. 215v, 220r]).

[157] See at nn 144–6, along with William de Langworth's other connections with Durand's family: Peter, son of Master Durand de Lincoln, was underage when Bardney Abbey first presented him to Sotby. It was William de Langworth who undertook to hold the benefice *in commendam* until Peter attained his maturity (Rolls and Reg. Sutton, I, 1, 95). This Peter's parentage is rather unclear. An archdeacon with an (acknowledged) son is a somewhat surprising find in the 1280s, and Peter is generally styled, a little ambiguously, as "Petrus Durandi," so one hesitates to identify Master Durand de Lincoln, archdeacon of Stow, as the father of this Peter, son of Master Durand de Lincoln. (For this form of his name, see Rolls and Reg. Sutton, VI, 50, 105, 119, 149, VIII, 190 [LAO, Episcopal Register I fos. 173r, 190r, 197r, 344r]). There seems to have been some relationship, however, since after their deaths, Peter's executors were in conflict with those of Durand over the "goods of the deceased Master Durand de Lincoln and of Peter, son and executor of the will of the same" ("bona quondam magistri Durandi de Linc' ac Petri filii et executoris testamenti ipsius") (Rolls and Reg. Sutton V, 141 [LAO, Episcopal Register I f.138v]). One might also note here, in a different vein, that Durand the archdeacon of Stow had an indirect connection with Robert Chafford, an episcopal penitentiary. Both men received benefices from Bullington Priory (Rolls and Reg. Sutton, I, 75, VIII, 17–18). Sutton commissioned Robert, vicar of St. Albans, Spridlington, as his joint penitentiary in the deanery of Aslackhoe, in 1292 (ibid., IV, 46). The vicar was presumably Robert de Chafford, instituted to this vicarage in 1288 (ibid., VIII, 17–18).

[158] Rolls and Reg. Sutton, IV, 160; *The Registrum Antiquissimum of the Cathedral Church of Lincoln*, ed. C. W. Foster and Kathleen Major, Lincoln Record Society 27–28, 32, 34, 41, 46, 51, 62, 67 (Hereford and Gateshead, 1931–73), X, no. 2881.

[159] LAO, Dii/82/1/20 (= LAO, A/1/8 no. 876 [f. 215v]). Robert de Burton appears as Sutton's sequestrator in the years 1291–6, when he received many ad hoc commissions, some of them joint, to deal with testamentary matters (Rolls and Reg. Sutton, III, 95, 101, 141, 147, 156–7, 197, IV, 4, 17, 21, 26, 76, 80, 85–6, 103, 129, 138, 140, 166, V, 45, 47–8, 53, 55, 59, 61, 157 and see V, 4). He also received many ad hoc commissions regarding sequestrations in these years (ibid., IV, 65–6, 74, 79–80, 122, 157–8, V, 21, 25). Sutton commissioned him to get some parishioners to contribute to the repair of their church in 1291 (ibid., III, 113, 125), to decide whether a rector needed a coadjutor in 1292 (ibid., III, 187), and in 1294 to receive an altar stolen from the bishop (ibid., V, 47–8). The entry concerning him at ibid., III, 189 needs no correction. The MS in fact has "Robert,"

A position in the bishop's household could make some clerks especially suitable agents of men who could not be present at their own institution, throwing light on social connections that would otherwise be invisible. John de Schalby, the bishop's registrar, performed this service on a number of occasions (indeed, more than anyone else in Sutton's entourage).[160] He acted as the proctor for Robert de Pratellis and Philip de Swayfield, both of whom received the bishop's patronage, as well as for Robert de Swillington and Henry de Nassington, two episcopal agents.[161] John de Schalby also served as the proctor of John le Fleming, an important episcopal servant, and once John's fellow in the bishop's household, in his institution to Ambrosden.[162] This connection was strengthened by John's similar service for one Richard de Palgrave, presented to a benefice by John le Fleming in his capacity as proctor of St. Fromund's Priory, Séez.[163] Along with his colleague in the household and episcopal service, John de Schalby was sufficiently trusted by Simon de Ghent, archdeacon of Oxford, to be chosen by the archdeacon to determine the revenues due him from a certain vicarage.[164] John fell within the network provided by the benefice system as well, sharing a patron in the priory of Markby (whose own officers received several episcopal commissions)

---

not "John," de Burton (LAO, Episcopal Register I, f. 100r). In the entry at Rolls and Reg. Sutton, V, 100, read "Robert Bernard" for "Robert Burton" (LAO, Episcopal Register I, f. 130v).

[160] A similar case from Exeter is that of Roger de Dartford. Roger, steward of Bishop Bronscombe's household (Reg. Bronscombe, nos. 417, 954–5), acted as the proctor of Richard Paz and Roger Rufus (or le Rus) (ibid., nos. 847–8) at their institutions. Roger Rufus should probably be considered an episcopal clerk, as he received collation from the bishop (indeed, this very instance). The evidence is stronger for Richard Paz, as he not only received several benefices from the bishop (ibid., nos. 659, 848, 942, 1005, 1273, 1336), but also served as the bishop's proctor at the Court of Arches and as his ad hoc commissary (ibid., nos. 1017, 1123, and see no. 1181).

[161] Rolls and Reg. Sutton, II, 58, VIII, 58, 83, 128. A similar service was provided by Robert de Kibworth, another member of the bishop's household, for Durand de Lincoln, soon to become archdeacon of Stow (ibid., VIII, 7; LN Lincoln, 47). Sutton collated two benefices to Robert de Pratellis (Rolls and Reg. Sutton, VIII, 18, 23, and see 128). For Henry de Nassington as Sutton's *officialis*, see Chapter 8, n 50.

[162] Rolls and Reg. Sutton, VIII, 200. For John Le Fleming's service to Sutton, see Chapter 9, n 34.

[163] Rolls and Reg. Sutton, I, 205.

[164] Ibid., VIII, 195–7. Simon eventually became bishop of Salisbury. As such he would collate benefices to Roger de Martival, Sutton's archdeacon of Leicester, and William de Bosco, Sutton's sequestrator (Reg. Martival, viii–ix). Roger de Martival in turn left a silver-gilt cup to Bishop Gravesend of Lincoln's grandnephew, Stephen de Gravesend (Emden, *Biographical Register of the University of Oxford*, II, 806). William de Bosco appears as Sutton's sequestrator in 1285 (Rolls and Reg. Sutton, VIII, 99–100).

with Thomas de Perariis, a minor but fairly active ad hoc commissary of the bishop.[165] Another man, Benedict de Hallam, the official of William de Estiniaco, archdeacon of Lincoln, shared the patronage of Shelford Priory with John de Fledborough, a minor commissary of the bishop, himself connected with William de la Gare, archdeacon of Lincoln.[166] That connection appears only in a rather unusual document – a short, deathbed narrative issued by the dying William de la Gare, in which he claimed John de Fledborough as his "socius."[167] Such discoveries bring home how little evidence has survived for the social connections of these men.

Yet, the ties among episcopal clerks presumably meant that a bishop who threatened one of their number took a risk. True, a clerk who angered his bishop might find his social world disrupted. But, as William Pikeril's disappearance from Bishop Giffard's service suggests, episcopal clerks might side with their friends and colleagues against their bishop. Indeed, two of Bishop Swinfield's men, friends of Poncius de Cors, against whom Swinfield was proceeding for pluralism, interceded with Swinfield on Poncius's behalf.[168] Poncius was not one of Swinfield's clerks, but the episode shows how a bishop might heed the appeal of his men, hinting at the solidarity that might rein in a bishop, or any lord for that matter. After all, men with the right administrative skills were in short supply. Bishop Bronscombe of Exeter may have been appalled by the behavior of some of his predecessor's clerks. But in the end he took some of them into his service anyway.[169]

All told, the discipline bishops meted out to their clerks was not impressive. This was not because bishops had no disciplinary tools to

---

[165] Markby had tried to present Thomas to Mumby, but withdrew when the advowson was contested. On winning its case, the priory allowed Thomas the commend of Mumby, followed by John de Schalby's institution (Rolls and Reg. Sutton, I, 193–5). Sutton commissioned Thomas jointly to discharge executors in 1291 (ibid., III, 96) and five times jointly to grant probate in the years 1294–8 (ibid., V, 83, 111, 185, VI, 109).

[166] Ibid., I, 1, 89. Bishop Sutton jointly commissioned Benedict de Hallam to discharge executors in 1290 (ibid., III, 21). In 1291 he took an oath to Sutton as archidiaconal official of Lincoln (ibid., III, 93, and see IV, 36). Sutton commissioned John de Fledborough jointly to discharge executors in 1291 (ibid., III, 145).

[167] *Registrum Antiquissimum*, IX, no. 2482. The document is in fact a sort of testamentary *addendum*, in which William announces that one of his executors approached him to ask whether he had made certain provisions in his testament regarding some houses, and that he thereupon gave instructions regarding them. The structure (a narrative) is, however, rather unusual.

[168] Reg. Swinfield, 248.

[169] See Chapter 9 at n 7.

hand. Bishops could have sequestrated their clerks' benefices, held them to their oaths, thrown them in prison, bound them with bonds, excommunicated them, and inflicted humiliatingly public penances upon them. But bishops rarely took any of these steps. And although bishops might, by cutting off their clerks, sever them from a social world, the world of the see's *clerici episcopi*, that sword was a double-edged one. Secure in their benefices and independence, clerks might choose to go with the exile rather than stay with their bishop. The bishops' easier course was simply not to reach for the rod. I suspect they did not often even consider it.

PART III

CONSEQUENCES

8

Patronage Hunger

Bishops, I have argued, needed to give benefices. Certainly one reason was their own bottom line: supporting hangers-on with benefices meant not having to do so out of pocket. It is this desire to cut costs that has drawn the attention of historians.[1] But the pressure on bishops was greater than this. Bishops also faced demand from below: clerks wanted the security and prestige that came with benefices. Hence, benefice hunger helped drive bishops' patronage hunger. Fortunately for bishops, their control over the machinery of diocesan governance also positioned them to extend their patronage. Pressured by their own need to bestow benefices, bishops in turn pressured those below them, in particular religious houses. Predatory bishops thus acquired either advowsons or the use of them. The degree to which bishops felt this pressure presumably varied. Bishops whose cathedrals were occupied by monastic chapters lacked the supply of prebendal benefices enjoyed by their colleagues with secular chapters. Simple circumstance could mean that a bishop might have more or fewer vacant benefices at his disposal at any one time. But while the degree of such pressure varied, pressure there was. As seen in Chapter 7, bishops also increased the value of the benefices already in their gift by increasing their endowments.

---

[1] E.g., R. N. Swanson, "Learning and Livings: University Study and Clerical Careers in Later Medieval England," *History of Universities* 6 (for 1986–7) (1987), 88 (a discussion which in some other respects is very sensitive to the position of those seeking benefices); Frederic Cheyette, "Kings, Courts, Cures, and Sinecures: The Statute of Provisors and the Common Law," *Traditio* 19 (1963), 297; W. A. Pantin, *The English Church in the Fourteenth Century* (Cambridge, 1955), 41–2; C. R. Cheney, *English Bishops' Chanceries 1100–1250* (Manchester, 1950), 9.

Acquiring Advowsons

By the end of the twelfth century, the right to nominate clergy to churches had become a saleable right, fully distinct from the estate to which it might originally have been attached. Bishops who wanted to extend their patronage thus had the option of purchasing advowsons like any other would-be patron.[2] But bishops had an alternative means of acquiring patronage not available to other lords. From the later twelfth century, monasteries in every diocese sought to appropriate the rectories to which they either held the advowson or which lay lords sought to give them. Such appropriations required the approval of the bishop, who had to ordain the vicarage. Normally, the appropriating monastery received the advowson of the new vicarage, just as it had held the advowson of the old rectory.

But normally was not always. Christopher Harper-Bill's studies of the diocese of Norwich show bishops from the late twelfth century appropriating churches to local monastic houses on condition that one of the bishop's clerks be presented as the next vicar. And in the thirteenth century the bishops of Norwich went further: these bishops' ordinations of vicarages, while giving revenue to the appropriating monastery, conferred the advowson of the vicarage entirely on the bishop and his successors. Indeed, rather than claiming the advowson for themselves, bishops could also leave the advowson nominally in the hands of the appropriator, but ordaining that the appropriator was to present to the bishop – a clerk to be named by the bishop.[3]

As Harper-Bill observes in regard to these maneuvers, bishops of Norwich were short on patronage of their own. Burdened with a monastic chapter that did not provide the cathedral prebends in the gift of bishops blessed with secular chapters, those anxious bishops had to turn elsewhere.[4] Other bishops so burdened followed suit. When appropriating Brasted to Keynsham Abbey, Archbishop Langton took care to reserve the collation of the church to himself and his successors.[5] Bishop

---

[2] For a grant of an advowson to a bishop, see Rot. Gray, 131–2.
[3] Christopher Harper-Bill, "The Struggle for Benefices in Twelfth-Century East Anglia," in *Anglo-Norman Studies XI: Proceedings of the Battle Conference 1988*, ed. R. Allen Brown (Woodbridge, 1989), 130–1; Harper-Bill, "The Diocese of Norwich in the Early Thirteenth Century: Sources and Themes," in *Counties and Communities: Essays on East Anglian History Presented to Hassell Smith*, ed. Carole Rawcliffe, Roger Virgoe, and Richard Wilson (Norwich, 1996), 25–6; EEA 21: Norwich, xxvii, lviii–lix.
[4] Harper-Bill, "The Struggle for Benefices," 129, 131. Harper-Bill refers to the desperation of the bishops of Norwich to find revenues for their clerks (ibid., 124).
[5] *Acta Stephani Langton*, no. 25.

Giffard of Worcester did the same when ordaining a vicarage in Wolford.[6] Appropriation to a religious house with the patronage going to the bishop could also be the kind of compromise in which each party benefited in order to resolve a dispute. Both Archbishop Langton and the Hospital of St. John in Jerusalem claimed the advowson of Tilmanstone. The parties made peace when Langton appropriated Tilmanstone to the hospital, the archbishop gaining the right to institute vicars there without the hospital's consent (i.e., effectively the right to collate the vicarage).[7]

But such shifts were not confined to bishops whose sees had monastic chapters. Bishop Neville of Chichester ordained that the vicarage of Cocking was to be at the disposal of the bishops of Chichester when appropriating that church.[8] Chichester, of course, was a poor see.[9] Better-off bishops with secular chapters, however, made similar moves. When Bishop Gravesend of Lincoln appropriated the church of Glen to Alcester Abbey, he ordained that the vicar was henceforth to be named by the bishop and that Alcester must present the nominee to the bishop for institution.[10] Bishop Gravesend then nominated Walter de Eylesbury, his own *capellanus*, to the vicarage of Glen, to which Alcester Abbey, the patron, then presented him. The same bishop later nominated to Glen John de Stounesby, who is to be found witnessing the acts of both Gravesend and his vicar-general.[11]

---

[6] Reg. Giffard of Worcester, 42. Unusually, however, this vicarage was not ordained as a part of an appropriation. Instead, the perpetual vicarage was created in a church held by a secular as rector.

[7] *Acta Stephani Langton*, no. 125.

[8] EEA 22: Chichester, no. 54. For what appears to have been a similar arrangement in effect by 1253 for Cuckfield, see ibid., no. 159.

[9] See Diana Greenway's comments, LN Chichester, xvii–xviii.

[10] Rot. Gravesend, 146.

[11] Ibid., 147. For Walter as the bishop's chaplain, Rot. Gravesend, 241, as witness to Gravesend's acts: Rot. Gravesend, 31, 145, 146, 193, 244, 246; *The Registrum Antiquissimum of the Cathedral Church of Lincoln*, ed. C. W. Foster and K. Major, Lincoln Record Society 27–8, 32, 34, 41, 46, 51, 62, 67 (Hereford and Gateshead, 1931–73), III, no. 1015; Rot. Gravesend, 53, 199 [300], 178 [318]; LAO, Dii/69/1/36, Dii/69/1/53). As witness to the vicar-general: ibid., 48, 117. One may, perhaps, understand such a situation to have been behind the institution to Snarford of John le Gentil, "upon whom the lord bishop [Hugh of Wells], with the *consent* of the prior and convent of Elsham, the patrons of Snarford, conferred it, and to the same [church] he was admitted and in it canonically instituted parson" (emphasis mine) (Rot. Wells, I, 229: "cui dominus episcopus, de consensu Prioris et conventus de Ellesham, patronorum ecclesie de Snarteford, contulit, ad eandem admissus est, et in ea canonice persona institutus"). There is no evidence, however, of any formal arrangement made for Snarford like that for Glen, and I have not found any further connection between John and Bishop Hugh.

Bishop Richard Poore of Salisbury resisted appropriating churches, instead preferring to grant monastic patrons a benefice in the church. But these arrangements also often included a transfer of the advowson from the monastic patron to the bishop and his successors. Hence, for example, Breamore Priory received a part of the tithes from the church of Ebbesborne Wake "nomine beneficii," while the patronage was to be the bishop's in perpetuity.[12] And at Salisbury, too, a number of appropriations were accompanied by the advowson of the vicarage going to the bishop.[13] The act of appropriation gave Archbishop Gray of York the opportunity to go even further and gain the entirely free disposal of churches in (the heretofore unlicensed?) possession of the abbot and convent of Aumale; the abbey got ordained appropriations of some of its other churches out of this transaction.[14]

Bishops thus effectively sometimes took a cut for using their authority to appropriate churches to monasteries of the diocese. Such arrangements were part of a larger pattern of bishops exploiting the opportunity afforded by appropriation to benefit themselves and their cathedrals. Those benefits could be spiritual. Bishop Bronscombe of Exeter ordained that the vicarage of West Alvington, appropriated to the dean and chapter of Salisbury, was to render four marks a year to support prayers for the souls of Bronscombe and his successors.[15] Of course, the prayers of the religious themselves, as well as those of a chantry priest, could be worth having. As bishop of Worcester, Walter de Gray appropriated Rowing to Reading Abbey, noting that his father was interred there; the appropriation was to benefit his father's soul.[16] Bishop Peter des Roches, the consummate politician, appropriated a church to his own foundation at Titchfield for the good of his own soul and the souls of all the other bishops of Winchester, of King Henry III, and Henry's father and uncle.[17] Bishop

---

[12] EEA 19: Salisbury, no. 267. For discussion of other instances, see EEA 18: Salisbury, lix.
[13] EEA 36: Salisbury, cxv–cxvi.
[14] Rot. Gray, 22. See also the comments of the rolls' editor, ibid., xxv.
[15] Reg. Bronscombe, no. 809, and see 810.
[16] EEA 34: Worcester, no. 172. In the late twelfth century, the bishop of Hereford appropriated the church of Holy Cross and the chapel of Hope to Leominster Priory for the good of the souls of himself and his parents and other relations, among others (EEA VII: Hereford, no. 216). Another version of this *actum* does not, however, include the language about benefit to souls (ibid., n).
[17] EEA IX: Winchester, no. 69. For des Roches's "canny opportunism" regarding his foundations and in other respects, see Nicholas Vincent, *Peter de Roches: An Alien in English Politics 1205–1238* (Cambridge, 1996), 65, 359. For Titchfield's founding, ibid., 257. Titchfield itself lay on a manor granted to Peter by Henry (ibid., 228). For des Roches's facilitation of other grants in King John's memory, ibid., 132.

Richard Poore of Salisbury appropriated Sturminster Marshall to the hospital of Pont-Audemer. "Having God alone before his eyes," he asked that the brothers and sisters intercede with God for him and the church of Salisbury.[18] Poore similarly arranged for the monks of Malmesbury to celebrate his obit in the grand style – with full pontificals – when appropriating the chapel of Norton to Malmesbury's infirmary.[19]

Collation by Lapse

In 1179, the Third Lateran Council laid down that when a benefice had been vacant for six months, the bishop should collate it. From this derived thirteenth-century bishops' habit of collating benefices by lapse, or, as the episcopal registers often describe it, "by authority of the council."[20] Various circumstances might keep a benefice vacant for six months: a patron might neglect to present; the patron might present unqualified candidates; or the patronage itself might be in dispute for longer than six months.

Such occasions offered bishops an opportunity to reward their own clerks with benefices not in their gift. That does not mean that bishops always took it. The early Lincoln rolls make this clear. Grosseteste collated Northmoor to Thomas Gaylhun "by authority of the council" but also, his rolls attest, at the instance of the prior of Deerhurst, who appears to have been the patron.[21] That bishop also collated Hardwick to William de Biggleswade by authority of the council; the patron later presented William to the same church, to which the bishop instituted him.[22] Clearly, Grosseteste had done the patron a courtesy here, but it is unclear how far this courtesy extended. True, instituting William following his collation made no difference to who held the church. But by accepting the presentation following the collation, the bishop was protecting the patron's advowson in the future. The patron could point to an exercise of the advowson if at some later point the patron's ownership of the advowson

---

[18] EEA 19: Salisbury, no. 343.
[19] Ibid., no. 325.
[20] For an interesting discussion of the procedure, see R. H. Helmholz, *The Oxford History of the Laws of England I: The Canon Law and Ecclesiastical Jurisdiction from 597 to the 1640s* (Oxford, 2004), 172–3.
[21] Rot. Grosseteste, 465. An earlier institution had been carried out on the prior's presentation, as was a later instance (Rot. Wells, II, 31; Rot. Gravesend, 222).
[22] Rot. Grosseteste, 241. The later presentation is not be explained because William had proceeded to higher orders after his collation. He appears to have been a priest on the occasion of his collation (ibid.).

should be challenged; an action of darrein presentment would go in this patron's favor. But it is also quite possible that Grosseteste's solicitude went further, and that he had collated the church to the patron's candidate in the first place. Whether William de Biggleswade was the bishop's man or the patron's is unclear, but the case provides a possible instance of a bishop collating by authority of the council in such a way as to serve the patron's interest rather than his own. The situation is even more ambiguous regarding Sibbertoft, which Grosseteste's predecessor collated to William Blund de Lincoln by lapse. The bishop then instituted Blund to Sibbertoft on the presentation of Sulby Abbey, which had by then vindicated its ownership of the advowson in court.[23] While the institution protected Sulby, Blund was also one of Bishop Hugh's men.[24]

Various reasons for episcopal generosity to patrons in these matters might apply. The patron could be influential, either locally or nationally, and so worth pleasing. But it could also be that the benefice was a bad match for the bishop's men at the time of the collation. It may have been that none of the bishop's clerks needed another benefice, or that the income of the benefice was too small compared with benefices the bishop's clerks already enjoyed, or that it came with cure of souls. Rewarding one's men with benefices was always a matter of contingency; the right benefice for the right man had to fall open at the right time. That was the case for benefices in the gift of other patrons as well as a bishop's own. The fact that a benefice was an integrated package of income whose owner (normally) had to die or resign for the benefice to be conferred meant that a benefice was sticky, and thus much less flexible than a cash stipend would have been. This fact may well lie behind bishops' occasional willingness to put their incidental patronage at the disposal of others. Archbishop Pecham notably allowed the bishop of Worcester to collate Hampton St. Peter, Broadway, and Benington; these churches had fallen to the archbishop by lapse.[25] The fact was that these ecclesiastical incomes were not fluid, but came in sometimes awkward, defined packets. That inflexibility was, of course, an aspect of the security of tenure that so added to a benefice's appeal for clerks.

---

[23] Rot. Wells, II, 104, 193.

[24] He obtained the archdeaconry of Leicester and the chancellorship of the cathedral during Hugh's episcopate, and so presumably by collation by Hugh (LN Lincoln, 17, 34). But Blund either had his own connection to Sulby or perhaps established one by gaining Sibbertoft, for Sulby later presented him to another benefice (Rot. Wells, II, 187, 271).

[25] Reg. Pecham, II, 244. Pecham also put the nomination of a presentation to Partney, which had fallen to him by lapse, in the hands of William de Corneria, his commissary general (ibid., 139).

But the vacancy of a benefice for six months or more also allowed bishops to swoop in on behalf of their own men. A dispute over patronage allowed Bishop Sutton of Lincoln to collate Saunderton to his clerk, William de Swayfield.[26] Archbishop Pecham collated Chipping Norton to his clerk Richard de Gloucester, by right of devolution.[27] David Smith has identified seven of Hugh of Wells's clerks who received churches in this way.[28] In the diocese of Hereford, Bishop Swinfield collated Fownhope to his clerk, William de Morton, and two collations by lapse went to men who are likely to have been in Swinfield's service.[29] Such collations did not have to mean that a bishop was careless of the long-term rights of the true patron. When Bishop Ghent of Salisbury collated Donhead to his clerk by lapse, he issued a letter stating that the collation was not to prejudice the future rights of the abbess and convent of Shaftsbury to the advowson.[30]

Episcopal Pressure and Control of Process

But bishops could appear in a more sinister light. The prior of Lewes sued the bishop of Ely, who after a six-month vacancy (and so presumably by authority of the council), had collated the church of Caxton, in the prior's gift, to the bishop's own clerk. The prior had in fact presented a candidate within the six-month period, but the bishop had refused him, claiming the candidate was unqualified.[31] The seneschal of Bishop Ralph Neville of Chichester let his absent master know that a prebend in Hastings, in his diocese, had fallen vacant. The vigilant servant suggested that Neville might want to ask the patron to present one of Neville's clerks, "as he is your friend."[32] What a bishop could portray as an exercise in

[26] Rolls and Reg. Sutton, VIII, 126.
[27] Reg. Pecham, I, 108.
[28] *Acta of Hugh of Wells*, xxxiii.
[29] William de Morton appears as the bishop's clerk and seneschal (Reg. Swinfield, 112, 138), and attested a number of his acts (ibid., 162, 175, 182, 222, 226, 238, 240, 249, 252, 282). The candidates are Adam de Aylinton, and Richard de la Sole. As a notary, Adam witnessed episcopal acts at Bosbury in 1306 and again in 1316 (ibid., 476, 512). Richard de la Sole carried out Swinfield's command as dean of Weobbley in 1307 (he is called Richard, rector of Whitney, which church was collated to Richard de la Sole in 1285) (ibid., 525 and, for details missing from ibid., 439, see Hereford Record Office AL 19/2, f. 158r). For the collations by lapse, see Reg. Swinfield, 525–6, 537).
[30] Reg. Gandavo, I, 115.
[31] See *Year Books of the Reign of King Edward I*, ed. Alfred J. Horwood (RS) (London, 1866–79), IV, 30–2.
[32] *Royal and Historical Letters Illustrative of the Reign of Henry III*, ed. Walter Waddington Shirley (RS) (London, 1862–6), I, no. 229: "quoniam amicus vester est, ut credo."

reform – saving a church from falling into the hands of an unworthy clerk – could appear to a patron as a cynical manipulation of the system in order to seize patronage. Which it was cannot always be known.³³

Other actions by bishops are open to such dark suspicions. The Dunstable chronicler appears to have had some. Dunstable Priory had illegally farmed out a church. When Bishop Gravesend discovered this – and that the incumbent was said to be dead – he expelled both farmer and incumbent and, it was noted at Dunstable, gave custody to his own clerk instead.³⁴ The bishop of Bath and Wells obtained from the pope a command – it appears in the papal registers among a series of favors to this bishop – to warn pluralists in the diocese to resign their excess benefices and empowering the bishop to collate the benefices thus vacated. An earlier chapter has recounted how Archbishop Winchelsey, whose court expelled an incumbent from Haddenham, in the gift of Ramsey Abbey, asked the abbot to present the archbishop's own chaplain to the now vacant church.³⁵ And a bishop could act even more directly. Archbishop Pecham may well have complained that he was unable to provide enough benefices for his clerks, but his suffragans complained in turn that the archbishop himself was collating benefices, including those in their own collation, declared vacant by his court.³⁶

Indeed, bishops might claim patronage in return for conferring office on the patron himself or herself. In the early fourteenth century the bishop of Worcester wrote to the abbot of Cirencester that, on examining "the old books of our register …, we find that abbots and priors on receiving episcopal benediction used to promise promotion to one of our predecessor's clerks as an act of gratitude."³⁷ This right, assuming it in fact

---

33 For hostility between bishop and patron regarding collations by devolution, see Adam J. Davis, *The Holy Bureaucrat: Eudes Rigaud and Religious Reform in Thirteenth-Century Normandy* (Ithaca, 2006), 108–9, 132. Archbishop Rigaud may have been a reformer, but contemporaries sometimes saw a predator. For a contemporary speculation that a bishop might delay examination of a presentee for six months in order then to collate by lapse, see *Year Books of Edward II*, eds. F.W. Maitland et al., Selden Society 17- (London, 1903-), III, 274.
34 *Annales Monastici*, III, 276. The chronicler implies that the expelled occupant was alive – his proctor, he says, could do nothing – but also says that the priory successfully presented another candidate, thus losing the fruit of this church for a year. These events do not appear in Gravesend's rolls.
35 *Reg. Winchelsey*, 443–4.
36 Pecham, *Epistolae*, I, 278, 331, 334.
37 "in registri nostri codicibus reperiamus antiquis Abbates et priores … post munus benediccionis assumptum ad promocionem unius clericorum predecessorum nostrorum intuitu gratitudinis obligari" (*The Register of Thomas de Cobham, Bishop of Worcester 1317–1327*, ed. E. H. Pearce, Worcester Historical Record Society 40 [London, 1930], 195).

existed,[38] is reminiscent of that claimed by the archbishop of Canterbury to nominate a clerk for presentation to a benefice in the gift of a suffragan bishop-elect immediately after the archbishop's confirmation of the election.[39]

Of course, the exercise of patronage by one party in favor of another could be said to show not benefice hunger, but benefice surfeit. After all, if I am willing to present someone else's clerk to a church in my gift, presumably I do not need the use of the advowson myself. But patronage thus used seems to have been a matter of the advowsons of the less influential being used to favor the clerks of the more powerful, like bishops. An uncommon case of a bishop presenting clerks other than his own to benefices in his gift suggests this phenomenon. Several benefices in the gift of Robert of York, bishop-elect of Ely, appear in possession of clerks of the papal legate Guala. The bishop was a vulnerable man. He had not yet been consecrated bishop, his election itself was disputed (and would be ultimately quashed), and he was reputed to have sympathized with the rebels against King John, who were now on the outs. He was ill-placed to resist any suggestion that he exercise his advowsons on behalf of the clerks of the papal legate to England. The bishop-elect either did not resist or himself sought out Guala's clerks to curry favor in the right places. Whether the impetus came from Guala or from Robert, the drift of patronage upward is evident.[40] Another exception is the benefices claimed by new archbishops of Canterbury from their suffragans (noted earlier). One may note a study for a later, better documented period, that shows that the pressures on the prior of Durham to exercise his patronage on behalf of other people's clerks came largely from men in high places.[41]

Indeed, by the early fourteenth century, monastic complaints about bishops who pressured them into presenting candidates of the bishop's choice for institution had percolated up to the great councils of

---

[38] It is not entirely clear from E. H. Pearce's discussion of this incident to what extent this request was fulfilled (E. H. Pearce, *Thomas de Cobham, Bishop of Worcester, 1317–37* [London, 1923], 54).

[39] Irene Churchill, *Canterbury Administration* (London, 1933), I, 350 and 350 n 1. It is interesting that these customs were not (or do not appear to have been) considered vaguely simoniacal.

[40] *The Letters and Charters of Guala Bicchieri, Papal Legate in England 1216–1218*, ed. Nicholas Vincent, Canterbury and York Society 83 (Woodbridge, 1996), liii.

[41] R. Donaldson, "Sponsors, Patrons, and Presentations to Benefices – Particularly those in the Gift of the Priors of Durham – During the Later Middle Ages," *Archaeologia Aeliana* (fourth series) 37 (1960), 172. Although one should note the caveat raised by Barrie Dobson, *Durham Priory 1400–1450* (Cambridge, 1973), 146.

the church.[42] Monasteries were more vulnerable to such pressure than lay patrons, who tended to be at least gentry, if not of the higher nobility. After all, monks and nuns were subject to a great deal of episcopal supervision. Their heads were approved or rejected by bishops. They were subject to episcopal visitation and correction. Bishops set the terms on which they enjoyed appropriated benefices. It is true that reform-minded bishops may have cooperated in the appropriation of benefices to monasteries, hoping that the monks would accept such rewards in return for fostering reform, presenting suitable, unmarried, and pastorally oriented vicars.[43] Patronage-minded bishops, however, could well have seen appropriation as opening up more benefices to their own clerks by creating vicarages in the gift of authorities more subject to their will than the laity.

The pressure exerted by bishops on monastic patrons, or the attempt by monasteries to gain influence with bishops by rewarding episcopal servants, appears to have been ad hoc. This is evident in the fact that monasteries which themselves were in episcopal patronage were not particularly liable to furnish benefices to episcopal servants. That, at least, is the conclusion to be drawn from a survey of the large diocese of Lincoln over the course of several episcopates in the thirteenth century. There the houses in the bishop's patronage – the abbeys of Dorchester and Eynsham, St. Katherine's Priory, Lincoln, and the hospital of St. John, Northampton, all of the bishop's own patronage – seem to have contributed comparatively few of the benefices held by the bishops' major servants.[44] From the time the episcopal rolls begin in the early thirteenth century to the century's end, neither of the benefices in Dorchester's patronage (Sherburn and Warpsgrove)[45] went to men traceable as socially or bureaucratically connected with the bishop or his men. Only twice in the same period is St. Katherine's Priory, Lincoln, known to have gone to

---

[42] The council of Vienne (1311–13), Chapter 30: *Decrees of the Ecumenical Councils I: Nicaea I to Lateran V*, ed. Norman Tanner (Washington, DC, 1990), 386.

[43] Hence the suggestion of Ulrich Rasche, "The Early Phase of Appropriation of Parish Churches in Medieval England," *Journal of Medieval History* 26 (2000), 234.

[44] Although one should certainly note the problem with this procedure regarding the uncertainty of identifying all episcopal servants. The hospital of Mere, also in the bishop's patronage (Churchill, *Canterbury Administration*, II, 44; Rolls and Reg. Sutton, II, 96), does not appear to have held any advowsons, at least, not within the diocese of Lincoln. For monasteries presenting men to benefices at their patrons' behest, see Susan Wood, *English Monasteries and Their Patrons in the Thirteenth Century* (London, 1955), 112–14.

[45] Rolls and Reg. Sutton, VIII, 183; Rot. Grosseteste, 484–5.

such men.⁴⁶ Eynsham Abbey was more generous – or more aggressive or more bullied – presenting to benefices Robert de Kibworth and Richard de Pocklington, servants of Bishops Sutton and Grosseteste, respectively, as well as William de la Pommery, who received collation from Bishop Gravesend, and William de Wells, perhaps a relative of Bishop Hugh of Wells.⁴⁷ St. John's hospital, Northampton, does not appear to have presented any episcopal servants to benefices.⁴⁸ Such presentations of men connected with Bishop Sutton are, indeed, substantial, but not especially remarkable when compared to those made by other monastic patrons to Bishop Sutton's servants alone.⁴⁹ Moreover, this was not simply for want

---

⁴⁶ William de la Gare and William de Newark both received Stapleford on the priory's presentation (Rot. Gravesend, 43; Rolls and Reg. Sutton, I, 57–8). William de la Gare first appears as archdeacon of Lincoln under Gravesend, ca. 1277 (LN Lincoln, 26) and was also Gravesend's vicar-general and chancellor (A. B. Emden, *A Biographical Register of the University of Oxford to A.D. 1500* [Oxford, 1957], sub nom.). William de Newark probably first appears as archdeacon of Huntingdon in 1276 and very possibly remained in the archdeaconry until 1284 (LN Lincoln, 29). He appears as Gravesend's *officialis* on January 26, 1276 (Rot. Gravesend, 228).

⁴⁷ Rot. Wells, II, 37; Rot. Grosseteste, 457, 461; Rot. Gravesend, 193, 220 (and 332); Rolls and Reg. Sutton, VIII, 193. Bishop Gravesend collated Hockliffe to William de la Pommery by lapse. As a professor of canon law, William would have been valuable to any ecclesiastical patron (Rot. Gravesend, 193). William de Wells shares his name (a cognomen? a toponymic?) with Bishop Hugh of Wells, in whose episcopate he was presented by Eynsham. The link here is stronger, as the bishop himself collated a benefice, by authority of the council, to William's clerk, Robert de Dunholm (Rot. Wells, I, 126). Robert de Kibworth received custody of certain documents in the bishop's *camera* at Theydon Mount in 1296 (Rolls and Reg. Sutton, VI, 14). He had charge of supplying money to Robert de Warsop, the bishop's proctor at the Roman court, in 1298 (ibid., V, 64). He was probably a member of Sutton's household in the years 1290–8. In these years he attested on twenty-nine out of sixty-two days (i.e., 47%) on which Sutton issued dated acts attested by persons below the rank of canon of Lincoln, at fifteen locales (Michael Burger, "Intimacy and Lordship: The Creation of a Bureaucracy in the Diocese of Lincoln, ca. 1186–1299," PhD Dissertation, University of California, Santa Barbara [1991], 394). For Richard de Pocklington and Grosseteste, see Kathleen Major, "The *Familia* of Robert Grosseteste," in *Robert Grosseteste: Scholar and Bishop*, ed. D. A. Callus (Oxford, 1955), 233.

⁴⁸ Although it is conceivable that the William "de Br*u*mpton," deacon in 1282 when Sutton collated Little Bytham to him (and not otherwise traceably connected with the bishop), was the same man as the William "de Br*a*mpton," priest, instituted to Piddington on the hospital's presentation in 1295 (Rolls and Reg. Sutton, I, 4,19, II, 120).

⁴⁹ Peterborough Abbey, for example, aimed some of its patronage at Sutton's servants. Henry de Nassington received Pytchley on Peterborough's presentation in 1287; he became *officialis*, and is first connected with the bishop in 1280 (Rolls and Reg. Sutton, I, 8 [and inspeximus of same in BL, 35296, f. 365r-v], II, 58, and also Matthew Sullivan, "The Role of the Nassington Family in the Medieval English Church," *Nottingham Medieval Studies* 37 [1993], 54). Henry Sampson the younger was instituted to Bringhurst on Peterborough's presentation in 1298, the same year he acted as a joint ad hoc commissary of the bishop

of advowsons. In the thirteenth century, St. Katherine's Priory held rights to eight benefices, Eynsham to seventeen, St. John's hospital, to three.[50]

Of course, monastic patrons could and did also present episcopal clerks to benefices for the same reasons bishops collated benefices to their clerks: they wanted their skilled service, even leaving aside any influence

(Rolls and Reg. Sutton, VI, 111, VIII, 68–9). Nicholas de Appletree is traceable in Sutton's service (for joint and single ad hoc commissions issued by Sutton to Nicholas 1294–9, including administering the vacant archdeaconry of Buckingham, see ibid., V, 10, VI, 44, 115, 143, 148, 161, 186) before and after he received Barnack on Peterborough's presentation (ibid., II, 138). St. Neot's Priory aimed its patronage at major episcopal servants in Sutton's *familia*. The priory presented John de Clipston and John de Bayton, both of whom were of Sutton's houschold, as well as Roger de Sixil, a third member of the household, albeit one who cannot be found rendering actual service to the bishop. (Roger de Sixil resigned Wing in 1295, upon which St. Neot's Priory presented to the benefice [ibid., II, 130]. Presumably the *Robert* de Sixil instituted to Wing in 1287 [ibid., II, 58] is a mistake for Roger, who witnesses in 1291 as rector of Wing [ibid., III, 116]. See also "Robert, alias Roger of [Sixhills]" in the index of persons and places in Rolls and Reg. Sutton, II.) Roger is most evident in Sutton's household in the years 1290–2, when he attested on twelve of the twenty-one days (i.e., 57%) on which Sutton issued dated acts with attestors lower than the rank of canon of Lincoln (see Michael Burger, "*Officiales* and the *familiae* of the Bishops of Lincoln, 1258–99," *Journal of Medieval History* 16 [1990], 40–2, for the issue of rank in these witness lists; lists that do not descend below the ranks of the canons, a rank Roger never reached, cannot be used to determine whether Roger was present). For the lists in which Roger appears 1290–2: LAO, Episcopal Register I, f. 354, correcting "Robert of Sixhills" for "Roger de Sixhills" at Rolls and Reg. Sutton, VIII, 205, regarding Buckden; LAO, Episcopal Register I, f. 354v, correcting Rolls and Reg. Sutton VIII, 205–6, regarding archdeaconry of Stow; Rolls and Reg. Sutton, III, 7, 15, 103–4, 116, 121, 172, 182, VIII, 143, 204, 206. These twelve occasions were at nine different places. For all the lists of this period (with corrections noted earlier): ibid., II, 80, 86, 91, III, 7, 15, 73, 86–8, 103–4, 116, 171–2, 186, IV, 34, VIII, 17, 121, 128, 131, 136, 143, 176, 204–7, 209; LAO, Dii/62/1/4; LAO, Dii/62/1/8. In addition, Roger appears as a witness on nine different dates in the years 1292–5 at five different places (Rolls and Reg. Sutton, III, 182, IV, 121, 191, VIII, 143, 206, 211, 217). He had also earlier appeared in a list of 1288 (LAO, Roll III, m 4, correcting Rolls and Reg. Sutton, VIII, 18, regarding Nettleham). Sutton created John de Clipston a notary public on papal authority in 1293 (Rolls and Reg. Sutton, IV, 130–1 and see 110). John drew up documents for the bishop in 1295, 1296, 1297, and 1299 (ibid., V, 110, VI, 13, 166, VIII, 218). He examined candidates for ordination on the bishop's behalf in 1297 and 1299 (ibid., VII, 99, 115, 119). John de Bayton appears as *marescallus episcopi* in 1290 (ibid., III, 7) and so should be included in the bishop's household. He later became a clerk.

[50] St. Katherine's Priory held the advowsons of Bracebridge, Canwick, Stapleford, Newton on Trent, Alford, and Friskney (Rot. Wells, I, 225, III, 168, 209; Rolls and Reg. Sutton, I, 14, 25, 57–58). Eynsham held those of Whitfield, Lower Heyford, South Stoke, Merton, Woodeaton, Westcott Barton, Cassington, Combe, Brize Norton, Little Rollright, Sarsden, St. Ebbe (Oxford), Souldern, Staunton, Charlbury, Yarnton, and Eynsham (Rot. Wells, I, 52–3, II, 9–10, 12, 18, 26, 35, 45; Rot. Grosseteste, 445–6; Rolls and Reg. Sutton, II, 38–9, VIII, 172, 175, 193, 201–2). St. John's Hospital, Northampton, held those of Piddington, Helmdon, and Slipton (Rot. Grosseteste, 218, 238, 244; Rot. Gravesend, 119; Rolls and Reg. Sutton, II, 28, 80, 82, 120).

they could provide in the operations of the diocese. Lincoln again provides some evidence for this. Under Grosseteste, John de Riston, a clerk of the archdeacon of Lincoln and recipient from the bishop of orders to induct, was presented to St. Peter's, Stamford, by St. Fromund's Priory, which later enjoyed his services as proctor.[51] Robert de Kirmington, a minor commissary of Bishop Sutton in 1293, had, in 1290, been instituted to Brigsley on the presentation of the proctor of the prior of Ravendale, himself acting for Beauport Abbey.[52] Robert had earlier served as the prior of Ravendale's proctor, who in turn was Beauport's proctor.[53] William de Sausthorpe, brother of the archdeacon of Stow, also received a minor ad hoc commission from Bishop Sutton in 1293. He had already received the commend of a rectory in the gift of Bardney Abbey, and before that had done the abbey a favor in acting as the convent's proctor in securing the abbot-elect's confirmation from the bishop.[54] (William's particular service to Bardney, and his blood tie with Sutton's first appointee to Stow, help bring home the [potential] value to patrons of men with ties to episcopal government.)[55] Even (or especially) a cathedral chapter could seek such benefits. In 1292–3, the chapter of Lincoln compensated Walter de Fotheringhay, an active episcopal ad hoc commissary, for dealing with the bishop regarding Ailby and Gosberton.[56]

---

[51] Rot. Grosseteste, 117. For his connection with Grosseteste, see Major, "*Familia* of Robert Grosseteste," 236.

[52] Rolls and Reg. Sutton, I, 155, IV, 112.

[53] Ibid., I, 115–16.

[54] Ibid., 2–3, 60.

[55] Although I have not noticed any clear evidence that the bishop was more pliable when dealing with parties who gave gifts to his men. It may have been that expectations were generally greater than effects. R. M. T. Hill has discussed Sutton's impartiality in policy regarding the institution of heads of religious houses, although she does not appear to consider the possible consequences of monastic patronage of episcopal servants ("Bishop Sutton and the Institution of Heads of Religious Houses in the Diocese of Lincoln," *English Historical Review* 58 [1943], 202–6).

[56] LAO, Bi/5/5/13/2/m. 1. Sutton commissioned him jointly to discharge executors on three occasions in 1293 (Rolls and Reg. Sutton, IV, 106, 111–12, 115), and to hear a case in 1294 (ibid., V, 3). The following year he received two joint commissions to grant probate (ibid., V, 98, 110). Sutton commissioned him jointly to hear two cases and jointly to grant probate on two occasions in 1296 (ibid., V, 141–2, 146, 157, 165, and see 162). He received four joint commissions to grant probate in 1297, as well as a commission to visit a priory (ibid., V, 215, VI, 7, 40, 44, 50). He received eight joint commissions to grant probate in 1298 as well as a joint commission to settle a dispute (ibid., VI, 58, 67, 72, 83, 109, 116, 123–4). Sutton commissioned him jointly to audit certain accounts, to grant probate, and to hear a case in 1299 (ibid., VI, 139, 165, 191, 203–4).

Creating Benefices and a Move for Reform

Demand for benefices led bishops to divert their own wealth into creating more benefices to give. Hence bishops moved to endow new colleges with prebends, such as the college the archbishops of Canterbury tried to establish at Lambeth.[57] True, historians have sometimes seen such moves as attempts to create a collegiate body to displace, or at least to play off of, the cathedral chapters with which bishops were periodically in conflict. This view surely has some truth to it, explaining why cathedral chapters viewed the foundation of colleges by their bishops with such hostility.[58] A college could also be a source of prayers for one's soul and simply a source of prestige. Presumably another motive behind such colleges was, however, the creation of a supply of prebendal benefices – that is, benefices without cure of souls.[59] After all, living in a land of monastic cathedral chapters, a bishop whose sole goal was to erect a rival cathedral chapter could have founded a monastery, even if monastic chapters were less fashionable than they used to be. Moreover, a monastery could furnish prayers and prestige. Yet, Bishop Bek of Durham explicitly cited a shortage of advisors to assist him when he founded a prebendal college at Chester-le-Street, and this was only one of the colleges he founded, fostered, or reordered.[60] Indeed, in 1189, the bishop of Coventry and Lichfield had violently invaded his priory of Coventry and replaced the monks with secular canons. An account hostile to the monks even claims

---

[57] See Charles Fonge, "Patriarchy and Patrimony: Investing in the Medieval College," in *The Foundations of Medieval English Ecclesiastical History: Studies Presented to David Smith*, ed. Philippa Hoskin, Christopher Brooke, and Barrie Dobson (Woodbridge, 2005), 78–9 and material cited there. Of course, lay patrons also fostered such prebendal colleges, mostly for reasons similar to those of bishops (e.g., St. Mary's, Warwick, for which see ibid., 80–2, and the "Introduction" to *The Cartulary of St. Mary's Collegiate Church, Warwick*, ed. Charles Fonge [Woodbridge, 2004]). Royal establishments claimed exemption from episcopal jurisdiction by asserting direct subjection to the pope (J. H. Denton, *English Royal Free Chapels 1100–1300: A Constitutional Study* [Manchester, 1970]). With papal appeal in theory thus open, incumbents might have been able to seek protection against their royal patron. Whether that was so in practice is uncertain.

[58] Fonge, "Patriarchy and Patrimony," 78–9.

[59] As noted ibid., 79–80. Fonge also points to other motives for founding colleges: a means to safeguard property (a twelfth-century practice); spiritual return and prestige; a way of delegating the cost of managing lands; a way of attracting lay investors to the bishop's ventures (ibid., 80–2, 90–1). His stress on the demand for prebends from clerical hangers-on (ibid., 83–4) is exactly mine here.

[60] *Records of Antony Bek, Bishop and Patriarch: 1283–1311*, ed. C. M. Fraser, Surtees Society 162 (London, 1953), no. 6; C. M. Fraser, *A History of Antony Bek, Bishop of Durham, 1283–1311* (Oxford, 1957), 115–18.

that the bishop's blood was spilled at the altar. Only in 1197, as the bishop was dying and repentant, did the monks return.⁶¹

Less ambitious bishops, if they were fortunate enough to have secular cathedrals, created prebends in already existing cathedral chapters. This strategy could result in ersatz benefices, formed not out of tithes or a landed endowment but from a fixed cash payment from the bishop. By the early thirteenth century, the bishop of Lincoln had constituted £10 annually due him from the archdeacon of Lincoln as a prebend of Lincoln cathedral: "Decem Librarum."⁶² In the later twelfth century, the bishops of Salisbury were contributing 100s a year *de camera* to two prebends in Salisbury cathedral, a fact caught in the sources only by the king's administration of the bishop's temporalities *sede vacante* in 1185–8.⁶³ Of course, finding the money elsewhere was always appealing. The bishop of Coventry and Lichfield carved out a "prebenda bursalis" from the common fund of the chapter of Lichfield, yielding 100s annually to the recipient.⁶⁴ But when Bishop Hugh of Wells of Lincoln collated Decem Librarum to Peter de Chevermunt, he did so only until he would provide for him suitably (*competenter*) in the cathedral.⁶⁵ This unusual condition for a collation suggests that Peter would have preferred something else, perhaps something with a more independent endowment.⁶⁶

Of course, the pope was the greatest ecclesiastic in need of patronage. Increasingly in the twelfth and thirteenth centuries the papacy had found means to transfer the patronage of benefices from local hands to its own. Not surprisingly, the losers saw papal provision of benefices as an abuse. But the system was arguably a reform, putting benefices in the hands of men chosen less according to the whim of local potentates.⁶⁷ A path to

---

[61] M. J. Franklin, "The Bishops of Coventry and Lichfield, c. 1072–1208," in *Coventry's First Cathedral: The Cathedral and Priory of St. Mary's, Papers from the 1993 Anniversary Symposium*, ed. George Demidowic (Stamford, 1994), 135–7; D. E. Desborough, "Politics and Prelacy in the Late Twelfth Century: The Career of Hugh de Nonant, 1188–1198," *Historical Research* 64 (1991), 6–8.

[62] LN Lincoln, 65; *Registrum Antiquissimum*, II, nos. 350–2. At some point in the twelfth century, a bishop of Lincoln also permanently granted about 50s annually from sums owed him by the archdeacon of Lincoln to the prebend of Carlton Kyme, which otherwise had a landed endowment (LN Lincoln, 57).

[63] LN Salisbury, 4, 136–7.

[64] *The Great Register of Lichfield Cathedral Known as Magnum Registrum Album*, ed. H. E. Savage (Kendal, 1926), no. 634.

[65] *Registrum Antiquissimum*, II, no. 352.

[66] Indeed, the terms of this collation bring to mind the grants of pensions in lieu of benefices discussed in Chapter 5.

[67] Geoffrey Barraclough, *Papal Provisions: An Aspect of Church History, Constitutional, Legal and Administrative, in the Later Middle Ages* (Oxford, 1935).

a different kind of reform lay in altering the material support of papal bureaucrats. The late twelfth and earlier thirteenth centuries saw a series of proposals to reform the papal curia at a stroke by finding its members income other than gifts offered by suitors. Strikingly, the first of these plans was proposed, not by the pope, but by the Emperor Henry VI in 1197: to reserve benefices across Christendom on a systematic basis for clerks in papal service.[68]

But once the plan was revived at papal hands, it was recast to decouple curial revenues from benefices altogether. Innocent III proposed that the papal court receive a tenth of the income from every cathedral in Christendom; curial officers would be paid out of that.[69] This plan, which not only threatened local income but also proposed to strike at the root of the independence offered by reward through benefices, went nowhere, even when proposed by an Innocent III. The pope failed to prevail at the Fourth Lateran Council when he unveiled this proposal, opposed by the greater part of the clergy there.[70] Yet, Innocent's plan offered a way out of the problems that rewarding servants with benefices posed bishops, including the patronage hunger they themselves felt in the face of benefice hunger. As papal provisions suggest, popes felt this hunger too. Honorius III revived the plan in 1225. On this occasion the sources are fuller. Unfortunately, none of the surviving arguments against the proposal originated from the curia. Resistance among bishops and collegiate chapters was in terms of their own loss of benefices or income. (Honorius's plan would have taxed bishops for the common fund too.)[71] So one cannot know what papal *curiales* thought about the scheme. But it is noteworthy that the pope converted a plan systematically to reserve benefices for papal clerks into a more liquid fund from which to salary those clerks. The move, had it been executed, would have strengthened the pope's control over his own *curiales*.

English bishops had been among those to whom Innocent and Honorius made their proposals. Indeed, Honorius's plan was aimed specifically at the English and French churches; English clergy met twice to deliberate on the matter.[72] Yet, while English prelates may have been

---

[68] See Chapter 6 at n 130.
[69] Richard Kay, "Gerald of Wales and the Fourth Lateran Council," *Viator* 29 (1998), 79, 93.
[70] Ibid., 93. Unfortunately, the grounds for its rejection are left unstated in the major source.
[71] Richard Kay, *The Council of Bourges, 1225: A Documentary History* (Aldershot, 2002), 175–232; Kay, "An Eyewitness Account of the 1225 Council of Bourges," *Studia Gratiana* 12 (1967), 63–79.
[72] Kay, *Council of Bourges*, 215–29.

driven by patronage hunger, none proposed at home the kind of reform that might have ended that hunger by changing the system of rewards through benefices. That failure makes sense. Most of them, after all, were themselves products of that system, rising from benefice to benefice until attaining nearly the grandest of all, a bishopric. The mental habits of the better part of a lifetime are hard to break. Moreover, their own clerks had even more invested in the reliance on benefices rather than revocable payments as a reward for service.

9

Continuity and Discontinuity of Service

In 1259, a new bishop of Exeter arrived in his see to discover scandal. Walter Bronscombe found that on the death of his predecessor, Richard Blund, certain men, "contrary to the knowledge and command of the venerable father Richard ... [Bronscombe's] deceased predecessor, dictated letters in the name of the deceased for the collation of benefices and other matters, wrote them, sealed them, [and] gave fraudulent assent to the sealing."[1] Two of the conspirators confessed. Their account is worth quoting *in extenso*:

> There appeared before the lord bishop Sir Walter de Loddiswell, priest, chancellor and chamberlain to Richard of blessed memory, late bishop of Exeter, at the time of his death, and Master Richard de Totnes, clerk and notary to the same.
>
> Returning to their senses under the influence of repentance, they took oath of their own free will, in the presence of the lord bishop ... and they confessed that, in the year of the Lord 1257, on being summoned, they entered the bishop's room by night where they found various members of the household gathered together, both clerks and laymen. These told them that the bishop was in a failing condition, and that they were engaged in disposing of the bishop's property, conferring benefices and drawing up and sealing letters on these matters; after each of them had given his word that he would never reveal the deed, they all reached agreement, assigned benefices, wrote and sealed letters. On being asked whether the bishop was

---

[1] Reg. Bronscombe, no. 78: "preter conscientiam et mandatum venerabilis patris R[icardi] predecessoris sui defuncti, super collationibus beneficiorum et aliis rebus disponendis sub nomine defuncti litteras dictaverunt, scripserunt, consignarunt, consignationi fraudulenter consenserunt." I have reproduced the editor's translation. Later entries make clear that these forgeries were concocted after Bishop Blund's death (see next n).

then dead or was still alive in his bed, they say that they did not know, but that they did not afterwards see him either living or speaking.²

Walter and Richard named names. Among them was that of Master John fitz Robert, then *officialis* who, along with another clerk, dictated the letters. Richard de Totnes himself was guilty of acting as scribe and one Henry the chaplain applied the bishop's seal. And the account explicitly states that "many letters were written and sealed after they knew the bishop was dead."³

This episode reveals that a bishop's death could be a time of high anxiety. The rewards and punishments discussed in preceding chapters help explain why. I have argued that when it came to their administrators, bishops preferred carrots, largely in the form of permanent gifts, and they used sticks, small anyway, sparingly. In particular, benefices were the chief reward bishops had to offer, but benefices came with a security of tenure that made it hard for bishops to discipline the bureaucrats who received them. At least bishops and bureaucrats could try to exploit whatever ties of sentiment bound a bishop who gave benefices and the clerk who received them (more on such ties in the next chapter). But once death had removed a bishop, his clerks faced an incoming man, his identity not certain until he took office, with whom they might or might not have cultivated such ties.⁴ Clerks who had already gained their benefice(s) could afford to face the new situation with some equanimity. After all, they had a secure income and standing to go with it. Indeed, their bishop's death may have been in one sense welcome, making it easier to explore other possibilities, from transferring to service in another diocese, to focusing on alternative activities as a member of collegiate chapter, to simply retiring from administrative work altogether. Their less fortunate colleagues, however, had reason to worry. Would the new bishop want their services? Would he prove to be a good patron? Bishop Blund's men avoided the problem by gaining benefices by fraud. The fact that the *officialis*, a man already securely beneficed in the diocese,⁵ took part also suggests the solidarity that might tie together a bishop's clerks (discussed in Chapter 7),

---

² Ibid., no. 83, and see no. 92.
³ Ibid., no. 83.
⁴ Of course, the death of a secular patron could still leave a clerk feeling bereft, even if he had a benefice: see Peter of Blois's response to the death of Henry II (John D. Cotts, *The Clerical Dilemma: Peter of Bois and Literate Culture in the Twelfth Century* [Washington, DC, 2009], 38–40).
⁵ This was John, son of Robert, for whom see LN Exeter, 56.

although it could be that the *officialis* benefited from letters "on other matters" mentioned in the register's first entry concerning this episode.

The aftermath of the extraordinary scene in Bishop Blund's chamber was also extraordinary. Not surprisingly, Bronscombe excommunicated the culprits, suspending one.[6] But as Frank Barlow has noted, two of the guilty parties went on to serve Bronscombe himself.[7] Why did Bronscombe take them in? He presumably needed clerks, but that might be the case of any bishop. His move suggests how understandable, if not permissible, their actions had been.

An account – even if partly spurious – of another bishop's death points to similar anxiety. Matthew Paris tells the story. As Edmund of Abingdon, archbishop of Canterbury, lay dying, his *ministri* approached him, lamenting that his death would leave them high and dry. The archbishop was on the road to Rome, apparently voluntarily, so Paris's explanation that Edmund was in exile must throw some doubt on his story. Matthew has Edmund's clerks complain that, on their return to England, they would face penury, not to mention the hostility of king and magnates.[8] According to Paris, the archbishop went ahead and wrote letters of recommendation for them, at least one addressed to the bishop of Norwich.[9] Paris produces that letter, so presumably this element of the account can be trusted. In this case, the archbishop may not have had any vacant benefices to hand. Arranging their service elsewhere, with some living lord, was the only licit option. Indeed, any dying bishop might act in these matters. In his will, Bishop Suffield of Norwich commended those who had faithfully served him and his church to his successor.[10] Perhaps the drama of a bishop's death added to the tension, from the breaking of his

---

[6] Reg. Bronscombe, nos. 78, 83.

[7] EEA XI: Exeter, lxxix n3.

[8] Matthew Paris, "Vita S. Edmundi" in C. H. Lawrence, *St. Edmund of Abingdon: A Study of Hagiography and History* (Oxford, 1960), 267. See Lawrence's discussion, ibid., 168–76, debunking this exile. I am not sure how to treat these (partially fictionalized?) *ministri*'s claim that they are unaccustomed to business (*negocia*). These do not sound like administrators. But Archbishop Edmund wrote letters of recommendation for them. Matthew reproduces one of these letters. It is a letter for Robert de Essex addressed to the bishop of Norwich, asking the bishop to take Robert into his *obsequium*, commending the good *servicium* Robert had rendered Edmund (ibid., 268). This suggests administration of some sort. Perhaps Matthew was determined to give Edmund's ministers a rather monastically unworldly cast. But, as was his practice, Matthew reproduces the archbishop's letter in toto. It can be taken as reliable. Lawrence notes that only one of the monks of Christ Church, Canterbury, seems to have been of Edmund's household (ibid., 148–9).

[9] Ibid., 262–8.

[10] EEA 32: Norwich, no. 138.

seal to the drawn out obsequies. Unfortunately, the dry prosopography of clerical administration does not capture the hopes and anxieties of such men the way the evidence cited here does.[11]

Although the degree of continuity of administrators from one episcopate to the next was a live issue in the thirteenth century, historians have not until recently given it much focused treatment. That has begun to change, most notably at the hands of Philippa Hoskin and Nicholas Vincent. Vincent notes that a bishop's demise could be depressing for his clerks. He explains that the death of a bishop removed his clerks' source of patronage, while Hoskin notes that such a picture is indeed implicit in historians' discussions.[12] Vincent uses a discussion of the clerk Elias de Dereham to point out that men like Elias – steward to several bishops of different dioceses – were few and valued for the skills they possessed, whereas "the vast majority of close episcopal familiars passed their lives in service to one particular bishop; or in lateral moves within the same diocese as newly elected bishops reconstituted their households around an existing core of experienced administrators."[13] Hoskin argues that there was great continuity in the administrative personnel of the bishops of Durham across the thirteenth century. But she holds that this continuity was unusual, arguing that it was the peculiarly weighty secular responsibilities of the bishops of Durham for their Palatinate that gave their households the high degree of continuity to be found among those of great secular lords.[14] Finally, a number of short examinations of continuity of service are dispersed among the accumulating volumes of the *English Episcopal Acta* series, which with its third volume (1986) began to cover the thirteenth century.[15]

Was continuity of service to one bishop after another normal? Or did a change of bishop mean a change in administrative personnel? The picture – complicated by evidentiary problems discussed later – is mixed. When a bishop died, some of his clerks left the diocese to serve other

---

[11] See the remarks of Cotts, *Peter of Blois*, 95.
[12] Nicholas Vincent, "Master Elias of Dereham (d. 1245): A Reassessment," in *The Church and Learning in Later Medieval Society: Essays in Honour of R.B. Dobson, Proceedings of the 1999 Harlaxton Symposium* (Donington, 2002), 139; Philippa Hoskin, "Continuing Service: The Episcopal Households of Thirteenth-Century Durham," in *The Foundations of Medieval Ecclesiastical History: Studies Presented to David Smith*, ed. Philippa Hoskin, Christopher Brooke, and Barrie Dobson (Woodbridge, 2005), 126.
[13] Vincent, "Master Elias of Dereham," 157.
[14] Hoskin, "Continuing Service," 135–8 and see EEA 29: Durham, xxxix.
[15] EEA III: Canterbury. These discussions tend to be ad hoc: e.g., a couple clerks of one bishop of Carlisle noted to have been inherited by his successor (EEA 30: Carlisle, xliv).

bishops. Some went on to serve their bishop's successor. And some left diocesan administration altogether. What all this suggests is that diocesan administrators were, in a sense, free agents. So were their bishops. A clerk's decisions to serve this or that bishop was an ad hoc one, as was that of a bishop to accept him. The result might on occasion have been a kind of core of administrators who provided continuity across episcopates, but such occasions were negotiated occasions. The "core," when there was one, was a by-product of who chose to stay, and whom the bishop wished to stay, rather than some sort of standing entity.

Continuity and Discontinuity in the Diocese of Lincoln

This fluidity is evident in the episcopates of the five bishops of Lincoln whose episcopates stretch across most of the thirteenth century. One should begin, however, by noting some facts of evidence. For most of the century, the most fruitful means of identifying diocesan administrators at Lincoln is to find their frequent appearances as witnesses to episcopal *acta* or their appearances as witnesses in memoranda of episcopal acts, very often the collation of benefices by the bishop to clerks as recorded in his rolls of institutions to benefices. As supplement one can add the identification of men as canons of Lincoln, presumably through collation by the bishops (often when listed as witnesses); the explicit designation of a man as the bishop's clerk or chaplain (again often as a witness to the bishop's acts); and the occasional mention of a clerk as an episcopal agent in other sources (e.g., the royal rolls of letters close and patent). But nothing approaching a systematic record of administrative orders given out by the bishops is preserved at Lincoln until 1290, when Bishop Sutton did historians a favor by replacing rolls with a more secure register as a means of preserving business. As a result, it is easier to identify men in episcopal service at Lincoln after 1290 than before. After all, a bishop's clerk who spent most of his time outside the household receiving administrative orders by letter would infrequently witness that bishop's acts. That rarity would also cut down the number of occasions on which a source might explicitly refer to him as the bishop's clerk. If such a clerk did not happen to have been caught by, say, an appearance in one of the king's letters patent, one would never know he served the bishop. His reception of a benefice from the bishop would indicate a connection, but only at one point in time; the historian cannot know how long the connection lasted. (E.g., if a clerk received a benefice in 1240 as the bishop's man, can one still assume a connection with the bishop in, say, 1245, in the absence of any other evidence?)

All this means that the sources from the diocese of Lincoln – and indeed of most thirteenth-century dioceses most of the time – are likely to understate the number of men who served successive bishops of a diocese. For a man who can be identified as the clerk of one bishop might have served his successor or predecessor, but have been rarely in that bishop's household, and so less likely to be identifiable as that bishop's servant.

How to overcome these evidentiary problems? One approach is not to worry too much about them and simply establish what the evidence can show. Historians have sometimes taken this course, and there is something to be said for doing so. One has only the evidence one has. Another approach is to try to trace the activities of episcopal clerks after their bishop's death. If they cannot be found in the service of the succeeding bishop, can they be found doing other things instead? If so, depending on the nature of those activities, one can presume (and presume only) that they left diocesan administration. In this way, historians can arrive at positive evidence for discontinuity to set against the positive evidence for continuity presented by men identifiable as episcopal clerks under consecutive bishops.

Finally, in considering continuity it is necessary to beware archdeacons. For once a man became an archdeacon, he held a benefice which made him ex officio a diocesan officer. In the following discussion, I have excluded archdeacons, who automatically served the next bishop simply by surviving his predecessor.

Lincoln, despite lacunae, presents the single best documented diocesan administration for the bulk of the thirteenth century. By good fortune, surviving cartularies furnish a large number of *acta* from Bishops St. Hugh of Avalon (1186–1200) and William of Blois (1203–6). Moreover, the bishops' ongoing records of institutions to benefices are the earliest in England, surviving from the year 1214 or 1215 under Bishop Hugh of Wells (1209–35).[16] In roll or register form, they run continuously to the end of the century and beyond. The survival of a register dedicated to the vicarages ordained by Hugh of Wells bolsters the number of Hugh's attested *acta*.[17]

---

[16] David M. Smith, *Guide to Bishops' Registers in England and Wales, a Survey from the Middle Ages to the Abolition of Episcopacy in 1646* (London, 1981), 103–7 and for the date in particular, Smith, "The Rolls of Hugh of Wells, Bishop of Lincoln 1209–35," *Bulletin of the Institute of Historical Research* 45 (1972), 155–95.

[17] Printed as *Liber Antiquus de Ordinationibus Vicarium Tempore Hugonis Wells, Lincolniensis Episcopi, 1209–1235*, ed. A. Gibbons (Lincoln, 1888). For the *acta*, however, see *Acta of Hugh of Wells*.

David Smith has identified several servants inherited by Bishop William of Blois (1203–6) from his predecessor, Bishop Hugh of Avalon (1186–1200): Roger Bacon, Hugh de St. Edward, Alexander de Bedford, Alexander de Elstow, Gerard de Rowell, and Geoffrey de Deeping.[18] Smith has also carefully identified the administrative personnel of the next bishop, Hugh of Wells (1209–35).[19] He observes that Hugh of Wells inherited Thomas de Fiskerton, active under William of Blois, as a datary, and that Hugh promoted other clerks of William – Hugh de St. Edward, Adam de St. Edmund, and William son of Fulk – to archdeaconries.[20] Professor Smith has more recently put forward three other names – Adam de St. Edmund, Richard de Linwood, and Gilbert de Mablethorpe – as men who served both Hugh of Wells and at least one of his two immediate predecessors.[21] Three of Hugh's clerks are in turn traceable as servants of Hugh's successor, Robert Grosseteste (1235–53): Thomas de Ashby, Stephen de Castello, and John de Crakehall.[22] Thomas, it should be noted, served Grosseteste only until about February 1237, after which point he appears to have become resident in the cathedral chapter at Lincoln.[23] Richard and John, however, served Grosseteste for a number of years.[24] Yet, several men in Hugh's service at the end of his episcopate disappear from diocesan service with his death. This suggests a degree of discontinuity, but since their fate is unknown, some caution is in order.[25] Against the men

---

[18] EEA IV: Lincoln, xxvii.
[19] In David M. Smith, "The Administration of Hugh of Wells, Bishop of Lincoln, 1209–35," PhD Thesis, University of Nottingham (1970), I, 216–57. His subsequent publication of a revised edition of Hugh's *acta* occasionally adds to the information presented in his thesis.
[20] *Acta of Hugh of Wells*, xxxii–xxxiii.
[21] EEA IV: Lincoln, xxviii, n 29.
[22] Smith, "The Administration of Hugh of Wells," I, 220, 228, 231–2. These men are also so identified by Kathleen Major, "The *Familia* of Robert Grosseteste," in *Robert Grosseteste: Scholar and Bishop*, ed. D. A. Callus (Oxford, 1955), 219–20, 224–6.
[23] Major, "*Familia* of Robert Grosseteste," 220. Major speculates from this short service that he may have stayed on under Grosseteste "only for the purpose of ensuring continuity and handing over the business to the new men" (ibid., 219–20). It is also possible that Thomas had a falling out with his new bishop. To Major, add his attestations of charters dealing with members of the chapter or chapter business in the years after 1237: Registrum Antiquissimum, IV, no. 1451, X, no. 2499, X, nos. 2692, 2799, 2800, 2864; LAO, A/1/8/463, f. 147v.
[24] Stephen as late as 1244, John to the very end (ibid., 224–5).
[25] E.g., Geoffrey de Moris, Richard de Oxford, Richard de Wyndesor (Smith, "Administration of Hugh of Wells," I, 244–5, 254–5). Smith also notes that some of William of Blois's clerks appear to have retired to reside as canons at Lincoln, but he does not provide examples (*Acta of Hugh of Wells*, xxxii).

who went on to careers under Grosseteste, one can also point to a similar number who after Bishop Hugh's death began to reside at Lincoln as members of the chapter: Robert de Bolsover, Robert de Gravele, Hugh de Wells (not to be confused with his namesake the bishop), and William de Winchecombe.[26] One might also add Ralph de Waraville, canon of Wells, who seems to have gone back to Wells on Grosseteste's accession.[27]

Judging continuity following Grosseteste's death presents a special problem. Grosseteste's episcopate was followed by the short episcopate of Henry de Lexington (1254-8), and Lexington's pontificate is poorly documented. An institution roll survives for only one out of the eight archdeaconries, and so his administrative personnel are very hard to identify.[28] Lexington was followed by Bishop Richard Gravesend (1258-79), whose administrative activities are documented on a level comparable with those of Hugh of Wells and Grosseteste. Given the near documentary hiatus presented by Lexington's pontificate, the best approach is to consider together continuity between the pontificates of Grosseteste and Lexington, and between those of Grosseteste and Gravesend.

Here the case for continuity is stronger than for that between Hugh of Wells and Robert Grosseteste. Three men moved from Grosseteste's to Lexington's service: Robert de St. Agatha and, on weaker evidence, G(ilbert) de Leicester and Peter de Stamford.[29] It has been suggested that a third man, John de Riston, served both Lexington and Gravesend, but the evidence is, I think, too thin for confidence regarding his service to

---

[26] Smith, "Administration of Hugh of Wells," I, 225, 236-7, 250-4.
[27] Ibid., 249.
[28] The roll is printed at Rot. Grosseteste, 508-14.
[29] Robert de St. Agatha is not listed by Major as Grosseteste's servant (Major, "*Familia* of Robert Grosseteste"). He jointly examined, presumably on the bishop's commission, the election of the prioress of Studley, confirmed June 1250-June 1251 (Rot. Grosseteste, 499). His service to Lexington is much better attested: he served as Lexington's *officialis* in 1255 (*The Registrum Antiquissimum of the Cathedral Church of Lincoln*, ed. C. W. Foster and K. Major [Lincoln Record Society 27-8, 32, 34, 41, 46, 51, 62, 67] [Hereford and Gateshead, 1931-73], III, no. 832). He first appears as a canon of Lincoln, presumably on Lexington's collation, in 1256 (LN Lincoln, 141). Major identifies G. de Leicester as Grosseteste's man and suggests he served Lexington also. The evidence for the latter service is attestations to Lexington's acts on two different dates, in two different places; one of these attestations is by a Gilbert de Leicester (Major, "*Familia* of Robert Grosseteste," 230-1). The evidence for service under Lexington is thus quite thin. Of course, so is the evidence for this episcopate in general. Similarly, Peter de Stamford, who served Grosseteste (ibid., 238), can be connected with Bishop Lexington by his attestation of one of Lexington's *acta* (Rolls and Reg. Sutton, I, 69-70).

either bishop.³⁰ William de Southwell clearly served both Grosseteste and Gravesend.³¹ There is also reason to conclude that two other men, Richard de Bromholm and Robert de Marisco, moved from Grosseteste's to Gravesend's service.³² All told, there is solid evidence for four "crossovers" of this kind from Grosseteste's service to that of a successor. But given that two successors are considered here (Lexington and Gravesend), this is not impressive evidence for continuity of administrative personnel. Indeed, the scale of this continuity is similar to that from Hugh of Wells's episcopate to Grosseteste's. I have not, however, found much evidence of Grosseteste's servants retiring to the cathedral on Grosseteste's death. Perhaps that bishop's very bad relations with his chapter made the prospect unpalatable, although Robert de Marisco, Grosseteste's *officialis* and vicegerens in the bishop's absence, would eventually be elected dean of the cathedral, albeit seven years after Grosseteste's death.³³

The case for continuity is as strong between the episcopates of Gravesend and his successor, Oliver Sutton (1280–99) as it was at the beginning of the century, between the episcopates of William of Blois and Hugh of Avalon.

[30] The only evidence connecting John to Lexington and Gravesend is John's appearance among the witnesses to one act of Lexington's and two of Gravesend's (done on the same date) (Major, "*Familia* of Robert Grosseteste," 235).
[31] Ibid., 237. Major notes that he was Gravesend's *officialis* in 1260 (ibid.); he still held this position in 1261 (BL, Harley 4714, f. 132v).
[32] Richard de Bromholm does not appear in Kathleen Major's list ("*Familia* of Robert Grosseteste") as a servant of Grosseteste, but he did enjoy Grosseteste's patronage, receiving the collation of Brinkhill (Rot. Grosseteste, 84, 94). He first appears as canon of Lincoln, presumably on Grosseteste's collation, in 1249 (LN Lincoln, 83). His only traceable connection with Gravesend is his inquiry, presumably on the bishop's commission, regarding the presentation of a vicar in 1263 (Rot. Gravesend, 102–3). For Robert de Marisco's (Marsh's) service to Grosseteste, see Major, "*Familia* of Robert Grosseteste," 231. As newly elected dean of Lincoln, he acted as Gravesend's agent in confirming two newly chosen priors in Gravesend's first year (Rot. Gravesend, 1, 98). He also received an order as Gravesend's vicegerens (*Calendar of the Patent Rolls Preserved in the Public Record Office (1232–1509)* [London, 1891–1916], V [for 1258–1265], 9 and see *Close Rolls of the Reign of Henry III (1227–72)* [London, 1902–38], [for 1259–61], 279).
[33] Major, "*Familia* of Robert Grosseteste," 231; LN Lincoln, 11. For relations with the chapter, see R. W. Southern, *Robert Grosseteste: The Growth of an English Mind in Medieval Europe,* 2nd ed. (Oxford, 1992), 264–5; J. H. Srawley, "Grosseteste's Administration of the Diocese of Lincoln," in *Robert Grosseteste: Scholar and Bishop,* 171–7. It is also the case that in Grosseteste's last years a couple of his clerks, rather unusually, and perhaps inspired by their saintly master, entered religion, and so became unavailable for service. Benedict de Burgo entered the priory of Dunstable while William de Pocklington, most appropriately, joined the Franciscans (Major, "*Familia* of Robert Grosseteste," 222, 233).

Six men clearly served both Gravesend and Sutton: John le Fleming,[34] Richard de Horton,[35] Richard de Rothwell,[36] Simon de Luda,[37] Walter de

[34] John le Fleming first appears as canon of Lincoln, presumably by Gravesend's collation, in 1275 (LN Lincoln, 70) and was serving as Gravesend's chancellor in 1278 (Rot. Gravesend, 187, 320). In 1293, Sutton commissioned him to hear suits which would come before the *officialis* or his commissary and then commissioned him jointly to hear suits due before the bishop in a four-day period (Rolls and Reg. Sutton, IV, 119–20, 145–6). In that year, he also instituted to a benefice as Sutton's representative (ibid., VIII, 122). Sutton commissioned him jointly to hear a dispute and several times to grant probate in 1296 (ibid., V, 141–2, 185–6). He received several ad hoc commissions in 1297 (ibid., V, 217, VI, 10, 52). In 1298, he instituted to a benefice as Sutton's commissary (ibid., VIII, 122). From 1293 through 1294, he is occasionally to be found examining candidates for ordination (ibid., VII, 8, 26, 39, 54).

[35] Richard de Horton inquired, presumably on Gravesend's commission, regarding a presentation to a vicarage that culminated in institution in 1273 and three years later instituted a clerk to a vicarage, again presumably on Gravesend's commission (Rot. Gravesend, 68, 279). Gravesend also collated Quarrington to him (ibid., 37). Gravesend presumably collated to him his canonry and treasurership of the cathedral (LN Lincoln, 20, 85). Sutton commissioned him jointly to discharge executors in 1290 (Rolls and Reg. Sutton, III, 21). In the following year, Richard received commissions jointly to discharge executors, to investigate a complaint, and to examine some executors and make a report to the bishop (ibid., III, 95, 148, 154). In 1292, he was jointly to reconcile a churchyard (ibid., IV, 46). He received two more such commissions in the following year (ibid., IV, 69, 138). In 1294, Sutton commissioned him jointly to execute a papal provision, to grant probate, and to settle a dispute (ibid., I, 192, IV, 177, V, 44). Richard received an order jointly to hear a divorce case in 1295 (ibid., V, 54). He generally received commissions simply as the treasurer of Lincoln, which post he held in these years (LN Lincoln, 20). He also attested acts of the bishop on two dates (Rolls and Reg. Sutton, VIII, 117, 215; *Registrum Antiquissimum*, II, no. 607).

[36] Richard de Rothwell is identified as the bishop's clerk, and in one case, chaplain, in documents of 1274–8 (Rot. Gravesend, 135, 281, 285). Gravesend collated to him Castle Bytham, Winwick, and apparently a canonry in Lincoln cathedral (Rot. Gravesend, 60, 13; LN Lincoln, 51). Sutton commissioned Richard jointly to discharge executors in 1293 and to grant probate in 1295 (Rolls and Reg. Sutton, IV, 57, V, 111). Richard also attested Sutton's acts on two dates in different places (ibid., VIII, 17, 117).

[37] Simon is referred to as Gravesend's clerk on the occasions of the collation of Aylesby and Castle Bytham to him in 1277 and 1278 (Rot. Gravesend, 73, 82, 285, 287). He was active as an ad hoc commissary for Sutton. That bishop commissioned him jointly to discharge executors in 1290 and again in 1291 (Rolls and Reg. Sutton, III, 41–2, 93). In 1293, Sutton commissioned Simon jointly to examine an election (ibid., I, 199; IV, 119) and he received two commissions in that year to discharge executors (ibid., IV, 112). Sutton twice commissioned him jointly to grant probate in 1296 and also to hear a case in that year (ibid., V, 156–7, 163). In some of these commissions he is merely called Simon, rector of Aylesby. But he is identified explicitly as Master Simon de Luda, rector of Ailby in 1293, and had received Ailby in 1278 (Rot. Gravesend, 82; Rolls and Reg. Sutton, I, 199, IV, 112, 119). The entry in the edition, which calls him "William of Louth, rector of Aylesby," is in error: the manuscript reads "Simoni de Luda," rector of Ailby (Rolls and Reg. Sutton, V, 64 [LAO, Episcopal Register I, f. 118r]). Simon also appears as a witness to Sutton's acts on three dates at three locales early in the episcopate (Rolls

Malling,[38] and William de Thornton.[39] And there are less certain cases.[40] As after Grosseteste's death, I have not been able to identify canons in Gravesend's service in his last years who appear to have concentrated their energies on the cathedral chapter after their bishop's death. Weaker evidence of discontinuity comes in the form of John de Authoy and John de Leicester, clerks of Gravesend's later years who never rose to canonries and who do not appear to have served Sutton.[41]

The continuity of episcopal servants in the diocese across the thirteenth century should also be seen in the context of the origins of these pontiffs. After Hugh of Wells, these bishops all had enjoyed connections with the administration of the diocese before their elevations to the episcopate. Grosseteste had been archdeacon of Leicester under Hugh of Wells, a career cut idiosyncratically short in 1232 by his resignation; even

and Reg. Sutton, I, 2, 7, 8 (=BL Add. MS 35296, f. 365r-v). For his service to the bishops, see also Nicholas Bennett, "Pastors and Masters: The Beneficed Clergy of North-East Lincolnshire, 1290–1340," in *The Foundations of Medieval English Ecclesiastical History: Studies Presented to David Smith*, ed. Philippa Hoskin, Christopher Brooke, and Barrie Dobson (Woodbridge, 2005), 40, 62.

[38] Walter de Malling was acting as Gravesend's commissary regarding the presentation to a vicarage in 1276 and had presumably received his canonry of Lincoln from Gravesend (Rot. Gravesend, 183; LN Lincoln, 81). Sutton commissioned Walter jointly to discharge executors on three occasions in 1291–3 (Rolls and Reg. Sutton, III, 95, 108, IV, 81). He received two joint commissions to discharge executors in 1294, and four joint commissions to grant probate in 1295 (ibid., IV, 166, V, 83, 110–11).

[39] William de Thornton was the bishop's chancellor in 1276 and had received the commend of Woburn, in the bishop's patronage, in 1269 (Rot. Gravesend, 228, 244). He first appears as canon of Lincoln, presumably by Gravesend's collation, in 1270 (LN Lincoln, 99). William was one of Sutton's greater ad hoc commissaries. In 1290, he received a commission to hear jointly a case and two commissions jointly to grant probate (Rolls and Reg. Sutton, III, 48–9, 54 and see 159). Sutton commissioned him jointly to grant probate once in 1291, and to represent the bishop in a usury case in the following year (ibid., III, 159, IV, 10). Sutton commissioned him twice jointly to discharge executors in 1293 (ibid., IV, 80–1, but see 112). The bishop further commissioned him jointly to discharge executors in 1294 (ibid., IV, 166). In 1296, he received three joint commissions: to resolve a dispute, to grant probate, and to deal with problems posed by some executors (ibid., IV, 133, V, 142, 171). Sutton commissioned him jointly to deal with a dispute arising from a will in 1297 (ibid., V, 211). In the years 1297–8, he also received five commissions jointly to grant probate (ibid., V, 216, VI, 52, 75, 97, 124). He witnessed Sutton's acts on two dates, both at Lincoln (ibid., VIII, 117, 217–18).

[40] E.g., William de Anlauby, whose only connection with Gravesend is the church collated to him by that bishop (Rot. Gravesend, 240, 256). He served as notary to Sutton (Rolls and Reg. Sutton, III, 90, IV, 73) and examined candidates for ordination as acolyte on two occasions for Sutton (ibid., VIII, 9–10).

[41] John de Authoy appears as Gravesend's clerk when the bishop collated Clifton to him in 1279 (Rot. Gravesend, 212, 328). John de Leicester first appears as Gravesend's clerk in 1274, usually continuing to do so until his last appearance, in 1278, when he received the collation of Wheathampstead (ibid., 69, 73, 129, 156, 200, 228, 287, 320, 326).

then, he retained his place in the cathedral chapter as canon.[42] Gravesend had served as archdeacon of Oxford under Grosseteste.[43] Oliver Sutton's connection with the administration of the diocese had been looser than those of his two immediate predecessors, but he would still have been a fairly well known quantity to Gravesend's men, having been a member of the cathedral chapter from perhaps as early as 1270, and its dean since 1275.[44] Indeed, while membership in the chapter could serve as a kind of distraction from diocesan administration, as an alternative focus for one's time, in this situation it could also create ties with the man who would turn out to be of the next bishop, and so foster continuing service after the current bishop died. Of the six men who went on from Gravesend to serve Sutton, all but one (Simon de Luda) had been members of the chapter under Sutton as dean.[45] They not only knew Sutton when he became bishop, but they had had experience as his subordinates. Indeed, the chapter elected him bishop unanimously.[46]

There is also another kind of discontinuity to examine. I identified those episcopal clerks active in diocesan service in a bishop's last years who evidently did not serve his successor. But there were other episcopal servants who did not even serve in their bishop's later years, but who retired to cathedral activities long before their bishop died. For example, Roger de Bohun, sprung from a significant noble and ecclesiastical family in Bishop Hugh of Wells's home diocese of Bath and Wells, served as Hugh's attorney and is often to be found in his household between 1214 and late 1218. He appears to have received his canonry in the cathedral from Hugh, sometime before January 9, 1218. But after 1218 those four years of service were followed by at least twelve years of residence at Lincoln and deeper involvement in the affairs of the cathedral; Roger eventually served as the provost of the chapter's common fund.[47] Stephen de Chichester[48] and Geoffrey Scot[49] also fit this pattern. The evidence is weaker, but still suggestive, in the case of Roger de Bristol[50] and Theobald

---

[42] LN Lincoln, 77.
[43] Ibid., 37.
[44] Ibid., 11, 88.
[45] See at nn 34–40.
[46] Rolls and Reg. Sutton, III, xviii.
[47] From 1219 he witnesses Hugh's *acta* only when done in Lincoln either in chapter or with the consent of the dean and chapter: LN Lincoln, 94; Smith, "Administration of Hugh of Wells," 224–5; *Registrum Antiquissimum*, X, lvii; *Acta of Hugh of Wells*, nos. 150–1, 180, 186–8, 198–9, 234, 245, 280, 320.
[48] LN Lincoln, 145; Smith, "Administration of Hugh of Wells," I, 230.
[49] LN Lincoln, 124; Smith, "Administration of Hugh of Wells," I, 245–6.
[50] LN Lincoln, 95; Smith, "Administration of Hugh of Wells," I, 226.

de Kent,[51] who, although they do not feature in many charters of the cathedral, after a certain point appear in the bishop's acts only when the business concerns the chapter, either at Lincoln or at Stow Park, after an immobile Hugh was confined there in his last years. John de Banbury, in possession of a rectory not from Hugh but on the presentation of St. James's Abbey, Northampton, simply took the cross.[52] Other men, all beneficed, seem to have disappeared from Bishop Hugh's service years before Hugh's death, but their subsequent activities are untraceable in any significant degree: Oliver Chesney,[53] Nicholas de Evesham,[54] Richard de Fingest.[55]

The next episcopates also produced these kinds of Lincoln diocesan dropouts: under Grosseteste, Thomas de Ashby[56] and Richard de Wisbech.[57] Another man departed too, but to serve a different master. Roger de Buscot (*alias* Burwardescote) left to become Bishop Robert de Bingham of Salisbury's archdeacon of Wiltshire, to which diocese Nicholas Tessun, canon of Salisbury, also departed.[58] One can add from Henry de Lexington's short and ill-documented episcopate Robert de St. Agatha's departure in 1256 to become archdeacon of Durham.[59] As under Hugh, other men seem simply to have disappeared from Grosseteste's service, but there is no positive evidence as to how they then spent their time: Roger Blund,[60] Robert de Cadney,[61] Remigius de Pocklington,[62] and Richard de Pocklington.[63]

Such men can also be found among Gravesend's servants. William de Southwell, canon of Lincoln, served as Gravesend's *officialis* in 1259 and 1260 but was serving as the provost of the chapter's common fund

---

[51] LN Lincoln, 145; Smith, "Administration of Hugh of Wells," I, 240.
[52] Smith, "Administration of Hugh of Wells," I, 220–21; Rot. Hugh of Wells, II, 222. Hugh must not have begrudged his departure, as he took John's church under his protection during John's absence on crusade (Smith, "Administration of Hugh of Wells," I, 220).
[53] Ibid., 229. He survived into Gravesend's episcopate (ibid.).
[54] Smith, "Administration of Hugh of Wells," I, 234–5. Smith wonders whether he went to the diocese of Wells, where he also was a member of the chapter (ibid.).
[55] Ibid., 235.
[56] See above note 23.
[57] Major, "*Familia* of Robert Grosseteste," 240. He later went to the curia on chapter business (ibid.).
[58] Ibid., 222–3, 238–9.
[59] LN Lincoln, 141. For his service to Lexington, see n 29.
[60] Major, "*Familia* of Robert Grosseteste," 221–2.
[61] Ibid., 223.
[62] Ibid., 233.
[63] Ibid.

sometime in the years 1262–72.⁶⁴ Richard de Bromholm, already canon of Lincoln, inquired regarding the presentation of a vicar on Gravesend's behalf and is also later to be found serving as provost of the common fund.⁶⁵ Or, again, a man could simply disappear, his later activities invisible to the historian. John de Lindsey served as Gravesend's *officialis* and sometimes as his vicar-general between 1263 and 1268, and is last found in Gravesend's service in 1269.⁶⁶ He lived at least four more years, but how he spent them is unrecoverable.⁶⁷ A lesser such man was the clerk John de Stounesby, who in the period November 1265–December 1273 witnessed the bishop's acts on eleven different days out of the twenty-four or twenty-five dates on which the witnesses to Gravesend's acts are recorded in that time. The fact that these eleven dates place John with the bishop in nine different places, including Durham and London, confirm that the connection was real.⁶⁸ But that connection seems to have been severed, or at least is untraceable, from 1274 on, although the vicarage John received at Gravesend's behest was vacated by his death only by the summer of 1287.⁶⁹ A similar lesser man is John de Dunstaple, who heard a lawsuit on Gravesend's behalf in the 1260s and held the rectory of Winwick, which appears to have been in the bishop's gift. He disappears from episcopal service after 1264, but Bishop Sutton would have to wait until John's death to collate Winwick in 1298.⁷⁰

---

⁶⁴ LN Lincoln, 50; *Registrum Antiquissimum*, X, lviii. He attests a charter of Gravesend's that can be dated no more narrowly than Gravesend's episcopate (LAO, Dii/69/2/36).

⁶⁵ LN Lincoln, 83; Major, "*Familia* of Robert Grosseteste," 237–8. William was involved in several final concords regarding land near Lincoln ("in the suburb") starting in Grosseteste's final year (LAO, A/1/6/709, 710, 711 [f. 108v]). For activities in the vicinity in later years, see LAO, VC 2/1, f. 71r (no. 348), f. 71 r-v (no. 349); LAO, Dii/52/2/1.

⁶⁶ BL, Cotton Vespasian E xx, fos. 228–9; *Registrum Antiquissimum*, III, no. 1034; Rot. Gravesend, 22–4, 72, 108.

⁶⁷ For his death, LN Lincoln, 85.

⁶⁸ Rot. Gravesend, 31, 53, 119, 145–6, 178, 193, 244, 246; *Registrum Antiquissimum*, III, no. 1015; LAO, Dii/69/1/36, 53. For the dates in this period in which John is absent from the lists of witnesses: Rot. Gravesend, 48, 115, 151, 240, 241, 259, 262; *Registrum Antiquissimum*, II, no. 454, III, nos. 833, 1007; *Calendar of the Close Rolls (1272–1485)* (London, 1902–38), I, 41. One of Gravesend's *acta*, LAO, Dii/88/3/44, appears to have been issued in March 1273, but a hole in the manuscript makes a more precise date impossible to establish; the place where it was given is not stated. Thus this document might or might not have been issued the same date as the activities recorded at Rot. Gravesend, 178. See also LAO, Dii/88/3/43.

⁶⁹ Rot. Gravesend, 147; Rolls and Reg. Sutton, VIII, 37.

⁷⁰ *Records of Harrold Priory*, ed. G. H. Fowler, Bedfordshire Historical Records Society 17–18 (no place, 1935), nos. 41, 47*; Rolls and Reg. Sutton, II, 154.

Men also left Sutton's employ. Sometimes the evidence is explicit on this point, sometimes only implicit. Henry de Nassington, in receipt of a canonry from Sutton and the bishop's *officialis*, transferred to the service of the archbishop of Canterbury, becoming his dean of Arches.[71] Richard de Rothwell, a holdover from the previous episcopate, ceases to be found in Sutton's service after 1295; he became provost of the chapter's common fund by the time of Sutton's death and met his own only ca. 1315.[72] Roger de Sixil, explicitly called Sutton's clerk in 1290, was attached to Sutton's household in the years 1290–5.[73] In these years he also enjoyed Sutton's patronage.[74] After his last year in Sutton's household, he received the church of Laughton on the presentation of Thornholm Priory and no more is heard of him in Sutton's register.[75]

Other Dioceses

This discussion of the diocese Lincoln allows a better assessment of the most comprehensive analysis of continuity of diocesan administrative personnel in England at large, that of Philippa Hoskin. Her invaluable survey of the bishops of Durham between 1242 and 1311 presents a picture of what she concludes was unusual continuity in that diocese. The rest of England, except for the archdiocese of Canterbury, serves as a foil for that continuity. She notes that part of this picture may simply be an effect of an especially rich body of sources at Durham compared with thinner material from other sees. But she traces the chief root of the contrast in the bishop of Durham's secular standing as lord of a palatinate, making for the greater continuity from one bishop's household to the next comparable to that found among the households of great secular lords.[76]

Hoskin indeed shows that a number of men served successive bishops of Durham. Here it is worth noting that some of these men were the episcopal knights,[77] a point that highlights her suggestion that the secular

---

[71] Matthew Sullivan, "The Role of the Nassington Family in the Medieval English Church," *Nottingham Medieval Studies* 37 (1993), 54.
[72] See n 36 and *Registrum Antiquissimum*, X, lix, no. 2702; LN Lincoln, 51.
[73] For "bishop's clerk," see Rolls and Reg. Sutton, VIII, 204. For Roger in Sutton's household, see Chapter 8, n 49.
[74] Rolls and Reg. Sutton, VIII, 23.
[75] Ibid., 27–8.
[76] Hoskin, "Continuing Service," 133–8.
[77] Ibid., 130, 132.

aspect of the bishops' position fostered continuity across pontificates. The target of this book, however, is bishops' clerical adherents. Excluding seculars such as knights and foresters[78] still leaves examples of continuous service at Durham. But how many? While it is necessary to lay out the identification and description of diocesan personnel in prose, comparing the degree of continuity in one diocese with that of another ultimately requires the reduction of people to numbers. Hoskin examines continuity over five changes of bishop. By my count, five men who served Bishop Nicholas Farnham (1243–9) served a previous bishop.[79] Five of the servants of Bishop Walter Kirkam (1249–60) served his predecessor.[80] Four of the servants of the next bishop, Robert Stichill (1261–74), had served Bishop Kirkham.[81] Three of Stichill's men served his successor, Robert of Holy Island (1274–83).[82] And five men who served Bishop Robert served the last bishop of the century, Antony Bek (1283–1311).[83]

These figures are, however, quite comparable to those for the thirteenth-century diocese of Lincoln. To reconsider the previous discussion, one finds that the earliest bishop, William of Blois, inherited six clerks from his predecessor, Hugh of Avalon. William in turn bequeathed four men to his successor, Hugh of Wells.[84] Three of Hugh's clerks can be found among the servants of the next bishop, Robert Grosseteste. The next pontificate, that of Bishop Lexington, is problematic. Four of Grosseteste's clerks went on to serve Lexington or his successor, Richard Gravesend.[85]

[78] Ibid., "Continuing Service," 131.
[79] John de Romsey, William de Blockley, Robert de Saint Meldred, Philip de Saint Helen, and Walter de Selby (ibid., 129, 131).
[80] Philip de Saint Helen, Martin de St. Cross, Walter de Selby, John Gylet, and William de Merrow (ibid., 129, 131–2). The "Walter of Merrow" Hoskin mentions in this connection (131) must be an error for William. The *acta* cited for Walter's connection with the bishops in fact have William as an attestor (EEA 29: Durham, nos. 47, 56, 58, 77, 78, 91, 112, except for no. 55, which mentions neither name, and also add no. 54 and see 75 n). No Walter de Merrow appears among the *acta* of the bishops of Durham in these years. I have also found no mention of William's service as Bishop Kirkham's proctor (Hoskin, "Continuing Service," 131) although he did serve as Bishop Stichill's proctor (EEA 29: Durham, nos. 122–3).
[81] John Gylet, Roger de Auckland, Roger de Seaton, and William de Merrow (Hoskin, "Continuing Service," 132).
[82] Alexander de Biddick, Thomas de Levesham, and Robert de Driffield (ibid., 132–3).
[83] Thomas de Levesham, Guichard de Charron, Robert Avenal, Alan de Easingwold, and Peter de Thoresby (ibid., 133).
[84] Or perhaps more. I am not including here the three men whom Smith identifies as servants of either Hugh of Avalon or William of Blois who went on to serve Hugh of Wells.
[85] I have not counted John de Riston here, as the evidence for him seems particularly weak (see at n 30).

And, finally, six men survived Gravesend to serve his successor, Oliver Sutton. Comparing the two dioceses, roughly the same range of crossovers appears in each: between three and five crossovers between episcopates at Durham, between one and six at Lincoln – but between three and six if one consolidates the episcopate of Gravesend with the short and badly documented one of Lexington. To engage in a little arithmetic, this comes to an average of 4.4 men serving successive bishops at Durham versus an average of 4.7 at Lincoln.[86] This degree of precision is, of course, excessive when dealing with such small numbers. That is especially the case given the evidentiary problems noted earlier.[87] More elaborate manipulation would be inappropriate. But this exercise in quantification does not instill the conviction that clerks were more likely to serve successive bishops of Durham than to serve successive bishops of Lincoln.

It is true, of course, that the historian can point to men who served more than two bishops at Durham: William de Merrow and Thomas de Levesham, all servants to three bishops, and John Gylet, who served four.[88] Lincoln furnishes no such cases. But it is also worth noting that bishops of Lincoln often lived rather longer than did bishops of Durham. (The relevant episcopates at Durham ran seven, eleven, thirteen, and nine years compared with three, twenty-six, eighteen, four, and twenty years at Lincoln).[89] It was fairly easy for a youngish man to outlive a couple of bishops of Durham. Surviving two bishops of Lincoln was a greater challenge. It should come as no surprise that not many men, perhaps not any, were up to it.[90]

---

[86] The total number of "crossovers" is divided by the number of changes of bishops, five at Durham, six at Lincoln.

[87] The fragility of the evidence for service at Lincoln should be evident from my discussion. Some of the evidence for service at Durham is also a bit delicate. Martin de St. Cross's service to Bishop Kirkham relies solely on his appearance as witness to one of Kirkham's *acta* (Hoskin, "Continuing Service," 131, relying on EEA 29: Durham, no. 64), whereas Walter de Selby's and Philip de St. Helen's service to that bishop relies on three *acta* – undated and with no place given – all thought possibly to have been produced on the same occasion (Hoskin, "Continuing Service," 131, relying on EEA 29: Durham, nos. 108, 114–15).

[88] See at nn 80–3.

[89] For each see, the length of the last episcopate is irrelevant to the argument here, and so is not listed.

[90] In actuarial terms, the best opportunity would have been for a man to enter Grosseteste's service in his later years, serve the short-lived Bishop Lexington on Grosseteste's death, and then continue on under Gravesend. For this reason, Lexington's missing rolls may play an especially large role in obscuring continuing service by bishops' men at Lincoln.

The proposition that the diocese of Durham experienced unusual continuity of administrative personnel because of the secular nature of its palatinate is thus doubtful because it is not clear that Durham did experience unusual continuity. At this point, it is worth considering the evidence adduced to support this explanation. Some years ago it was suggested that the archbishops of Canterbury may have been served by a "nucleus of 'permanent civil servants'" who continued on after the man who happened to be archbishop died.[91] The evidence here is an archdeacon (a somewhat problematic figure for this question for reasons I have noted), and sound evidence for three or four other men.[92] One of these clerks, however, is Elias de Dereham, whose frequent moves from diocese to diocese, and simultaneous service to more than one bishop, make him look more like a man with skills in high demand – nearly an administrative superstar – than a member of a standing nucleus of diocesan administrators at Canterbury.[93] At any rate, the continuity here is on the same order of magnitude as that demonstrable at Lincoln as well as Durham. The reason Hoskin compares Durham to Canterbury, however, is that there is evidence that the archbishops of Canterbury relied on a council. Thus, she argues, the archbishops did business like a great secular magnate, making them like the bishops of the Durham palatinate.[94] I suspect there were indeed similarities here, but not because the bishops of Durham and Canterbury had unusual secular responsibilities. Rather, all English bishops – except perhaps Rochester – had significant landed endowments as well as political and legal problems that would have made an advisory council attractive to them. Archbishops of Canterbury may have been in the lead among English bishops in establishing a formal council, or this impression may simply be an accident of evidence. The earliest reference to an episcopal council comes from Canterbury. But it is revealing that the next diocese to have one in the evidentiary record is, to judge from modern discussions, not Durham, but Worcester, hardly a powerhouse among bishoprics in

---

[91] Lawrence, *St. Edmund of Abingdon*, 140.
[92] Ibid., 141–3: Thomas de Freckenham, Elias de Dereham, Aaron de Kent, and William de St. Edmund, of whom Lawrence has some doubt, but I think should be counted in. Lawrence points to Walter de Somercote as another possibility, but only his attestation of a single one of Archbishop Abingdon's *acta* connects him with that archbishop (ibid., 142).
[93] For his links to multiple bishops, see in particular Vincent, "Master Elias of Dereham," 133–58.
[94] Hoskin, "Continuing Service," 135–6.

terms of secular authority or landed endowment.[95] Salisbury and Bath and Wells soon followed.[96]

Some degree of continuity has been noted between episcopates at various other thirteenth-century dioceses. Four (perhaps three) ecclesiastics who served Bishop des Roches's predecessor at Winchester went on to serve des Roches.[97] Two clerks have been found serving two bishops of Chichester in a row.[98] These numbers, of course, are not large. F. R. H. Du Boulay found that estate administrators of the archdiocese of Canterbury both served successive bishops and easily moved from the archdiocese to find new masters.[99] That fluidity fits the picture of episcopal clerks that emerges in this chapter. The pipe rolls of the diocese of Winchester, unusual in their chronological span, provide evidence of continuity of estate officers across episcopates there;[100] it would be interesting to see those sources mined for a systematic study of continuity and discontinuity of diocesan personnel, especially in conjunction with the series of registers that starts there in the later thirteenth century.

Historians have noted here and there that one source of newcomers in a diocese's administration was a new bishop from outside the diocese, who brought clerks with him. Bishop Raleigh of Norwich brought men with him from Devon, his home turf.[101] When Ranulph

---

[95] From 1300 on: Roy Martin Haines, *The Administration of the Diocese of Worcester in the First Half of the Fourteenth Century* (London, 1965), 97. Elizabeth E. Levett asserts that both the bishops of Durham and Ely had councils by the mid-thirteenth century, but regrettably cites no sources ("Baronial Councils and Their Relation to Manorial Courts," in *Melanges offerts à M. Ferdinand Lot* [Paris, 1925], 424–5).

[96] Haines, *Administration of the Diocese of Worcester*, 98. I have not come across earlier instances.

[97] EEA IX: Winchester, xl–xli. About one of these four, Philip de Fauconberg, there may be some doubt. The evidence of his connection to Bishop des Roches is his attesting three of the bishop's *acta* and his presence on one occasion at one of the bishop's manors (ibid., 195–6). Since two of these *acta* were also witnessed by Philip's kinsman, Eustace de Fauconberg (ibid., 195), an undoubted adherent of des Roches, it may be that Eustace's presence alone explains those two appearances.

[98] EEA 22: Chichester, l.

[99] F. R. H. Du Boulay, *The Lordship of Canterbury: An Essay on Medieval Society* (New York, 1966), 268–9.

[100] Nicholas Vincent, "The Politics of Church and State as Reflected in the Winchester Pipe Rolls, 1208–1280," in *The Winchester Pipe Rolls and Medieval English Society*, ed. Richard Britnell (Woodbridge, 2003), 171–2. Vincent also suggests broader continuity: review of *Foundations of Medieval Ecclesiastical History* in *Journal of Ecclesiastical History* 58 (2007), 129.

[101] EEA 21: Norwich, liii. When he was translated to Winchester, he may well have again brought along at least one of his men from Norwich. Raleigh appears to have twice collated archdeaconries to Roger Pincerna while at Norwich (LN Monastic Cathedrals,

de Warham, formerly the bishop of Norwich's *officialis*, rose to be bishop of Chichester, clerks from his old diocese appeared among his clerks in his new one.[102] It may be that John de Alvechurch's departure from the diocese of Worcester, where he had been Cantilupe's *officialis*, to that of Norwich to serve as *officialis* (and later archdeacon) of Bishop Walton, stemmed from an acquaintance with the future bishop of Norwich from the time John was active at Worcester.[103] I have noted Bishop Hugh of Wells of Lincoln's introduction of clerks from his old stomping grounds.

Sometimes the previous connections of new clerks with a new bishop are simply a matter of supposition from the fact that new men suddenly appear. Bishop Giles de Braose of Hereford made nearly a clean sweep of his predecessor's clerks.[104] Although his father held extensive Welsh lands, Giles does not seem to have had an ecclesiastical role in the diocese before his elevation, and so was probably an outsider. Brian Kemp has stressed that the lack of continuity between the servants of Bishop Jocelin de Bohun of Salisbury and those of his successor, Hubert Walter, may have resulted not just from the long vacancy between their pontificates, but also from "Walter's determination to have his own men around him."[105] Bishop William of Blois of Worcester had been a stranger to his new diocese; he brought in outsiders, a move that did not endear him to the cathedral priory.[106] When Walter Cantilupe became bishop of Worcester, he appears to have effected a complete change in personnel stemming from his dislike of his predecessor, with the exception of one estate steward; he did, however, recruit from within the diocese, pleasing his cathedral convent.[107] Cathedral politics could well have played a role in a new bishop's decisions about his clerks, a point that may illuminate the kind of continuity discussed regarding Lincoln, with its succession of chapter members in the see.

68, 70). As bishop of Winchester, the connection continued, to judge (at least) from the bishop dispensing Roger for pluralism (CPL, I, 210).

[102] EEA 22: Chichester, xlviii.
[103] EEA 13: Worcester, xxxviii; EEA 32: Norwich, xli–xlii.
[104] EEA VII: Hereford, lix.
[105] EEA 18: Salisbury, lxxi. Or, a perhaps less lord-centered explanation: that de Bohun's clerks were not inclined to serve Walter.
[106] Philippa Hoskin, "Diocesan Politics in the See of Worcester 1218–1266," *Journal of Ecclesiastical History* 54 (2003), 432. Hoskin also notes other reasons for the prior and convent's dismay in this fine study (ibid., 433).
[107] EEA 13: Worcester, xxxviii, xxxv, although n.b. comments regarding the paucity of the evidence linking these men to their bishops.

And, like Lincoln, other dioceses furnish examples of episcopal clerks whose interests and activities changed. Alan de Beccles, *officialis* to Bishop Pandulph of Norwich in the 1220s, ceased to serve in 1227, leaving to study and teach at Paris. Beneficed, he lived another fourteen years.[108] Richard Wyche, Archbishop Abingdon's chancellor, left to study at Orléans on Abingdon's death, a move that his benefices no doubt helped make possible.[109] Another clerical career illustrates that the decision to stay in diocesan administration still left choices as to master and diocese. Geoffrey de Ferring emerges as an episcopal clerk of Archbishop Abingdon, but before the archbishop's death in 1240, Geoffrey had begun to serve Bishop Raleigh of Norwich. When Raleigh himself moved on to become bishop of Winchester, Geoffrey went with him.[110] Or a clerk might serve in a succession of dioceses, moving only with the death of his bishop.[111]

That last move of Geoffrey de Ferring shows that while a bishop lived, his clerk's service to him might continue, and indeed that a clerk's service was to his bishop rather than to the diocese. Other men's careers suggest the same. In the later twelfth century, Master Silvester served Roger, bishop of Worcester and then Roger's successor at Worcester, Baldwin of Forde, only to leave for Canterbury when Baldwin was promoted to the archdiocese.[112] Such moves could throw an incoming bishop uncomfortably back on his own resources. Hugh of Avalon, on becoming bishop of Lincoln in 1186, discovered that, following his predecessor's translation to Rouen and years of Lincoln being vacant besides, he could find no suitable clerks to help him administer the diocese. Moreover, Hugh had been a Carthusian without extensive experience in England. Such a conspiracy of circumstance helps explain Hugh's request to the archbishop of Canterbury to supply him clerks as assistants.[113]

---

[108] EEA 21: Norwich, xliv–xlv; Emden, *A Biographical Register of the University of Oxford*, sub nom.

[109] EEA 22: Chichester, xxxvii, and for the benefices see Emden, *A Biographical Register of the University of Oxford*, sub nom.

[110] EEA 21: Norwich, xlvi.

[111] Andrew de Kilkenny, for example, served as Bishop Merton of Rochester's *officialis*. On Merton's death, he moved to Exeter as Bishop Bronscombe's *officialis*. Two years after Bronscombe's death he is to be found in the archbishop of Canterbury's service as the dean of Arches (*Early Rolls of Merton College Oxford*, ed. J. R. L. Highfield [Oxford, 1964], 55, 58).

[112] Mary G. Cheney, *Roger, Bishop of Worcester 1164–1179* (Oxford, 1980), 102.

[113] David M. Smith, "Hugh's Administration of the Diocese of Lincoln," in *St. Hugh of Lincoln: Lectures delivered at Oxford and Lincoln to celebrate the eighth century of St. Hugh's consecration as bishop of Lincoln*, ed. Henry Mayr-Harting (Oxford, 1987), 27–8; EEA IV: Lincoln, xx–xxii.

The death of a bishop also furnished some bishops' clerks opportunity as well as anxiety. I have already pointed to men at Lincoln who became more active in their cathedral chapter and other men who returned to the schools. Administrative moves also awaited. Luke de Bré served as Thomas Cantilupe of Hereford's trusted agent, his *officialis* and vicar-general. But on Cantilupe's death, he entered the service of Cantilupe's mortal enemy, Archbishop Pecham.[114] John de Beccles, Cantilupe's proctor at the curia, followed suit.[115]

In addition, of course, as at Lincoln, men did not have to wait for their bishop to die before leaving his service. John de London, like many of the bishop of Durham's other clerks holding a benefice in the gift of the cathedral priory, nonetheless departed for the service of the bishop of Winchester.[116] Archbishop Geoffrey of York (1189–1212) could be such a difficult master that Master Honorius moved from his service to that of his rival, Archbishop Hubert Walter of Canterbury.[117] Peter de Leicester and William Pikeril left the service of the irascible Bishop Giffard of Worcester. But such moves could also come as the end neared. Archbishop Pecham was clearly in decline in 1288–9, when a member of his household wrote to the prior of Christ Church, Canterbury, that Pecham's violent changes of mind were astounding those around him. Indeed, the writer said, one of the archbishop's clerks had left the lord archbishop's hall against Pecham's will, and another was preparing to do so.[118]

---

[114] David M. Smith, "Thomas Cantilupe's Register: The Administration of the Diocese of Hereford 1275–1282," in *St. Thomas Cantilupe Bishop of Hereford: Essays in His Honour*, ed. Meryl Jancey (Leominster, 1982), 87–8.

[115] Ibid., 88, n 16.

[116] EEA 24: Durham, xlvi. And other instances: Robert de Ruddeby left Archbishop Hubert Walter's service for that of John de Gray, bishop of Norwich (C. R. Cheney, *English Bishops' Chanceries 1100–1250* [Manchester, 1950], 16). (A David de Ruddeby, possibly a relative and also in Walter's service, entered Gray's service after Walter's death [ibid.]). John de Alvechurch, *officialis* of the bishop of Worcester, left before that bishop's death to serve Simon de Walton, the new bishop of Norwich, in the same office; Bishop Simon's previous Worcester connections probably help explain John's decision (EEA 13: Worcester, xxxviii–xxxix).

[117] Stephan Kuttner and Eleanor Rathbone, "Anglo-Norman Canonists of the Twelfth Century," *Traditio* 7 (1949–1951), 305–8; C. R. Cheney, *Hubert Walter* (London, 1967), 165.

[118] Decima L. Douie, *Archbishop Pecham* (Oxford, 1952), 322–3. The clerks were Adam de Hailes, who had served as Pecham's *officialis* at the very start of the episcopate, and John de Beccles, Pecham's notary and registrar (ibid., 53, 60; *Historical Manuscripts Commission Report on Manuscripts in Various Collections I* [London, 1901], 252). Adam had been devoted enough to lead an armed attack on the archbishop of York's party, destroying York's cross and defending Pecham's honor (Douie, *Archbishop*

Some Observations

A bishop's death could be a frightening time for his clerks and for good reason. Benefices had a lot to do with this. The widespread use of benefices to reward administrators itself likely fostered an expectation of security, a belief that lifetime financial independence was a natural outcome of the administrative life. For those clerks who had not achieved that security by the time their bishop passed on, his death, and the prospect of finding and cultivating a patron all over again, were especially troubling. At least servants of secular lords could know who the heir would be and trim their sails accordingly in their present lord's lifetime.[119] Servants of bishops did not enjoy that kind of predictability. Indeed, they might well face hostility. In 1296, Archbishop Winchelsey heard complaints that the new bishop of Coventry and Lichfield was harassing the clerks of the previous bishop.[120] I discussed in Chapter 4 attempts by bishops to expel men from benefices collated by their predecessors.

But security of tenure in a benefice also meant, for those who had one, a certain independence. That independence might mean leaving the service of one bishop for another, taking one's benefice or benefices with one, like a snail with its shell. Or it might mean leaving diocesan administration altogether to follow other interests, either before one's bishop's death or, more decorously, after it.[121] Or it could mean staying on after a bishop died to serve his successor.

The account of the last two paragraphs is clerk-centered rather than bishop-centered. But of course a bishop was an equal party to the decision of whether a clerk would serve him. The forces molding a bishop's

---

Pecham, 229). Adam, it should be noted, was beneficed (LN Chichester, 56). So was the notary John de Lewis, who also left Pecham's service at about this time (Douie, *Archbishop Pecham*, 323; Reg. Pecham, I, 56–7, 105). John de Beccles, however, was not (C. R. Cheney, *Notaries Public in England in the Thirteenth and Fourteenth Centuries* [Oxford, 1972], 32).

[119] Michael Hicks stresses the long-term connections between families of lords and those of their retainers, from heir to heir (*Bastard Feudalism* [London, 1995], 93–104). In her study of secular noble households, Kate Mertes also finds a strong degree of continuity from one lord's *familia* to that of his heir, and also contrasts this with bishops' households. She relies, however, for the episcopal side of the equation on a study based on late fourteenth-century sources (Kate Mertes, *The English Noble Household 1200–1600* [Oxford, 1988], 64–5). It must be said, however, that she also finds strong continuity among monastic households as well (ibid.), where the election of a new abbot must have been an uncertain affair, although perhaps more predictable than the selection or election of a new bishop.

[120] Reg. Winchelsey, 129.

[121] See the instance of Peter of Blois (Cotts, *Peter of Blois*, 240).

decision were as multiform as those that shaped clerks' decisions. Did he have men of his own already? Could taking on men already in the diocese, and especially already members of the cathedral chapter, bring special expertise or local political support that he could use? Where did the simple interplay of individual personality of bishop and clerk lead? Such questions were, of course, the specifics that made clerks uncertain of what to expect when a bishop died; for them the answers were incalculable. Having a benefice would have provided some comfort. But the fact that both a new bishop and beneficed clerks had such strong bargaining positions from which to consult their own needs and desires helps explain the fluidity revealed in this chapter.

Finally, this fluidity indicates a world in which clerks served bishops, not dioceses. Clerks followed translated bishops from one diocese to another. Clerks left the bishop of one diocese to serve that of another, either before their current bishop's death or after it. True, a number of men also served bishop after bishop in one see. But in the context of other clerical careers, this continuity looks like a result of individual decisions taken under individual circumstance rather than a loyalty to the diocese transcending the bishops at its head.

10

Affection and Devotion

It may be well to warn the reader of ... [Pope Innocent III's letters] against two dangers. In the first place it is natural for a twentieth-century reader to tire of the verbosity, the piling up of epithets, the elaborate expressions of humility and affection – natural for him to discount the tropes as mere verbiage which meant little or nothing to the correspondent. But the exuberant literary form represented a long tradition; it is unlikely that it affected contemporaries as it affects us.[1]

English bishops often expressed affection for their underling – so often, in fact, that the language in which they did so was conventional, even rule-bound. While bishops proclaimed their love and friendship for subordinates, however, subordinates were circumspect about returning the favor, declaring instead their devotion to their bishop. But these points do not mean that such language was *only* a matter of convention, although some modern historians have argued that medieval representations of emotion were representations only, even a kind of cultural game played with no real emotions at stake. And even though expressions of affection and devotion were used to try to manipulate those at whom they were aimed, this does not mean that they were solely instrumental. Bishops' wills show episcopal affection for their clerks in action – and not, it may be noted, only in a representation of action, as the historian might find in a chronicle or saint's life. Bishops were much more likely to leave sentimentally charged legacies to their clerks than to their lay adherents. But bishops' tendency to leave such legacies to individual clerks by name

---

[1] "Introduction," *Selected Letters of Pope Innocent III Concerning England (1198–1216)*, ed. C. R. Cheney and W. H. Semple (London, 1953), xv.

Affection and Devotion

suggests limits to the pull of any generalized policy of affection toward their clerks. For their part, bishops' clerks – at least some of them – acted on their devotion, taking on the sometimes grueling work of executing their bishops' final testaments. Here, too, clerks acted – and were presumably chosen – selectively, just as clerks decided whether devotedly to continue to serve their living bishops, or to move on (on which, see Chapter 9).

Expressions of Affection and Devotion

To judge from the language one finds there, to open a bishop's register is to enter a world of love and friendship (even if – as here – one discounts those occasions when the affection is said to be "in Christ," and so arguably too spiritual to be of concern in this book). Such expressions of affection are evident from the top. Pope Honorius III wrote to Archbishop Gray of York that he loved the dean and chapter of York with sincere affection, proceeding to explain his decision regarding the right of Honorius's chaplain and his "beloved son" to the chapter common.[2] In a letter traveling along the hierarchy in the opposite direction, a later archbishop of York wrote Master Benedict, apostolic notary, his "most loving and heartfelt and kind friend," regarding the archbishop's conflict with the archbishop of Canterbury over York's right to have a cross carried before him in the southern province.[3]

English bishops spoke this way to each other too. The bishop of Durham found himself described as "friend, if it pleases, full of faith beyond the rest," by Archbishop Winchelsey who, although not omitting to mention his status as primate of all England, wrote as the bishop's cherished one (*carus*) and offered the bishop his greeting and embrace of sincere love.[4] Winchelsey was writing to ask the bishop to use his influence to block any suggestion that the king send the archbishop on a diplomatic mission to France. Winchelsey also reminded the bishop that "the bond of friendship, rightly conceived, desires that a friend most frequently search out the situation of a friend with ardent zeal."[5] Such expressions of affection ran further down. Bishop Cantilupe of Hereford

---

[2] Rot. Gray, 154: "sincere diligentes affectu"; "dilectum filium."
[3] Reg. Wickwane, 181: "amantissimo et precordiali, benivolo et amico suo."
[4] Reg. Winchelsey, 126–27: "amico si placet pre ceteris confidenti."
[5] Ibid., 126: "Fedus amicicie rite concepte desiderat ut amicus amici statum ardenti studio sepius investiget."

asked the chapter of Hereford, "venerable men and discreet brothers and dearest friends," to work to resolve the disputed election to the deanery of the cathedral.⁶ Archbishop Wickwane of York announced to the clergy and laity of the archdeaconry of Cleveland his appointment of a new archdeacon – whom he ordered them to obey – "considering and turning over in our heart the glowing zeal and affection which our loving and intimate son ... has with deep feeling maintained and laboriously laid out for the honor and exaltation of our church of York."⁷

In this book, I have argued that the effectiveness of material rewards and punishments applied by bishops to their clerks was limited. It would have made sense, therefore, for bishops to turn to other means of cultivating their subordinates. Bishops could love them, or at least say they did. Certainly doing so was natural in the loving ambience suggested by the letters cited here, whose language is not atypical of that found in bishops' registers generally.

Indeed, bishops often invoked affection when exercising authority over their subordinates. Archbishop Giffard of York required of his subordinates, in a friendly way ("amiciter") that his animals and grain, and their custodians, not be molested, "pro amore nostro."⁸ Archbishop Wickwane, commanding his dean of Christianity of York to induct a presentee to custody of the Hospital of Saint Nicholas there, addressed the dean as "your love."⁹ Bishop Cantilupe of Hereford similarly sent an order to hold court to his seneschal, "with sincere love."¹⁰ Bishop Gray of Norwich ordered his *officialis*, "most cherished son," to take action regarding the income of the vicar of Woolpit.¹¹ The bishop of Carlisle warned, with paternal affection, the officials, deans, and other clergy of the diocese to support the claims of the Hospital of St. Peter's York to grain from the diocese.¹² Archbishop Winchelsey, with a more elaborate expression of affection, commanded the abbot of Waverley to collect a

⁶ Reg. Cantilupe, 3.
⁷ Reg. Wickwane, 125: "Attendentes at intime revolventes in corde zelum fervidum et affectum quem ad honorem et exaltacionem ecclesie nostre Eboracensis amantissimus et intimus filius noster, magister Thomas de Grimestone, visceraliter optinet et operose pretendit." Archbishop Giffard of York, on informing his *officialis* of his excommunication of Robert de Balliol, noted that Robert was one "whom we formerly loved deeply as one of our own" ("quem visceraliter nuper dileximus sicud nostrum") (Reg. Giffard of York, no. 898 [p. 299]).
⁸ Ibid., no. 660 (p. 181).
⁹ Reg. Wickwane, no. 5 (p. 33): "tue dileccione."
¹⁰ Reg. Cantilupe, 3: "cum dileccione sincera."
¹¹ EEA VI: Norwich, no. 336: "fili carissime."
¹² EEA 30: Carlisle, no. 36.

tax, noting "your love in whom we affectionately have confidence."[13] Archbishop Pecham had earlier ordered his "beloved son," the former dean of Arches, to deliver the deanery's seal and all pertinent materials to the new dean, also the archbishop's "beloved son."[14] Not surprisingly, bishops expressed such feelings when giving gifts to their own men. The bishop of Coventry and Lichfield granted advowsons to one of his archdeacons, he said, out of love (*amor*) for him – and so that the grant went to him alone, and not his successors.[15]

Assertions of affection were in fact a clerical commonplace. At the end of the twelfth century, the archdeacon of Bedford wrote to the dean of Lincoln, "his most cherished friend."[16] The archdeacon and the dean similarly addressed all the remaining archdeacons of the diocese as their most cherished friends, ordering them to announce an excommunication.[17] Someone, probably Henry de Sandford, clerk of the chancellor of York cathedral, wrote to tell his correspondents that frequent letters are a great solace to absent friends, saying, "most cherished ones, if you prosper, I prosper; if you rejoice, I rejoice … so much the fervor of my greater affection burns as I always hunger for your increase with a very genuine spirit."[18] The chancellor himself – or perhaps Henry writing in his name – also employed some of the same language ("most cherished one, if you prosper, I prosper, if you rejoice, I rejoice") to ask for help in getting certain tithes restored to him.[19]

These thirteenth-century bishops and clerks were not writing in very original terms. For example, twelfth-century readers would have found familiar the concern with overcoming distance between distant friends, apparent in the letters discussed. Indeed, the problem of bridging physical

---

[13] Reg. Winchelsey, 420: "dileccionem vestram de qua confidimus affectuose."
[14] Pecham, *Epistolae*, I, no. 60.
[15] EEA 17: Coventry and Lichfield, no. 37. Archbishop Romeyn of York licensed the rector of Heslerton's nonresidence "on account of the particular affection we bear you." (Reg. Romeyn, no. 614: "ob specialem affeccionem quam erga te gerimus").
[16] *Twelfth-Century English Archidiaconal and Vice-Archidiaconal Acta*, ed. Brian Kemp, Canterbury and York Society 92 (Woodbridge, 2001), no. 67: "amico karissimo."
[17] Ibid., no. 139: "karissimis amicis suis."
[18] "Letters of William Wickwane, Chancellor of York, 1266–1268," ed. C. R. Cheney, *English Historical Review* 48 (1932), reprinted with corrections and additions, in C. R. Cheney, *The English Church and Its Laws 12th–14th Centuries* (London, 1982), article XIII, 627, 634 n 3, 634–6: "Karrissimi, si prosperamini prosperor, gaudeo si gaudetis … tanto me maioris affeccionis fervor accendit quanto vestrum sinceriori semper appeto animo incrementum."
[19] "Letters of William Wickwane," 631: "Karissime, si prosperamini prosperor, gaudeo gaudetis."

distance through letters, of making friends intimate when in fact they were not, had become a standard, and elaborate, trope of the *ars dictamen* by the thirteenth century.[20] It sprang from the larger, lively cult of friendship that flowed from antiquity into the Carolingian period, and ran vigorously in monastic circles in the later eleventh and twelfth centuries.[21] By the end of the twelfth century, secular clerks were also celebrating friendship – and the love that did not seem clearly distinct from it – in their letters.[22] Indeed, so common are expressions of friendship and affection in medieval letters that such language was long seen as too pedestrian to be worthy of study. Now, however, it has spawned a small industry among scholars ready to take it seriously.[23]

Expressions of affection also suffused the letters of thirteenth-century English bishops. There were, however, some differences in context and form. When historians study twelfth-century friendship, they generally do so using either contemporary treatises on friendship or, more often, medieval letter collections. Such collections were themselves intended as works of art, put together for the edification of later readers, for some literary

[20] McGuire, *Friendship and Community: The Monastic Experience 350–1250* (Kalamazoo, 1988), 386. The concern continued well into the thirteenth century (e.g., see Grosseteste, *Epistolae*, no.2).

[21] For Carolingian developments and later, see C. Stephen Jaeger, *Ennobling Love: In Search of a Lost Sensibility* (Philadelphia, 1999). For the monastic context, see McGuire, *Friendship and Community*. On the influence of Cicero in the twelfth century, see Jan Ziolkowski, "Twelfth-Century Understandings and Adaptation of Ancient Friendship," in *Mediaeval Antiquity*, ed. Andreis Wekenhuysen, Herman Braet, and Werner Verbeke (Louvain, 1995), 59–81. Like other medieval intellectual traditions rooted in antiquity, academic discussions of friendship received a new dose of Aristotelian thought in the thirteenth century (Bénédicte Sère, *L'amitié au Moyen Age: Étude historique des commentaries sur les livres VIII et IX de l'Éthique à Nicomaque* [Turnhout, 2007]).

[22] See in particular John McLoughlin, "*Amicitia* in Practice: John of Salisbury and his Circle," in *England in the Twelfth Century: Proceedings of the 1988 Harlaxton Symposium*, ed. Daniel Williams (Wolfeboro, New Hampshire, 1990), 165–81. On the tie between medieval love and friendship, and contrasting modern attitudes that clearly distinguish between these two categories of relationship, see the remarks of Julian P. Haseldine, "Love, Separation and Male Friendship: Words and Actions in Saint Anselm's Letters to His Friends," in *Masculinity in Medieval Europe*, ed. D. M. Hadley (London, 1999), 240–41, and, for courtly love and twelfth-century friendship, Ziolkowksi, "Twelfth-Century Understandings," 60–81.

[23] For the abundance of such expressions, see Walter Ysebaert, "Medieval Letter-Collections as a Mirror of Circles of Friendship? The Example of Stephen of Tournai, 1128–1203," *Revue belge de philologie et d'histoire/Belgisch tidschrift voor philology en geschiedenis* 83 (2005), 288. For dismissals of medieval friendship contrasted with recent studies of the subject, and a rapid tour of those studies, see Margaret Mullett, "Power, Relations and Networks in Medieval Europe," ibid., 255–7.

purpose, to illustrate well-known personalities, or simply to divert.[24] The samples of thirteenth-century bishops' letters assembled here, however, nearly all come from bishops' registers. Such registers were put together for business: a reference for a bishop or his successors, or his clerks. The closest a register came to functioning like a letter collection was as a source of models for writing other letters.[25]

This difference in context also accounts for a difference in form. The instances of affection in twelfth-century letters that receive the most modern attention tend to be fairly elaborate. To judge from bishops' registers, when thirteenth-century English bishops wrote that they loved someone, they usually did so briefly. Some examples are the expressions of episcopal affection noted previously. The most elaborate such invocations are usually to be found in bishops' letters addressed to recipients who were not their subordinates: to colleagues, to men who may have been their lessers in dignity but over whom the bishop lacked jurisdiction, and to men who, in some sense, can be regarded as their superiors, in terms of dignity or general influence, although not in the sense of enjoying formal jurisdiction over the bishop who is writing. Archbishop Winchelsey addressed Boniface VIII's vice-chancellor, as, "if it pleases, an intimate friend," going on to say that he trusted in their friendship, asking for the vice-chancellor's help in restoring the privileges granted by Boniface's generous predecessor.[26] Bishop Grosseteste turned down the chancellor of York cathedral's request for a benefice for his relative by citing the law of friendship and the bond of love, which were powerful, but could not lead to sin. On examination, the chancellor's candidate had turned out to be insufficiently literate, and Grosseteste took the trouble to send along the results of the examination to prove it. Calling on his correspondent's love, he asked "humbly and with all my might and earnestly, with all the

---

[24] Giles Constable, *Letters and Letter-Collections*, Typologie des sources du moyen âge occidental 17 (Turnhout, 1976), 60–2.

[25] This function could be explicit: see, for example, the letters in Reg. Bronscombe III, nos. 489, 531, 536, 541, marked "EXEMPLUM DISPENSATIONIS," "FORMA," and "COLLATIO CUM FORMA."

[26] Reg. Winchelsey, 516: "amico se placet intime." A cardinal's chamberlain was addressed in similar terms regarding the same business: "having confidence in your friendship, we ask from the heart" for your help (ibid., 518: "de amicicia vestra confisi vos ex corde requirimus"). Winchelsey also asked the pope's physician, his "most cherished friend," to whom he sent "greeting and an embrace of sincere love" for help in a legal struggle with the abbey of St. Augustine's, Canterbury, begging for a continuation of the addressee's affection in this business (ibid., 655: "amico suo karissimo ... salutem et sincere dileccionis amplexum").

affection of my spirit that the sincerity of your love for me not be lessened on account of your cause touched on above, nor that the light of your countenance be obscured from me."²⁷

On a few occasions, bishops called on the language of affection in these more elaborate terms when writing to their own subordinates. Notable in this regard is Robert Grosseteste's very long letter to the cathedral chapter of Lincoln. The letter was simply one move in Grosseteste's epic campaign to conduct a visitation of his own cathedral. The bishop writes to his recalcitrant canons not as friends, but as sons. He nonetheless begins by noting that carnal sons owed their parents love (*amor*), among other things, and that such an obligation applied to spiritual sons as well, professing his own paternal affection for them; no tree can bear good fruit without such affection.²⁸ In another letter – really a treatise – addressed to the chapter concerning the same subject, Grosseteste points out that sons, carnal and especially spiritual, should lovingly and obediently accept the correction meted out by fathers.²⁹ And, indeed, expressing affection in another way, Grosseteste compares a bishop to a bird who, spreading the word of God in his diocese, arouses his friends (including the chapter).³⁰ The archdiocese of York yields more mundane cases. Archbishop Wickwane commissioned Robert de Lafford, "our beloved, with heartfelt feeling, commensal clerk," to deal with conflicts in the diocese of Durham.³¹ Archbishop Romeyn wrote to Master Adam de Copeland, "deeply (loved) son and friend," to have him instigate a tax inquiry.³² In a very different cause, Bishop Swinfield of Hereford addressed his man John de Ros, as "your friendship, with all the affection we can" to ask John to forward the case for the canonization of Swinfield's predecessor.³³

---

²⁷ Grosseteste, *Epistolae*, no. 19: "humiliter et obnixe tota mentis affectione, quatinus vestrae dilectionis sinceritas erga me vestram ob causam praetactam non minuatur, nec vultus vestri lumen ad me obtenebretur." Elsewhere, Bishop Cantilupe of Hereford wrote to ask a favor of the pope's penitentiary, "if it may please, his own friend," thanking him for the love he would show the bishop's proctor at the curia – and promising his own paternal affection for a relative of the penitentiary who had a benefice in the bishop's diocese (Reg. Cantilupe, 272–3: "si placet, speciali amico").
²⁸ Grosseteste, *Epistolae*, 199–200.
²⁹ ibid., 405.
³⁰ ibid., 414.
³¹ Reg. Wickwane, 155: "dilecto et precordiali ac commensali clerico nostro." Or another York instance: Archbishop Giffard announced to the world that he absolved Thomas, "our dear son, and deeply loved," of all claims concerning his accounts (Reg. Giffard of York, 111: "dilectus et precordialis noster").
³² Reg. Romeyn, I, 73–4: "precordiali filio et amico."
³³ Reg. Swinfield, 428–9: "vestram amiciciam omni qua possumus affeccione." Swinfield would collate the prebend of Moreton Parva to him, and John later appears as archdeacon

Affection and Devotion 217

Other bishops were briefer. Cantilupe of Hereford thanked his proctor at Rome, "necnon et amico speciali," for his services, reassuring him that the new proctor the bishop was sending was not to replace him, but to help him.[34] The bishop of Norwich ordered his *officialis*, "most cherished son," to arrange the income of the vicarage of Woolpit.[35]

So bishops sometimes addressed their subordinates in elaborately affectionate terms. Most of the time, however, they expressed such affection in the briefest of ways. That should not be surprising. After all, most of the surviving letters of bishops are administrative; they can be called business letters. But bishops nonetheless insinuated affection, and thus the cultural tradition associated with it, into such letters. Archbishop Pecham might occasionally refer to men as "our most cherished son" (*filius noster karissimus*) or "beloved son, our most cherished" (*dilectus filius, carissimus noster*).[36] When insisting that a nonresident rector of the archdiocese, who also happened to be a papal chaplain, attend to the cure of souls in his parish, Pecham wrote his "beloved son" as, he said, a friend.[37] Such letters are less common, however, than those of another sort. Pecham routinely – although not invariably – addressed the recipients of his letters as *nostri filii dilecti* or referred to some clerk of his in the same terms.[38] The register of Archbishop Gray of York yields similar results. The archbishop granted a pension to the *nepos* of his most cherished (*karissimus*) friend, the papal *hostiarius*, and he confirmed a grant of his beloved (*dilectus*) son to the cathedral, for whom he desired to provide with affection (*affectio*).[39] But most subordinates

---

of Hereford under Swinfield, and so presumably by Swinfield's collation (John Le Neve, *Fasti Ecclesiae Anglicanae 1300–1541 II: Hereford*, compiled by Joyce M. Horn [London, 1962], 7, 35).

[34] Reg. Cantilupe, 213 (and see 215).

[35] EEA VI: Norwich, no. 336: "fili carrissime." From Canterbury, Archbishop Winchelsey called on Reginald de St. Albans, his proctor at Rome, "beloved son and heartfelt friend," sending "greeting, blessing, and the grace of the savior with intimate love," to ask for help in getting Reginald's own proctor to obey the archbishop's order (Reg. Winchelsey, 518: "dilecto filio ac precordiale amico ... cum intima dileccione salutem benediccionem et graciam salvatoris"). For Reginald's standing as proctor, see ibid., 303–4, 545–8, 564, 583–91, 671.

[36] Reg. Pecham, 87, 116, and see 165.

[37] Ibid., 156.

[38] E.g., ibid., 40, 46, 50–1, 54–5, 59–61, 64–5, 67, 70, 72, 74, 78, 80, 85, 88–9, 97, 104, 118, 121, 123, 128, 134, 138, 144, 147, 149, 152–4, 156–7, 159–60, 162–5, 167–8, 174–5, 178–9, 183–4, 186–94, 196, 198–200, 202–3, 205–7, 211–12, 216–17, 219–20, 222–3, 225, 230, 235. At times Pecham addressed his recipients as *dilecti*, but not *filii*: e.g., ibid., 25, 27, 41, 43, 90, 138–9, 162.

[39] Rot. Gray, 142, 262.

to whom the archbishop showed affection, either in direct address or by referring to them in the third person, were simply his *dilecti filii*.[40] This was not an iron formula. Gray could vary his language, as grants to his *dilectus serviens*, his *dilectus* (carnal) brother, and his *dilectus et fidelis* attest.[41] At Winchester, Bishop Pontoise frequently addressed his letters to his *dilecti filii*, sometimes also referring to third parties in these terms.[42] Again, Pontoise, or his chancery, was capable of variation – *dilectus nobis* and *dilectus* [name] *clericus*.[43] To judge from the letters printed in Latin in the edition of his register – most of them – Bishop Bronscombe of Exeter invariably adopted *dilectus filius* to show affection to subordinates, except for the rare occasion when the affection was "in Christ."[44] This pattern is common, but not absolute. To judge from the Latin entries in the edition of his rolls and register, Bishop Sutton always expressed affection for his subordinates by noting that they were his *dilecti filii*, but his *dilectii filii* in Christ.[45] Certainly these general conclusions here about the use of *dilectus* by bishops fits the practice of the bishops of Carlisle, who were more likely to style subordinates as *dilecti filii* (in Christ or not) than anything else.[46]

Subordinates could return such affection and invoke the affection bishops offered them, to judge from their letters to bishops. Richard, called "de Douaie," addressed Bishop of Neville of Chichester as his most loving ("precipue diligendo") lord, offering his "service and love, with reverence and subjection."[47] Simon de Senliz, Neville's steward, addressed him on more than one occasion as his "most cherished lord."[48] In a very

---

[40] Ibid., 27, 40, 51–2, 59, 64, 67, 69, 71, 103, 140, 153, 224, 270.
[41] Ibid., 234–5, 251, 264.
[42] Reg. Pontissara, 17, 8, 17, 21–4, 29, 33–4, 38, 40, 42–3, 55–6, 69, 77, 88, 91, 94–5, 98, 114–17, 122–3, 125–6, 133–5, 140–4, 152, 163, 165, 168, 171, 177–81, 251, 257, 267, 273, 275, 287, 300, 312, 317, 324, 330, 348, 350, 459–60, 462, 473, 568, 576, 586, 588, 801–2, 821, 831. For *dilecti filii* for third person: ibid., 17, 20, 38, 41, 181, 245–6, 314, 463, 712.
[43] Reg. Pontissara, 67, 317.
[44] Reg. Bronscombe, nos. 531, 818, 841, 868, 925, 971, 983, 987, 990, 1012, 1024–5, 1038, 1044, 1053, 1058, 1069, 1091–2, 1101, 1110, 1124, 1175, 1222, 1239, 1242, 1248, 1255, 1262, 1274, 1277, 1312, 1342, 1429, and see also Appendix I, B. For *dilectus* son or friend in Christ: Reg. Bronscombe, nos. 976, 1013, 1262, 1313, 1324.
[45] Rolls and Reg. Sutton, especially III–VI.
[46] EEA 30: Carlisle, xlix–l.
[47] TNA, SC1/6/56: "obsequium et dileccione, cum reuerencia et suieccione."
[48] *Royal and Historical Letters Illustrative of the Reign of Henry III*, ed. Walter Waddington Shirley (RS) (London, 1862–6), I, no. 234: "domine carissimi"; TNA, SC1/6/88: "karrissime domini"; letters printed by Jacques Boussard, "Ralph Neville, Éveque de Chichester

different (and partially fictionalized) context (discussed in Chapter 9), Matthew Paris has Archbishop Abingdon's *ministri* lament the coming death of their most cherished (*karrissimus*) lord. Paris has the archbishop responding to one of this chorus as his *amicus*.[49]

But such expressions are relatively uncommon. To judge from their letters, the affection between bishop and subordinate was one-sided. Bishops often loved their subordinates, and might also declare their friendship, but subordinates did not usually address their bishops in such terms. Instead, when subordinates expressed any sort of attitude on their part, they did so by stressing their dedication to their bishop. Bishops said they loved their subordinates (most often by describing them as *dilecti filii*), but the subordinates most often said they were devoted to the bishop, that is, that they were the bishop's *devoti*. Bishop Pontoise of Winchester was frequently addressed by people who described themselves as his *devoti*. Sometimes these were his own clerks, sometimes his subordinates within the diocese, sometimes people of lesser status but not his subordinates, like the prior and convent of Christ Church, Canterbury.[50] The address could include a more elaborate expression of devotion. The dean of Guildford sent his report on his inquiry at the bishop's command regarding a clerk from the deanery to Bishop Pontoise. The dean was Pontoise's "humble and devoted dean, sending greeting as much owed as devoted to such a paternity, and reverence and obedience with honor."[51] Archbishop Pecham's subordinates, too, could describe themselves as his *devoti* or offer their obedience and/or devotion.[52] The same language crops up in letters from subordinates, including diocesan administrators, to Bishop Sutton of Lincoln.[53] And, like the bishop of Winchester, Sutton was addressed in such terms by men who were not his subordinates; the prior and chapter of Christ Church, Canterbury, offered him the service of devotion (*devotionis obsequium*), and even the bishop of Chichester,

---

et chancellier d'Angleterre (†1244) d'après sa correspondence," *Revue historique* 166 (1935), 227, nn 1, 4.

[49] C. H. Lawrence, *St. Edmund of Abingdon: A Study of Hagiography and History* (Oxford, 1960), 267. For C. H. Lawrence's suspicions regarding this episode, see Chapter 9, n 8.

[50] Reg. Pontissara, 73, 76, 79, 240, 283, 285, 316, 347, 369, 576.

[51] Ibid., 576: "suus humilis et devotus ... Decanus de Guldeford," sending "salutem tam debitam, quam devotam tante Paternitati reverenciam et obedienciam cum honore."

[52] Reg. Pecham, II, 39; Pecham, *Epistolae*, I, nos. 236, 245, II, no. 443.

[53] Rolls and Reg. Sutton, III, 101, 175, 205, VI, 41, 42, 69; Crowland Cartulary (Spalding Gentlemen's Society MS), f. 111r; Bodleian Library, MS Top Linc. d 1, f. 61r-v; LAO, Dii/84/1/6. For an *officialis* to his archbishop, see Rot. Giffard of York, 174 and for an archdeacon to his archbishop, ibid., 73.

his *devotus*, offered up his service.⁵⁴ Indeed, administrators below the bishop were addressed in similar terms, such as the official of the archdeacon of Lincoln, who was addressed by "suus ubique deuotus" the dean of Holland, acknowledging reception of the official's mandate.⁵⁵ The formula was not set in stone, hence the letter to his most reverend Walter de Langton (before his elevation to the bishopric of Coventry and Lichfield), from "suus clericus de Esthan" (who may not have called himself *devotus*, but nonetheless anxiously assured Walter that his failure was due to illness and promised not to sleep while laboring on Walter's behalf).⁵⁶ And the terminology of devotion was used by other ecclesiastics to other clergy who were not their ordinaries or lords, sometimes with some hesitation, e.g., the rector of Cornwell to the dean and chapter of Lincoln: "suus si placet deuotus clericus," offering his "salutem, reuerenciam, obsequium et honorem."⁵⁷

As C. R. Cheney's warning quoted at the start of this chapter suggests, it is tempting to dismiss the language of affection in these letters as meaningless verbiage. That is perhaps especially so when it comes to the briefest mention of love to be found in most thirteenth-century bishops' letters, those addressed to episcopal *dilecti filii*. But, as Cheney notes, such a dismissal would be a mistake.

Certainly, it is true that the use of *dilectus filius* by ecclesiastics to refer to subordinates was extremely common, common enough to count as a common form. Innocent III laid down that the papal custom of referring to bishops as brothers and all others as sons (with exceptions, such as royal figures) was to be adhered to in papal letters. Such formulae would help unmask forgeries, and Innocent's pronouncement found its way into the canon law.⁵⁸ The gloss on the pope's statement raises the issue of *dilectus filius* by describing the instance that prompted the pope's statement as being one in which the pope much wondered at the forgery referring to a bishop as *dilectus filius* when the term was reserved for non-bishops.⁵⁹ Indeed, the Cheneys note that Innocent III and other popes generally

---

⁵⁴ Rolls and Reg. Sutton, IV, 60, 180–1.
⁵⁵ BL, Add. MS 35296, fos. 327v–328r, and see 324v–325r.
⁵⁶ Historical Manuscripts Commission, *Fourteenth Report: Lincoln, Bury St. Edmunds, and Great Grimsby Corporations and the Deans and Chapters of Worcester, Lichfield &c* (London, 1895), 231.
⁵⁷ LAO, Dii/38/2/36.
⁵⁸ X.5.22.6.
⁵⁹ *Corpus juris canonici emendatum et notis illustratum. Gregorii XIII. pont. max. iussu editum* (Romae: In aedibus Populi Romani, 1582), gloss on X.5.22.6, col. 1750–1, consulted in http://digital.library.ucla.edu/canonlaw.

followed this form, including the usage of *dilectus filius*.⁶⁰ Leaving aside worries about authentication, such forms may, as Jane Sayers suggests, have allowed some mental relaxation while long documents were read out loud.⁶¹ But they certainly often appear in short documents, like many of those cited in this chapter.

In fact, the forms followed by thirteenth-century English ecclesiastics had been set long before. They are standard elements of the *ars dictaminis* developed in the eleventh and twelfth centuries. The Bolognese school of letter-writing in particular came to influence English letters by the end of the twelfth century.⁶² Hugh of Bologna's treatise provides sample salutations between bishops and their subjects, including *dilectus filius* from a bishop to his subject and *amoris affectum* between bishops.⁶³ The anonymous *Rationes dictandae* of Bologna of 1135 more explicitly lays out how prelates should greet their subjects, allowing them to express affection when such greetings are also between friends.⁶⁴ The *Rationes* also notes terms suitable for subjects to use in addressing their prelates: *obedientia, subjectio, deuotio* – but includes no terms expressing affection on the list.⁶⁵ Indeed, a manual attributed to Peter of Blois is careful to explain that writing between equals is distinct from writing between persons of different ranks.⁶⁶

So, were such affectionate formulae mere verbiage, the equivalent of a modern letter that begins "Dear Resident"? Not so. Consider how one papal pronouncement was taken when it was received in England. In 1265, Pope Clement IV had to inform a papal legate in England, that no,

---

⁶⁰ *The Letters of Pope Innocent III (1198–1216) Concerning England and Wales*, ed. C. R. Cheney and Mary G. Cheney (Oxford, 1967), xi–xii. Jane Sayers observes that in Honorius III's letters to English recipients, other than archbishops, "all other important persons, laymen and ecclesiastics, were his sons and daughters" (Jane E. Sayers, *Papal Government and England during the Pontificate of Honorius III (1216–1227)* [Cambridge, 1984], 99).

⁶¹ Ibid., 97.

⁶² James J. Murphy, *Rhetoric in the Middle Ages: A History of Rhetorical Theory from Saint Augustine to the Renaissance* (Tempe, 2001), 226; *Five English Artes Dictandae and Their Tradition*, ed. Martin Camargo (Binghamton, 1995), 1–34.

⁶³ *Briefsteller und Formelbücher des eilften bis vierzehnten Jahrhunderts*, ed. Ludwig Rockinger (Munich, 1863–4), I, 62.

⁶⁴ Ibid., I, 14. The *Rationes* also provides a second section for salutations between *amici propinqui* (ibid., 15). The attribution of this work by its editor to Alberic of Monte Cassino is in error (see Murphy, *Rhetoric in the Middle Ages*, 220, and references there).

⁶⁵ *Briefsteller und Formelbücher*, I, 14. A manual attributed to Peter of Blois gives nearly the same list, substituting *fidelitas* (from laypeople) for *famulamen* ("Libellus de arte dictandae rhetorice," in *Five English Artes Dictandae*, 54).

⁶⁶ "Libellus de arte dictandae rhetorice," in *Five English Artes Dictandae*, 52.

although the pope had addressed, "in the common, usual style," certain English clerks as *dilecti filii*, and had sent them his apostolic benediction, that fact did not release them from the sentences of excommunication, suspension, or interdict under which they might labor.[67] Of course, these particular papal *dilecti filii* had reason to try to stretch a point, but they tried nonetheless, and even a papal legate felt it necessary to refer the question back to Rome rather than laughing it out of court. The more emphatic language of friendship also meant enough to have potential real-world consequences. When, in the letter referred to here, Archbishop Pecham warned an absentee rector of his archdiocese, his *dilectus filius*, that he wrote as a friend, he was careful to note that the familiar nature of his letter should not be taken to revoke the solemnly made citation of him to reside in his parish.[68] It was such potential that presumably lay behind the tentativeness of some expressions of affection, such as the instance in which Bishop Cantilupe addressed the papal penitentiary as "if it pleases, his own friend."[69] If bishops could feel some constraint in using such expressions, that suggests that the words were not mere verbiage devoid of meaning.[70]

So talk of affection meant something. But what? It will be noticed that in most of the episcopal professions of love and friendship noted here, the bishop wanted something from his correspondent. In most cases, he wanted obedience to his command. In others, especially those marked by more elaborate expressions of affection addressed to men not in his jurisdiction, he wanted some sort of favor. In other words, it is tempting to regard such pronouncements as simply instrumental: tools to wheedle the recipients of letters into doing what the sender wanted.

---

[67] *Les registres de Clément IV (1265–1268)*, ed. Edouard Jordan, Bibliothèque des Ecoles françaises d'Athènes et de Rome (second series) 11 (Paris, 1893–1945), no. 238 (p. 20). Papal offerings of apostolic benediction were indeed also common form in the salutations of papal letters. For an example of the expectation that the formula of a greeting would be read carefully – in this case, for an offering of obedience as well as devotion – see C. R. Cheney, "Gervase, Abbot of Prémontré: A Medieval Letter-Writer," in Cheney, *Medieval Texts and Studies* (Oxford, 1973), 261.

[68] Reg. Pecham, II, 156.

[69] Reg. Cantilupe, 272–3. For a similar instance, see Archbishop Winchelsey to a cardinal, "amantissimo, si placet" (Reg. Winchelsey, 662–3).

[70] For a brief examination of such expressions in secular letters, see Peter Coss, "An Age of Deference," in *A Social History of England 1200–1500*, ed. Rosemary Horrox and W. Mark Ormrod (Cambridge, 2006), 45–6. It is worth noting that even apparently purely formulaic descriptions in royal charters of witnesses as "dearest brother" and "most beloved son," in the time of Edward I, were not devoid of meaning (Douglas Biggs, "Royal Charter Witness Lists for the Reign of Henry IV, 1399–1413," *English Historical Review* 119 [2004], 414–15).

Affection and Devotion

This employment had a long tradition and, indeed, was rooted in the twelfth-century cult of friendship. That cult had been deployed to political ends, ends that went beyond the emotional lives of its participants.[71] Indeed, such uses applied even within the cloister – or, to be precise, between cloisters, as monks relied on friendship to defuse conflicts. But as Julian Haseldine notes, while these friendships had political effects, that does not mean that they were simply a product of political considerations.[72] Simple reductionism is dangerous here. At the same time, the pragmatic function of friendship and affection should not be ignored.

The convention that superiors express affection for subordinates, but not the other way around – and the determined maintenance of that convention – suggest that superiors were more interested in invoking affection when dealing with subordinates than vice versa.[73] The implication is

---

[71] Giles Constable, "Dictatores and Diplomats in the Eleventh and Twelfth Centuries," *Dumbarton Oaks Papers* 46 (1992), 39.

[72] Julian Haseldine, "Friendship and Rivalry: The Role of Amicitia in Twelfth-Century Monastic Relations," *Journal of Ecclesiastical History* 44 (1993), 411–12 and instances explored by Haseldine, "Thomas Becket: Martyr, Saint – and Friend?" in *Belief and Culture in the Middle Ages: Studies Presented to Henry Mayr-Harting* (Oxford, 2001), 305–17. See also the discussion, regarding a later period, of Philippa Maddern, "'Best Trusted Friends': Concepts and Practices of Friendship among Fifteenth-Century Norfolk Gentry," in *England in the Fifteenth Century: Proceedings of the 1992 Harlaxton Symposium* (Stamford, 1994), 101–5. It is possible to see expressions of emotions such as affection as purely cultural constructions deployed in order to send signals to other people (e.g., Barbara Rosenwein, "Controlling Paradigms," in *Anger's Past: The Social Uses of an Emotion in the Middle Ages*, ed. Barbara H. Rosenwein [Ithaca, 1998], 236–7, 242, 247, and in particular, Richard E. Barton, "'Zealous' Anger and the Renegotiation of Aristocratic Relationships in Twelfth-Century France," ibid., 153–70; also, Barbara Rosenwein, "Worrying about Emotions in History," *American Historical Review* 107 [2002], 837). Certainly commentators distinguished between true friendship and friendship feigned for the sake of gain, and condemned the latter: McGuire, *Friendship and Community*, 380–2; P. Delhaye, "Deux adaptations du 'De Amicitia' de Ciceron au xii^c siècle," *Recherches de theologie ancienne et medievale* 43 (1928), 316–18, and, for some sensitive observations, Jaeger, *Ennobling Love*, 19, 23. False friendship, however, was not necessarily a matter of a lack of feeling, but the absence of an appropriate end, a point expressed very clearly by Julian Haseldine, "The Monastic Culture of Friendship," in *The Culture of Medieval English Monasticism*, ed. James G. Clark (Woodbridge, 2007), 178 n 7, and for emotional language of friendship that was arguably neither instrumental nor an expression of real (personal) affection, see Haseldine, "Understanding the Language of *Amicitia*: The Friendship Circle of Peter of Celle (c. 1115–1183)," *Journal of Medieval History* 20 (1994), 237–60. For a discussion arguing for real affection in the friendships of at least some members of the twelfth-century nobility, see John Meddings, "Friendship among the Aristocracy in Anglo-Norman England," in *Anglo-Norman Studies XXII: Proceedings of the Battle Conference 1999*, ed. C. Harper-Bill (Woodbridge, 2000), 187–204.

[73] It may also be that convention in such matters was more powerful in the Middle Ages than a later age would expect: Julian Haseldine, "Introduction," *Friendship in Medieval Europe*, ed. Julian Haseldine (Phoenix Mill, 1999), xviii–xix.

that there was a tension between the exercise of power, on the one hand, and affection on the other, a tension that was keener for subordinates than superiors.[74] Moreover, while both superiors and subordinates had something to gain by expressing affection, superiors had more to gain. After all, as has been seen, their disciplinary tools when dealing with clerical subordinates were limited. Subordinates, on the other hand, had less need to express their love for superiors because they could express service and devotion, options not open to superiors when addressing subordinates.

Affection and Devotion in Action

The letters discussed earlier concern the representation of emotional ties between bishops and their men. But did representations reflect an emotional reality? Were such ties evident in action? A place to investigate the lived impact of affection and devotion – and so a way out of the evidentiary cul-de-sac of representations – is bishops' wills and their execution.* Composing his testament gave a bishop an opportunity to mark out who was important to him and to, at least by implication, recognize his friends. This could be done by simply leaving a cash legacy, the value of which itself gauges the importance of the relationship. Or a bishop could leave an object, even a cherished one, thereby suggesting a more sentimental attachment. Most testaments of thirteenth-century bishops have perished. What do the survivors show about the relations between bishop and bureaucrat?

On the whole, bishops do not appear to have felt enough affection to remember their clerks both systematically *and* by name. Instead, on a few occasions bishops left a blanket, standardized legacy to their clerks,

---

[74] These observations suggest that the tension between Adam Marsh's "obsequiousness" and Robert Grosseteste's affection, noted in their correspondence by C. H. Lawrence, was a sharper version of a more general phenomenon (*The Letters of Adam Marsh*, ed. C. H. Lawrence [Oxford, 2006–10], I, xx–xxi). On such a tension among twelfth-century Cistercians, although without the suggestion that subordinates felt it more than superiors, see Caroline Walker Bynum, *Jesus as Mother: Studies in the Spirituality of the High Middle Ages* (Berkeley and Los Angeles, 1982), 110–69.

* The collection of *Testamentary Records of the English and Welsh Episcopate 1200–1413: Wills, Executors Accounts and Inventories, and the Probate Process*, ed. C. M. Woolgar, Canterbury and York Society 102 (Woodbridge, 2011) was unfortunately published too late for me to consult in writing this book. A quick survey of its contents suggests that it does not, however, add to the testamentary evidence for thirteenth-century bishops examined in this chapter. This admirable volume will, however, allow a more systematic study of the executors of bishops' wills than I have been able to carry out here.

unnamed. More usually, bishops left legacies to a few of their clerks individually. The latter legacies look like gifts stemming from a stronger sense of connection, especially as they were usually objects like cups or books, in contrast with the cash usually left to lay servants. Hence, the affection bishops expressed in death may serve as an index of expectations, and perhaps anxiety, but does not indicate that these bishops loved their clerks indiscriminately, with utterly institutionalized *affectio*. The contrast between personal legacies left to bishops' clerks and lay servants does, however, suggest that bishops felt stronger ties to the former than the latter. Bishops evidently were especially moved by ties with their clerks, a material response to the ideology of clerical solidarity promoted by the Gregorian Reform. True, the Bibles and books of canon law that cluster among episcopal legacies would have been unsuitable gifts for lay subordinates. But the wills confirm that bishops had plenty of other similar possibilities for lay followers, from beds to horses. The testamentary evidence also indicates that while bishops felt the pull of affection for their clerks, they did so with discrimination. Like the clerks in the previous chapter, they made decisions. And what about the objects of episcopal affection? Bishops' clerks frequently took on the onerous job of executing bishops' testaments. It was a last act of devotion, usually for no reward. In drawing such conclusions, I have set aside legacies to episcopal clerks who were also relatives of the bishops or who were to receive the legacy as an inducement to execute the will.

A first examination shows that episcopal clerks certainly received bequests from their bishops.[75] Bishop Gravesend of London left various objects to his clerks: a silver cup to John de Bedford, his archdeacon of London; part of his *Decretum* to Richard de Newport, his *officialis*; a decorated silver cup to John de Saint Clare; a piece of silver plate to Robert de Farleye, his chaplain; and a silver vessel plus a mazer with a silver foot to John de Stebbenheath, his clerk.[76] Moreover, other clerks appear receiving bequests – in one case cash; these may have been episcopal

---

[75] One will, that of Bishop Neville of Chichester, is of no help in this survey. As its editor notes, only excerpts, largely of interest to the dean and chapter of Chichester, survive (EEA 22: Chichester, no. 106).

[76] *Account of the Executors of Bishop Richard of London 1303, and of the Executors of Thomas Bishop of Exeter 1310*, ed. W. H. Hale and H. T. Ellacombe, Camden Society (new series) 10 (London, 1874), 112, 114. John de Bedford first appears as archdeacon while Gravesend was bishop, and so presumably received the archdeaconry from him (LN London, 7). John de Saint Clare similarly first appears as canon of London in Gravesend's time, and so presumably had the canonry by the bishop's collation (ibid., 85).

servants but they are not easily identifiable as such in the absence of a surviving register.[77]

Bishop Cantilupe of Hereford's will does not survive. But his executors received acknowledgments from a number of his clerks: Adam de Fileby (a silver offertory box and three fleur-de-lis bench covers); Robert de Redeswell (10 marks, a mule, and a Bible); John de Clara (40 marks, a mule, and a whole piece of dark-blue cloth); John de Kemesey (20 marks, a winter robe with a mantle furred in miniver, a black cloak with two hoods); Robert de Wyse (20 marks, a piece of white cloth, a furred cloak with a hood, and Ash the horse); Nicholas de Oxford (a summer robe of white cloth with a hood and a cloak of blue cloth with a hood).[78]

Bishop Nicholas de Longespee of Salisbury, however, presents a less convincing picture of a bishop remembering his clerks. William de Abingdon, his vicar while the bishop was overseas, did receive a silver cup while William de Braybrok, evidently a recipient of a canonry of Salisbury from the bishop, received the same, 100s, and the rather secular gift of armor for himself and his horse.[79] Another canon of Salisbury, Richard de Sottwell, who received a silver cup and 100s, had been the bishop's beloved household clerk.[80] But Longespee named two of these three clerks as his executors.[81] Longespee's testament yields fewer merely plausible candidates than the accounts of Gravesend's executors.[82] The last testament of Peter de

---

[77] Hence Simon, rector of Orsethe (silver cup); Henry de Grafton, rector of Horkelseye (silver cup); Walter de London, rector of Haringay (a piece silver plate); Stephen, vicar of Broxbourne (a dark-blue cap with fur); John de Littlinton, rector of Gilling (silver cup); William de Marisco, rector of Fairstead (a piece of silver plate) (*Account of the Executors of Bishop Richard of London*, 113–14). One should probably include the bishop's namesake and nephew, Richard Gravesend, who was also a clerk, and who received 40s (ibid., 114; Rot. Gravesend, v–vi).

[78] Hereford Dean and Chapter Archives. no. 1414. I am grateful to the Dean and Chapter Archives for providing me a photograph of this document. For these clerks' service, see Reg. Cantilupe, lxix–lxxi, with the exceptions of Robert de Redeswell, for whom see ibid., 266, and Robert de Wyse, for whom see Chapter 2, at nn 18–20.

[79] EEA 37: Salisbury, no. 450; EEA 36: Salisbury, lxxxviii. For William de Abingdon's service, see *Calendar of the Patent Rolls Preserved in the Public Record Office (1232–1509)* (London, 1891–1916), II (for 1281–92), 448. For William de Braybrok's first appearance as canon of Salisbury, see LN Salisbury, 43. William is called "rector of Wittenham" in the will, so he is not some layman of the same name as the canon.

[80] EEA 37: Salisbury, no. 450. He had received his canonry before the bishop's accession (LN Salisbury, 114).

[81] EEA 37: Salisbury, no. 450: William de Braybrok and Richard de Sottewell.

[82] The most plausible is Robert, vicar of Ramsbury, who received eight marks (ibid.). Adam, the treasurer of Salisbury's vicar, Robert de Iernumue, the vicar (choral?) of Salisbury, and the man who was "my vicar [choral?] in the church of Salisbury" all received bequests in order to pray for the bishop's soul, and do not look like diocesan administrators (ibid.).

Aquablanca, bishop of Hereford, leaves a similar picture. "Bartholomew our clerk" received a good 30 marks, while William the clerk got the nag he usually rode, along with 5 marks, and James de Aosta, his notary, received 20 marks and his usual horse. Two other legatees might have been among the bishop's clerks: William the chaplain received 20 marks and his usual nag while Jordan de London, chaplain, received the bishop's best robe, namely, the blue tunic and supertunic "de bloy sive de perse" and the mantle of same. The bishop of Maurienne was to have a new silver alb and ewer.[83] Otherwise, the only legatees identifiable as clerks, albeit not explicitly as Aquablanca's own clerks, are men who were also his relatives and whose legacies may be better understood in those terms: John de Aquablanca, dean of Hereford; Aimeric, chancellor of Hereford; and Aymo, precentor of Hereford, all nephews of the bishop.[84]

Although the episcopate of Bishop Godfrey Giffard of Worcester is much better documented by a surviving register, identifying episcopal clerks in his will is no easier. Master J. de Ebroycis, who received a miter the bishop had himself received from his brother the archbishop of York, a ring, and the bishop's smaller Bible, had also enjoyed the bishop's patronage in a benefice. But he was Giffard's *nepos*, and that alone might account for such a sentimentally freighted legacy.[85] Thomas de Wycheford had been Giffard's cross-bearer and had been promoted to the priesthood and benefices (although not clearly ones in the bishop's gift), and so likely should be counted among his clerks; he received a goblet worth 100s.[86] In addition to his executors, Giffard remembered other clerks: his commensal clerks were each to have one length of silk cloth; those clerks of his chapel who were not beneficed were to have 40s apiece.[87] Giffard's

---

(It should also be noted that Longespee had long been treasurer of Salisbury, and these bequests may thus reflect that association.) An unnamed clerk of the bishop's chapel received six marks (ibid., 526).

[83] EEA 35: Hereford, no. 124; "The Will of Peter, of Aigueblanche, Bishop of Hereford," ed. C. Everleigh Woodruff, in *Camden Miscellany* 14, Camden Society (third series) 37 (London, 1926), 4–5. The bishop's previous will survives (EEA 35: Hereford, no. 123), but does not leave legacies to individuals.

[84] "Will of Peter, of Aigueblanche," 4–5; EEA 35: Hereford, no. 124, and for the family relationships, "Will of Peter, of Aigueblanche," xi. John and Aymeric did engage in administrative service for the bishop (*Calendar of the Close Rolls*, X [for 1256–9], 465–6; *Calendar of the Patent Rolls*, V [for 1258–66], 332).

[85] Reg. Gainsborough, 52. For his reception of a prebend from Giffard, Reg. Giffard of Worcester, 362.

[86] For his legacy, Reg. Gainsborough, 53. For the rest, Reg. Giffard of Worcester, 28, 40, 45, 128, 495.

[87] Reg. Gainsborough, 53.

clerks do appear prominently among his executors, and they received their legacies *as* his executors: each was to have a jewel worth 100s and a piece of silver plate.[88] Among these five executors were Walter de Berton, rector of Bredon; John de Redberrow, rector of Hartlebury; and John de Staneway, rector of Ripple, all of whom rendered the bishop administrative service.[89]

Bishop Hugh of Wells of Lincoln left two testaments. The first dates to 1212; Hugh had not actually served in his diocese but was still in exile during Innocent III's interdict of England. Not having had a chance to build much of an administration, Hugh would have had few clerks at Lincoln to whom to leave anything.[90] John de York was to receive 100 marks unless the bishop had beneficed him; William the bishop's scribe was to receive 10 marks.[91] Hugh's second will dates to 1233, near the end of his episcopate. It is, as one might expect, more extensive. But episcopal clerks are again barely in evidence as legatees. The canon of the prebend of Leicester (unnamed) was to have 40 marks for building in his prebend unless he received the money before Hugh's death, a bequest that reads more like a concern for the prebend than its incumbent, who had, however, indeed been among Hugh's diocesan servants.[92] Otherwise, Hugh's second will is devoid of legacies to episcopal clerks or even likely candidates as episcopal clerks. Boniface of Savoy, archbishop of Canterbury, did not remember any of his clerks in his will,

---

[88] Ibid., 53–4.

[89] Ibid., 53–4. Walter de Berton was steward of Giffard's household and later, apparently, of his lands, enjoying one or perhaps two benefices from the bishop (Reg. Giffard of Worcester, 28, 40, 72, 362, 481). Although the collation of Bredon to him is not recorded, the bishop collated this rectory on another occasion, and it was in his gift in 1291 (ibid., 305; Online Taxatio of Pope Nicholas IV http://www.hrionline.ac.uk/taxatio, sub nom.). John de Redberrow received his rectory by collation from Giffard (Reg. Giffard of Worcester, 367, 370, 455) and received a number of ad hoc commissions from him (ibid., 425, 518–19, 531, 539, 547). John de Staneway received Ripple from Giffard and the commendation of another benefice, and was explicitly called Giffard's clerk (ibid., 192, 270, 354, and see 362).

[90] He seems largely to have ignored his clerks from his days in the royal chancery.

[91] *Acta of Hugh of Wells*, no. 2. A Welsh will looks similar in this respect. Bishop Anian II of St. Asaph left the better of his chickens to Griffin, archdeacon of St. Asaph. Unless some of the friars mentioned in his will and the canon of St. Asaph (who was also the bishop's nephew) were also the bishop's clerks, this is the only bequest to one of the bishop's administrative subordinates (Christ Church, Canterbury, Dean and Chapter *Sede Vacante* Register 2, no. 187). Of course, as the chickens suggest, St. Asaph's was a poor see.

[92] *Acta of Hugh of Wells*, no. 408. The incumbent was Robert Grosseteste, to whom Hugh had already collated the archdeaconry of Leicester (LN Lincoln, 77).

although at least two were among his executors and present at the will's composition.[93]

Bishop Walter Suffield of Norwich, however, followed the larger pattern. He bequeathed rings to an (unnamed) archdeacon of Colchester and to Hervey de Feckenham, his clerk.[94] Some lesser clerks also received bequests. Giles the chaplain got a mazer, a well-furred cap, a particular missal given the bishop, a silver goblet, and five silver spoons, while Matthew the chaplain got 5 marks and one of the bishop's better robes.[95] William, clerk of the chapel, received 40s and the book of canticles that had been John Bygot's.[96] William de Foceston, clerk, who does not otherwise seem to be connected with Suffield, was to have a silver goblet.[97] Otherwise, the clerks who benefited under Suffield's will were also his executors. Unlike Giffard, however, Suffield did not dangle bequests before his executors like carrots to perform their duties. William de Pakenham, the bishop's proctor, received a silver goblet with a stand and the bishop's psalter.[98] Two clerks are never explicitly named as being in the bishop's service, but both were his executors and perhaps should be counted among his clerks: William de Whitwell was to have the image of Mary given the bishop by Roger de Raveningham; Hugh de Corbrig was to receive a goblet with a stand and the bishop's large (*spissam*) Bible, beautiful but false; William de Wychingham got a goblet with a stand and 100s.[99]

Bishop Richard Wyche of Chichester's will is similar. Half of the legatees identifiable as clerks, and perhaps as the bishop's clerks, were also his

---

[93] L. Wurstenberger, *Peter der Zweite Graf von Savoyen, Markgraf in Italien, sein Haus und seine Landa: ein Charakterbild des dreizehnten Jahrhunderts* (Bern, 1856–1858), IV, 342–4. Among the archbishop's executors, also present at the drawing up, were Stephen (de Monte Luelli) (who first appears as archdeacon during Boniface's pontificate; his predecessor held the archdeaconry into Boniface's pontificate [LN Monastic Cathedrals, 13]); and P(eter) de Auxon, the archbishop's *officialis* and vicar-general (*The Medieval Court of Arches*, ed. F. Donald Logan, Canterbury and York Society 95 [Woodbridge, 2005], 197 and n 9; Wurstenberger, *Peter der Zweite*, IV, 343–4).

[94] EEA 32: Norwich, no. 138. For Hervey as Suffield's clerk: ibid., nos. 88–9, 108.

[95] Ibid., no. 138.

[96] Ibid.

[97] Ibid.

[98] Ibid. For his work as attorney: ibid., nos. 118 n, 228–9.

[99] Ibid., no. 138. For William de Whitwell as clerk: ibid., nos. 43, 77, 83, 109, 118. For Hugh as clerk: ibid., nos. 9, 77. For William de Wychingham as clerk: ibid., nos. 69, 87. Hugh Corbrigg attested the bishops' *acta* on five different dates (ibid., nos. 9, 22, 77, 87, 91) and William de Whitwell had done so on at least nine different dates (ibid., nos. 26, 43, 77, 83, 87, 94, 109, 111, 118).

executors: Simon de Tarring, Walter de Campeden, William de Selsey, John Mansel, and Hugh de St. Edmunds.[100] Others who were not executors were Robert de Crowhurst, the bishop's clerk (to receive £20); William de Kempsey, the bishop's proctor (£20); Robert de Hastings, the bishop's *officialis* (appropriately, the bishop's *Decretals*); William de Bramber, chaplain (a silver goblet and a book concerning the vices); Henry, clerk of the chapel (10 marks).[101] Perhaps Philip (called *magister*, and so presumably a clerk), who received a particular footed goblet, £20, and a nag fit for harness, should be counted among the bishop's clerks, but only his appearance as a legatee in the will connects him with Bishop Wich.[102]

Archbishop Winchelsey's testament departs from this pattern of named clerks receiving objects as legacies when they received legacies at all. The bishop left a number of monetary bequests to named clerks: to Thomas de Cobham, William de Passele, John de Twytham, Laurence de Mause, William de Schelving, and Geoffrey de Brochamton, 10 marks apiece; to Stephen Ambrois, £20; and to John de Aqua de Maidstone, and Richard, clerk and almoner, 20 marks apiece. Since these were men to whom Winchelsey thought he might give benefices should he live, they presumably should be counted as his clerks.[103] To their number one can probably add John de Croindene, to whom Winchelsey left 70s.[104] (Two special cases are the bishop of Llandaff, the archbishop's vicar-general [100 marks], and John de Winchelsey, the archbishop's nephew [a Bible

---

[100] EEA 22: Chichester, no. 188.
[101] Ibid. Robert de Crowhurst, whom the bishop called "our clerk," witnessed two of the bishop's *acta*, perhaps on different dates (ibid., nos. 119, 159). (Ibid., no. 159 reads "de Cilahurst" whereas *Saint Richard of Chichester: The Sources for His Life*, ed. David Jones, Sussex Record Society 79 (Lewes, 1995 for 1993), 39 reads "de Croihurst." The pertinent copy here is faint where Robert's name appears [West Sussex Record Office, Ep. I/1/1, f. 178v], but I am inclined to follow the latter reading. This late fourteenth-/early fifteenth-century copyist cannot have been expected to have been too particular in rendering this witness's name. I am grateful to the West Sussex Record Office for providing an image of this ms.) For William de Kempsey as proctor: *Saint Richard of Chichester: The Sources for His Life*, 70 n 8. For Robert de Hastings as *officialis*: EEA 22: Chichester, lvi–lvii. The chaplain William de Bramber is not found connected with the bishop unless this William is the William, rector of Bramber, who attests one of the bishop's *acta* (EEA 22: Chichester, no. 159, following *Saint Richard of Chichester: The Sources for His Life*, 70 n13).
[102] EEA 22: Chichester, no. 188.
[103] Reg. Winchelsey, 1342. Of course, Richard should be thus counted simply because he is described as (Winchelsey's) almoner. John de Aqua de Maidstone is elsewhere explicitly called the archbishop's clerk (ibid., 1343). Thomas de Cobham had received the commend of the archdeaconry of Lewes on Winchelsey's nomination (ibid., 733–4).
[104] He was rector of Keston, at whose presentation is not recorded (ibid., 962). But Winchelsey's predecessor had collated Keston as in his own gift (Reg. Pecham, I, 50).

bound in black leather with the archbishop's concordances].)[105] And all the archbishop's "greater clerks" (*clerici nostri majores*) were to have a covered silver cup, according to their grade.[106] None of the men named earlier was among the bishop's executors, who were also each to have 40 marks for their labors.[107]

What can one make of this evidence? Giffard's and Winchelsey's testaments suggest one reason that named clerks might have been generally so uncommon among bishops' legatees. Giffard left 40s each to the clerks of his chapel who were not beneficed. Winchelsey left more legacies to clerks by name than any of his thirteenth-century colleagues, but most of these were to be given only if they had not received a benefice from the archbishop. Indeed, in his first testament, Hugh of Wells left 100 marks to John de York, one of only two clerks who received legacies in that will, but John was to receive the money only if Hugh had not given John a benefice before the bishop's death. Episcopal clerks generally did get benefices during their bishops' lifetimes. Giffard and Winchelsey, and on a lesser scale Hugh of Wells (although with a very large sum of money), simply attempted to take care of some of the exceptions. A gift of a benefice while the bishop was alive was seen to be enough.

This tendency to limit the number of named clerks who received bequests does not mean that individual clerks could not stand out. Some did for each bishop, in particular, Gravesend and Winchelsey – hence the individual bequests mentioned earlier.[108] Suffield of Norwich indeed expressed tender feelings in this regard. Suffield described William de Whitwell, who was to receive a certain image of Mary, as "my cherished and faithful one."[109] William de Pakenham was to receive not only a silver footed cup and Suffield's psalter but also the emotive sentiment that "nothing but death could separate us," and so the wish that William would work for the good of Suffield's soul.[110] Another legatee, the cathedral's seneschal Geoffrey de Lodnes and not clearly one of the bishop's clerks, received several bequests and was faithful enough that Suffield

---

[105] Reg. Winchelsey, 1341. For John as Winchelsey's nephew: ibid., xxxii. Winchelsey had also collated Newenden to him (ibid., 1207).
[106] Ibid., 1341.
[107] Ibid., 1342.
[108] Perhaps Cantilupe of Hereford should be included here too. However, the surviving source is not Cantilupe's will but the record of what legatees received at the hands of executors. The specifics of the benefaction may reflect some discretion on the executors' part rather than the bishop's will.
[109] "fideli et caro meo": EEA 32: Norwich, no. 138.
[110] "nichil nisi mors nos separare": ibid.

thought Geoffrey would benefit Suffield's soul.[111] The bishop of Norwich was not entirely alone in this. Edmund of Abingdon, archbishop of Canterbury, bequeathed "our cup to our beloved chancellor whom we have long viscerally embraced," although this statement is from a source open to question.[112] Archbishop Boniface appears to have left nothing to lay servants; the archbishop was more generous to important figures like his niece, the queen of England.[113]

Strikingly, however, with the exception of Winchelsey's list of clerks who might not have received a benefice and the possible exception of a number of Gravesend's legatees, where clerks are remembered in the wills in larger numbers, they are not remembered individually, but collectively. All Giffard's commensal clerks were to receive silk cloth; all the unbeneficed clerks of his chapel were to receive 40s. All Winchelsey's greater clerks were to have a covered silver cup – according to rank. If these are actions rooted in sentiment, in affection, they are not the individualized affection one expects to flow from real feeling. Rather, these bequests echo the sort of affection by policy found in bishops' letters. Indeed, Winchelsey did intend his legacies of covered silver cups to unnamed clerks to have emotional weight; the recipients, he said, were to use them "in memory of us."[114]

One way to get a handle on the bequests of bishops to their clerks is to compare such bequests by those bishops to lay servants, many of them menials, by name. Men identified as cooks, bakers, messengers, marshals, and the like crowd episcopal testaments. Here I have assumed that if a legatee's name appears among such lay servants, that legatee was a lay servant also, even if his occupation is not mentioned.[115] The least marked instances are the wills of Bishops Longespee and Wyche, in which such lay servants roughly equal in number the legatees who were, or possibly

---

[111] Ibid.
[112] "Legamus dilecto ... cancellario nostro, quem iam diu nobis invisceravimus cuppam nostram" (*Saint Richard of Chichester: The Sources for His Life*, 93). Saint Edmund's will does not survive. His chancellor's *vita* quotes this line from Edmund's will in order to strengthen the tie between Saint Edmund, and his chancellor, Saint Richard. The author's need to show that saints are loved by saints means the quotation needs to be treated with some caution.
[113] Wurstenberger, *Peter der Zweite*, IV, 342–4.
[114] Reg. Winchelsey, 1341: "in nostri memoriam qua utatur."
[115] This seems a safe procedure, although it does turn up one discrepancy: Richard de Gravesend, Bishop Gravesend of London's legatee, whose name appears among lay servants although he was a clerk (*Account of the Executors of Bishop Richard of London*, 114; Rot. Gravesend, v–vi).

were, episcopal clerks.¹¹⁶ Gravesend of London remembered many more clerks by name than he did lay servants.¹¹⁷ For the other bishops, such lay servants easily outnumber legatees who were or possibly were episcopal clerks. Hence, for example, Archbishop Winchelsey named twelve legatees who were his clerks or possibly so, the largest such number. Yet he remembered seventeen lay servants by name: Godard his cook (50 marks); Richard his marshal (40 marks); John de Ros (30 marks); Geoffrey the cook (£20); Richard de Grosherst (£20); William his tailor (20 marks); Roger the doorkeeper (*hostiarius*) (20 marks); Yvo of the buttery (20 marks); Robert de Sanford (£10); John, formerly his barber in the archbishop's time of persecution (50s); Adam the scullion who similarly served (40s); Ralph le Weyte (presumably the watchman) (100s); Nicholas the doorkeeper (*janitor*) (100s); Andrew the cook (50s); Adam the pantler (£4); Thomas the baker (50s); and Stephen of the buttery (50s).¹¹⁸ Moreover, these bequests do not appear to have been a matter of spreading a lesser total sum among many lesser legatees. Most of the legacies to these men are on the same scale as those Winchelsey left his clerks: five received 40s or 50s, comparable to the 70s Winchelsey left to the clerk John de Croindene. The others received sums between £10 and 50 marks, compared with 20 marks to £20 left to the clerks (excluding the 100 marks left to the bishop of Llandaff who was, after all, a bishop).¹¹⁹

On the whole, then, legacies to lay servants confirm the impression that bishops did not remember their clerks widely when making bequests.

---

[116] Longespee of Salisbury left legacies to three clerks who appear to have been in his service, and four more who may have been (see at nn 79–84). His will appears to record legacies to six laymen, all recipients of small amounts of cash except Lambert. Bishop Wyche of Chichester left roughly as many legacies to lay servants (for whom see Appendix 2) as to clerks or likely clerks. The sums bequeathed to these laymen are substantial but rather below what Wyche's clerks or likely clerks received. Moreover, they are all monetary, whereas the clerks were more likely to receive objects. M. M. Sheehan remarks that the wills of the "well-to-do" (among whom bishops must be included) stressed monetary bequests (*The Will in Medieval England, From the Conversion of the Anglo-Saxons to the End of the Thirteenth Century* [Toronto, 1963], 283). There is, however, a possible notable exception: Lambert the chamberlain. If he was a layman – and he might have been a clerk – he would be an exception who tests the rule, in that the bishop also describes Lambert as his *alumpnus* (EEA 37: Salisbury, no. 450) and his haul of money and objects was very great (see Appendix 2), more than that of most legatees of any description in thirteenth-century episcopal wills.

[117] Twelve clerks (see at nn 76–7) versus seven lay servants (Appendix 2).

[118] Reg. Winchelsey, 1341–2.

[119] As for the other bishops, see Appendix 2.

Yet they also highlight the sentimental nature of those bequests to clerks. Bishops' clerks were more likely to receive objects, such as silver cups or books, than lay servants, who almost always received cash. Hence, while bishops did not feel the pull of affection systematically when making bequests to their clerks, they did feel it nonetheless.

So much for the affection of bishops for their clerks. What about clerks' devotion to their bishops? Just as bishops' wills afforded opportunities for bishops not just to express affection but to do something about it, so too a bishop's death gave his clerks an opportunity to serve their bishop one last time, to be truly *devoti*, when their bishop could no longer do them any good.

Certainly acting as a bishop's executor could serve as a test of devotion. As noted earlier, Bishop Giffard of Worcester thought it necessary to offer inducement from beyond the grave, and so he left legacies to his executors in return for their service.[120] Winchelsey left his executors 40 marks each for their labors, whereas Longespee left 100s.[121] But Wyche simply, but "devotedly" (*devote*) asked his executors faithfully and diligently to carry out his wishes, while Gravesend begged that they be good disposers of his goods by the aspersion of Christ's blood.[122] The other bishops' wills examined here do not even go that far.[123] For their part, bishops seem to have counted on their executors' good will and little else. This could be a mistake;[124] three of Winchelsey's executors declined the work, even at the cost of their 40 marks.

In naming executors, bishops were asking a great deal. Being an executor was potentially a long-term job. Carrying out bishops' wills was no exception. On the one hand, affairs sometimes passed easily. The estate of Bishop Sutton of the large and wealthy diocese of Lincoln was wrapped up in a mere five months.[125] On the other hand, the executors of Bishop Cantilupe of Worcester, who passed from this earth in 1266, were freed from their work only in 1294.[126] The estate of Archbishop Winchelsey, who died in 1313, was still in probate in 1325, by which time all but one

---

[120] See at nn 88–90.
[121] Reg. Winchelsey, 1342; EEA 37: Salisbury, no. 450.
[122] EEA 22: Chichester, no. 160; *Account of the Executors of Bishop Richard of London*, 115.
[123] EEA 32: Norwich, no. 138; *Acta of Hugh of Wells*, nos. 2, 408; Wurstenberger, *Peter der Zweite*, IV, 342–4; EEA 35: Hereford, no. 124; "The Will of Peter de Aigueblanche, Bishop of Hereford," 8.
[124] Reg. Winchelsey, xxxiv.
[125] Rolls and Reg. Sutton, III, lxxxvi.
[126] Reg. Giffard of Worcester, 448.

of the archbishop's executors had themselves died; one of the legatees pleaded, with devout prayers, to the current archbishop to bring the business to an end.[127]

And, of course, there was work to be done. A bishop was a major magnate, with estates and goods scattered across a diocese and beyond. Even Bishop Merton of tiny Rochester left nine larger manors or churches for which inventories had to be drawn up, in addition to other personally held properties.[128] All this sent executors shooting across the country, as they visited each manor multiple times (to check on stock and on grain harvests and sales) as well as dealing with various legal authorities.[129] True, most of a bishop's property was that of the diocese, and so not subject to his testamentary disposition. But that fact meant that the bishop's personal property had to be disentangled from that of the see. Indeed, the issue was sensitive enough that bishops routinely asked for royal permission even to make wills.[130]

So even if the administration of a bishop's estate went smoothly, his executors' labors could be extensive. And all might easily not go smoothly.[131] Bishop Bronscombe of Exeter informed the executors of his predecessor Bishop Blund that Blund's property was sequestrated, as Blund's creditors planned to sue. Evidently the matter had risen to the pope's notice, often a signal of trouble and expense, as Bronscombe acted on receiving a papal letter about the matter.[132] Like any executor, a bishop's executor also inherited the job of collecting debts owed the deceased and might have to go to law to collect.[133] A bishop's actions in his official capacity could also easily leave legal fallout for his executors. The executors of Bishop de la Wyle of Salisbury found themselves sued by a rector who claimed to have been unjustly excommunicated, and his rectory sequestrated, by the bishop.[134] Moreover, ecclesiastical lawsuits

[127] Reg. Winchelsey, xxxiv, 1347–8.
[128] *Early Rolls of Merton College*, 56.
[129] Ibid., 56. In the years 1277–82, the duties of John de Merston, for example, carried him from London to the diocese of Durham three times; from London to Basingstoke, from Basingstoke to Salisbury; from Chalfont to Chedington, and, of course, to Rochester (ibid., 127–8, 133–4).
[130] Sheehan, *Will in Medieval England*, 246. By the end of the thirteenth century, they were also asking for papal permission (ibid., 247).
[131] On the various labors of the executors of Bishop Gravesend of London, see *Account of the Executors of Bishop Richard of London*, xx–xxiii.
[132] Reg. Bronscombe, no. 26. For what seems a similar case, see Reg. Swinfield, 96.
[133] Hence the suit of Bishop Aquablanca of Hereford's executors against a rector for 40 marks (*Select Cases from the Ecclesiastical Courts of the Province of Canterbury*, 154).
[134] Ibid., 145.

might always entail excommunication of the parties, which may explain the otherwise unexplained excommunication of some of Bishop Merton of Rochester's executors.[135] Furthermore, executors could fall out with each other. Master Ewell, for example, may have been a clerk, but he also represented Bishop Merton's family among Merton's executors. His conflicts with his colleagues, drawn from among the bishop's other followers, helped spin out the execution of the will for five years.[136]

Bishops usually chose some of their clerks to undertake these difficulties. Of course, one reason for them to do so was expertise. Clerks were more literate and numerate than laity, and so better suited to execute a will. They also might have the connections to smooth over difficulties. Master Elias de Dereham, a high flyer, was named as executor by two archbishops of Canterbury, a bishop of Durham, and a bishop of Lincoln.[137] Moreover, a bishop's clerks were likely to be experienced in dealing with probate as judges, as bishops often delegated such business to them. And, of course, episcopal clerks were also on the receiving end of a language of affection from their bishops.

The issue here is whether episcopal clerks did in fact take up such duties. Were they, really, *devoti*? They were, although not all of them were. The discussion of the legacies of bishops Giffard, Suffield, and Wyche points to these bishops naming some of their clerks as executors. Moreover, episcopal clerks can be detected carrying out their duties as executors for bishops throughout the century. The diocese of Durham provides a succession of examples. The testament of Bishop Richard Poore of Durham was executed by his steward, who may have followed the bishop from his previous see.[138] Robert de St. Agatha, presumably made archdeacon of Durham by Bishop Kirkham of Durham, acted as that bishop's executor after his death.[139] Episcopal clerks found executing Bishop Stichill's will include Roger de Seaton and Thomas de Levesham, while executors of Bishop Robert of Holy Island's will include Robert Avenal and, once again, Thomas de Levesham.[140]

---

[135] *Early Rolls of Merton College*, 57.

[136] Ibid., 54–5, 58. Michael Sheehan points out that executors often failed to work together harmoniously ("English Wills and the Records of the Ecclesiastical and Civil Jurisdictions," *Journal of Medieval History* 14 [1998], 8).

[137] Vincent, "Master Elias de Dereham," 139, 143, 147, 153.

[138] EEA 29: Durham, xxxix.

[139] Ibid., no. 163.

[140] Ibid., lii and no. 189 n. Roger served Stichill as an itinerant justice (ibid., xlviii). Thomas attested four of Bishop Stichill's *acta* and was described by Stichill as his clerk, and later attested ten of Bishop Robert of Holy Island's *acta* (ibid., xlix, li, no. 166). Robert Avenal was Bishop Robert of Holy Island's chancellor (ibid., lii).

Other dioceses also turn up cases. Archbishop Hubert Walter's executors included not only the ubiquitous Elias de Dereham (Walter's steward), but also James Salvagius, another of the archbishop's clerks.[141] Master Thomas de Freckenham, Archbishop Langton's *officialis*, served him in death as an executor.[142] Thomas did not survive his last master, Archbishop Abingdon, but that archbishop's proctor, Master John de Wich, served as his executor.[143] The executors of Bishop Cantilupe of Hereford included his clerks Richard de Swinfield, Walter de Rudmarley, William de Montfort, and Robert de Wyse.[144] Both clerks who acted as executors of the will of Bishop March of Bath and Wells appear to have been the bishop's clerks.[145] Of course, a bishop could choose wrong. Archbishop Pecham complained that his predecessor's executor was failing in his duty, noting for good measure that the deceased had collated benefices to him.[146] Archbishop Pecham complained regarding the "notorious negligence" of Bishop Kilkenny of Ely's executors.[147]

There are other occasional signs that bishops were held in affection by their clerks that went beyond language or even serving as an executor of a bishop's will. The archdeacon of Berkshire arranged for masses for his own soul and that of his bishop.[148] Similarly, Thomas de Hertford, archdeacon of Totnes, considering the benefices he had received "as a

---

[141] EEA III: Canterbury, 307. For Elias as Walter's steward: Vincent, "Master Elias of Dereham," 133.

[142] Kathleen Major, "The 'Familia' of Archbishop Stephen Langton," *English Historical Review* 48 (1933), 538–40.

[143] Ibid., 141, 151.

[144] Reg. Swinfield, 12, 96. Swinfield says he had been in Cantilupe's household for about eighteen years (ibid., 234). Robert de Wyse (alias de Wyche and de Gloucester) served as Cantilupe's *officialis* (Reg. Cantilupe, lxix) and William de Montfort as his vicar-general (ibid.). Walter de Rudmarley was a guardian of the temporalities of the see while the bishop was away and an auditor (ibid., lxix–lxx).

[145] Reg. Winchelsey, 441. Master Peter de Avebari appears to have received the archdeaconry of Taunton from Bishop March, for Peter first appears as archdeacon during March's episcopate (LN Bath and Wells, 94). Anthony de Bradeney similarly first appears as canon of Wells while March was bishop, and later received another prebend in the cathedral under March (ibid., 54, 71).

[146] Pecham, *Epistolae*, III, 828, and see 889.

[147] Ibid., I, 110.

[148] EEA 19: Salisbury, no. 283. For a likely Welsh case, see the establishment by Bishop Richard de Carew of St. David's of a chantry for the benefit of the souls of his mother, his carnal father, his venerable father Bishop Thomas Wallensis, and his own (*St. David's Episcopal Acta, 1085–1280*, ed. Julia Barrow, South Wales Record Society 13 [Cardiff, 1998], no. 143). Richard first appears as canon of St. David's during Bishop Thomas's episcopate, his predecessor in the see (ibid., 13), and so quite possibly was canon by Bishop Thomas's collation, although it should be noted that the diocese's documentation is very sparse.

grateful man should," worked to have a church appropriated to the dean and chapter of Exeter for the good of the souls of himself, of Exeter's current bishop, and of the previous two.[149] Richard Gravesend had, earlier in his career, been made canon of London, presumably by Henry de Sandwich, then bishop of London. When Gravesend himself died as bishop of London, he asked that he be interred in the cathedral next to Henry, *promotor meus*.[150]

Death clarifies. The ties that bound bishop and clerk are revealed when the senior partner perished. Bishops' bequests indicate that their ties to their servants were real and might transcend departure from this world.[151] Indeed, bishops entrusted the health of their very souls to their executors. Provisions for the spiritual benefit of the deceased were commonplace in thirteenth-century wills,[152] and bishops' wills were no exception. The affection felt by bishops – or at least expressed by bishops – evoked the devotion of their clerks, and sometimes, at least, bishops got it.[153]

[149] Reg. Bronscombe, no. 841.
[150] *Account of the Executors of Bishop Richard of London*, 111.
[151] The fact that the terms of thirteenth-century wills were generally secret during the life of the testator (Sheehan, *Will in Medieval England*, 183, 189–90) strengthens the notion that these were gifts of the testator bestowed altruistically (although perhaps not so when the legatee was also an executor).
[152] Ibid., 258, 261.
[153] C. Stephen Jaeger argues that the power a lord exercised over his subordinates heightened the impact of lordly expressions of affection for subordinates. Such subordinates in turn felt especially bound to their lords (Jaeger, *Ennobling Love*, 21–2). This psychology is plausible, but presumably applies only weakly here, in that beneficed clerks were not so vulnerable to their lords. For a strong statement along these lines regarding medieval friendship, perhaps not intended to be of universal application, see Gerd Althoff, *Family, Friends and Followers: Political and Social Bonds in Medieval Europe*, trans. Christopher Carroll (Cambridge, 2004), 68. On the use of emotion to manipulate, see also Rosenwein, "Worrying about Emotions in History," 839–40 and the works cited there. If I am correct, bishops certainly expressed affection they did not feel in just this way. But this chapter also suggests that bishops were indeed sometimes moved by affection for their clerks. As Paul Hyams remarks about expressions of royal anger, expressions of affection had to be close enough to the real thing – and there had to be a real a thing – in order to be effective (Paul Hyams, "What Did Henry III of England Think in Bed and in French about Kingship and Anger," in *Anger's Past*, 102). Indeed, we today are not unacquainted with feigned friendship, love, or even anger, used instrumentally. Such practices do not require that people not also on other occasions really feel such emotions. Barbara Rosenwein's discussion of emotions in the early Middle Ages presumes that emotions expressed formulaically on parchment were felt, at least sometimes, and had some reference to actual emotional experience (*Emotional Communities in the Early Middle Ages* [Ithaca, 2006], 193). Regarding English royal diplomatic letters, not so far off from the bishops' letters considered here, Pierre Chaplais notes that the term *amicus* could refer simply to an ally "but it could also be used to express ties of friendship of a more personal and less definable kind" (*English Diplomatic Practice in the Middle Ages* [Hambledon, 2003], 106).

11

Conclusions

Culture and Context

> Other people are other. They do not think the way we do.... We constantly need to be shaken out of a false sense of familiarity with the past, to be administered doses of culture shock.[1]
>
> It is not only the case that attention to the past may change one's grasp of the present; ignorance of our own era may also subvert our understanding of the past.[2]

A simple account of rewards and punishments may seem to reflect too thin a psychology to explain what drove the clerks who made a thirteenth-century diocese work. "What about culture?" one might ask. In particular, "What about religion?"

In England's case, the last question has a particular edge. Decades ago, in his *Two Churches*, Robert Brentano compared the English and Italian churches in the thirteenth century.[3] Although his book concentrated on administration and institutions, it also in fact centered very much on religion. Brentano's central thesis was that the English expressed their spiritual concerns through diocesan institutions, through administration, whereas a hotter Italian spiritual life avoided such institutional forms, explaining the comparative weakness of Italian ecclesiastical institutions.[4] Moreover,

---

[1] Robert Darnton, *The Great Cat Massacre and Other Episodes in French Cultural History* (New York, 1985), 4.
[2] Anton Powell, *Athens and Sparta: Constructing Greek Political and Social History from 478 B.C.* (London, 1988), 406.
[3] Robert Brentano, *Two Churches: England and Italy in the Thirteenth Century* (Princeton, 1968; reprint with an additional essay, Berkeley and Los Angeles, 1988).
[4] Brentano acknowledges that he had a thesis (although he called it the "wrong word," preferring "idea") (ibid., 358). It must be confessed that Brentano also said that he meant

a decade later, in his examination of English ecclesiastical administration, Robert E. Rodes argued that the High- and Late-Medieval Church was hamstrung in attempts to reform itself not by an excessive attention to law and administration over spirituality, but by a canon law that was tender, too tender, regarding the individual's spiritual life. That law thus nudged prelates toward forgiving clergy for their lapses where the rod would have produced better results; secular law was more effective.[5] The law and institutions of the English Church should not be seen as devoid of pastoral concern, even spirituality. Diocesan administration could express a deeply religious life.

But even if Brentano was right – and I think his argument should be taken seriously – I do not think his position undermines the approach taken here, an attendance on rewards and punishments. A pastorally minded clerk in thirteenth-century England had options other than diocesan administration. He could always engage in more obviously pastoral work, especially if he were an incumbent of a benefice with cure of souls. If more spiritually minded, he could, once beneficed, devote himself to contemplation or study. Moreover, of course, even if a clerk chose to dedicate himself to the administrative life, either for its own sake or as an act of pastoral care, that would not explain why he might remain in the service of one bishop or move to that of another. Rewards and punishments, mundane or no, still appear to be part of the picture.

Then there is the way in which quotidian demands distract from the larger aims and ideals of an organization. The phenomenon is known well enough today. In the modern academy, the business of broadcasting good news and suppressing the bad, of cultivating donors and the political powers that be, of recruiting and keeping students, can take precedence over actually teaching students and producing scholarship. In the modern corporation, the work of tending to similarly ancillary concerns can take precedence over the business of business, profit. And in such substitutions, the human desire to take care of oneself, to build one's comforts, plays a role. The medieval church experienced similar distractions; indeed, they were some of the chief targets of reformers.[6] Ideals,

Two Churches to be elusive, even "unintelligible" (ibid., 354). The perplexed may find it useful to read Chapter 3 ("Bishops and Saints") before the rest of the book.

[5] Robert E. Rodes, *Ecclesiastical Administration in Medieval England: The Anglo-Saxons to the Reformation* (Notre Dame, 1977), 89–99.

[6] For moves against pluralism and nonresidence, see Marion Gibbs and Jane Lang, *Bishops and Reform 1215–1272, with Special Reference to the Lateran Council of 1215* (Oxford, 1932), 168–73. On clerical selfishness and materialism as the targets of reform, see J. R. H. Moorman, *Church Life in England in the Thirteenth Century* (Cambridge, 1955), 215–17.

it is true, can be powerful, but over the long term they need periodic renewal. So far as the thirteenth-century English Church was concerned, saintly bishops were the agents of that renewal. Then as now, however, the staying power of self-interest should never be underestimated. The willingness of even active diocesan administrators to engage in pluralism – and of even reform-minded bishops to tolerate it[7] – points to the inevitable gap between ideals and self-interest.

So a stress on reward and punishment may not be so thin a psychology after all. It fits modern and medieval experience. That point does not, however, mean that culture is insignificant in understanding the universe in which diocesan clerks operated. An important element of the cultural world that emerges from the preceding discussion is that it was one that stressed reward over punishment. Diocesan clerks enjoyed various revenue streams. The most critical was provided by the benefice, which brought not only income, but secure income, income that would be kept even if one left one diocese to administer another or left diocesan administration altogether. Certainly the law and the courts fostered this situation. The law restricted the occasions on which bishops could deprive their beneficed clerks of their benefices. Courts of appeal further limited bishops' ability to act arbitrarily in such matters. But bishops made little use even of the tools the law gave them. Attempts to deprive clerks of their benefices on the grounds of violation of their oaths of fidelity were rare, perhaps nonexistent. Bishops largely ignored measures like commendation that offered a way around the protection full collation gave their clerks. Bishops sometimes invoked oaths of loyalty when dealing with their own clerks, but did not think such oaths required the systematic attention that they gave such oaths when sworn by other people, even other clerks. Bishops were also reluctant to exploit other weapons against misbehavior that they more easily used against others: bonds, excommunication, and sequestration. When it came to a bishop's clerks, punishment was simply not the done thing.

The point about the culture in which diocesan administration operated can be refined. That culture assumed that gifts like benefices were for service and that recipients should be grateful for them.[8] That makes sense in a gift-giving culture, in which exchanges were expected to create

---

[7] Even Grosseteste: *The Letters of Adam Marsh*, ed. C. H. Lawrence (Oxford, 2006–10), I, xxvii. See also Chapter 4 at nn 208, 210–11.
[8] See Chapter 3.

longer-term relationships.⁹ Moreover, bishops and their clerks also operated in a tradition that stressed friendship – more specifically, affection and devotion – and permitted friendship between superior and subordinate. That culture of friendship provided the form in which the ties created by gifts were manifest. Friendship of that kind could certainly operate instrumentally, in a way that recalls modern discussions of ancient Roman *amicitia*.¹⁰ But that did not mean that such friendships had to be cool. How warm the temperature was varied according to individuals; the culture of friendship did not have an iron grip. Nevertheless, a culture of friendship can help account for, and in turn fostered, a cozy ambience among bishops and their clerks, one in which reward overshadowed punishment. Indeed, when bishops did attempt to deprive incumbents of benefices in their gift, the incumbents tended to be men who had received the collation from a previous bishop. In other words, the clerks bishops pursued were not their friends.

This culture of friendship also helped diocesan administration operate as well as it did. Here there is a modern analogy, imperfect, certainly, but useful. My own friend and teacher once pointed out to me that it was all very well to argue that security of tenure made benefices poor tools of accountability, but that modern university faculty get lifetime tenure and still keep working. She was right – even if some tenured faculty may seem retired. But *why* do tenured professors keep working hard rather than sleepwalk through their contractually required teaching and drop everything else? It is not, by and large, the money, and certainly not the danger

---

⁹ Lester Little has argued that the gift economy of the Early Middle Ages was displaced by a profit economy in the High Middle Ages – and that that change explains the Gregorian Reform's castigation as simoniacal transactions earlier seen as licit (*Religious Poverty and the Profit Economy in Medieval Europe* [Ithaca, 1987]). The discussion in Chapter 3 indicates that new and old attitudes toward exchanges coexisted for a long time when it came to benefices. Medievalists' discussions of gift-giving ultimately derive some inspiration from the anthropological investigations of Marcel Mauss. Mauss observed that in some societies, although gifts and counter-gifts "take place under a voluntary guise they are in essence strictly obligatory" (Mauss, *The Gift: Forms and Functions in Exchange in Archaic Societies*, trans. I. Cunnison [London, 1954], 3 and see 17–18), a point that may go to the ambiguity of benefices (legally not encumbered with administrative responsibilities, yet sometimes felt to be so) discussed here. Mauss, however, devotes most of his attention to the obligatory nature of gift-giving rather than to its voluntary nature.

¹⁰ For Roman *amicitia*, see, e.g., Peter Garnsey and Richard Saller, *The Roman Empire: Economy, Society and Culture* (Berkeley and Los Angeles, 1987), 152–6; Lily Ross Taylor, *Party Politics in the Age of Caesar* (Berkeley and Los Angeles, 1961), 7–8. It has been argued that Roman letters did not distinguish between friendship in private matters and instrumental friendship in public ones (Stanley Stowers, *Letter Writing in Greco-Roman Antiquity* [Philadelphia, 1986], 19, 29).

of losing it. The tenured toil often because they work in a certain culture with certain expectations (e.g., that status, if not money, comes with publication or a reputation for excellent teaching). So did thirteenth-century diocesan bureaucrats. Among those expectations was devotion to one's superiors and the affection of superiors for subordinates.[11] Those expectations contrast with those under which modern tenured faculty and academic administrators operate – perhaps to the relief of all parties. But affection is not always the strongest of ties. Clerks could not count on it. Hence, the independence offered by benefices was especially valuable.

Clerks were rewarded with benefices for their past service. Were they likewise expected to render continued service as a consequence of receiving a benefice? It is counterintuitive to think that they were not. A recent analysis of the secular patronage of Edward I, however, raises the question. Andrew Spencer notes that early fourteenth-century theorists held that gifts should be given for service already received, not to ensure future service, and argues that Edward's gift-giving fits the theorists' descriptions.[12] There is some reason to suspect that the same might be said of clerks and their benefices. The abbot and convent of Eynsham granted a pension to one John de Farleye, "dilecto clerico nostro," who would have his two marks annually, until he received a benefice from Eynsham "or from others."[13] Here the critical thing was not who gave the benefice (which would fit an expectation of future service), but simply that it was received. The attitude may have been less that benefices bought future service than that they simply provided "promising men in the standard of comfort to which they had been [or wished to] become accustomed."[14]

Indeed, talk of honoring clerks with benefices further softened the economic aspect of the transaction (see Chapter 3). Clerks not uncommonly received a benefice from the bishop they served, only to leave that bishop's service, yet keeping the benefice. The fact that they generally did so without apparent reproach lends credence to the idea that benefices

---

[11] I suspect an allied element was ideas about the episcopal *familia*, a topic I hope to explore in a future study.
[12] Andrew M. Spencer, "Royal Patronage and the Earls in the Reign of Edward I," *History* 93 (2008), 44, and his comments regarding the gifts given by Edward I and Edward III at 42.
[13] "& hoc quousque eidem per nos uel per alios in ecclesiastico prouideatur beneficio" (*The Cartulary of the Abbey of Eynsham*, ed. H. E. Salter, Oxford Historical Society 49, 51 [Oxford, 1907–8], I, no. 336). See also the bishop of Exeter's grant of a pension of 20s annually in lieu of a richer benefice, to be supplied by the bishop or someone else in the diocese; the relationship between grantor and grantee here is, however, unclear (Reg. Bronscombe, no. 727).
[14] F. M. Powicke, *The Thirteenth Century*, 2nd ed. (Oxford, 1962), 487.

were given not to ensure future activity but to reward past service. The fact that benefices were given for many reasons other than service – as a way to support relatives, for example – further blurred the connection between benefices and service. The tendency to use the language of friendship and devotion outside the relationship between superior and subordinate had the same effect. So did the drive to avoid simony. The move to decouple reward from service is also evident in bishops' attempts to limit clerical fees to cover expenses (for which, see Chapter 6), obviating profit for work.

There is also reason to doubt this decoupling – see the discussion of medieval double-think regarding simony in Chapter 3. Thirteenth-century epsicopal registers produce a couple of instances of bishops explicitly invoking their hopes of future service from recipients when collating benefices.[15] The rules against simony increase the value of these instances as evidence; bishops stating rationales so in conflict with the law and official morality probably meant them. It could also be urged that the canon law permitted deprivation should a clerk violate his oath of fidelity and obedience to his prelate.[16] But this argument is problematic. The failure of bishops to make much use of this stick offered by the law when dealing with their clerks suggests that Spencer's observations, with some reservation, apply to bishops and their clerks too. Bishops and their men lived in a contradictory world, one that denied a connection between benefices and service even as it quite naturally connected these very things. To the extent that connection was weak, bishops relied on the fragile reeds of friendship and devotion. They were strong enough for a diocese to work, but not perhaps for one to do so with maximum effectiveness.

The power of affection and devotion should not, however, be underestimated. My discussion of these ties in action focuses on what clerks did after their bishops died. But presumably the dangers clerks undertook on behalf of their living bishops (see Chapter 2) also indicate some measure of devotion. Perhaps the trust that bishop and clerk put in one another also reflects their perceptions of affection and devotion. And if affection and devotion greased the track to trust, they in that way also greased the operations of diocesan governance. Bishops needed not just clerks, but clerks they could trust, especially given bishops' lack of sanctions against beneficed clerks. But trust is, and was, a two-way street.[17] And

---

[15] Reg. Winchelsey, 292–3; Reg. Pontissara, 792. For these, see Chapter 3 at nn 28–30.
[16] See Chapter 4.
[17] See Chapter 7 at n 20.

not trusting one's clerks might lead to trouble – look at Bishop Giffard of Worcester. Unlike other bishops, he extracted bonds from his own clerks.[18] He appears to have engaged in some sharp practice with his own clerk, if he indeed attempted to extinguish his proctor's pension with a doubtful benefice.[19] Perhaps this – and a bad temper (more on this later) – account for his moves to deprive two of his other clerks.[20]

For bishops, benefices were poor tools of accountability in diocesan administration.[21] Yet is that description accurate? Strictly speaking, yes. But when it came to benefices, did bishops and their clerks themselves actually think in terms of "accountability"? The line of argument I have pursued suggests they usually did not. The practical, institutional situation – a canon law and courts of appeal that limited the ability of bishops to deprive their clerks – discouraged bishops from disciplining their clerks through deprivation. That situation fostered the expectation that benefices were irrevocable gifts. But such sentiment in turn led courts further to discourage bishops from disciplining their clerks through deprivation. Bishops' own backgrounds probably helped them accept these limitations. They, after all, had themselves generally made their administrative careers as beneficed clerks, just as they had earlier offered their devotion and received a bishop's friendship.

Indeed, the great exceptions – attempts by bishops to deprive their own clerks – are worth special attention. Those exceptions were produced by bishops who were particularly difficult men.

Consider Archbishop Geoffrey of York. He dogged his former clerk, Master Honorius, archdeacon of Richmond, although Honorius's deprivation, if deprivation it was, seems ultimately have come as a result of royal action.[22] Honorius ultimately left Geoffrey's service for that of a better master, Archbishop Hubert Walter. Moreover, while Geoffrey collated

---

[18] See Chapter 7 at nn 15–16.
[19] See Chapter 5 at n 94.
[20] M. Burger, "Peter of Leicester, Bishop Godfrey Giffard of Worcester, and the Problem of Benefices in Thirteenth-Century England," *Catholic Historical Review* 95 (2009), 453–73.
[21] Robert Berkhofer III (*Day of Reckoning: Power and Accountability in Medieval France* [Philadelphia, 2004]), who examines other techniques of governance in his account of twelfth-century monastic administration, couches his investigation of medieval governance in terms of accountability. Thomas N. Bisson, focusing on the secular world, sees accountability as emerging uneasily in the High Middle Ages (*The Crisis of the Twelfth Century: Power, Lordship, and the Origins of European Government* [Princeton, 2009], 17, 382, and for a comment on the papacy, 420). He appears to see this development as being in tension with personal ties.
[22] See Chapter 4 at n 174.

the archdeaconry of Cleveland to Ralph de Kyme, once his *officialis*, Ralph found he could not count on the archbishop's support, and may ultimately have also left Geoffrey's service.²³ These were, moreover, only two in a series of broken relationships that perhaps only a Plantagenet's temperament could leave in its wake.²⁴

Bishop Giffard of Worcester is less well known. He appears in this book primarily in the context of his long battle to deprive his steward, Peter de Leicester, but Giffard also moved similarly against another of his clerks, Nicholas de Chilbauton.²⁵ As with Archbishop Geoffrey, personality mattered. Giffard was bad tempered.²⁶ He was often sick and gouty.²⁷ To make matters worse, by the time of his conflicts with Peter and Nicholas, he had been bishop of Worcester for twenty years, a time by which many bishops were dead. Perhaps the power that corrupts judgment had done its work. His actions may reflect a bishop who had himself grown too secure.²⁸ Nicholas de Chilbauton died in 1284, preserving him from the miseries of this earth. But Peter de Leicester lived on. Giffard could not quite give up harassing him even after reaching a perhaps brokered settlement in 1293 over Bishop's Cleeve, of which he had attempted to deprive Peter.²⁹ When, in 1297, the abbot and convent of Tewkesbury presented Peter to Thornbury, Giffard refused to institute Peter, and put in his own

---

²³ EEA 27: York, lxiv–lxv.
²⁴ Ibid., xxxvii–lvii.
²⁵ See Chapter 4 at nn 91–3.
²⁶ On his irritability, see the *Oxford Dictionary of National Biography*, ed. H. C. G. Matthew and B. H. Harrison (Oxford, 2004), sub nom., and Susan Jane Davies, "Studies in the Administration of the Diocese of Worcester in the Thirteenth Century," University of Wales PhD Thesis (1971), 6. The Worcester annalist, admittedly not a friendly source, noted that after Giffard failed to get the prior and convent's cooperation regarding Westbury, he left *iratus* (*Annales Monastici*, IV, 504). If an allegation by a proctor opposed to Giffard is to be believed, Giffard's belligerence antedated his ascension to the episcopate. The proctor accused him of spurning an offer to talk over a dispute regarding a benefice to which Giffard and another clerk had rival claims. Giffard preferred to fight in court (Hereford Dean and Chapter Archives, no. 2921; I am grateful to this archive for supplying me an electronic photograph of this document). For an account more sympathetic to the bishop, see Reg. Giffard of Worcester, xxii.
²⁷ See the *Oxford Dictionary of National Biography*, sub nom., and Davies, "Studies in the Administration of the Diocese of Worcester," 68–99. The year before the rupture with Peter, Giffard was excusing himself from attending Convocation on grounds of gout (Reg. Giffard of Worcester, 295).
²⁸ Although there are signs of the attitude starting early. From his first year as bishop, Giffard's personal estate was being conflated with that of the bishopric (Christopher Dyer, *Lords and Peasants in a Changing Society: The Estates of the Bishopric of Worcester, 680–1540* [Cambridge, 1980], 58).
²⁹ On the episode, Burger, "Peter of Leicester," 453–73.

choice.³⁰ (As before, a superior jurisdiction came to Peter's rescue, and Peter got Thornbury on appeal to the court of Canterbury.)³¹ And there are signs that Giffard continued to pursue William Pikeril, the man who appears to have left Giffard's service with Peter.³²

Thirteenth-century secular life offers useful analogies for understanding the lives of clerks and their bishops. That makes sense. The two worlds were intimately tied.³³ I have already pointed to the likelihood that ideas about past and future service were the same in each sphere. The security of tenure that clerks enjoyed in their benefices also had an instructive secular analogue.

The High Middle Ages was a time of burgeoning administration effectively governing larger and larger territories. Royal authority extended more widely and deeply. At the same time, so did papal authority, fostering a more articulated hierarchy of pope, metropolitan, bishop, archdeacon, and rural dean. In both cases, a prime expression of this administrative growth was judicial. Indeed, it has been argued that medieval governance most naturally took judicial form.³⁴ These conditions are significant for understanding property and lordship. Historians have given great attention to estates in land under the Common Law. Lords may have given fiefs to their men, but that did not mean they could easily take them back. The Common Law protected the fee simple, guaranteeing tenants lifetime tenure and, indeed, heritability. In other words, royal courts served as a venue in which tenants could call on royal power and authority to prevent their lords from displacing them except in restricted circumstances. That much is clear, although there has been great controversy as to how early this development took place, and whether it also marked a conceptual, rather than a simply practical, revolution regarding the relations between lord and tenant.³⁵

---

³⁰ *Reg. Giffard of Worcester*, 489.
³¹ Ibid., 493; WRO, Rf.x716.093 BA 2648/1[i], fos. 422–423 (pp. 869–71). For good measure, he leveled a complaint that Giffard had been illicitly consuming Thornbury's fruits in the meantime (ibid., fos. 422–3 [pp. 869–71]).
³² See Chapter 7 at nn 123–33.
³³ For an analogy between the rise of monastic appropriation of churches and seigneurial direct management of estates – both responses to economic changes of the late twelfth century – see Ulrich Rasche, "The Early Phase of Appropriation of Parish Churches in Medieval England," *Journal of Medieval History* 26 (2000), 225–7.
³⁴ Berkhofer, *Day of Reckoning*, 168–9; J. E. A. Joliffe, *Angevin Kingship*, 2nd ed. (Oxford, 1963), 32–3; and perhaps Alan Harding, *Medieval Law and the Foundations of the State* (Oxford, 2002).
³⁵ Fortunately it is not necessary here to enter the lists. For an argument that the Angevin "great leap forward" transformed conceptions of relations between lord and tenant: S.

Ecclesiastical courts of appeal operated similarly. They provided a venue in which clerks dispossessed of benefices, including bishops' clerks, could appeal to an authority that thus intervened between bishop and clerk. The courts guaranteed, within the limits of the canon law – and even beyond those limits – clerks' security of tenure against their lords just as the royal courts guaranteed tenants' security of tenure in lay fees against their lords. From a bishop's point of view, the emergence of a system of ecclesiastical courts was not an entirely good thing.[36] In the thirteenth century, central authorities thus had a significant role in checking lords' control over their subordinates by protecting their property. The impact of that limitation on bishops and their clerks has been a theme of this book. But those clerks and bishops were not alone. Indeed, in both cases, that security of tenure and the independence that went with it may have bolstered the holder's status irrespective of income.[37]

It has also been argued that the rise of royal authority gave lords, or at least greater lords, new tools with which to reward their followers. Administrative kingship yielded kings a basket of favors from which to give.[38] Magnates could and did use their access to the king to become the channel through which such favors ran from the crown to their own men.[39] In this way, while the king with one hand undermined lords'

F. C. Milsom, *The Legal Framework of English Feudalism* (Cambridge, 1976); Robert C. Palmer, "The Origins of Property in England," *Law and History Review* 3 (1985), 1–50, and for a lucid exposition of their views, Paul Brand, "The Origins of English Land Law: Milsom and After," in Brand, *The Making of the Common Law* (Rio Grande, 1992), 203–25. For emphatic arguments that the Angevin great leap forward was in fact Anglo-Norman, or even echoed Anglo-Saxon conditions, see Patrick Wormald, *The Making of English Law, King Alfred to the Twelfth Century I: Legislation and Its Limits* (Oxford, 1999); John Hudson, *The Formation of the English Common Law* (London, 1996) and Hudson, *Land, Law, and Lordship in Anglo-Norman England* (Oxford, 1994).

[36] Charles Duggan, in fact, stressed the way in which the canon law came to constrain bishops: "Papal Judges Delegate and the Making of the 'New Law,'" in *Cultures of Power: Lordship, Status, and Process in Twelfth-Century Europe*, ed. Thomas N. Bisson (Philadelphia, 1995), 194–5.

[37] Regarding secular landholding, see S. D. Church, "Rewards of Royal Service in the Household of King John: A Dissenting Opinion," *English Historical Review* 110 (1995), 295.

[38] C. Warren Hollister, *Henry I*, ed. and completed by Amanda Clark Frost (New Haven, 2001), 335, 343–4; Judith Green, *The Government of England under Henry I* (Cambridge, 1986), 74, 173, although see comments at 190–1; W. L. Warren, *Henry II* (Berkeley and Los Angeles, 1973), 181–4.

[39] For the thirteenth century, in particular magnate influence in the courts, see P. R. Coss, "Bastard Feudalism Revised," *Past and Present* no. 125 (1989), 51–7. Regarding magnates' use of influence with the king to gain favors for followers in the twelfth century: David Crouch, "Bastard Feudalism Revised," *Past and Present* no. 131 (1991), 173, 177,

authority over their men, he strengthened that authority with the other. A similar tension marked ecclesiastical governance. The papacy may have been ready to stay the hands of bishops against their own clerks. But bishops were better placed than most of their clerks to lobby at Rome for favors, such as those described in Chapter 6. The centralization of authority thus strengthened as well as weakened bishops in their dealings with their clerks.

Here, however, it is important to note that both the weakening and strengthening worked in the same direction: they both put a premium on ties of sentiment, on affection and devotion. For what was weakened was bishops' coercive power over their clerks: the ability to punish. What was strengthened, however, was bishops' capacity to give their clerks favors: the ability to reward. These observations apply equally to royal power and magnates' relations with their subordinates. I have argued that the weight of reward over punishment pushed bishops to find more rewards to give their followers and bolstered the significance of a culture of affection and devotion in diocesan administration. Were these things true of secular administration?

and Stephanie Mooers Christelow, "The Royal Love in Anglo-Norman England: Fiscal or Courtly Concept?" *Haskins Society Journal* 8 (1999), 36. Bishops, of course, could use influence at the king's curia in the same way as at the pope's curia. Bishop Peter de Aquablanca, close to Henry III, gained an exemption for a member of the episcopal *familia* from service on royal assizes, juries, and recognitions (EEA 35: Hereford, liv).

APPENDIX I

Handlist of Pensions Granted by Thirteenth-Century Bishops

This list does not include allusions to grants of pensions, but only documents rehearsing the grants themselves or memoranda of such grants.

Pensions in Lieu of Benefices

Bath and Wells
1248–64: Bishop William (de Bitton I) appoints Master John de Cheam, a chaplain of the pope, as his clerk at a "salary" of £20 a year, or until other or better ecclesiastical appointment be provided for him (*Two Cartularies of the Priory of St. Peter at Bath*, ed. William Hunt, Somerset Record Society Publications 9 [London, 1893], 54–5).

September 26, 1261: Bishop (William de Bitton I), grants pension to Master G. [Gilbert de St. Leofardo] of 10 marks a year until a prebendal benefice be provided for him. (*Calendar of the Manuscripts of the Dean and Chapter of Wells*, I, 141).

September 27, 1262: Bishop W(illiam de Bitton I) grants to W. de Smalebrok, clerk, a pension until he shall be provided with a prebend or other benefice (*Two Cartularies of the Priory of St. Peter at Bath*, 52).

January 12, 1263: Bishop W(illiam de Bitton I) grants to Master William le Rus de Bristol, clerk, an annuity until he shall provide him a benefice (ibid., 49).

March, 1268: Bishop William (de Bitton II) grants Magister Thomas de Bitton, canon of Wells, upon resigning the office of precentor, £20 a year *de camera*, until he be provided with a benefice of equal value (*Calendar of the Manuscripts of the Dean and Chapter of Wells*, I, 104).

Canterbury

September 24, 1279: At the king's instance, Archbishop Pecham grants Stephen de Suchie, clerk, 100s a year until Pecham or someone else provides a benefice; this entry is canceled (Reg. Pecham, I, 14).

No date (1295?): At the king's instance, Archbishop Winchelsey grants 5 marks a year *de camera* to Ralph de Watervile, until the archbishop provides him a benefice (Reg. Winchelsey, 43).

Carlisle

September 28, 1276: Bishop Robert de Chaury grants a pension of 20s *de camera* to William de Insula until the bishop or his successors, or the prior and convent of Carlisle, provide a benefice (EEA 30: Carlisle, no. 151; Reg. Halton, I, 56).

April 21, 1282: Bishop Ralph de Ireton of Carlisle grants a pension of 40s a year and robes and caps to Magister Adam de Copeland, his proctor at York, until the bishop or his successors provide a competent benefice; Adam is to enjoy the fruit of the benefice "without dispute and with effect" (EEA 30: Carlisle, no. 173; Reg. Halton, I, 31 and see 32).

Coventry and Lichfield

1296–1321 (document undated, and so dated by episcopate): Bishop Langton grants a pension of 10 marks *de camera* to "dilecto filio N. de B." until Langton provides a benefice that N. is willing to accept (*Liber Epistolaris of Richard de Bury*, ed. Noel Denholm-Young [Oxford, 1950], no. 417, sub no. 14). Given the nature of the source in which this grant appears, "N. de B." can be taken to be no one in particular. Langton's register offers no clear candidates. An uncompelling case could be made for Nicholas de Blaston, clerk, who held Tarvin on the presentation of Walter de Clipston, the bishop's nephew; Nicholas had also received a favor from the bishop in being allowed to hold the sequestration of Tarvin before being instituted to it (Reg. Langton, nos. 523, 528, 547, 821, and see xxv).

October 28, 1299: Bishop Langton grants a pension of 5 marks *de camera* to Richard de Wolvy, clerk, until he is provided a benefice worth 60 marks by the bishop or another person (ibid., no. 76).

Exeter

March 10, 1258: Bishop Bronscombe grants Peter de Vienne £10 a year *de camera* until the bishop makes better provision; this is done at the instance of Boniface, archbishop of Canterbury, and is a renewal of the pension (Reg. Bronscombe, no. 444).

Appendix 1

June 22, 1258: Bishop Bronscombe grants 10 marks a year *de camera* to Thomas de Windsor until provision is made by the bishop or his successors of a competent benefice to Thomas or any suitable clerk he chooses (Reg. Bronscombe, no. 56).

November 20, 1264: Memorandum that Bishop Bronscombe granted Geoffrey de Bisimano a pension of 20 marks a year *de camera* until he provides Geoffrey a benefice without cure of souls (Reg. Bronscombe, no. 574).

December 6, 1265: Bishop Bronscombe grants Michael de Fiennes 40 marks a year *de camera* for life, or until he becomes a bishop or a monk, on his resignation of Paignton (ibid., no. 606).

February 4, 1269: Bishop Bronscombe grants William de Hancot 20s a year until he shall be provided a richer benefice by the bishop or by someone else in the diocese (ibid., no. 727).

October 22, 1275: Bishop Bronscombe grants John de Lardario 40s a year until he receives a more adequate benefice from the bishop or from another on the bishop's behalf (ibid., no. 1115, and see no. 1169).

1280–91: Bishop Quivil grants John de Bamfeld 1 mark a year until he provides him a benefice (Reg. Quivil, 314).

July 27, 1281: Bishop Quivil grants Anselm de Esquerra 5 marks a year *de camera* until the bishop provides him a competent benefice (ibid., 326).

July 28, 1281: Bishop Quivil grants Walter de Bauntone, his clerk, 40s a year until he gives a competent benefice (ibid., 315).

August 21, 1281: Bishop Quivil grants Richard de Gryndeham 40s a year *de camera* until he provides an acceptable benefice (ibid., 331).

October 7, 1281: Bishop Quivil grants Nicholas Castelle, king's clerk, 20s a year *de camera* until he provides a competent benefice (ibid., 319).

October 15, 1281: Bishop Quivil grants John de la Wade 10 marks a year and two robes according to the rest of the clerks of his condition, until the archbishop provides a prebendal benefice or another benefice that John is willing to accept; John is to be rewarded for he does the bishop's business and lawsuits according to his oath (ibid., 381).

February 7, 1282: Bishop Quivil grants Durand, son of Nicholas Elys, 40s a year *de camera* until the bishop or his successors provide a competent benefice; Durand may have the sheriff distrain for lack of payment (ibid., 325).

February 18, 1282: Bishop Quivil grants Salvagius de Florence 100s a year *de camera* until he provides a benefice "which he will be willing to accept" (ibid., 372).

February 20, 1282: Bishop Quivil grants Hugh de Lumynster 40s a year *de camera* until he provides a benefice (ibid., 362).

April 9, 1282: Bishop Quivil grants James de Hispania 100s a year *de camera* until he be provided a benefice, considering his knowledge of letters, noble birth, mores, and probity (ibid., 335).

November 24, 1282: Bishop Quivil grants Philip de St. Austolo 40s a year until he provides a benefice "which he will be willing to accept" (ibid., 372–3).

February 4, 1283: Bishop Quivil grants Richard de Fremyngham 4 marks a year until he provides a prebendal benefice (ibid., 328).

May 3, 1283: Bishop Quivil grants Adam de "Pileley" (recte, Adam de Fileby), archdeacon of Salop, 5 marks a year *de camera* until he provides a prebendal benefice (ibid., 366).

April 30, 1286: Bishop Quivil and the dean and chapter of Exeter grant Peter *dictus* Haverwell 100s a year until he is provided a benefice of the same value or a prebendal benefice worth 6 marks (ibid., 389).

Lincoln

April 3, 1294: Bishop Sutton grants, on the king's recommendation, to Theobald de Bar, the Count of Bar-le-Duc's brother, £20 a year until the provision of a prebend worth 60 marks (Rolls and Reg. Sutton, IV, 183).

Salisbury

October 28, 1302: At the king's instance, Bishop Ghent grants a pension of 10 marks a year *de camera* to Roger de Bello Campo until he provides Roger a competent benefice (Reg. Gandavo, 152).

January 4, 1309: At the queen's instance, Bishop Ghent grants a pension of 100s a year "de nostra speciali gracia" to Bochard de Vernon, the queen's chaplain, until the bishop provides Bochard a competent benefice (ibid., 173).

Winchester

November 18, 1293: Bishop Pontoise grants a pension of 100s a year to Philip le Say, clerk, kinsman of Roger le Estrange, justiciar of the king, until the bishop provides him a benefice (Reg. Pontissara, 353–4).

January 24, 1294: Memorandum of "consimilem litteram" issued to Hugh de Nottingham, king's clerk, for a pension of 5 marks a year (ibid., 354).

January 24, 1294: Memorandum of "consimilem litteram" issued to John Bacoun, clerk of the king's justiciary, for 90s a year (ibid., 354).

June 5, 1295: Bishop Pontoise grants a pension of 10 marks a year *de camera* to Theobald, brother of the count of Bar-le-Duc, until the bishop provides Theobald a competent benefice (ibid., 195).

April 13, 1303: Bishop Pontoise grants Aymo, archdeacon York, son of the count of Savoy, a pension of 10 marks a year *de camera* until the bishop provides Aymo a competent benefice (ibid., 150).

Worcester

July 20, 1286: Bishop Giffard grants Mag. John de Butterley, 40s a year *de camera* to be paid to him or his proctor until the Bishop provides John an ecclesiastical benefice "valente communibus annis" 30 marks (Reg. Giffard, 291; WRO, Rf.x716.093 BA 2648/1(i), f. 255v="p. 502").

November 18, 1293: Bishop Giffard grants John de Sola Villa 100s a year *de camera* until the bishop provides John a competent benefice (Reg. Giffard 438; WRO, Rf.x716.093 BA 2648/1(i), [f. 375] [p. 741]).

York

(June 17, 1227: Archbishop Gray grants 10 marks a year *de camera* to Godfrey de Ludham, "until we should provide him better," but with no specific mention of a benefice (Rot. Gray, 9). Although two years later Gray collated a benefice to Godfrey (ibid., 26), I have not counted this grant in the total of pensions granted in lieu of a benefice.

September 5, 1234: Archbishop Gray grants Master Stephen the goldsmith a pension of 10 marks a year *de camera* until the Archbishop has provided Stephen to a certain benefice (ibid., 63).

December 5, 1247: Archbishop Gray grants 5 marks a year *de camera* to Guido, rector of West Kerle, *nepos* of Master Boethius the papal chancellor, until the archbishop provides a better benefice (ibid., 102).

November 13, 1249: Archbishop Gray grants 40s a year *de camera* to John Bonet, until the archbishop has provided Bonet a better benefice (ibid., 258).

June 19, 1250: Archbishop Gray grants 10 marks a year *de camera* to Richard son of Richard de Lat until he is provided a benefice by the archbishop or by the lord W. de Gray, son of the archbishop's late brother, the lord Robert de Gray (ibid., 263).

November 15, 1250: Archbishop Gray grants Roger son of Adam, *nepos* of Brother William, papal *hostiarius*, 40s a year until the archbishop provides Roger a better benefice (ibid., 262).

February 9, 1252: Archbishop Gray grants 20s a year *de camera* to John Bonet, until the archbishop has provided Bonet a better benefice (ibid., 263).

September 9, 1267: Archbishop Giffard grants 40s a year to William, rector of Gatintone, clerk of Queen Eleanor, until the archbishop provides William a benefice (Reg. Giffard of York, 101).

November 2, 1268: Archbishop Giffard grants a pension of 100 marks a year, payable by the archbishop and the dean and chapter of York, to Ancher, cardinal-priest of St. Praxedis (in lieu of an annual pension of 80 marks from the archbishop alleged by Ancher to have been granted to Ancher by authority of papal letters until he be provided to a benefice in the church of York), by papal authority; this is a settlement of suit between Ancher, on the one hand, and the archbishop and William, chancellor of York, on the other, regarding the prebend of Neubald; there will be a fine of 10 marks for each year of arrears of the pension; Ancher renounces his claims on Neubald (ibid., 6–7).

October 2, 1281: Archbishop Wickwane grants Ralph de Hengham £10 a year *de camera* until Ralph is provided a suitable benefice (Reg. Wickwane, 329).

January 27, 1282: Archbishop Wickwane grants Master Robert de Ros £10 a year *de camera* until Robert is provided a suitable benefice or prebend (ibid., 329).

March 15, 1282: Archbishop Wickwane grants William de Bolington £10 a year *de camera* until William is provided a suitable benefice or prebend (ibid., 329).

March 8, 1283: Archbishop Wickwane grants Gerard de Grandisson, *nepos* of the lord O. de Grandisson, king's counselor, 50 marks a year until the archbishop provides Gerard a prebend in the church of York (ibid., 329).

May 10, 1287: Archbishop Romeyn grants William de Saham, royal justice, a pension, 100s a year until he can honor him with a benefice (Reg. Romeyn, II, 160–1).

Simple Pensions

Bath and Wells

February 17, 1256: Bishop W[illiam de Bitton I] grants £20 annually, from himself and his successors, to John de Cheam, papal chaplain (*Two Cartularies of the Priory of St. Peter at Bath*, 34–5).

Canterbury

January 1, 1285: Archbishop Pecham grants £20 a year *de camera* to Cardinal Matthew Orsini (Pecham, *Epistolae*, III, 872–3).

No date (so January 1, 1285?): memorandum of a pension conceded in the same form regarding 20 marks a year to James de Sabello (ibid., 873).

No date (so January 1, 1285?): memorandum of a pension conceded in the same form regarding 20 marks a year to Jordan, cardinal deacon of St. Eustace's (ibid.).

January 1, 1285: memorandum of a pension conceded in the same form regarding 20 marks a year to Gervase, cardinal-priest of St. Martin's (ibid.).

No date (so January 1, 1285?): memorandum of a pension of £10 a year granted by Archbishop Pecham to Peter de Grossis, vice-chancellor of the Roman Church (ibid.).

No date (so January 1, 1285?): memorandum of a pension of 40s a year granted by Archbishop Pecham to Master Raymond Hispanus, advocate in the curia (ibid.).

October 25, 1300: Archbishop Winchelsey grants £20 a year to Matthew, cardinal deacon of St. Mary's in Porticu (Reg. Winchelsey, 582–3).

October 25, 1300: memorandum of a "consimilem litteram" for 20 marks a year granted to John Monachus, cardinal deacon of St. Marcellinus's (ibid., 583).

October 25, 1300: memorandum of a "consimilem litteram" for 20 marks a year granted to Richard, cardinal deacon of St. Eustace's (ibid.).

March 9, 1302: Archbishop Winchelsey grants 100s a year to the lord William de Bereford, knight (ibid., 431).

March 9, 1302: memorandum of a "consimilis littera" conceded to the lord William Howard, knight, regarding such a pension (ibid.).

Carlisle

February 15, 1301: Bishop Halton grants £40 a year to John de Drokensford for life from himself and his successors (Reg. Halton, I, 138).

Coventry and Lichfield

November 11, 1298: Bishop Langton grants 6 marks per year *de camera* to Master William de Fotheringhay, advocate in the Court of Arches, "for as long as he attends the bishop's business in the same court" (Reg. Langton, no. 62).

November 11, 1298: memorandum of similar letters to Master John de Bruton for 5 marks a year (ibid.).

November 11, 1298: memorandum of similar letters to Master Henry de Derb' for 40s a year (ibid.).

November 5, 1299: Bishop Langton grants Philip Martel, advocate in Court of Canterbury, to deal with all the bishop's causes there in that court in London or elsewhere, 5 marks a year (an indenture) (ibid., no. 363).

No date (ca. 1309?): Bishop Langton grants Geoffrey de Eydon, his advocate at the Court of Arches, 40s a year "as long as he will be his advocate [there] and he is willing to present his defense counsel and aid for the bishop's business to be expedited in the same court" (ibid., no. 791).

No date (ca. 1309?): memorandum of similar letters to John de Bloye for 40s (ibid.).

No date (ca. 1309?): memorandum of similar letters to Andrew de Brugg for 40s (ibid.).

Durham

September 24, 1277: Bishop Robert of Holy Island grants Walter de Merton, former royal chancellor, £40 a year from the exchequer for life (EEA 29: Durham, no. 252).

Exeter

March 6, 1258: memorandum of a grant by Bishop Bronscombe of 15 marks a year to Peter de? (name missing), clerk. No benefice is mentioned, but this entry is largely illegible (Reg. Bronscombe, no. 9).

May 21, 1262: memorandum of a grant by Bishop Bronscombe of 20s a year to Walter de Wylburham (Reg. Bronscombe, no. 440).

June 2, 1268: Bishop Langton grants Peter de Vienne, dean of Sion, 20 marks a year, a pension formerly paid by the vicar of St. Merryn (ibid., no. 680, and see nos. 679, 681–2).

November 15, 1281: Bishop Quivil grants 100s a year to Master Emanuel, archdeacon of Cremona, as long as he will act as the bishop's advocate in the Court of Canterbury (Reg. Quivil, 322).

December 3, 1282: Bishop Quivil grants 4 marks a year for life *de camera* to R.[probably Robert] de Bremertone, Rector of Horsley (ibid., 317).

October 21, 1283: Bishop Quivil grants Master John de Shelvestone 6 marks a year as long as he will act as the bishop's advocate in the Court of Canterbury (ibid., 374).

Hereford

1268–1272: Bishop John le Breton and his successors grant Bodro de Scaccario Romano 40 marks a year *de camera* (Reg. Cantilupe, 21).

November 4, 1275: Bishop Cantilupe grants Hamo de Barre 20s a year *de camera*, for his homage and service (ibid., 22).

November 4, 1275: memorandum that the bishop "eodem modo" is bound to Alan de Walkynham for 40s (ibid., 22).

November 4, 1275: memorandum that the bishop "eodem modo" is bound to William de Stow for 20s (ibid.).

November 4, 1275: memorandum that the bishop "eodem modo" is bound to Adam de Ardern for 20s (ibid.).

November 4, 1275: memorandum that the bishop "eodem modo" is bound to John de Houton for 20s (ibid.).

October 17, 1287: Bishop Swinfield grants John de Canterbury, his clerk, 2 marks a year for as long as John serves as the bishop's proctor in the court of Canterbury (Reg. Swinfield, 156–7).

October 19, 1287: Bishop Swinfield grants 6 marks a year to Warin de Boys, the bishop's advocate in London (ibid., 157).

APPENDIX 2

Lay Servants Named as Legatees in Episcopal Wills

For the lay legatees of Robert Winchelsey, Archbishop of Canterbury, see Chapter 10 at n 118.

The will of Bishop Longespee of Salisbury records legacies to Walter the carpenter (10 marks), John the farrier (10 marks), and his (unnamed) sub-chamberlain (100s). Interspersed among these men are a John Drew (10 marks) and a John Walwain (100s), who probably had occupations of a similar status. If Lambert, the bishop's chamberlain and *alumpnus*, was a layman rather than a clerk, he is an exception to the pattern of cash bequests going to lay servants. He did very well indeed, receiving £100 sterling but also 16 oxen, 6 cows, 200 eggs, 20 pigs, an assortment of the bishop's plate, all the wooden vessels and implements of the bishop's chamber and kitchen, the coffers of his chamber and wardrobe, the bishop's better armor suitable to him, his horse to ride, and more (EEA 37: Salisbury, no. 450).

Bishop Wyche of Chichester left roughly as many legacies to lay servants as to clerks or likely clerks: Willard, formerly his cook (10 marks); Walter de Wyke (10 marks); Adam the butler (10 marks); Robert the baker (10 marks); Ralph the marshal (100s); Alexander, keeper of the palfreys (6 marks); Laurence the farrier (100s); Walter Gray (100s); William his messenger (*nuntius*) (100s) (EEA 22: Chichester, no. 188).

Bishop Gravesend of London names seven lay servants as legatees in his will: Richard his marshal (40s); Richard Filliol his valet (40s); Walter Lithfot of the buttery (1 mark); Jolanus his cook (40s); Roger of the pantry (10s); Roger Strik (one-half mark); William the barber (one-half mark) (*Account of the Executors of Richard Bishop of London 1303 and of the Executors of Thomas Bishop of Exeter 1310*, ed. W. H. Hale and H. T. Ellacombe, Camden Society Publications (second series) 10 [London, 1874], 114).

Hugh of Wells of the diocese of Lincoln left legacies to many lay servants, but to so few of his identifiable clerks that comparing sums does not say much. The lay servants named in his first will are Herbert of the chamber (1 mark); Roger the marshal (30 marks); Richard the marshal (40 marks); Walens the cook (30 marks); Richard of the chamber (10 marks); Matthew of the kitchen (3 marks); William the hodder (2 marks) (*Acta of Hugh of Wells*, no. 2). His second will included the following legacies to lay servants: John of the chamber (10 marks); Peter de Cotintone (10 marks); Hugh the cook (10 marks); Roger the marshal (10 marks); William, servant (*serviens*) of Buckden (100s); William Lupus (10 marks); William, servant (*serviens*) of Leicester (100s); William de Tunring (2 marks); William de Wodeford (2 marks); John, servant (*serviens*) of Esfordeby (3 marks); Reginald de Treilly (5 marks); Elias Kotele (5 marks); Richard de Ispania (2½ marks); Roger son of William (10 marks); Thomas the marshal (5 marks); William Cauchais de Tinghurst (5 marks); Gilbert of the chamber (2 marks); Walter the doorkeeper (1 mark); Bufetus the messenger (*nuntius*) (4 marks); Hankin of the bakery (1 mark); John the runner (*de curru*) (20s); Paganus (1 mark); Geoffrey Rom' (=Romipetus?) (1 mark); Thomas the carter (1 mark); Reginald the carter (1 mark) (ibid., no. 408).

Bishop Suffield of Norwich left the following to his lay servants: Hugh of the chamber (his bed); John the cook (5 marks); Gilbert the saucer (*salsarius*) (a livery of food and clothing appropriate for the hospital of St. Giles, to which the bishop left other legacies); Adam the groom (100s); Coleman (5 marks); Hugh the butler (5 marks); Wakke (4 marks); John the doorkeeper (*hostiarius*) (5 marks); Thoward (100s); Semman of the kitchen (5 marks); Gille (2 marks); Geoffrey de Lodn', formerly doorkeeper of the kitchen (2 marks); Ralph the doorkeeper of the chamber (3 marks); Geoffrey the baker (3 marks); Nicholas the brewer (20s); Capun (20s); little Simon (30s); John the carter (3 marks and one of the robes of secondary rank); Richard the carter (3 marks); Dusing (30s); Hobb the carter (20s); Roger the carter who was at Hoxne (3 marks); Simon the smith (3 marks); Geoffrey the watchman (1 mark); Matilda the laundress (the lone female servant in this material) (20s); Stephen the messenger (*nuntius*) (2 marks); Wyndelaboys (10s); William his own messenger (*nuntius meus proprius*) (100s); Buleys (10s); Peter the baker (20s) (and 20s for his unnamed companions); William the brewer (20s) (and 1 mark for his unnamed boys); Nicholas and William, his two pages

(10s); Baningham, caretaker of the bishop's bed ("qui custodit sumarium lecti mei") (1 mark); Martin of the kitchen (1 mark); Geoffrey the doorkeeper of the kitchen (1 mark); Godwin of the kitchen (10s); William the skinner (5s); Henry the cobbler (5s); Richard the cobbler (5s); Geoffrey of the chamber (20s); Trot (5s); Nicholas Syre (5s); Gwyliot (5s); Ward de Hasingham (3s); Ingeram (3s); naked Scot ("Scot nudo") (3s); Crust (3s) (and to the unnamed boy of the vigil, 3s) (EEA 32: Norwich, no. 138). These legacies, almost all sums of money (large and small), are not so comparable with the many objects, usually goblets, Suffield left his clerks or men likely to have been his clerks.

Bishop Giffard of Worcester left more legacies to lay servants by name than to his clerks or likely clerks: to Simon Sauage his butler, whom Giffard notes had served him a long time (20 marks); Geoffrey de Hembury, his bailiff for his long service (£20); Nicholas his chamberlain (the bishop's bed along with one of the bishop's whole robes for his wife's use); Robert Tailor, his chamberlain (40s); Robert the brewer (5 marks); Andrew the hall doorkeeper (40s); Thomas the watchman (40s) (Reg. Gainsborough, 53).

In his final will, Bishop Aquablanca of Hereford also left more legacies to his lay servants than to his clerks and likely clerks combined: William of the bushels (20 marks); Bernard (20 marks); Geoffrey the cook (20 marks); Thomas *seccus* (20 marks) (and the horse he customarily rides to each of these men if he has none of his own); Gingoneccus the baker (5 marks); Guilloloccus the baker (5 marks); Willekin (5 marks); Gunieccus of the kitchen (5 marks); Merinecus (5 marks); Roger formerly keeper of the bishop's park (40s); Alan his messenger (*cursor*) (10s); James de Maurienne, formerly his messenger (*cursor*) (10s) (EEA 35: Hereford, nos. 124–5). The bishop's previous will mentions no individual legatees (EEA 35: Hereford, no. 123). Julia Barrow suggests that such legatees may have been ignored by its eighteenth-century copyist (ibid., n).

The legacies received from Bishop Cantilupe may not reflect solely his will, but decisions made by his executors – his will does not survive, only material recording its execution. Cantilupe's lay servants more often received objects than did legatees of other bishops, but were still more likely to receive only cash than his clerks: Nicholas de Hodenet (chamberlain: see Reg. Cantilupe, lxxi) (25 marks and a gray foal); John Parisuis (cook) (15 marks); John the marshal (20 marks and a white horse); Piccardus (3 marks); John de Baseyvill (25 marks and Butterleye the horse); Rubinettus the butler (26 marks and a furred robe for his wife); Richard the tailor (5 marks and the horse that was Rubinettus's); Robert the farrier (7½ marks); Peter the messenger (7½ marks); Robert Deynte (chamberlain: see ibid.) (20 marks and the bishop's bed with its accoutrements); William the doorkeeper (5 marks); Robert Harlond (10 marks); Thomas the baker (3 marks); Gille of the kitchen (3 marks); Walter the page (1 mark) (Hereford Dean and Chapter Archives, no. 1414).

Sources Cited

Primary Sources

Manuscript

Cambridge:
  Cambridge University Library
    MS Ee V 31
    Peterborough Dean and Chapter MS 23
Canterbury:
  Christ Church, Dean and Chapter Archives
    Dc MA 1
    Sede Vacante Register 2
Chichester:
  West Sussex Record Office
    Ep. I/1/1
Hereford:
  Hereford Dean and Chapter Archives
    No. 1414
    No. 1813
    No. 1856
    No. 2921
  Herefordshire Record Office
    AL 19/2
Lincoln:
  Lincoln Archives Office (LAO)
    A/1/6
    A/1/8
    Bi/5/5/13/2
    Dii/38/2/36
    Dii/52/2/1

Dii/56/1/7
Dii/56/1/67
Dii/62/1/4
Dii/62/1/7c
Dii/62/1/8
Dii/64/2/7
Dii/69/1/36
Dii/69/1/53
Dii/69/2/36
Dii/82/1/20
Dii/84/1/6
Episcopal Register I
Episcopal Register II
Episcopal Register III
Rolls of Bishop Oliver Sutton, Roll III
Rolls of Bishop Richard Gravesend, Roll I
VC 2/1

London:
  British Library (BL)
    Add. MS 35296
    Cotton Caligula A xii
    Cotton Vespasian E xx
    Cotton Claudius xii
    Harley 4714
  Lambeth Palace
    MS 241
  The National Archives (TNA)
    C 85/71
    C 85/100
    C 85/101
    CP 40/69
    CP 40/73
    SC1/6/56
    SC1/6/88
    SC1/15/120
    SC1/29/5
    SC1/33/119

Oxford:
  Bodleian Library
    MS Top Linc. d 1

Spalding:
  Spalding Gentlemen's Society
    Spalding Gentlemen's Society MS: The Crowland Cartulary

Worcester:
  Worcestershire Record Office (WRO)
    Rf.x716.093 BA 2648/1(i)

Online:

The Anglo-American Legal Tradition. www.aalt.law.uh.edu/aalt.html. Ed. Robert C. Palmer and Elspeth K. Palmer.

Taxatio of Pope Nicholas IV. Online edition. www.hrionline.ac.uk/db/taxatio.

Print

"A 1301 Sequestrator-General's Account Roll for the Diocese of Coventry and Lichfield." Ed. Jill B. Hughes. In *Chronology, Conquest and Conflict in Medieval England*, Camden Society Miscellany 34. Camden Society Fifth Series 10. London. 1997. 105–39.

Account of the Executors of Richard Bishop of London 1303 and of the Executors of Thomas Bishop of Exeter 1310. Ed. W. H. Hale and H. T. Ellacombe. Camden Society Second Series 10. London. 1874.

The Acta of Hugh of Wells, Bishop of Lincoln 1209–1235. Ed. David M. Smith. Lincoln Record Society 88. Woodbridge. 2000.

Acta Sanctorum Quotquot Toto Urbe Coluntur vel a Catholicis Scriptoribus Celebrantur. Ed. J. Stiltingo et al. Paris. 1866. 66 vols.

Acta Stephani Langton Cantuariensis Archiepiscopi A.D. 1207–1128. Ed. Kathleen Major. Canterbury and York Society 50. Oxford. 1950.

Adam of Eynsham. *Magna Vita Sancti Hugonis*. Ed. D. L. Douie and D. H. Farmer. 2nd ed. Oxford. 1985. 2 vols.

"Annales Londinienses." In *Chronicles of the Reigns of Edward I and Edward II*. Ed. William Stubbs. Rolls Series. London. 1882–3.

Annales Monastici. Ed. Henry Richards Luard. Rolls Series. London. 1864–9. 4 vols.

Babee's Book. Ed. Frederick J. Furnival. Early English Text Society Publications Old Series 32. London. 1868.

Briesfsteller und Formelbücher des eilften bis vierzehnten Jahrhunderts. Ed. Ludwig Rockinger. Munich. 1863–4. 2 vols.

Calendar of Ancient Correspondence Concerning Wales. Ed. J. G. Edwards. Cardiff. 1935.

Calendar of the Close Rolls (1272–1485). Ed. H. C. Maxwell Lyte et al. London. 1892–1954. 45 vols.

A Calendar of the Earlier Hereford Cathedral Muniments. Ed. B. G. Charles and H. D. Emanuel. National Library of Wales. Reproduced Typescript. 1955. Consulted at Lambeth Palace Library. London. 3 vols.

Calendar of Entries in the Papal Registers Relating to Great Britain and Ireland. Ed. W. H. Bliss et al. London. 1893–.

Calendar of Inquisitions Post Mortem. London. 1904–.

Calendar of the Manuscripts of the Dean and Chapter of Wells. Ed. W. H. B. Bird and W. P. Baildon. Royal Commission on Historical Manuscripts. London. 1907–1914. 2 vols.

Calendar of the Patent Rolls Preserved in the Public Record Office (1232–1509). London. 1891–1916. 52 vols.

Canterbury Professions. Ed. Michael Richter. Canterbury and York Society 67. Torquay. 1973.

The Cartulary of the Abbey of Eynsham. Ed. H. E. Salter. Oxford Historical Society 49, 51. Oxford. 1907–8. 2 vols.

The Cartulary of Daventry Priory. Ed. M. J. Franklin. Northamptonshire Record Society 35. Northampton. 1988 for 1987.

The Cartulary of St. Mary's Collegiate Church, Warwick. Ed. Charles Fonge. Woodbridge. 2004.

The Cartulary of the Treasurer of York Minster and Related Documents. Ed. Janet E. Burton. York. 1978.

Charters and Records of Hereford Cathedral. Ed. William W. Capes. Cantilupe Society for 1908. Hereford. 1908.

The Chartulary of the High Church of Chichester. Ed. W. D. Peckham. Sussex Record Society 46. Lewes. 1946 for 1942 and 1943.

Chronicle of Walter of Guisborough. Ed. Harry Rothwell. Camden Society Third Series 89. London. 1957 for 1955–6 and 1956–7.

Chronicon Abbatiae Rameseiensis. Ed. W. Dunn Macray. Rolls Series. London. 1886.

Chronicon Petroburgense. Ed. Thomas Stapleton and John Bruce. Camden Society Old Series 47. London. 1849.

Close Rolls of the Reign of Henry III (1227–72). London. 1902–38. 14 vols.

Councils and Synods with Other Documents Relating to the English Church, II, A.D. 1205–1313. Ed. F. M. Powicke and C. R. Cheney. Oxford. 1964. 2 vols.

Corpus juris canonici emendatum et notis illustratum, Gregorii XIII. Pont. Max. iussu editum (Rome, 1582). Electronic edition: UCLA Digital Library Program: Corpus Juris Canonici, 1582. http://digital.library.ucla.edu/canon-law. 3 vols.

Curia Regis Rolls. Ed. C. T. Flower et al. London. 1922–.

Decrees of the Ecumenical Councils I: Nicaea to Lateran V. Ed. Norman P. Tanner. Washington, DC. 1990.

"De Diversis Ordinibus Hominum." In *The Latin Poems Attributed to Walter Mapes*. Ed. T. Wright. Camden Society First Series 16. London. 1841. 229–55.

Diplomatic Documents Preserved in the Public Record Office I: 1101–1272. Ed. Pierre Chaplais. London. 1964.

Durham Annals and Documents of the Thirteenth Century. Ed. Frank Barlow. Surtees Society 155. Durham. 1945.

The Earliest English Law Reports. Ed. Paul Brand, Selden Society 111, 112, 122, 123. London. 1996–2007. 4 vols.

The Early Rolls of Merton College Oxford. Ed. J. R. L. Highfield. Oxford. 1964.

English Episcopal Acta I: Lincoln 1067–1185. Ed. David M. Smith. Oxford. 1980.

English Episcopal Acta II: Canterbury 1162–1190. Ed. C. R. Cheney and B. E. A. Jones. Corrected edition. Oxford. 1991.

English Episcopal Acta III: Canterbury 1193–1205. Ed. C. R. Cheney and Eric John. Corrected edition. Oxford. 1991.

English Episcopal Acta IV: Lincoln 1186–1206. Ed. David M. Smith. Oxford. 1986.
English Episcopal Acta VI: Norwich 1070–1214. Ed. Christopher Harper-Bill. Oxford. 1990.
English Episcopal Acta VII: Hereford 1079–1234. Ed. Julia Barrow. Oxford. 1993.
English Episcopal Acta IX: Winchester, 1205–1238. Ed. Nicholas Vincent. Oxford. 1994.
English Episcopal Acta X: Bath and Wells 1061–1205. Ed. Frances M. R. Ramesey. Oxford. 1995.
English Episcopal Acta XI: Exeter 1046–1184. Ed. Frank Barlow. Oxford. 1996.
English Episcopal Acta XII: Exeter 1186–1257. Ed. Frank Barlow. Oxford. 1996.
English Episcopal Acta 13: Worcester 1218–1268. Ed. Philippa M. Hoskin. Oxford. 1997.
English and Episcopal Acta 17: Coventry and Lichfield 1183–1208. Ed. M. J. Franklin. Oxford. 1998.
English Episcopal Acta 18: Salisbury 1078–1217. Ed. B. R. Kemp. Oxford. 1999.
English Episcopal Acta 19: Salisbury 1217–1228. Ed. B. R. Kemp. Oxford. 2000.
English Episcopal Acta 21: Norwich 1215–1243. Ed. Christopher Harper-Bill. Oxford. 2000.
English Episcopal Acta 22: Chichester 1215–1253. Ed. Philippa M. Hoskin. Oxford. 2001.
English Episcopal Acta 23: Chichester 1254–1305. Ed. Philippa M. Hoskin. Oxford. 2001.
English Episcopal Acta 24: Durham 1153–1195. Ed. M. G. Snape. Oxford. 2002.
English Episcopal Acta 25: Durham 1196–1237. Ed. M. G. Snape. Oxford. 2002.
English Episcopal Acta 27: York 1189–1212. Ed. Marie Lovatt. Oxford. 2004.
English Episcopal Acta 29: Durham 1241–1283. Ed. Philippa M. Hoskin. Oxford. 2005.
English Episcopal Acta 30: Carlisle 1133–1292. Ed. David M. Smith. Oxford. 2005.
English Episcopal Acta 32: Norwich 1244–1266. Ed. Christopher Harper-Bill. Oxford. 2007.
English Episcopal Acta 34: Worcester 1186–1218. Eds. Mary G. Cheney, David Smith, Christopher Brooke, and Philippa Hoskin. Oxford. 2008.
English Episcopal Acta 35: Hereford 1234–1275. Ed. Julia Barrow. Oxford. 2009.
Episcopal Registers, Diocese of Worcester: Register of Bishop Godfrey Giffard, September 23rd 1268 to August 15th 1301. Ed. J. W. Bund. Worcestershire Historical Society 15. Oxford. 1898–1902. 2 vols.
Five English Artes Dictandae and Their Tradition. Ed. Martin Camargo. Binghamton. 1995.

Gerald of Wales. *De Invectionibus.* Ed. W. S. Davies. *Y Cymmrodor: The Magazine of the Honourable Society of Cymmrodorion* 30. 1920.

Giraldi Cambrensis Opera. Ed. J. S. Brewer. Rolls Series. London. 1861–3. 8 vols.

Speculum Duorum or a Mirror of Two Men. Ed. Yves Lefèvre and R. B. C. Hughes. trans. Brian Dawson. Cardiff. 1974.

"Gesta Innocentii PP. III." In *Patrologiae Cursus Completus.* Ed. J.-P., Migne. Paris. 1844–55. CCXIV. cols. xvii–ccxxviii.

The Great Register of Lichfield Cathedral Known as Magnum Registrum Album. Ed. H. E. Savage. Kendal. 1926.

Historia et Cartularium Monasterii Sancti Petri Gloucestriae. Ed. William Henry Hart. Rolls Series. London. 1863–7. 3 vols.

Historiae Dunelmensis Scriptores Tres. Ed. James Raines. Surtees Society 9. London. 1839.

Historical Manuscripts Commission. *Fourteenth Report: Lincoln, Bury St. Edmunds, and Great Grimsby Corporations and the Deans and Chapters of Worcester, Lichfield &c.* London. 1895.

Historical Manuscripts Commission, *Reports on Manuscripts in Various Collections I.* London. 1901.

Historical Papers and Letters from the Northern Registers. Ed. James Raine. Rolls Series. London. 1873.

Household Accounts from Medieval England. Ed. C. M. Woolgar. Oxford. 1992–3. 2 pts.

John Lydford's Book. Ed. Dorothy M. Owen. London. 1974.

John of Salisbury. *Ioannis Saresberiensis Episcopi Carnotensis Policratici sive de Nvgis Cvrialivm et Vestigiis Philosophorvm Libri VIII.* Ed. Clemens I. Webb. Oxford. 1909.

The Letters and Charters of Cardinal Guala Bicchieri, Papal Legate in England 1216–1218. Ed. Nicholas Vincent. Canterbury and York Society 83. Woodbridge. 1996.

The Letters and Charters of Gilbert Foliot. Ed. Adrian Morey and C. N. L. Brooke. Cambridge. 1967.

The Letters of Pope Innocent III (1198–1216) Concerning England and Wales. Ed. C. R. Cheney and Mary G. Cheney. Oxford. 1967.

"Letters of William Wickwane, Chancellor of York, 1266–1268." Ed. C. R. Cheney. *English Historical Review* 47. 1932. 626–42. Reprinted with corrections and additions, in C. R. Cheney. *The English Church and Its Laws 12th–14th Centuries.* London. 1982. article XIII.

Liber Antiquus de Ordinationibus Vicarium Tempore Hugonis Wells, Lincolniensis Episcopi, 1209–1235. Ed. A. Gibbons. Lincoln. 1888.

The Liber Epistolaris of Richard de Bury. Ed. Noel Denholm Young. Oxford. 1950.

Liber Memorandorum Ecclesie de Bernewelle. Ed. John Willis Clark. Cambridge. 1907.

Llandaff Episcopal Acta 1140–1287. Ed. David Crouch. Cardiff. 1988.

Lyndwood, William. *Provinciale, (seu Constitutiones Angliae) continens constitutiones provinciales quatuordecim archiepiscoporum cantuariensium.* Oxford. 1679. 2 pts.

Marsh, Adam. *The Letters of Adam Marsh*. Ed. C. H. Lawrence. Oxford. 2006–10.

The Medieval Court of Arches. Ed. F. Donald Logan. Canterbury and York Society 95. Woodbridge. 2005.

The Memoranda Roll for the Michaelmas Term of the First Year of the Reign of King John (1199–1200). Ed. H. G. Richardson. Pipe Rolls Society New Series 21. London. 1943.

Original Papal Documents in England and Wales from the Accession of Pope Innocent III to the Death of Pope Benedict XI (1198–1304). Ed. Jane E. Sayers. Oxford. 1999.

Die Päpstlichen Kanzleiordnungen von 1200–1500. Ed. Michael Tangl. Innsbruck. 1894.

Paris, Matthew. *Chronica Majora*. Ed. H. R. Luard. Rolls Series. London. 1872–83. 7 vols.

Peter of Blois. *The Later Letters of Peter of Blois*. Ed. Elizabeth Revell. Oxford. 1993.

Records of Antony Bek, Bishop and Patriarch: 1283–1311. Ed. C. M. Fraser. Surtees Society 162. Oxford. 1953.

Records of Convocation III: Canterbury 1317–1377. Ed. Gerald Bray. Woodbridge. 2005.

Records of Harrold Priory. Ed. G. H. Fowler. Bedfordshire Historical Records Society Publications 17–18. No place. 1935. 2 vols.

Regesta Honorii Papae III Iussu et Mvnificentia Leonis XIII Pontificis Maximi ex Vaticanis Archetypis aliisque Fontibvs. Ed. Petrus Presutti. Rome. 1888–95. Reprint Hildesheim. 1978. 2 vols.

Regesta Pontificum romanorum ab condita ecclesia. Compiled by Philipp Jaffé. 2nd ed. Directed by W. Wattenbach et al. Leipzig. 1885–8. 2 vols.

Die Register Innocenz' III. Ed. Othmar Hageneder et al. Graz. 1964–.

The Register of John de Halton, Bishop of Carlisle A.D. 1292–1324. Ed. W. N. Thompson. Canterbury and York Society 12–13. London. 1913. 2 vols.

The Register of John Le Romeyn, Lord Archbishop of York, 1286–1296. Ed. W. Brown. Surtees Society 123, 128. Durham. 1913–17. 2 vols.

The Register of John Pecham, Archbishop of Canterbury, 1279–1292. Ed. F. N. Davis, D. L. Douie, et al. Canterbury and York Society 64–65. Torquay. 1908–69. 2 vols.

The Register of Thomas de Cantilupe, Bishop of Hereford (A.D. 1275–1282). Ed. R. G. Griffiths, with an Introduction by W. W. Capes. Canterbury and York Society 2. London. 1907.

The Register of Thomas de Cobham, Bishop of Worcester 1317–1327. Ed. E. H. Pearce. Worcester Historical Record Society 40. London. 1930.

The Register of Walter Bronscombe, Bishop of Exeter, 1258–1280. Ed. O. F. Robinson. Canterbury and York Society 82, 87, 94. Woodbridge. 1995–2003. 3 vols.

The Register of Walter Giffard, Lord Archbishop of York, 1266–1279. Ed. W. Brown. Surtees Society 109. Durham. 1904.

The Register of Walter Langton, Bishop of Coventry and Lichfield, 1296–1321. Ed. J. B. Hughes. Canterbury and York Society 91, 97. Woodbridge. 2001–7. 2 vols.

The Register of Walter Reynolds, Bishop of Worcester, 1308–1313. Ed. R. A. Wilson. Worcestershire Historical Society 39. London. 1927.

The Register of William de Geynesburgh, Bishop of Worcester, 1302–1307. Ed. J. W. Willis Bund with an introduction by R. A. Wilson. Worcestershire Historical Society 22. Oxford. 1907–22.

The Register of William Wickwane, Lord Archbishop of York, 1279–1285. Ed. W. Brown. Surtees Society 114. Durham. 1907.

The Register, or Rolls, of Walter Gray, Lord Archbishop of York: With Appendices of Illustrative Documents. Ed. J. Raine. Surtees Society 56. Durham. 1872.

The Registers of Henry Burghersh 1320–1342. Ed. Nicholas Bennett. Lincoln Record Society. 87, 90. Woodbridge. 1999–.

The Registers of Roger Martival, Bishop of Salisbury, 1315–1330. Ed. K. Edwards, C. R. Elrington, S. Reynolds, and D. Owen. Canterbury and York Society 55–9, 68. Oxford and Torquay. 1959–75. 6 vols.

The Registers of Walter Bronscombe (A.D. 1257–1280), and Peter Quivil (A.D. 1280–1291), Bishops of Exeter, with Some Records of the Episcopate of Bishop Thomas de Bytton (A.D. 1292–1307); also the Taxation of Pope Nicholas IV, A.D. 1291. Ed. F. C. Hingeston-Randolph. London. 1889.

Les Registres de Boniface VIII. Ed. A. Thomas et al. Bibliothèque des Ecoles françaises d'Athènes et de Rome Second Series 4. Paris. 1884–1939. 4 vols.

Les Registres de Clément IV (1265–1268). Ed. Edouard Jordan. Bibliothèque des Ecoles françaises d'Athènes et de Rome Second Series 11. Paris. 1893–1945.

Les Registres de Clément V. Ed. The Benedictines. Rome. 1884–94. 8 vols.

Les Registres de Grégoire IX. Ed. Lucien Auvray et al. Bibliothèque des Ecoles françaises d'Athènes et de Rome Second Series 9. Paris. 1896–1955. 4 vols.

Les Registres d'Innocent IV (1243–54). Ed. E. Berger et al. Bibliothèque des Ecoles françaises d'Athènes et de Rome Second Series 1. Paris. 1884–1921. 4 vols.

Les Registres de Nicholas IV (1288–1292). Ed. F. Soehnée et al. Bibliothèque des Ecoles françaises d'Athènes et de Rome Second Series 5. Paris. 1887–93. 2 vols.

Les Registres d'Urbain IV (1261–1264). Ed. J. Guiraud and S. Clémencet. Bibliothèque des Ecoles françaises d'Athènes et de Rome Second Series 13. Paris. 1892–1958. 4 vols.

The Registrum Antiquissimum of the Cathedral Church of Lincoln. Ed. C. W. Foster and Kathleen Major. Lincoln Record Society 27–28, 32, 34, 41, 46, 51, 62, 67. Hereford and Gateshead. 1931–73. 10 vols.

Registrum Epistolarum Fratris Johannis Peckham, Archiepiscopi Cantuariensis. Ed. C. T. Martin. Rolls Series. London. 1882–5. 3 vols.

Registrum Henrici Woodlock, diocesis Wintoniensis, A.D. 1305-1316. Ed. A. W. Goodman, Canterbury and York Society 43–4. Oxford. 1940–1. 2 vols.

Registrum Johannis de Pontissara, Episcopi Wintoniensis, A.D. MCCLXXX–MCCCIV. Ed. C. Deedes. Canterbury and York Society 19, 30. London. 1915–24. 2 vols.

Registrum Ricardi de Swinfield, Episcopi Herefordensis, A.D. MCCLXXXIII–MCCCXVIII. Ed. W. W. Capes. Canterbury and York Society 6. London. 1909.

Registrum Roberti Winchelsey Cantuariensis Archiepiscopi. Ed. Rose Graham. Canterbury and York Society 51, 52. Oxford. 1952–6. 2 vols.

Registrum Simonis de Gandavo, Diocesis Sarisberiensis, A.D. 1297–1315. Ed. C. T. Flower and M. C. B. Dawes. Canterbury and York Society 40–1. Oxford. 1934. 2 vols.

Registrum sive Liber Irrotularius et Consuetudinarius Prioratus Beatae Mariae Wignorniensis. Ed. William H. Hale. Camden Society First Series. 91. London. 1865.

"Robert Grosseteste at the Papal Curia, Lyons 1250: Edition of the Documents." Ed. Servus Gieben. *Collecteana Franciscana* 41. 1971. 340–93.

Roberti Grosseteste Episcopi Quondam Lincolniensis Epistolae. Ed. H. R. Luard. Rolls Series. London. 1861.

A Roll of the Household Expenses of Richard de Swinfield, Bishop of Hereford during Part of the Years 1289 and 1290. Ed. John Webb. Camden Society First Series 59. London. 1854–5. 2 vols.

The Rolls and Register of Bishop Oliver Sutton, 1280–1299. Ed. R. M. T. Hill. Lincoln Record Society 39, 43, 48, 52, 60, 64, 69, 76. Hereford, Lincoln, Woodbridge. 1948–86. 8 vols.

The Rolls of the Shropshire Eyre of 1256. Ed. Alan Harding. Selden Society 96. London. 1981 for 1980.

Rotuli Hugonis de Welles, Episcopi Lincolniensis, A.D. MCCIX–MCCXXXV. Ed. W. P. W Phillimore, F. N. Davis, et al. Canterbury and York Society 1, 3–4. London. 1907–9. 3 vols.

Rotuli Ricardi Gravesend, Diocesis Lincolniensis. Ed. F. N. Davis with additions by C. W. Foster and Alexander Hamilton Thompson. Canterbury and York Society 31. Oxford. 1925.

Rotuli Roberti Grosseteste, Episcopi Lincolniensis, A.D. MCCXXXV–MCCLIII. Ed. F. N. Davis. Lincoln Record Society 11. Horncastle. 1914.

Royal and Other Historical Letters of the Reign of Henry III. Ed. W. W. Shirley. Rolls Series. London. 1862–6. 2 vols.

Sacrorum Conciliorum Nova et Amplissima Collectio. Ed. Joannes Dominicus Mansi. Padua. 1767. 31 vols.

St. David's Episcopal Acta, 1085–1280. Ed. Julia Barrow. South Wales Record Society 13. Cardiff. 1998.

Saint Richard of Chichester: The Sources for His Life. Ed. David Jones. Sussex Record Society 79. Lewes. 1995 for 1993.

Select Cases in the Court of King's Bench under Edward II. Ed. G. O. Sayles. Selden Society 45, 47–8, 74, 76, 82, 88. London. 1936–71. 7 vols.

Select Cases from the Ecclesiastical Courts of the Province of Canterbury c. 1200–1301. Ed. Norma Adams and Charles Donahue Jr. Selden Society 95. London. 1981 for 1978–9.

Selected Letters of Pope Innocent III Concerning England (1198–1216). Ed. C. R. Cheney and W. H. Semple. London. 1953.

Testamentary Records of the English and Welsh Episcopate 1200–1413: Wills, Executors' Accounts and Inventories, and the Probate Process, ed. C. M. Woolgar, Canterbury and York Society 102 (Woodbridge, 2011).

Twelfth-Century English Archidiaconal and Vice-Archidiaconal Acta. Ed. Brian Kemp. Canterbury and York Society 92. Woodbridge. 2001.

Two Chartularies of the Priory of St. Peter at Bath. Ed. William Hunt. Somerset Record Society 9. London. 1893.

The White Book of Peterborough: The Registers of Abbot William of Woodford, 1295–99 and Abbot Godfrey of Crowland, 1299–1321. Ed. Sandra Raban. Northampton. 2001.

"The Will of Peter, of Aigueblanche, Bishop of Hereford." Ed. C. Everleigh Woodruff. In *Camden Miscellany* 14. Camden Society Third Series 37. London. 1926.

William of Malmesbury. *De Gesta Pontificum Anglorum*. Ed. N. E. S. A. Hamilton. Rolls Series. London. 1870.

Year Books of Edward II. Ed. F.W. Maitland et al. Selden Society 17- (passim). London, 1903–.

Year Books of the Reign of King Edward I. Ed. Alfred J. Horwood. Rolls Series. London. 1866–79. 5 vols.

Secondary Sources

Addleshaw, G. W. O. *Rectors, Vicars, and Patrons in Twelfth and Early Thirteenth Century Canon Law*. Saint Anthony's Hall Publications 9. York. 1956.

Althoff, Gerd. *Family, Friends and Followers: Political and Social Bonds in Medieval Europe*. Trans. Christopher Carroll. Cambridge. 2004.

Barraclough, Geoffrey. *Papal Provisions: Aspects of Church Constitutional, Legal and Administrative History in the Later Middle Ages*. Oxford. 1935.

Barlow, Frank. *The English Church 1000–1066*. 2nd ed. London. 1979.
   Thomas Becket. Berkeley and Los Angeles. 1986.

Barrow, Julia. "Cathedrals, Provosts and Prebends: A Comparison of Twelfth-Century German and English Practice." *Journal of Ecclesiastical History* 37. 1986. 536–64.

   "Why Forge Episcopal Acta?" In *The Foundations of Medieval English Ecclesiastical History: Studies Presented to David Smith*. Ed. Philippa Hoskin, Christopher Brooke, and Barrie Dobson. Woodbridge. 2005. 18–39.

Barton, Richard E. "'Zealous Anger' and the Renegotiation of Aristocratic Relationships in Twelfth-Century France." In *Anger's Past: The Social Uses of an Emotion in the Middle Ages*. Ed. Barbara H. Rosenwein. Ithaca. 1998. 153–70.

Baumann, Daniel. *Stephen Langton: Erzbischof von Canterbury im England der Magna Carta (1207–1228)*. Leiden. 2009.

Bean, J. M. W. *From Lord to Patron: Lordship in Medieval England*. Philadelphia. 1989.

Bennett, Nicholas. "Pastors and Masters: The Beneficed Clergy of North-East Lincolnshire, 1290–1340." In *The Foundations of Medieval English Ecclesiastical History: Studies Presented to David Smith*. Ed. Philippa Hoskin, Christopher Brooke, and Barrie Dobson. Woodbridge. 2005. 40–62.

Berkhofer, Robert F. III. *Day of Reckoning: Power and Accountability in Medieval France*. Philadelphia. 2004.
Biggs, Douglas. "Royal Charter Witness Lists for the Reign of Henry IV, 1399–1413." *English Historical Review* 119. 2004. 161–77.
Bisson, Thomas N. *The Crisis of the Twelfth Century: Power, Lordship, and the Origins of European Government*. Princeton. 2009.
Boase, T. S. R. *Boniface VIII*. London. 1933.
Boyle, Leonard. "The Constitution 'Cum ex eo' of Pope Boniface VIII: Education of Parochial Clergy." *Mediaeval Studies* 24. 1962. 263–302.
Boussard, Jacques. "Ralph Neville, Évêque de Chichester et chancellier d'Angleterre (†1244) d'après sa correspondence." *Revue historique* 166. 1935. 217–33.
Brand, Paul. "Medieval Legal Bureaucracy: Clerks in the King's Courts in the Reign of Edward I." In Brand. *The Making of the Common Law*. London. 1992. 169–201.
— "The Origins of English Land Law: Milsom and After." In Brand. *The Making of the Common Law*. Rio Grande. 1992. 203–25.
— *The Origins of the English Legal Profession*. Oxford. 1992.
Brentano, Robert. *York Metropolitan Jurisdiction and Papal Judges Delegate (1279–1296)*. Berkeley and Los Angeles. 1959.
— *Two Churches: England and Italy in the Thirteenth Century*. Princeton. 1968.
Brett, Martin. *The English Church under Henry I*. Oxford. 1975.
Brooke, C. N. L. *Churches and Churchmen in Medieval Europe*. London. 1999.
Brooke, Z. N., and C. N. L. Brooke. "Hereford Cathedral Dignitaries in the Twelfth Century." *Cambridge Historical Journal* 8. 1944–6. 1–21, 179–85.
Brown, Sandra. *Medieval Courts of York Minster Peculiar*. Borthwick Papers 66. York. 1984.
Brundage, James A. "Taxation Costs in Medieval Canonical Courts." In *Forschungen zur Reichs-, Papst-, und Landesgeschichte, Peter Herde zum 65. Geburtstag von Freunden, Schülern und Kollegen dargebracht*. I. Ed. Karl Borchardt and Enno Bünz. Stuttgart. 1998. 565–74.
— "The Ethics of Advocacy: Confidentiality and Conflict of Interest in Medieval Canon Law." In *Grundlagen des Rechts: Festchrift für Peter Landau zum 65. Gerburtstag*. II. Ed. Richard H. Helmholz, Paul Mikrat, and Michael Stolleis. Paderborn. 2000. 453–66.
— *The Medieval Origins of the Legal Profession: Canonists, Civilians, and Courts*. Chicago. 2008.
Buck, Mark. *Politics, Finance and the Church in the Reign of Edward II: Walter Stapeldon, Treasurer of England*. Cambridge. 1983.
Burger, Michael. "*Officiales* and the *familiae* of the Bishops of Lincoln, 1258–99." *Journal of Medieval History* 16. 1990. 39–53.
— "Intimacy and Lordship: The Creation of a Bureaucracy in the Diocese of Lincoln, ca. 1186–1299." PhD Dissertation. University of California, Santa Barbara. 1991.
— "Peter of Leicester, Bishop Godfrey Giffard of Worcester, and the Problem of Benefices in Thirteenth-Century England." *Catholic Historical Review* 95. 2009. 453–73.

Butler, L. A. S. "Suffragan Bishops in the Medieval Diocese of York." *Northern History* 37. 2000. 49–60.
Bynum, Caroline Walker. *Jesus as Mother: Studies in the Spirituality of the High Middle Ages*. Berkeley and Los Angeles. 1982.
Carpenter, David. "St. Thomas: His Political Career." In *Saint Thomas Cantilupe Bishop of Hereford: Essays in His Honour*. Ed. Meryl Jancey. Leominster. 1982. 57–72.
Chaplais, Pierre. *English Diplomatic Practice in the Middle Ages*. Hambledon. 2003.
Cheney, C. R. "The Punishment of Felonous Clerks." *English Historical Review* 51. 1936. 215–36.
English Bishops' Chanceries 1100–1250. Manchester. 1950.
From Becket to Langton, English Church Government 1170–1213. Manchester. 1956.
Hubert Walter. London. 1967.
Notaries Public in England in the Thirteenth and Fourteenth Centuries. Oxford. 1972.
"Gervase, Abbot of Prémontré: A Medieval Letter-Writer." In Cheney. *Medieval Texts and Studies*. Oxford. 1973. 242–76.
"The Letters of Pope Innocent III." In Cheney. *Medieval Texts and Studies*. Oxford. 1973.
Pope Innocent III and England. Stuttgart. 1976.
Episcopal Visitations of Monasteries in the Thirteenth Century. 2nd ed. Manchester. 1983.
Cheney, Mary G. *Roger of Worcester*. Oxford. 1980.
Cheyette, Frederic. "Kings, Courts, Cures, and Sinecures: The Statute of Provisors and the Common Law." *Traditio* 19. 1963. 295–349.
Chodorow, Stanley. "Custom, Roman Canon Law, and Economic Interests in Late Twelfth-Century England." In *Grundlagen des Rechts: Festschrift für Peter Landau zum 65. Geburtstag*. II. Ed. Richard H. Helmholz, Paul Mikat, Jörge Müller, and Michal Stolleis. Paderborn. 2000. 291–9.
Christelow, Stephanie Mooers. "The Royal Love in Anglo-Norman England: Fiscal or Courtly Concept?" *Haskins Society Journal* 8. 1999. 27–42.
Church, S. D. "Rewards of Royal Service in the Household of King John: A Dissenting Opinion." *English Historical Review* 110. 1995. 277–302.
Churchill, Irene Josephine. *Canterbury Administration: The Administrative Machinery of the Archbishopric of Canterbury Illustrated from Original Records*. London. 1933. 2 vols.
Clanchy, M. T. *From Memory to Written Record, England 1066–1307*. 2nd ed. Oxford. 1993.
Clarke, Peter D. *The Interdict in the Thirteenth Century: A Question of Collective Guilt*. Oxford. 2007.
Constable, Giles. *Letters and Letter-Collections*. Typologie des sources du moyen âge occidental 17. Turnhout. 1976.
"Dictatores and Diplomats in the Eleventh and Twelfth Centuries." *Dumbarton Oaks Papers* 46. 1992. 37–46.

Coss, Peter. "An Age of Deference." In *A Social History of England 1200–1500*. Ed. Rosemary Horrox and W. Mark Ormrod. Cambridge. 2006. 31–73.
——— "Bastard Feudalism Revised." *Past and Present* no. 125. 1989. 27–64.
Cotts, John D. *The Clerical Dilemma: Peter of Bois and Literate Culture in the Twelfth Century*. Washington, DC. 2009.
Crouch, David. "Debate: Bastard Feudalism Revised." *Past and Present* no. 131. 1991. 165–89.
——— "The Origin of Chantries: Some Further Anglo-Norman Evidence." *Journal of Medieval History* 27. 2001. 159–80.
——— *The Birth of Nobility: Constructing Aristocracy in England and France 900–1300*. Harlow. 2005.
Darnton, Robert. *The Great Cat Massacre and Other Episodes in French Cultural History*. New York. 1985.
Davies, Susan Jane. "Studies in the Administration of the Diocese of Worcester in the Thirteenth Century." PhD Thesis. University of Wales. 1971.
Davis, Adam J. *The Holy Bureaucrat: Eudes Rigaud and Religious Reform in Thirteenth-Century Normandy*. Ithaca. 2006.
Davnall, Sarah, Jeffrey Denton, Sheila Griffith, Dorothy Ross, and Beryl Taylor. "The *Taxatio* Database." *Bulletin of the Institute of Historical Research* 74. 1992. 89–108.
Delhaye, P. "Deux adaptations du 'De Amicitia' de Ciceron au xiie siècle." *Recherches de theologie ancienne et mediévale* 43. 1928. 304–31.
Denholm-Young, Noel. "Richard de Bury (1287–1345)." In Denholm-Young. *Collected Papers on Mediaeval Subjects*. Oxford. 1946.
——— *Seignorial Administration in England*. Oxford. 1937. Reprint. New York. 1964.
Denton, J. H. *English Royal Free Chapels 1100–1300: A Constitutional Study*. Manchester. 1970.
——— *Robert Winchelsey and the Crown 1294–1313: A Study in the Defence of Ecclesiastical Liberty*. Cambridge. 1980.
——— "The Valuation of Ecclesiastical Benefices of England and Wales." *Historical Research* 66. 1993. 231–50.
Desborough, Donald E. "Politics and Prelacy in the Late Twelfth Century: The Career of Hugh de Nonant, 1188–1198." *Historical Research* 64. 1991. 1–14.
Dickinson, J. C. *An Ecclesiastical History of England: The Later Middle Ages, from the Norman Conquest to the Eve of the Reformation*. London. 1979.
Dobson, Barrie. *Durham Priory 1400–1450*. Cambridge. 1973.
Dohar, William J. "Medieval Ordination Lists: The Origins of a Medieval Record." *Archives* 20. 1992. 17–35.
——— "*Sufficienter Litteratus*: Clerical Examination and Instruction for the Cure of Souls." In *A Distinct Voice: Medieval Studies in Honor of Leonard E. Boyle, O.P.* Ed. Jacqueline Brown and William P. Stoneman. Toronto. 1997. 305–21.
Donahue, Charles, Jr. "Proof by Witnesses in the Church Courts of Medieval England: An Imperfect Reception of the Learned Law." In *On the Laws and Customs of England: Essays in Honor of Samuel E. Thorne*. Ed. Morris S. Arnold et al. Chapel Hill. 1981. 127–58.

Donaldson, R. "Sponsors, Patrons, and Presentations to Benefices – Particularly Those in the Gift of the Priors of Durham – during the Later Middle Ages." *Archaeologia Aeliana*. Fourth series 37. 1960. 169–77.

Douie, Decima L. *Archbishop Pecham*. Oxford. 1952.

Du Boulay, F. R. H. *The Lordship of Canterbury: An Essay on Medieval Society*. New York. 1966.

Duggan, Anne. *Thomas Becket*. London. 2004.

Duggan, Charles. "Papal Judges Delegate and the Making of the 'New Law.'" In *Cultures of Power: Lordship, Status, and Process in Twelfth-Century Europe*. Ed. Thomas N. Bisson. Philadelphia. 1995. 172–99.

Dyer, Christopher. *Lords and Peasants in a Changing Society: The Estates of the Bishopric of Worcester, 680–1540*. Cambridge. 1980.

Standards of Living in the Later Middle Ages. Cambridge. 1989.

Edwards, Kathleen. *The English Secular Cathedrals in the Middle Ages: A Constitutional Study with Special Reference to the Fourteenth Century*. 2nd ed. Manchester. 1967.

Emden, A. B. *A Biographical Register of the University of Oxford to A.D. 1500*. Oxford. 1957.

Fryde, Natalie, and Dirk Reitz. "Introduction." In *Bischofsmord im Mittelalter/ The Murder of Bishops in the Middle Ages*. Ed. Natalie Fryde and Dirk Reitz. Göttingen. 2003. 7–11.

Finucane, R. C. "The Cantilupe-Pecham Controversy." In *St. Thomas Cantilupe Bishop of Hereford Essays in His Honour*. Ed. Meryl Jancey. Hereford. 1982. 103–22.

"Two Notaries and Their Records in England, 1282–1307." *Journal of Medieval History* 13. 1987. 1–14.

Fonge, Charles. "Patriarchy and Patrimony: Investing in the Medieval College." In *The Foundations of Medieval English Ecclesiastical History: Studies Presented to David Smith*. Ed. Philippa Hoskin, Christopher Brooke, and Barrie Dobson. Woodbridge. 2005. 77–93.

Frankforter, A. Daniel. "The Origin of Episcopal Registration Procedures in Medieval England." *Manuscripta* 26. 1982. 67–89.

Franklin, M. J. "The Bishops of Coventry and Lichfield, c. 1072–1208." In *Coventry's First Cathedral: The Cathedral and Priory of St. Mary's, Papers from the 1993 Anniversary Symposium*. Ed. George Demidowic. Stamford. 1994. 77–93.

Fraser, C. M. *A History of Antony Bek Bishop of Durham 1283–1311*. Oxford. 1957.

Garnsey, Peter, and Richard Saller. *The Roman Empire: Economy, Society and Culture*. Berkeley and Los Angeles. 1987.

Giandrea, Mary Frances. *Episcopal Culture in Late Anglo-Saxon England*. Woodbridge. 2007.

Gibbs, Marion, and Jane Lang. *Bishops and Reform 1215–1272, with Special Reference to the Lateran Council of 1215*. Oxford. 1932.

Given, James Buchanan. *Society and Homicide in Thirteenth-Century England*. Stanford. 1977.

Godfrey, C. J. "Pluralists in the Province of Canterbury in 1366." *Journal of Ecclesiastical History* 11. 1960. 23–40.

Rose Graham. "The Metropolitical Visitation of the Diocese of Worcester." In Graham. *English Ecclesiastical Studies*. London. 1929. 330–59.
"The Taxation of Pope Nicholas IV." In Graham. *English Ecclesiastical Studies*. London. 1929. 272–301.
Gray, J. W. "The Ius Praesentandi in England from the Constitutions of Clarendon to Bracton." *English Historical Review* 67. 1952. 481–509.
Green, Judith. *The Government of England under Henry I*. Cambridge. 1986.
Haines, R. M. *The Administration of the Diocese of Worcester in the First Half of the Fourteenth Century*. London. 1963.
Archbishop John Stratford: Political Revolutionary and Champion of the Liberties of the English Church, ca. 1275/80–1348. Toronto. 1986.
"The Appropriation of Longdon Church to Westminster Abbey." In Haines. *Ecclesia Anglicana: Studies in the English Church of the Later Middle Ages*. Toronto. 1989. 3–14.
"Canterbury versus York: Fluctuating Fortunes in a Perennial Conflict." In Haines. *Ecclesia Anglicana: Studies in the English Church of the Later Middle Ages*. Toronto. 1989. 69–105.
Ecclesia Anglicana: Studies in the English Church of the Later Middle Ages. Toronto. 1989.
Hallebeek, Jan. "Actio ex Iuramento: The Legal Enforcement of Oaths." *Ius Commune: Veröffentlichungen des Max-Planck-Instituts für europäische Rechtsgeschichte, Frankfurt am Main* 17. 1990. 69–88.
Hanawalt, Barbara A. *The Ties that Bound: Peasant Families in Medieval England*. Oxford. 1986.
Harding, Alan. *Medieval Law and the Foundations of the State*. Oxford. 2002.
Haren, Michael. *Sin and Society in Fourteenth-Century England: A Study of the Memoriale Presbiterorum*. Oxford. 2000.
Harper-Bill, Christopher. "The Struggle over Benefices in Twelfth-Century East Anglia." In *Anglo-Norman Studies XI: Proceedings of the Battle Conference 1988*. Ed. R. Allen Brown. 1989. 113–32.
"The Diocese of Norwich in the Early Thirteenth Century: Sources and Themes." In *Counties and Communities: Essays on East Anglian History Presented to Hassell Smith*. Ed. Carole Rawcliffe, Roger Virgoe, and Richard Wilson. Norwich. 1996. 21–35.
"The Diocese of Norwich and the Italian Connection, 1198–1261." In *England and the Continent in the Middle Ages: Studies in Memory of Andrew Martindale, Proceedings of the 1996 Harlaxton Symposium*. Ed. John Mitchell, assisted by Matthew Moran. Stamford. 2000. 75–89.
Hartridge, R. A. R. *A History of Vicarages in the Middle Ages*. Cambridge. 1930. Reprint New York. 1968.
Harvey, Margaret. "The Benefice as Property: An Aspect of Anglo-Papal Relations during the Pontificate of Martin V, 1417–31." *Studies in Church History* 24. 1987. 161–73.
Haseldine, Julian. "Friendship and Rivalry: The Role of Amicitia in Twelfth-Century Monastic Relations." *Journal of Ecclesiastical History* 44. 1993. 390–414.
"Understanding the Language of *Amicitia*: The Friendship Circle of Peter of Celle (c. 1115–1183)." *Journal of Medieval History* 20. 1994. 237–60.

"Introduction." In *Friendship in Medieval Europe*. Ed. Julian Haseldine. Phoenix Mill. 1999. xvii–xxiii.

"Love, Separation and Male Friendship: Words and Actions in Saint Anselm's Letters to His Friends." In *Masculinity in Medieval Europe*. Ed. D. M. Hadley. London. 1999. 240–1.

"Thomas Becket: Martyr, Saint—And Friend?" In *Belief and Culture in the Middle Ages: Studies Presented to Henry Mayr-Harting*. Ed. Richard Gameson and Henrietta Leyser. Oxford. 2001. 305–17.

"The Monastic Culture of Friendship." In *The Culture of Medieval English Monasticism*. Ed. James G. Clark. Woodbridge. 2007. 177–202.

Helmholz, R. H. "Ethical Standards for Advocates and Proctors in Theory and Practice." In Helmholz. *Canon Law and the Law of England*. London. 1987. 41–57.

The Ius Commune in England: Four Studies. Oxford. 2001.

The Oxford History of the Laws of England I The Canon Law and Ecclesiastical Jurisdiction from 597 to the 1640s. Oxford. 2004.

Herde, Peter. *Beiträge zum päpstlichen Kanzlei- und Urkundenwesen im dreizehnten Jahrhundert*. Munich. 1967.

Hicks, Michael. *Bastard Feudalism*. London. 1995.

Hill, R. M. T. "Bishop Sutton and the Institution of Heads of Religious Houses in the Diocese of Lincoln." *English Historical Review* 58. 1943. 201–9.

"Public Penance and the Problems of a Thirteenth-Century Bishop." *History* 36. 1951. 213–26.

Hollister, C. Warren. "Henry I and the Anglo-Norman Magnates." In Hollister. *Monarchy, Magnates, and Institutions in the Anglo-Norman World*. London. 1986. 93–107.

Henry I. Ed. and completed by Amanda Clark Frost. New Haven. 2001.

Holt, J. C. *Magna Carta*. 2nd ed. Oxford. 1992.

Hoskin, Philippa. "Diocesan Politics in the See of Worcester 1218–1266." *Journal of Ecclesiastical History* 54. 2003. 422–40.

"Continuing Service: The Episcopal Households of Thirteenth-Century Durham." In *The Foundations of Medieval Ecclesiastical History: Studies Presented to David Smith*. Ed. Philippa Hoskin, Christopher Brooke, and Barrie Dobson. Woodbridge. 2005. 124–38.

Hudson, John. *The Formation of the English Common Law*. London. 1996.

Land, Law, and Lordship in Anglo-Norman England. Oxford. 1994.

Hyams, Paul R. "Deans and Their Doings: The Norwich Inquiry of 1286." *Monumenta iuris canonici*. Series C. Subsidia 7. 1985. 639–43.

"What Did Henry III of England Think in Bed and in French about Kingship and Anger?" In *Anger's Past: The Social Uses of an Emotion in the Middle Ages*. Ed. Barbara H. Rosenwein. Ithaca. 1998. 92–124.

Rancor and Reconciliation in Medieval England. Ithaca. 2003.

Ireland, Richard W. "Theory and Practice in the Medieval English Prison." *American Journal of Legal History* 31. 1987. 56–67.

Jaeger, C. Stephen. *Ennobling Love: In Search of a Lost Sensibility*. Philadelphia. 1999.

Joliffe, J. E. A. *Angevin Kingship*. 2nd ed. Oxford. 1963.

Kay, Richard. "An Eyewitness Account of the 1225 Council of Bourges." *Studia Gratiana* 12. 1967. 63–79.

"Gerald of Wales and the Fourth Lateran Council." *Viator* 29. 1998. 79–93.

The Council of Bourges 1225: A Documentary History. Aldershot. 2002.

Keefe, Thomas K. "Counting Those Who Count: A Computer-Assisted Analysis of Charter Witness-Lists and the Itinerant Court in the First Year of the Reign of King Richard I." *Haskins Society Journal* 1. 1989. 135–45.

Kemp, Brian. "Towards Admission and Institution: English Episcopal Formulae for the Appointment of Parochial Incumbents in the Twelfth Century." In *Anglo-Norman Studies XVI: Proceedings of the Battle Conference 1993*. Ed. Marjorie Chibnall. Woodbridge, 1994. 155–76.

"The Acta of the English Rural Deans." In *The Foundations of English Ecclesiastical History: Studies Presented to David Smith*. Ed. Phillipa Hoskin, Christopher Brooke, and Barrie Dobson. Woodbridge. 2005. 139–58.

Kicklighter, Joseph A. "An Unknown Brother of Pope Clement V." *Mediaeval Studies* 38. 1976. 492–5.

Knowles, David. *The Religious Orders in England*. Cambridge. 1957. 3 vols.

Kuttner, Stephan, and Eleanor Rathbone. "Anglo-Norman Canonists of the Twelfth Century." *Traditio* 7. 1949–51. 279–358.

Lawrence, C. H. *St. Edmund of Abingdon: A Study of Hagiography and History*. Oxford. 1960.

Medieval Monasticism. 3rd ed. Harlow. 2001.

"The English Parish and Its Clergy in the Thirteenth Century." In *The Medieval World*. Ed. Peter Linehan and Janet L. Nelson. New York. 2003. 648–70.

Le Neve, John. *Fasti Ecclesiae Anglicanae 1066–1300 I: St. Paul's, London*. 3rd ed. Compiled by Diana Greenway. London. 1968.

Fasti Ecclesiae Anglicanae 1066–1300 II: Monastic Cathedrals. 3rd ed. Compiled by Diana E. Greenway. London. 1971.

Fasti Ecclesiae Anglicanae 1066–1300 III: Lincoln. 3rd ed. Compiled by Diana Greenway. London. 1977.

Fasti Ecclesiae Anglicanae 1066–1300 IV: Salisbury. 3rd ed. Compiled by Diana Greenway. London. 1991.

Fasti Ecclesiae Anglicanae 1066–1300 V: Chichester. 3rd ed. Compiled by Diana Greenway. London. 1996.

Fasti Ecclesiae Anglicanae 1066–1300 VI: York. 3rd ed. Compiled by Diana E. Greenway. London. 1999.

Fasti Ecclesiae Anglicanae 1066–1300 VII: Bath and Wells. 3rd ed. Compiled by Diana Greenway. London. 2001.

Fasti Ecclesiae Anglicanae 1066–1300 VIII: Hereford. 3rd ed. Compiled by Julia Barrow. London. 2002.

Fasti Ecclesiae Anglicanae 1066–1300 X: Exeter. 3rd ed. Compiled by Diana Greenway. London. 2005.

Fasti Ecclesiae Anglicanae 1300–1541 I: Lincoln Diocese. Compiled by H. P. King. London. 1962.

Fasti Ecclesiae Anglicanae 1300–1541 II: Hereford Diocese. Compiled by Joyce M. Horn. London. 1962.
Fasti Ecclesiae Anglicanae, or a Calendar of the Principal Ecclesiastical Dignitaries of England and Wales. 2nd ed. Corrected and continued by T. Duffus Hardy. Oxford. 1844.
Levett, Elizabeth E. "Baronial Councils and Their Relation to Manorial Courts." In *Melanges offerts à M. Ferdinand Lot*. Paris. 1925. 421–41.
Little, Lester K. *Religious Poverty and the Profit Economy in Medieval Europe*. Ithaca, NY. 1978.
Logan, F. Donald. *Excommunication and the Secular Arm in Medieval England*. Toronto. 1968.
Lunt, W. E. *The Valuation of Norwich*. Oxford. 1926.
Maddern, Philippa. "'Best Trusted Friends': Concepts and Practices of Friendship among Fifteenth-Century Norfolk Gentry." In *England in the Fifteenth Century: Proceedings of the 1992 Harlaxton Symposium*. Ed. Daniel Williams. Stamford. 1994. 100–17.
Maddicott, J. R. *Law and Lordship: Royal Justices as Retainers in Thirteenth- and Fourteenth-Century England*. Past and Present Supplement 4. 1978.
Maesschaele, James. "The Public Space of the Marketplace in Medieval England." *Speculum* 77. 2002. 383–421.
Major, Kathleen. "The 'Familia' of Archbishop Stephen Langton." *English Historical Review* 48. 1933. 529–33.
——— "The *Familia* of Robert Grosseteste." In *Robert Grosseteste: Scholar and Bishop*. Ed. D. A. Callus. Oxford. 1955. 216–41.
Mansfield, Mary C. *The Humiliation of Sinners: Public Penance in Thirteenth-Century France*. Ithaca, NY. 1995.
Matthew, D. J. A. "The Letter Writing of Archbishop Becket." In *Belief and Culture in the Middle Ages: Studies Presented to Henry Mayr-Harting*. Ed. Richard Gameson and Henrietta Leyser. Oxford. 2001. 287–304.
Mauss, Marcel. *The Gift: Forms and Functions in Exchange in Archaic Societies*. Trans. I. Cunnison. London. 1954.
Maxwell-Lyte, H. C. *Historical Notes on the Use of the Great Seal of England*. London. 1926.
McDonald, Peter. "Poor Clerks' Provisions: A Case for Reassessment?" *Archivum Historiae Pontificae* 30. 1992. 339–49.
McFarlane, K. B. "Bastard Feudalism." In McFarlane. *England in the Fifteenth Century: Collected Essays of K. B. McFarlane*. Ed. G. L. Harris. London. 1981. 23–43.
McGuire, Brian Patrick. *Friendship and Community: The Monastic Experience 350–1250*. Kalamazoo. 1988.
McHardy, A. K. "Ecclesiastics and Economics: Poor Priests, Prosperous Laymen, and Proud Prelates in the Reign of Richard II." *Studies in Church History* 24. 1987. 129–37.
——— "Some Patterns of Ecclesiastical Patronage in the Later Middle Ages." In *Studies in Clergy and Medieval Ministry in Medieval England*. Ed. David M. Smith. York. 1991. 20–37.
——— "The Churchmen of Chaucer's London: The Seculars." *Medieval Prosopography* 16. 1995. 57–87.

McLoughlin, John. "*Amicitia* in Practice: John of Salisbury and His Circle." In *England in the Twelfth Century: Proceedings of the 1988 Harlaxton Symposium*. Ed. Daniel Williams. Wolfeboro, NH. 1990. 165–81.

Meddings, John. "Friendship among the Aristocracy in Anglo-Norman England." In *Anglo-Norman Studies XXII: Proceedings of the Battle Conference 1999*. Ed. C. Harper-Bill. Woodbridge. 2000. 187–204.

Menache, Sophia. *Clement V*. Cambridge. 1998.

Mertes, Kate. *The English Noble Household 1200–1600*. Oxford. 1988.

Milsom, S. F. C. *The Legal Framework of English Feudalism*. Cambridge. 1976.

Mollat, G. "Bénéfices ecclésiastiques en Occident." In *Dictionnaire de droit canonique*. Ed. R. Naz. Paris. 1937. II. cols. 406–49.

Moorman, J. R. H. *Church Life in England in the Thirteenth Century*. Cambridge. 1955.

Morgan, M. M. "The Excommunication of Grosseteste in 1243." *English Historical Review* 57. 1942. 244–50.

Morris, Colin. "Letheringsett: The Early History of a Parish Church." *Bulletin of the Institute of Historical Research* 44. 1971. 116–20.

Mullett, Margaret. "Power, Relations and Networks in Medieval Europe." *Revue belge de philologie et d'histoire/Belgisch tidschrift voor philology en geschiedenis* 83. 2005. 255–59.

Murphy, James J. *Rhetoric in the Middle Ages: A History of Rhetorical Theory from Saint Augustine to the Renaissance*. Tempe. 2001.

Murray, Alexander. *Reason and Society in the Middle Ages*. Reprint with corrections. Oxford. 1985.

Newman, J. E. "Greater and Lesser Landowners and Parochial Patronage: Yorkshire in the Thirteenth Century." *English Historical Review* 92. 1977. 280–308.

Noonan, John T. Jr. *Bribes: The Intellectual History of a Moral Idea*. Berkeley and Los Angeles. 1984.

Norton, Christopher. "History, Wisdom and Illumination." In *Symeon of Durham: Historian of Durham and the North*. Ed. David Rollason. Stamford. 1998. 61–105.

Olsen, Glenn. "The Definition of the Ecclesiastical Benefice in the Twelfth Century: The Canonists' Discussion of Spiritualia." *Studia Gratiana* 11. 1967. 432–46.

Orme, Nicholas. "A Medieval Almshouse for the Clergy: Clyst Gabriel Hospital Near Exeter. *Journal of Ecclesiastical History* 39. 1988. 1–15.

——— "Sufferings of the Clergy, Illness and Old Age in Exeter Diocese 1300–1540." In *Life, Death, and the Elderly in Historical Perspective*. Ed. Margaret Pelling and Richard M. Smith. London. 1991. 62–73.

Ormrod, W. M. "Accountability and Collegiality: the English Royal Secretariat in the Mid-Fourteenth Century." In *Ecrit et pouvoire dans les chancelleries médiévales*. Ed. Kouky Fianu and DeLloyd Guth. Louvain. 1997. 78–85.

Oxford Dictionary of National Biography. Ed. H. G. C. Matthew and Brian Howard Harrison. Oxford. 2004. 60 vols.

Painter, Sidney. *Studies in the History of the English Feudal Barony*. Baltimore. 1943.

Palmer, Robert C. "The Origins of the Legal Profession in England." *The Irish Jurist*. New series 11. 1976. 126–46.

——— "The Origins of Property in England." *Law and History Review* 3. 1985. 1–50.

——— *Selling the Church: The English Parish Church in Law, Commerce, and Religion, 1350–1550*. Chapel Hill. 2002.

Pantin, W. A. *The English Church in the Fourteenth Century*. Cambridge. 1955.

Pearce, E. H. *Thomas de Cobham, Bishop of Worcester, 1317–37*. London. 1923.

——— "English Monastic Letter-Books." In *Historical Essays in Honour of James Tait*. Ed. J. G. Edwards, V. H. Galbraith, and E. F. Jacob. Manchester. 1933. 201–22.

Pegues, Franklin J. "A Monastic Society at Law in the Kent Eyre of 1313–1314." *English Historical Review* 87. 1972. 548–64.

Pennington, Kenneth. *Pope and Bishops: The Papal Monarchy in the Twelfth and Thirteenth Centuries*. Philadelphia. 1984.

Postles, Dave. "Penance and the Market Place: A Reformation Dialogue with the Medieval Church (c. 1250–c. 1600)." *Journal of Ecclesiastical History* 54. 2003. 441–68.

Powell, Anton. *Athens and Sparta: Constructing Greek Political and Social History from 478 B.C*. London. 1988.

Powicke, F. M. *Stephen Langton*. Oxford. 1928.

——— *The Thirteenth Century*. 2nd ed. Oxford. 1962.

Pugh, Ralph B. *Imprisonment in Medieval England*. Cambridge. 1968.

Ramsey, Nigel. "Retained Legal Counsel, c. 1275–c. 1475." *Transactions of the Royal Historical Society* 25. 1985. 95–112.

Rasche, Ulrich. "The Early Phase of Appropriation of Parish Churches in Medieval England." *Journal of Medieval History* 26. 2000. 213–37.

Richter, Michael. *Giraldus Cambrensis: The Growth of the Welsh Nation*. 2nd ed. Aberystwyth. 1976.

Ridgeway, H. W. "The Ecclesiastical Career of Aymer de Lusignan, Bishop Elect of Winchester, 1250–1260." In *The Cloister and the World: Essays in Honour of Barbara Harvey*. Ed. John Blair and Brian Golding. Oxford. 1996. 148–77.

Robson, Michael. "Franciscan Bishops *in Partibus Infidelium* Ministering in Medieval England." *Antonianum* 78. 2003. 547–73.

Rodes, Robert E. Jr. *Ecclesiastical Administration in Medieval England: The Anglo-Saxons to the Reformation*. Notre Dame. 1977.

Rosenthal, Joel. *Old Age in Late Medieval England*. Philadelphia. 1996.

——— "Retirement and the Lifecycle in Fifteenth-Century England." In *Aging and the Aged: Selected Papers from the Annual Conference of the Centre for Medieval Studies*. Ed. M. M. Sheehan. Toronto. 1990. 173–88.

Rosenwein, Barbara. "Controlling Paradigms." In *Anger's Past: The Social Uses of an Emotion in the Middle Ages*. Ed. Barbara Rosenwein. Ithaca, NY. 1998. 233–47.

——— *Emotional Communities in the Early Middle Ages*. Ithaca. 2006.

——— "Worrying about Emotions in History." *American Historical Review* 107. 2002. 821–45.

Rutledge, Elizabeth. "Lawyers and Administrators: The Clerks of Late-Thirteenth-Century Norwich." In *Medieval East Anglia*. Ed. Christopher Harper-Bill. Woodbridge. 2005. 83–98.
Ruud, Marylou. "Episcopal Reluctance: Lanfranc's Resignation Reconsidered." *Albion* 19. 1987. 163–75.
Saltman, Avrom. *Theobald, Archbishop of Canterbury*. London. 1955.
Saunders, P. C. "Royal Ecclesiastical Patronage from Winchelsey to Stratford." *Bulletin of the John Rylands Library* 83. 2001. 95–114.
Sayers, Jane. *Papal Judges Delegate in the Provincial Court of Canterbury 1198–1254: A Study in Ecclesiastical Jurisdiction and Administration*. Oxford. 1971.
Scammell, Jean. "The Rural Chapter in England from the Eleventh to the Fourteenth Century." *English Historical Review* 86. 1971. 12–21.
Schwarz, Brigide. *Die Organisation kurialer Schreiberkollegien von ihrer Entstehung bis zur Mitte des 15. Jahrhunderts*. Tübingen. 1972.
Sère, Bénédict. *L'amitié au Moyen Age: Étude historique des commentaries sur les livres VIII et IX de l'Éthique à Nicomaque*. Turnhout. 2007.
Sheehan, M. M. *The Will in Medieval England: From the Conversion of the Anglo-Saxons to the End of the Thirteenth Century*. Toronto. 1963.
    "English Wills and the Records of the Ecclesiastical and Civil Jurisdictions." *Journal of Medieval History* 14. 1988. 3–12.
Smith, David M. "The Administration of Hugh of Wells, Bishop of Lincoln, 1209–35." PhD Thesis. University of Nottingham. 1970. 2 vols.
    "The Rolls of Hugh of Wells, Bishop of Lincoln, 1209–35." *Bulletin of the Institute of Historical Research* 45. 1972. 155–95.
    Guide to Bishops' Registers of England and Wales: A Survey from the Middle Ages to the Abolition of Episcopacy in the 1646. London. 1981.
    "Suffragan Bishops in the Medieval Diocese of Lincoln." *Lincolnshire History and Archaeology* 17. 1982. 17–27.
    "Thomas Cantilupe's Register: The Administration of the Diocese of Hereford 1275–1282." In *Saint Thomas Cantilupe Bishop of Hereford: Essays in His Honour*. Ed. Meryl Jancey. Leominster. 1982. 83–101.
    "Hugh's Administration of the Diocese of Lincoln." In *St. Hugh of Lincoln: Lectures Delivered at Oxford and Lincoln to Celebrate the Eighth Century of St. Hugh's Consecration as Bishop of Lincoln*. Ed. Henry Mayr-Harting. Oxford. 1987. 18–47.
    "The 'Officialis' of the Bishop in Twelfth- and Thirteenth-Century England: Problems of Terminology." In *Medieval Ecclesiastical Studies in Honour of Dorothy M. Owen*. Ed. M. J. Franklin and Christopher Harper-Bill. Woodbridge. 1995. 201–20.
    "The Exercise of the Probate Jurisdiction of the Medieval Archbishops of York." In *Life and Thought in the Northern Church, c. 1100–c. 1700: Essays in Honour of Claire Cross*. Ed. Diana Wood. Woodbridge. 1999. 123–44.
Smith, Peter M. "The Advowson: The History and Development of a Most Peculiar Property." *Ecclesiastical Law Journal* 26. 2000. 320–39.
Smith, R. A. L. *Canterbury Cathedral Priory*. Cambridge. 1943.

"The Central Financial System of Christ Church, Canterbury, 1186–1512." In Smith. *Collected Papers*. London. 1947. 23–41.

Southern, R. W. *Robert Grosseteste: The Growth of an English Mind in Medieval Europe*. 2nd ed. Oxford. 1992.

Spencer, Andrew M. "Royal Patronage and the Earls in the Reign of Edward I." *History* 93. 2008. 20–46.

Srawley, J. H. "Grosseteste's Administration of the Diocese of Lincoln." In *Robert Grosseteste: Scholar and Bishop*. Ed. D. A. Callus. Oxford. 1955. 146–77.

Stewart, Susan. "What Happened at Shere?" *Southern History* 22. 2000. 1–20.

Stowers, Stanley. *Letter Writing in Greco-Roman Antiquity*. Philadelphia. 1986.

Sullivan, Matthew. "The Role of the Nassington Family in the Medieval English Church." *Nottingham Medieval Studies* 37. 1993. 53–64.

Summerson, Henry. "Fearing God, Honouring the King: The Episcopate of Robert de Chaury, Bishop of Carlisle, 1258–1278." *Thirteenth Century England X: Proceedings of the Durham Conference 2003*. Ed. Michael Prestwich, Richard Britnell, and Robin Frame. Woodbridge. 2005. 147–54.

Swanson, R. N. Church"Learning and Livings: University Study and Clerical Careers in Later Medieval England." *History of Universities* 6. 1987 for 1986–87. 83–103.

Church and Society in Late Medieval England. Manchester. 1989.

"Standards of Livings: Parochial Revenues in Pre-Reformation England." In *Religious Belief and Ecclesiastical Careers in Late Medieval England: Proceedings of the Conference Held at Strawberry Hill Easter 1989*. Ed. Christopher Harper-Bill. Woodbridge. 1991. 151–96.

"*Universis Christi Fidelibus*: The Church and Its Records." In *Pragmatic Literacy, East and West 1200–1300*. Ed. Richard Britnell. Woodbridge. 1997. 147–64.

Taylor, Lily Ross. *Party Politics in the Age of Caesar*. Berkeley and Los Angeles. 1961.

Thompson, A. Hamilton. *The Organization of the English Clergy in the Later Middle Ages*. Oxford. 1947.

"Pluralism in the Medieval Church, with Notes on Pluralists in the Diocese of Lincoln, 1366." Part 1. *Reports and Papers of the Architectural and Archaeological Societies of the Counties of Lincoln and Northampton* 33. 1915. 35–73.

The Premonstratensian Abbey of Welbeck. London. 1938.

Tout, T. F. *Chapters in the Administrative History of Mediaeval England*. Manchester. 1920–37. 6 vols.

Townley Simon. "Unbeneficed Clergy in Two English Dioceses." In *Studies in Medieval Clergy and Mininstry in Medieval England*. Ed. David M. Smith. York. 1991. 38–64.

Van Engen, John. "Sacred Sanctions for Lordship." In *Cultures of Power: Lordship, Status, and Power in Twelfth-Century Europe*. Ed. Thomas N. Bisson. Philadelphia. 1995. 203–30.

Vincent, Nicholas. "The Origins of the Winchester Pipe Rolls." *Archives* 21. 1994. 25–42.

"Master Elias of Dereham (d. 1245): A Reassessment." In *The Church and Learning in Later Medieval Society: Essays in Honour of R. B. Dobson, Proceedings of the 1999 Harlaxton Symposium*. Ed. Caroline M. Barron and Jenny Stratford. Donington. 2002. 128–59.

"The Murderers of Thomas Becket." In *Bischofsmord im Mittelalter/The Murder of Bishops in the Middle Ages*. Ed. Natalie Fryde and Dirk Reitz. Göttingen. 2003. 211–72.

Peter de Roches: An Alien in English Politics 1205–1238. Cambridge. 1996.

"The Politics of Church and State as Reflected in the Winchester Pipe Rolls, 1208–80." In *The Winchester Pipe Rolls and English Society*. Ed. Richard Britnell. Woodbridge. 2003. 157–81.

"The Strange Case of the Missing Biographies: The Lives of the Plantagenet Kings of England, 1154–1272." In *Writing Medieval Biography 750–1250: Essays in Honour of Frank Barlow*. Ed. David Bates, Julia Crick, and Sarah Hamilton. Woodbridge. 2006. 237–57.

Review of The Foundations of Medieval English Ecclesiastical History: Studies Presented to David Smith. Ed. Philippa Hoskin, Christopher Brooke, and Barrie Dobson. Woodbridge. 2005. *Journal of Ecclesiastical History* 58. 2007. 128–30.

Vodola, Elisabeth. *Excommunication in the Middle Ages*. Berkeley and Los Angeles. 1986.

Warren, W. L. *Henry II*. Berkeley and Los Angeles. 1973.

King John. Berkeley and Los Angeles. 1961.

Waugh, Scott L. "Tenure to Contract: Lordship and Clientage in Thirteenth-Century England." *English Historical Review* 101. 1986. 811–39.

Wertheimer, Laura. "Illegitimate Birth and the English Clergy, 1198–1348." *Journal of Medieval History* 31. 2001. 211–29.

"Clerical Dissent, Popular Piety, and Sanctity in Fourteenth-Century Peterborough: The Cult of Laurence of Oxford." *Journal of British Studies* 45. 2006. 3–22.

Wilshire, Leland Edward. "Boniface of Savoy, Carthusian and Archbishop of Canterbury 1207–1270." *Analecta Cartusiana* 31. 1977. 5–90.

Wright, Robert. *The Church and the English Crown 1305–1334: A Study Based on the Register of Archbishop Walter Reynolds*. Toronto. 1980.

Wood, Susan. *English Monasteries and Their Patrons in the Thirteenth Century*. London. 1955.

The Proprietary Church in the Medieval West. Oxford. 2006.

Woodcock, Brian L. *Medieval Ecclesiastical Courts in the Diocese of Canterbury*. Oxford. 1952.

Wood-Legh, Kathleen. *Perpetual Chantries in Britain*. Cambridge. 1965.

Wormald, Patrick. *The Making of English Law, King Alfred to the Twelfth Century I: Legislation and Its Limits*. Oxford. 1999.

Wurstenberger, L. *Peter der Zweite Graf von Savoyen, Markgraf in Italien, sein Haus und seine Lande: ein Charakterbild des dreizehnten Jahrhunderts*. Bern. 1856–8. 4 vols.

Yates, W. Nigel. "Bishop Peter de Aquablanca (1240–1268): A Reconsideration." *Journal of Ecclesiastical History* 22. 1971. 303–17.
Young, Charles. *Hubert Walter, Lord of Canterbury and Lord of England.* Durham, NC. 1968.
Ysebaert, Walter. "Medieval Letter-Collections as a Mirror of Circles of Friendship? The Example of Stephen of Tournai, 1128–1203." *Revue belge de philologie et d'histoire/Belgisch tidschrift voor philology en geschiedenis* 83. 2005. 285–300.
Ziolkowski, Jan. "Twelfth-Century Understandings and Adaptation of Ancient Friendship." In *Mediaeval Antiquity*. Ed. Andreis Wekenhuysen, Herman Braet, and Werner Verbeke. Louvain. 1995. 59–81.

Index

For unnamed rectors and vicars, see the name of their church. Bishops and modern authors only are listed under their toponyme/surname.

Aaron de Kent, 203 n92
Ab Kettelby, church, 78
Aberford, 20
Abingdon, Saint Edmund of (archbishop of Canterbury [1234–40]), 38, 128, 159 n139, 188, 203 n92, 206, 219, 232, 237
    chancellor of, 206, 232
Acomb, church, 121 n56
act (bishop's), defined, 8–9
acta (bishop's), defined, 8
Adam, butler of Bishop Wyche of Chichester, 260
Adam, groom of Bishop Suffield of Norwich, 261
Adam, *nepos* of Brother William, papal *hostiarius*, 256
Adam, pantler of Archbishop Winchelsey of Canterbury, 233
Adam, scullion of Archbishop Winchelsey of Canterbury, 233
Adam, vicar of the treasurer of Salisbury, 226 n83
Adam de Ardern, 259
Adam de Aylinton, 175 n29
Adam de Brampton, 163
Adam de Capella, 89
Adam de Copeland, 216, 262
Adam de Fileby, 98 n101, 226, 254
Adam de Hailes, 207 n118
Adam de Herwynton, 139
Adam de Lymmyng, 106
Adam Marsh, 37, 39, 224 n74
Adam de Pileby. *See* Adam de Fileby
Adam de Saint Edmund, 192
Adam de Shrewsbury, 120, 122
Adam de Stanford, 121 n56
Adam de Stratton, 56
Adam de York, 56
Adbury, church, 8 n3
Administrative church, 110
    culture of diocesan service, 239–47, 249
    episcopal clerks not a civil service, 187, 189–90, 203, 209
advowsons (in general)
    acquisition of by bishops, 170–2
    defined, 3
    value of, 33 n53
    saleable, 170
affection, 5, 95 n82, 123, 210–38, 242–5, 249
Agatha, wife of John le Cupper de Nottingham, 137 n3
Agen, canon of. *See* William Segin de Got
Ailby, church, 76 n197, 181, 195 n37
Aimeric, chancellor of Hereford cathedral, 227
Alan, *cursor* of Bishop Aquablanca of Hereford, 262
Alan de Beccles, 206
Alan de Easingwold, 201 n83
Alan de Frestone, 108–9
Alan de Walkynham, 259

Albano, bishop of, 104
  brother of, 104
Alberic of Monte Cassino, 221 n64
albs. *See* vestments
Alcester Abbey, 171
Alexander, keeper of the palfreys of Bishop Wyche of Chichester, 260
Alexander III, 27–8
Alexander de Bedford, 192
Alexander de Biddick, 201 n82
Alexander de Elstow, 192
Alexander de Holland, 77
Alexander de Swineshead, 77
Alford, church 180 n50
almhouses, 79 n217
Ambrosden, church, 164
Anagni, Saint Mary de Gloria, monastery of, 101
anathema, 114
Ancher, cardinal-priest of Saint Praxedis, 92, 256
Andover, church, 31 n43
Andrew, cook of Archbishop Winchelsey of Canterbury, 233
Andrew, hall doorkeeper of Bishop Giffard of Worcester, 262
Andrew de Brugg, 258
Andrew de Kilkenny, 107 n160, 127, 206 n111
Angers, Saint Nicholas's Abbey, 112
Anian II (bishop of Saint Asaph [1268–93]), 228 n92
annuities, 4, 11, 81, 99, 100, 108, 251.
  See also pensions
Anselm, archbishop of Canterbury (1093–1101), 115 n28
Anselm de Esquerra, 253
Anthony de Bradeney, 237 n146
Appleby, church, 162
Aquablanca, Peter de (bishop of Hereford [1240–68]), 16, 53, 60, 115, 138 n12, 226–7, 235 n134, 249 n39, 262
archdeacons, archdeaconries, 5–8, 31–2, 37 n86, 44, 47, 72–4, 130, 132, 191–2, 203, 204 n101, 205, 213, 229, 247. *See also* Bath; Bath and Wells; Bedford; Berkshire; Buckingham; Canterbury; Carlisle; Chester; Cleveland; Colchester; Cornwall; Cremona; Dorset; Durham; Exeter; Gloucester; Hereford; Huntingdon; Leicester; Lewes; Lincoln; London; Middlesex; Norfolk; Northampton; Oxford; Richmond; Saint Asaph; Salop; Stafford; Stow; Sudbury; Suffolk; Surrey; Totnes; Taunton; Wells, Wiltshire; Worcester; York
  officials of, 6, 77 n206, 114 n25, 131 n112, 132, 145, 157, 165, 220
Arches, Court of, 16, 44, 72, 87, 90 n48, 108, 143, 150, 164 n160, 257–8
  dean of, 93 n69, 102, 161, 200, 206 n111, 213
archives (bishop's), 6, 112–13
Aristotle, 214 n21
armor, 17 n21, 226, 260
ars dictamen, 214
Aslackhoe, deanery of, 163 n157
Asti, bishop of, 105
Aumale Abbey, 172
Aure, church, 139
Avalon, Saint Hugh of (bishop of Lincoln [1186–1200]), 191–2, 194, 201, 206
Aymo, archdeacon of York, 255
Aymo, precentor of Hereford, 227

B. de Sunting', 76
Badminton, church, 97 n94
bailiffs, 20, 156–7, 262
bakers, 232–3, 260–3
Bangor,
  bishop of, 103
  diocese of, 67 n136
Baningham, caretaker of Bishop Suffield of Norwich's bed, 262
Bar-le-Duc, count of, 254–5
barbers, 233
Bardney Abbey, 163 n157, 181
Barlings Abbey, 112
Barlow, Frank, 188
Barnack, church, 180 n49
Barnstaple Priory, 139
Barnwell Priory, 49, 108–9
Barrow, Julia, 262
Bartholomew, clerk of Bishop Aquablanca of Hereford, 227
Bartholomew de Gatesdene, 126
Basingstoke, 235 n130
bastard feudalism, 11, 81.
  See also pensions
bastardy, 36, 43, 117 n31, 118
Bath,
  archdeacon of, 122 n62
  prior/priory of, 84 n15, 90 n49

Index

291

Bath and Wells. *And see* Bath; Wells
   archdeacons of diocese of, 149.
      See also individual archdeaconries
   bishops of, 51, 69, 82 n9, 118, 119 n41,
      122 n62, 124, 176, 204.
      See also Bitton, William I; Bitton,
      William II; Jocelin; March, William
   diocese of, 197
Battle Abbey, 29, 137
Beatrix de Lindefield, 94
Beauport Abbey, 181
Becket, Thomas (archbishop of Canterbury
      [1162–70]), 40–1, 53, 129
   tomb of, 19
Bedford, archdeacons of, 131, 145, 213
beds, 187, 225, 261–3
Bek, Antony (bishop of Durham [1284–
      1311]), 13, 182, 201
bench covers (as legacies), 226
Benedict, Master, apostolic notary, 211
Benedict de Ferriby, 114, 146 n51
Benedict de Hallam, 157, 165
Benedict de Utterby, 162
benefices (concept, in general), 3–4, 7,
      11, 23–39, 82, 136–7, 237–8.
      See also honor; simony
   appropriation of, 31 n43, 47–8, 50,
      68–9, 121, 170–3, 178, 238
   augmentation of endowment of, 120–4
   clerks' demand for, 109, 169
   collation to, defined, 3
      collation by lapse, 51 n52, 98 n96,
         139, 151, 173–5, 176 n33, 179 n47
      collation, surreptitious, 153
      timing of collation, 174
   commendation of, 74–8, 87 n33, 163 n157,
      165 n165, 181, 230 n104, 241
   compared with pensions, 95–9
   competentes, 101, 103, 252–5
   dilapidations of, 24, 70, 71 n165
   distraint of, 161. *See also* benefices,
      sequestration
   endowed with other than tithes or land,
      183
   expectatives, 28, 29, 82, 93 n70
   information about vacancies of, 104
   legacies withheld from clerks who have
      received benefices, 227, 230–2
   residence/nonresidence in, 24–6, 71, 78,
      98, 101, 119–20, 121 n58, 138,
      151, 213 n15, 217, 222, 240 n6.
      See also benefices, pluralism

   institution to, defined, 3
   letters of, 36, 52, 113, 151, 153
   procedure, 35–6
   pluralism, 25–7, 32–3, 35, 39 n95, 43–4,
      57–9, 63, 71, 73, 77–8, 98, 101, 117–
      19, 141 n21, 142, 159, 165, 176,
      205 n101, 240 n6. *See also* benefices,
      residence/nonresidence in
   security of tenure in, 39–79, 104–5, 110,
      122, 124, 134, 166, 183, 185, 187,
      208–9, 238 n154, 241–2, 245, 248
   sequestration of, 70–2, 114, 136, 161,
      166, 241
   status pertaining to, 104–5, 109
   unbeneficed clergy, 34, 46, 99 n103.
      See also chantries
   value of, 99
      assessment of, 99 n105, 255
Benington, church, 174
Berkhofer, Robert F., 148, 150
Berkshire, archdeacon of, 237
Bermondsey Priory, 65–6
Bernard, legatee of Bishop Aquablanca of
      Hereford, 262
Bernard of Champagne, prior, 16
Beverley,
   bailiff of, 20
   college of, 142
   provost of, 20
Bibles. *See* books
Binewerk in Stamford, Saint Mary's,
      church, 55
Bingham, Robert (bishop of Salisbury,
      [1229–46]), 198
Bishop Middleham, church, 100, 105
bishops. *See* individual dioceses and
      bishops' names
Bishop's Cleeve, church, 53, 142, 246
Bitton, Thomas (bishop of Exeter [1292–
      1307]), 107
Bitton, William I (bishop of Bath and Wells
      [1248–64]), 92, 251, 256
Bitton, William II (bishop of Bath and
      Wells [1267–74]), 100, 251
Black Death, 34 n59
Blois, William of (bishop of Lincoln
      [1203–6]), 191–2, 194, 201
Blois, William of (bishop of Worcester
      [1218–36]), 205
Blund, Richard (bishop of Exeter
      [1245–57]), 186–8, 235
   officialis of, 187–8

Bochard de Vernon, 254
Bodmin Priory, 148
Bodro de Scaccario Romano, 259
Boethius, Master, papal chancellor, 255
Bogo de Clare, 32
Bohun, Jocelin de (bishop of Salisbury [1142–84]), 205
Boke of Nurture, 32
bonds, 18–19, 55 n68, 136–40, 142, 148, 166, 241
Boniface VIII, 67, 73
vice-chancellor of, 215
Boniface de Saluzzo, 154
books (as legacies), 225–7, 229–31, 234
Bosbury, 88 n33, 161, 175 n29
Bosham, prebend of, 67
Bottesford, 162
Boulton, church, 121
Bracebridge, church, 180 n50
Bradwell, 111
Bramber, church, 230 n102
Braose, Giles de (bishop of Hereford [1200–15]), 205
Brasted, church, 170
Braybrooke, church, 38
Breamore Priory, 172
Bredon, rector of. *See* Walter de Berton
Brentano, Robert, 148, 239–40
Breton, John le (bishop of Hereford [1269–75]), 259
brewers, 261–2
bribery, 4, 127, 133–6
Bridport, Giles (bishop of Salisbury [1257–62]), 74
Brigsley, church, 181
Bringhurst, 179 n49
Brinkhill, church, 194 n32
Brize Norton, church, 180 n50
Bromyard, portions of, 60 n101, 87 n33, 88 n33, 112
Bronscombe, Walter (bishop of Exeter [1258–80]), 67, 100, 111, 136, 139, 145, 164 n60, 165, 172, 186–8, 218, 235, 252–3, 258
officialis of, 111, 206 n111
Buckfast, 147
Buckingham, archdeacon/archdeaconry of, 111, 115 n27, 147 n52, 154, 180 n49
Budbrooke, church, 139
Bufetus, *nuntius* of Bishop Hugh of Wells of Lincoln, 261

Buleys, legatee of Bishop Suffield of Norwich, 261
Bullington Priory, 163 nn156–7
Burnel, Robert (bishop of Bath and Wells [1275–92]), 158
Bury St. Edmund's Abbey, 62
butlers, 260–2
Buxted, church, 125

Caldicot, church, 48 n37
Camberwell, church, 65–6
Canon Pyon, 87 n33
Canterbury, 236. *See also* Court of Arches
archbishops of, 5, 14–15, 73, 100, 108, 110, 120, 129, 149, 158 n131, 177, 182, 200, 211, 236. *See also* Abingdon, Edmund of; Anselm; Baldwin; Becket, Thomas; Dover, Richard of; Forde, Baldwin of; Jumièges, Robert of; Kilwardby, Robert; Langton, Stephen; Pecham, John; Savoy, Boniface of; Theobald; Walter, Hubert; Winchelsey, Robert
chancellor of, 118 n34, 129
officialis of archbishop of, 19, 69, 122 n63, 142, 161
registers of, 85
suffragans of, rights over, 177. *See also* courts, ecclesiastical; oaths; *officiales sede vacante*
archdeacon of, 99, 122
archdiocese of, 119 n41, 200, 203–4
Christ Church, Canterbury, 14, 16 n16, 18, 106, 122, 219
monk of, 188 n8
prior of, 91 n51, 103, 207. *See also* Henry Eastry
Council of 1329, 130
Court of, 15, 69, 90, 132, 258–9
Saint Augustine's Abbey, 99 n106, 103, 143 n33, 214 n21
canticles. *See* books
Cantilupe, Thomas (bishop of Hereford [1275–82]), 16–19, 59–60, 63, 72, 102, 128, 137–8, 146, 151, 153, 155–6, 161, 207, 211–12, 216 n27, 217, 222, 226, 231 n109, 237, 259, 262–3
officialis of, 155, 161, 207, 237 n145
register of, 85 n18, 155
vicar-general of, 237 n145

Cantilupe, Walter (bishops of Worcester [1237–66]), 32 n50, 118, 234
  officialis of, 118, 205
Canwick, 180 n50
Capes, W.W., 60
caps (as legacies). *See* clothing
Capun, legatee of Bishop Suffield of Norwich, 261
cardinals, 67, 92, 105, 177, 215 n26, 222 n69, 256–7
  cardinal's chamberlain, 215 n26
Carew, Richard de (bishop of Saint David's [1256–80]), 237 n149
carpenters, 260
carters, 89, 261
Carlisle, 17
  archdeacon of, 161
  bishop of *See also* Chaury, Robert de; Halton, John de; Ireton, Ralph) 5, 48, 76, 102, 119 n42, 125, 137, 212, 218
  officialis of, 17
  registers of, 85
  diocese of, 161
  prior and convent of, 252
Carlton Kyme, prebend, 183 n62
Cassington, church, 180 n50
Castle Bytham, Winwick, church, 195 nn36–7
cathedral chapter, 6, 102, 135, 205, 209. *See also* individual cathedrals
cathedral canons, 6, 26
cattle, 260
Cavenham, church, 37
Caxton, church, 175
Celestine V, 67
celibacy. *See* incontinence
Chaddesley Corbett, church, 159 n134
Chalfont, 235 n130
chamberlains, 7, 158 n131, 186, 215 n26, 233 n117, 260, 262–3
chancellors
  bishop's, 6, 17, 29, 118 n34, 129, 179 n46, 186, 195 n34, 196 n39, 206, 232, 236 n141
  Exchequer, 158 n131
  royal, 41 n6, 103, 134, 258
chantries/chantry priests, 34 n59, 50, 137 n3, 160, 172, 237 n149
chapels,
  bishops', 7, 89, 104, 127, 227, 229–32
  private, 111

chaplains (domestic), 6, 18, 57, 61, 120, 171 n11, 176, 187, 190, 195 n36, 225, 227, 229–32, 254
Charlbury, church, 180 n50
Charminster, 20
Chaury, Robert de (bishop of Carlisle [1258–78]), 252
Checkenden, church, 61
Chedington, 235 n130
Cheney, C.R., 9, 90, 220
Cheney, Mary G. 220
Chester, archdeaconry of, 121. *See also* Adam de Stanford
Chester-le-Street, college at, 182
Chichester, bishops of, 28–30, 37 n86, 112, 171, 204–5, 219–20. *See also* Neville, Ralph; Warham, Ranulph; Wyche, Richard
  dean and chapter of, 94
    common fund of, 142 n26
    precentor of, 142 n26
chickens, 228 n92
Chieveley, church, 54
Chipping Norton, church, 175
Christie, Agatha, 3, 10
Churchill, church, 58
Churchill, Irene, 132, 149
Cicero, 214 n21
Cirencester, Abbot of, 176
Cistercians, 51 n48, 224 n74
Clement, parson of Chaddesley Corbett, 159 n134
Clement IV, 221–2
Clement de Leake, 71 n165
Clericis laicos, 15
clerks (bishop's),
  defined, 7
  identifying, 7–8
  independence of, 5. *See also* benefices, security of tenure in
  social relations among bishops' clerks, 158–66, 187
Cleveland, archdeaconry of, 212. *See also* Ralph de Kyme
Clifton, church, 196 n41
cloaks (as legacies). *See* clothing
cloth (as legacy), 226–7, 232
clothing, 125, 150, 226–7, 229, 252–3, 261–2
coadjutors, 79, 163 n159
cobblers, 262
Cocking, church, 171

Coddington, 87 n33
Colchester, archdeacon of, 229
Coleman, legatee of Bishop Suffield of Norwich, 261
colleges, secular, 18, 25, 123, 142, 175, 182. *See also* individual colleges
Colton, church, 55 n69
Colonna family, 67, 73
Colwall, 125
   church, 87 n33
Combe, church, 180 n50
commercial activity, clerical, 135
Compton Bishop, prebend of, 120
Compton Verney, church, 123
compurgation. *See* oaths
confirmations of rights, 111–12, 114, 123
Conisholme, church, 77
cooks, 232–3, 260–2
Coreley, church, 87 n33
Cornwall,
   archdeacons/archdeaconry of, 100
   earl of, 14, 19
Cornwell, rector of, 220
Corringham, prebend of, 154
corrodies, 20, 79 n216
councils,
   church, 132, 177–8. *See also* Canterbury, Lambeth, London
     Fourth Lateran, 27 n15, 31 n43, 39, 46, 48, 53, 184
     Second of Lyons, 74–5, 78
     Third Lateran, 28, 130, 141, 173
   seigniorial/bishops', 149, 203–4
Cound, church, 76 n202
courts,
   ecclesiastical, 4, 6, 15, 32–3, 42, 44, 47, 49, 56–8, 63 n116, 64–5, 68–70, 72, 87, 88 n33, 90, 94 n76, 107, 110, 112 n9, 114, 116, 124, 128–30, 132, 138, 141–3, 159 n134, 160–2, 235–6, 241, 245, 247–8. *See also* Arches, Court of; Canterbury, Court of
   secular, 49, 51–2, 57, 81 n3, 94, 97, 99, 107–8, 128 n98, 129 n102, 130, 140, 142, 148, 155, 176, 247–8
   summons to, 13–14, 17, 20, 49, 142
Coventry, priory of, 182–3
Coventry and Lichfield
   bishop of, 76 n200, 114, 121, 123, 182–3, 208, 213. *See also* Langton, Walter; Weseham, Roger

officialis of, 55 n69
registers of, 85
diocese of, 74, 78 n213, 85, 119 n41
Credenhill, church, 122
Cremona, archdeacon of. *See* Emanuel, Master, archdeacon of Cremona
Crime and Punishment, 3
Crust, legatee of Bishop Suffield of Norwich, 262
cups, 126–7, 164 n164, 225–7, 229–32, 234, 262
cursores. *See* messengers

Dalderby, John (bishop of Lincoln [1300–20]), 58, 74 n183, 75–6, 78, 83, 91, 93, 102–4, 143, 157
   register of, 85
dangers of service to bishops, 13–20, 224
darrein presentment, 174
dataries, 192
Daventry Priory, 128
David de Ruddeby, 207 n116
David fitz-Reginald, 60 n102
Davis, Adam, 150
Decem Librarum, prebend of, 183
Deerhurst Priory, 173
Devon, 204
devotion, 5, 210–11, 219–21, 222 n67, 224–5, 234–8, 242–5, 249
dice, 115, 147
dictamen. *See* ars dictamen
discipline. *See* punishment
Diversis Ordinibus Hominum, 32, 38 n90
Doddington, chapel, 114
Donhead, church, 175
doorkeepers, 217, 233, 256, 261–3
Dorchester Abbey, 178
Dorset, archdeaconry of, 121 n56
Dover, 14, 126
   priory of, 80–1
Dover, Richard of (archbishop of Canterbury [1174–84]), 129
Du Boulay, F. R. H., 204
Dunre, church, 146
Dunstable Priory, 61, 131, 176, 194 n33
   chronicler of, 96, 137 n3, 176
Durand, son of Nicholas Elys, 253
Durand de Lincoln, 160–3, 164 n161
Durham, 199
   archdeacon/archdeaconry of, 55, 120–1. *See also* Robert de Saint Agatha; William de Lanham

bishops of, 5, 18–20, 25, 48 n34, 61, 97 n93, 117, 119, 124, 148, 189, 200, 207, 211, 236. *See also* Bek, Antony; Farnham, Nicholas; Holy Island, Robert of; Kirkham, Walter; Marsh, Richard; Poore, Richard; Stichill, Robert
longevity of, 202
officialis of, 61, 146
diocese of, 51 n48, 69 n147, 119 n41, 200–3, 204 n95, 216, 235 n130
prior/priory of, 13, 17, 19, 29, 55, 65, 91, 97 nn91 and 93, 100, 108, 115, 207
Dusing, legatee of Bishop Suffield of Norwich, 261

earl (as rank), 32
Ebbesborne Wake, church, 172
Eckington, church, 63
Edlesborough, church, 58
education, 35–7, 47, 75, 119, 134, 236, 253
Edward I of England, 15, 63, 67, 73, 91, 243
treasurer of, 158 n129
Edward II of England, 99 n101, 103
Edwards, Kathleen, 113
eggs, 260
Egloshayle, church, 76
Eleanor, queen of England, 256
Elias, chaplain of Jocelin, Bishop of Bath and Wells, 120
Elias de Chieveley, 54
Elias de Dereham, 189, 203, 236–7
Elias Kotele, 261
Ellesborough, church, 78
Ellisfield, church, 75
Elsham Priory, 171 n11
Ely, bishop of, 93 n69, 102, 118 n34, 175, 204 n95. *See also* Kilkenny, William of; Kirkby, John; York, Robert of
diocese of, 119 n41
Emanuel, Master, archdeacon of Cremona, 258
English Episcopal Acta project, 9, 189
Ernald Lovel, 125 n80
estate administrators, 204. *See also* bailiffs, seneschals
Evesham, abbey of, 28
Ewell, Master, executor of Bishop Merton of Rochester, 236
ewers, 227

Exchequer (royal),
chamberlain of, 158 n131
Chancellor of, 158 n131
excommunication, 14, 17 n24, 19, 35, 49, 115, 138, 141–7, 166, 188, 212 n7, 213, 222, 235–6, 241
Execrabilis, 141 n21
execution of wills. *See* executors
executors, 44, 107, 111 n2, 114 n25, 139, 146, 160, 163 n157, 165 nn165–6, 181 n56, 195 nn35–7, 196 nn38–9. *See also* probate
of bishops, 107, 211, 224–31, 234–8, 262
challenges faced by, 234–6
of bishops' clerks, 124, 160–3, 165 n167
exemptions, granted by bishops, 111, 116, 119, 123–4, 205 n101. *See also* papacy, dispensations/exemptions
Exeter, 126 n85
archdeacon of. *See* Pontoise, John
bishops of, 50, 68, 76, 102, 110, 132 n115, 134, 147–9, 243 n13. *See also* Bitton, Thomas; Blund, Richard; Bronscombe, Walter; Marshal, Henry; Quivil, Peter
chancellor of, 17
officialis of, 17, 76, 132 n115
registers of, 85
cathedral of, 17
dean and chapter of, 102 n125, 254
diocese of, 164 n160
Exeter, John de (bishop of Winchester [1262–8]), 68
Exford, church, 69
expenses of bishop's clerks, 20, 126
extortion, 4, 127–31, 133–4, 136
Eynsham
Abbey, 103, 178–80, 243
church, 180 n50

Fairstead, rector of. *See* William Marsh
familiaris/familiares, bishops', 7, 111 n2, 119, 125, 157 n125, 158, 222
Farlesthorpe, church, 162 n154
Farnham, Nicholas (bishop of Durham [1243–9]), 201
farriers, 260, 263
fees, 4, 91 n52, 112 n13, 127–8, 130–4, 244
Fladbury, church, 125
Flaxley, abbot-elect, 153

Foliot, Hugh (bishop of Hereford [1219–34]), 122 n62
Forde, Baldwin of (bishop of Worcester [1180–4], archbishop of Canterbury, [1184–90]), 18, 205–6
foresters, 201
Fownhope, prebend of, 87 n33, 88 n33, 175
Franciscans, 91 n52, 194 n33
freedom, granted for villeins, 125
friends/friendship, 38 n94, 60, 67, 69, 131, 165, 175, 210–17, 218 n44, 219, 221 n64, 222–4, 238 n154, 242–5. *See also* affection
Friskney, church, 180 n50

G. de Leicester, 193 n29
Gainford, church, 61, 69 n147
Garin de Boys, 87
Gatintone, church, 256
general commissary, 156
Gentham, church, 44
Geoffrey (Plantagenet) (archbishop of York [1191–1212]), 207, 245–6
  officialis of, 246
Geoffrey, baker of Bishop Suffield of Norwich, 261
Geoffrey, cook of Archbishop Winchelsey of Canterbury, 233
Geoffrey, cook of Bishop Aquablanca of Hereford, 262
Geoffrey, doorkeeper of the kitchen of Bishop Suffield of Norwich, 262
Geoffrey, watchman of Bishop Suffield of Norwich, 261
Geoffrey de Bisimano, 253
Geoffrey de Brochamton, 230
Geoffrey de Buguleun, 96
Geoffrey of the chamber of Bishop Suffield of Norwich, 262
Geoffrey de Deeping, 192
Geoffrey de Eydon, 258
Geoffrey de Ferring, 206
Geoffrey Gross, 39
Geoffrey de Hembury, 262
Geoffrey de Lodn', 261
Geoffrey de Lodnes, 231
Geoffrey de Moris, 192 n25
Geoffrey Rom'/Romipetus of Bishop Hugh of Wells of Lincoln, 261
Geoffrey Scot, 197
Geoffrey of Trani, 133 n120

Gerald of Wales, 16, 27, 34, 66, 128
Gerard, clerk of the archbishop of Canterbury, 114
Gerard de Grandisson, 256
Gerard de Rowell, 192
Gerard de Wesenham, 113 n17
Gervais, John, bishop of Winchester. *See* Exeter, John de
Gervase, cardinal priest of Saint Martin's, 257
Ghent, Simon (bishop of Salisbury [1297–1315] and archdeacon of Oxford), 150, 155 n101, 164, 175, 254
Giffard, Godfrey (bishop of Worcester [1268–1302]), 19, 35, 44, 53, 58–9, 69, 90 n48, 97 n94, 121, 124–5, 127, 134, 138–9, 142, 152, 158–9, 162, 165, 171, 207, 227–31, 234, 236, 245–7, 255, 262
  officialis of, 139 n15
Giffard, Walter (archbishop of York [1266–79]), 33, 37, 44, 51 n51, 92, 212 n7, 216 n31, 227, 256
  officialis of, 212 n7
gifts (other than benefices), 4, 27–8, 81, 88 n33, 110–11, 117–29, 131, 133–6, 184, 187, 213, 225–6, 241–3. *See also* land, grants of; papacy, papal dispensations/exemptions; wills of bishops
Gilbert, saucer of Bishop Suffield of Norwich, 261
Gilbert of the chamber of Bishop Hugh of Wells of Lincoln, 261
Gilbert de Leicester, 193
Gilbert de Mablethorpe, 192
Gilbert de Middleton, 93 n69
Gilbert de Saint Leofardo, 92, 251
Gilbert de Wycumb, 113 n17
Giles, king's clerk, 94
Giles de Avenbury, 53–4
Giles the chaplain, legatee of Bishop Suffield of Norwich, 229
Gille, legatee of Bishop Suffield of Norwich, 261
Gille of the kitchen of Bishop Aquablanca of Hereford, 263
Gilling, rector of. *See* John de Littlinton
Gingoneccus, legatee of Bishop Aquablanca of Hereford, 262
Given, James, 34

Glastonbury Abbey, 97 n91, 98, 101 n120
Glen, church, 171
Gloucester, 73
  archdeacon/archdeaconry of, 72, 152
Gloucester, Saint Peter's Abbey, 61, 64
Gnosall, church/college, 123
goblets. *See* cups
Godard, cook of Archbishop Winchelsey of
  Canterbury, 233
Godfrey de Crowland, 86
Godfrey de Ludham, 255
Godwin of the kitchen of Bishop Suffield
  of Norwich, 262
Goldcliff, William de (bishop of Llandaff
  [1219-29]), 48 n37
goldsmiths, 255
Goodnestone, church, 114
Gorwell, 120
Gorwell and Overby, prebend of, 122 n62
Gosberton, church, 53, 181
grants of land, 115 n28, 120, 122, 125
Gravesend, Richard (bishop of Lincoln
  [1258-79]), 74, 77, 164 n164, 171,
  193-4, 196-9, 200-2
  chancellor of, 196 n39
  officialis of, 179 n46, 194 n31, 198-9,
    199
Gravesend, Richard (bishop of London
  [1280-1303]), 107, 176, 193-4,
  225-6, 231-2, 235 n132, 238, 260-1
  chancellor of, 195 n34
  officialis of, 225
  vicegerens of, 194 n32
Gray, John (bishop of Norwich [1200-
  14]), 207 n116, 212
  officialis of, 212
Gray, Walter (archbishop of York
  [1215-1255]; bishop of Worcester
  [1214-15]), 23, 121 n56, 172, 211,
  217-18, 255-6
Gregorian Reform, 27, 30, 33, 41, 45-6,
  50, 131 n111, 225, 242 n9
Gregory IX, 48 n32, 100
Griffin, archdeacon of Saint Asaph,
  228 n92
grooms, 261
Grosseteste, Robert (bishop of Lincoln,
  [1235-53], archdeacon of Leicester),
  14, 31 n43, 37, 77-8, 113, 137,
  173-4, 179, 181, 192-4, 196-8,
  201, 202 n90, 215-16, 224 n74,
  228 n93, 241 n7

officialis of, 194
  vicegerens of, 194
Guichard de Charron, 201 n83
Guido, rector of West Kerle, 255
Guilden Morden, church, 49
Guildford, dean of, 219
Guilloloccus, baker of Bishop Aquablanca
  of Hereford, 262
Gunieccus of the kitchen of Bishop
  Aquablanca of Hereford, 262
Gussage All Saints, church, 121 n56
Gwyliot, legatee of Bishop Suffield of
  Norwich, 262

Haddenham, church 176
Haines, Roy Martin, 149
Hales in Lodden, Saint Andrew in, church,
  50 n43
Halton, John de (bishop of Carlisle
  [1292-1324]), 257
Hamo, rector of Letheringsett, 63
Hamo de Barre, 259
Hampton Bishop, church, 87 n33, 88 n33
Hampton Saint Peter, Broadway, church, 174
Hankin of the bakery of Bishop Hugh of
  Wells of Lincoln, 261
Haringay, rector of. *See* Walter de London
Hardwick, church, 173
Harper-Bill, Christopher, 170
Hartlebury, rector of. *See* John de
  Redberrow
Haseldine, Julian, 223
Hastings, prebend in, 175
Haughton le Skerne, church, 120
Helmdon, church, 180 n50
Heloise de Schelving, 126 n86
Henry II of England, 40, 187 n4
Henry III of England, 105, 172, 249 n39
  chancellor of, 103
Henry VI, emperor, 134, 184
Henry, clerk of the chapel of Bishop
  Richard Wyche of Chichester, 230
Henry, cobbler of Bishop Suffield of
  Norwich, 262
Henry, son of John (plaintiff in suit over
  church of Whixley), 63
Henry Bustard, 72
Henry de Camera, 163
Henry de Derb', 258
Henry Eastry, 86, 106
Henry de Grafton, 226 n78
Henry de Hacton, 125

Henry de Ho, 118 n34
Henry de Nassington, 164, 179 n49, 200
Henry Sampson, the younger, 145, 179 n49
Henry de Sandford, 213
Henry de Symplingham, 75
Henry de Tresgoz, 63 n116
Herbert of the chamber, legatee of Bishop
    Hugh of Wells of Lincoln, 261
Hereford,
  archdeacon/archdeaconry of, 16, 72–3,
      87 n33, 88 n33
  bishops of, 37, 118–20, 122, 125, 161,
      172 n16. See also Aquablanca,
      Peter de; Braose, Giles de; Breton,
      John le; Cantilupe, Thomas; Foliot,
      Hugh; Maidstone, Ralph; Swinfield,
      Richard
    officialis of, 54, 72, 87 n33, 88 n33
    register of, 85 n18
  canons of, 60, 120 n50
  chancellor/chancellorship of Hereford
      cathedral, 88 n33, 227
  dean/dean and chapter of, 102, 211, 227.
      See also Giles de Avenbury
    prebend in, 120. See also names of
        prebends
  diocese of, 119 n41
  officiales sede vacante, 156
  precentor/precentorship of, 87 n33, 227.
      See also Hervey de Boreham
  treasurership of Hereford cathedral,
      87 n33, 88 n33
Hervey de Boreham, 59 n96, 60 n101
Hervey de Feckenham, 229
Hervey de Threkeston, 162
Heslerton, church, 213 n15
Hillingdon, church, 121
Hinton, church, 87 n33, 88 n33
Hobb, carter of Bishop Suffield of
    Norwich, 261
Hockliffe, 179 n47
Holdgate Castle, portion of, 60 n101
Holland, dean of, 220
Holy Cross, church (diocese of Hereford),
    172 n16
Holy Island, Robert of (bishop of Durham
    [1274–83]), 201, 236, 258
  chancellor of, 236 n141
holy water carrier, 52, 98
honor, 10, 23, 38–9, 67, 105, 109,
    207 n118, 212, 219–20, 243

Honorius, Master, archdeacon of
    Richmond, 73, 207, 245
Honorius III, 23, 38, 46, 133 n121, 134,
    184, 211
Hope, chapel of (diocese of Hereford),
    172 n16
Hope Mansel, church, 60 n101
Horkesleye, rector of. See Henry de
    Grafton
Horsley, 258
horses, 14, 20, 126, 225–7, 230, 260, 262
Hoskin, Philippa, 189, 200–1, 203
hospitals, 18, 115 n27, 147 n52, 171, 173,
    178–80, 212, 261
Hospitallers. See Jerusalem, Hospital of
    Saint John in
hostiarii. See doorkeepers, papacy
households, 133 n120, 149
  of abbots, 208 n119
  accounts of, 86–9, 94, 106, 111,
      112 n9, 126
  of archdeacons, 147
  of bishops, 81, 88 n33, 114, 124, 128,
      144, 149, 159 n138, 164,
      179 n47, 180 n49, 188 n8, 189–90,
      200, 207, 226, 232, 249 n39.
      See also *familiaris*; households,
      accounts of; marshals; seneschals;
      stewards
  of the king of England, 96
  of the king of France, 96 n86
  of secular lords, 208 n119
Hoxne, 261
Hugh, butler of Bishop Suffield of
    Norwich, 261
Hugh, cook of Bishop Hugh of Wells of
    Lincoln, 261
Hugh of Bologna, 221
Hugh Burnel, 158
Hugh of the chamber of Bishop Suffield of
    Norwich, 261
Hugh de Corbrig, 229
Hugh Gerald, 102
Hugh de Leominster, 94 n73
Hugh de Lumynster, 254
Hugh de Merton, 56
Hugh de Nottingham, 254
Hugh de Saint Edmunds, 230
Hugh de Saint Edward, 192
Hugh de Wells, 193
humiliation, 146–7, 166

Huntingdon, archdeacon/archdeaconry of, 38, 73, 77 n207, 154 n94. *See also* Martival, Roger; Walter de Wooton; William de Newark
Huntington, prebend of, 88 n33
Hurlsey, church, 66

Imago Ecclesie, 31
incontinence, 43, 46, 136–7
Ingeram, legatee of Bishop Suffield of Norwich, 262
Ingham, church, 163 n156
Innocent III, 28–9, 54, 56, 68, 89, 130–1, 134, 150, 184, 210, 220, 228
Innocent IV, 53, 55 n68, 117
inspeximus. *See* confirmations of rights
interdict, 19, 43, 222, 228
Ipswich, Prior of Saint Peter's and Saint Paul's, 49
Ireton, Ralph (bishop of Carlisle [1280–92]), 90, 252
Italian church, 239

J. de Ebroycis, Master, 227
James, clerk and scribe of Pandulph, bishop of Norwich, 59, 143
James de Aosta, 227
James de Aquablanca, 63 n119, 72
James de Hyspania, 91–2, 254
James de Maurienne, 262
James de Sabello, 257
James Salvagius, 237
janitores. *See* doorkeepers
Jerusalem, Hospital of Saint John in, 108, 171
Jocelin, bishop of Bath and Wells (1206–42), 120, 122, 149
John, cook of Bishop Suffield of Norwich, 261
John, carter of Bishop Suffield of Norwich, 261
John, farrier of Bishop Longespee of Salisbury, 260
John, former barber of Archbishop Winchelsey of Canterbury, 233
John, *hostiarius* of Bishop Suffield of Norwich, 261
John, marshal of Bishop Aquablanca of Hereford, 262
John, runner of Bishop Hugh of Wells of Lincoln, 261

John, servant at Esfordby of Bishop Hugh of Wells of Lincoln, 261
John de Alvechurch, 205, 207 n116
John de Aqua de Maidstone, 230
John de Aquablanca, 227
John de Ardern, 139
John de Authoy, 196
John Bacoun, 255
John de Badminton, 97 n94
John de Bamfeld, 253
John the Baptist, 114
John de Baseyvill, 262
John Basing, 121 n56
John de Basing, 107 n160
John de Bayton, 180 n49
John de Beccles, 207
John de Bedford, 225
John de Bloye, 258
John Bonet, 256
John de Bridgenorth (alias de Ponte), 138
John de Bruton, 257, 164 n159
John de Butterley, 97 n94, 121, 255
John Bygot, 229
John de Camezan, 99
John de Canterbury, 87, 259
John of the chamber of Bishop Hugh of Wells of Lincoln, 261
John de Cheam, 251, 256
John de Clara, 226
John de Clipston, 144–5, 180 n49
John de Colonna, 73
John de Crakehall, 113 n17, 118 n34, 192
John de Croindene, 230, 233
John le Cupper de Nottingham, 137 n3
John Drew, 260
John de Drokensford, 257
John de Dunstaple, 199
John de Dyham, 113 n17
John of England, 172
John Ertruri de Cadomo, 90
John de Farleye, 243
John fitz Robert, 187
John de Fledborough, 165
John le Fleming, 164, 195
John de Fotheringhay, 143, 150
John le Gentil, 171 n11
John de Gloucester, 76
John Gylet, 201 nn80–1, 202
John de Haddenham, 61
John de Houton, 259

John de Kemesey, 87 n33, 111, 113, 121, 125-6, 226
John de Lacy, 13
John de Lardario, 253
John de la Wade, 90, 150, 253
John de Leake, 71
John de Leicester, 196
John de Lewis, 125, 208 n118
John de Lindsey, 199
John de Littlinton, 226 n78
John de London, 97 n93, 207
John Mansel, 230
John Marmiun, 61
John de Merston, 20, 235 n130
John Monachus, cardinal deacon of Saint Eustace's, 257
John de Normanby, 114, 146
John Parisuis, 262
John de Ponte (alias de Bridgenorth), 138
John de Redberrow, 111, 228
John de Redingate, 106
John de Riston, 77, 113 n17, 181, 193, 201 n85
John de Romsey, 201 n79
John de Ros, clerk of Bishop Swinfield of Hereford, 216
John de Ros, legatee of Archbishop Winchelsey of Canterbury, 233
John Russel. *See Boke of Nurture*
John de Saint Clair, 225
John de Saint Ebulo, 101
John of Salisbury, 133
John de Schalby, 77, 164, 165 n165
John de Schelving, 87 n33, 126
    niece of, 126
John de Selvestone, 106
John de Sola Villa, 255
John de Sotebi, 56-7
John de Standon, 76 n202
John de Staneway, 228
John de Stebbenheath, 225
John de Stokes, 113 n17
John de Stoteville, 63
John de Stounesby, 171, 199
John de Swinfield, brother of Bishop Swinfield of Hereford, 87 n33, 126
John de Swinfield, clerk of Bishop Swinfield of Hereford, 87 n33
John Talbot, 122
John de Twytham, 230
John de la Wade, 90, 150, 253
John Walwain, 260

John de Wich, 237
John de Willingham, 56-7
John de Winchelsey, 230
John de York, 228, 231
Jolanus, cook of Bishop Gravesend of London, 260
Jordan, cardinal deacon of Saint Eustace's, 257
Jordan de London, 227
Joseph de Whixley, 63
Jumièges, Robert of (archbishop of Canterbury [1051-2]), 41 n4
justices/justiciars, royal, 91-2, 96, 109

Kemp, Brian, 205
Keston, church, 230 n105
Kettering, church, 55 n68
Keynsham Abbey, 170
Kilkenny, William of (bishop of Ely [1255-6]), 237
Kilwardby, Robert (archbishop of Canterbury [1273-8]), 49
king of England, 41, 51 n51, 52 n53, 57 n82, 73, 93, 96, 103-5, 109, 124, 128 n98, 134, 144, 161, 188, 190, 211, 238 n154, 247-9, 252-6. *See also* Edward I; Edward II; Henry II; Henry III; John; Richard I
    chancellor of, 258
king of France, 96 n86
Kirkby, John (bishop of Ely [1286-90]), 158 n129
Kirkham, Walter (bishop of Durham [1249-60]), 201, 202 n87, 236
Knapwell, church, 60-1
knight (as rank), 31-2, 147
knights, of bishops, 85, 89, 200-1, 257

Lambert, chamberlain of Bishop Longespee of Salisbury, 233 n117, 260
Lambeth,
    college at, 182
    Council of, 148
Lancing, church, 62 n110
Langton, church, 117
Langton, Stephen (archbishop of Canterbury [1207-28]), 9, 27, 31 n42, 46, 122, 170-1
    officialis of, 237
Langton, Walter (bishop of Coventry and Lichfield [1296-1321]), 85 n20, 90, 123, 220, 252, 257-8

Index

Laughton, church, 200
laundresses, 261
Laurence, farrier of Bishop Wyche of Chichester, 260
Laurence de Mause, 230
Laverstock, church, 56
Law, See also courts
    canon law, 4, 33, 39, 42–5, 53, 55–61, 65, 66 n130, 74, 116–17, 118 n39, 119 n46, 130–1, 133, 137, 141–2, 148, 150, 173, 179 n47, 225, 230, 240–1, 244–5
    Common Law, 43, 46 n27, 51–2, 57, 81 n3, 174, 240–1, 247, 249
Lawrence, C.H., 34
lawyers, 44, 83 n13, 94–5, 150, 155, 197, 257–8. See also proctors
    professional ethics of, 95
lay servants, 225, 232. See also bailiffs; bakers; barbers; brewers; butlers; carpenters; carters; chamberlains; cooks; farriers; foresters; grooms; laundresses; messengers; pantlers; pages; scullions; tailors; watchmen
Leake, mediety of, 71 n165
Ledbury, prebend of, 60 n101, 87 n33
Legbourne Priory, 162
Leicester, archdeacon of, 156.
    See also Ghent, Simon; Grosseteste, Robert; Martival, Roger de
Leicester, prebend of, 228
Leominster Priory, 172 n16
Leonard de Dunwich, 78, 113 n17
Letheringsett, church, 63
letter collections, 214–15
Leverton, mediety of, 71
Lewes,
    archdeaconry of, 230 n104
    priory, of, 103, 112, 175
Lexington, Henry de (bishop of Lincoln [1254–8]), 193–4, 198, 201, 202
    officialis of, 193 n29
Lichfield cathedral,
    "bursal" prebend in, 183
    dean of, 114
Lincoln, 198, 199 n65. See also Lacy, Robert de
    archdeacon of, 71 n165, 76–7, 114, 154, 165, 179 n46, 181, 183.
    See also John de Riston; Peter, archdeacon of Lincoln; Roger de Fuldon; William de Estiniaco; William de la Gare; William Lupus
    official of, 131 n112, 165 n166, 220
    archdeaconries of, 193
    bishops of, 13, 55, 103, 111 n5, 114, 118 n34, 119 n41, 153–4, 183, 236.
    See also Avalon, Saint Hugh of; Blois, William of; Dalderby, John; Gravesend, Richard; Grosseteste, Robert; Lexington, Henry de; Sutton, Oliver; Wells, Hugh of
    longevity of, 202
    officialis of, 77 n207
    citizen of, 163
    dean and chapter of, 33, 220
    chapter of, 181, 192, 198 n57, 207, 216
    chancellor of cathedral, 174 n24
    dean of, 194 n32, 197, 213.
    See also Richard de Mepham
    prebends of, 122 n62, 183
    precentor of, 112 n11
    provost of chapter common fund, 197, 199–200
    treasurer, 195 n35
    vicars choral of, 128
    diocese of, 77–8, 119 n41, 178–80, 190–202, 206, 234
    officiales sede vacante, 156
    Saint Katherine's Priory, 80, 178
Lindridge, church, 121
Little Bytham, church, 179 n48
Little Malvern, prior of, 140 n20
Little Rollright, church, 180 n50
Littleborough, church, 50 n48
Llandaff, bishop of, 15, 230.
    See also Saltmarsh, William de; Goldcliff, William de
    officiales sede vacante, 156
Llanthony Priory, 48 n37
London, 126, 199, 235 n130, 259
    archdeacons of. See John de Bedford
    officiales sede vacante, 156
    bishops of, 73. See also Gravesend, Richard; Sandwich, Henry de
    cathedral of, 17, 101
    dean of. See Hervey de Boreham
    Councils of, 87 n33, 126 n83, 132
    Tower of, 17
Longespee, Nicholas (bishop of Salisbury [1292–97]), 226, 232, 233 n117, 234, 260
    vicar of, 226

lords/lordship, 36–7. *See also* secular lords
Lower Heyford, church 180 n50
Ludford Parva, church, 56–7
Luke, son of Peter, 103
Luke de Abingdon, 49
Luke de Bré, 161, 207
Luke de Cailly, 140 n20
Lusignan, Aymer de (bishop–elect and bishop of Winchester [1250–60, 1260]), 32–3, 68

Madley, prebend of, 88 n33
Maidstone, church of, 15
Maidstone, Ralph (bishop of Hereford [1234–9]), 37
Malmesbury Abbey, 54, 62, 173
  infirmary of, 173
March, William (bishop of Bath and Wells [1293–1302]), 237
Markby Priory, 164, 165 n165
Marple, Miss, 3, 10
marriage of heir, 125
Marsh, Richard (bishop of Durham [1217–26]), 65
Marshal, Henry (bishop of Exeter [1194–1206]), 50
marshals, of bishops' households, 180 n49, 232–3, 260–2
Martin Creuker, 76
Martin of the kitchen of Bishop Suffield of Norwich, 262
Martin de Saint Cross, 201 n80, 202 n87
Martival, Roger (bishop of Salisbury [1315–30], archdeacon of Huntingdon and Leicester), 111, 113, 164 n164
Mary, image of, 229, 231
Masca, Pandulph (bishop of Norwich [1222–6]), 59, 143
  officialis of, 206
Matilda, laundress of Bishop Suffield of Norwich, 261
Matthew, cardinal deacon of Saint Mary's in Porticu, 257
Matthew, chaplain of Bishop Suffield of Norwich 229
Matthew Orsini, 257
Matthew Paris, 17 n21, 72, 128 n95, 188, 219
Maurice de Arundel, 63 n119, 72
Maurienne, bishop of, 227

Medbourne, church, 78
Mere, Hospital of, 178 n44
Merinecus, legatee of Bishop Aquablanca of Hereford, 262
Merton, church, 180 n50
Merton, Walter (bishop of Rochester [1274–77], chancellor of the archbishop of York, royal chancellor), 20, 107, 118 n34, 127, 206 n111, 235–6, 258
  officialis of, 107, 206 n111
Merton Priory, 61
messengers, 261–3
Michael de Fiennes, 253
Michael de Leigh, 147
Mickleton, church, 58–9
Middlesex, archdeacon of. *See* Ralph de Malling
missals. *See* books
miter, 227
Modbury Priory, 50
monasteries, 71. *See also* individual houses
money (as legacy), 225, 230, 233–4
  individual money legacies, 226–31, 233, 260–3
Monnington on Wye, church, 62
Moorman, J.R.H., 10
Morbourne, church, 38
Moreton Parva, prebend of, 87 n33, 216 n33
Morton, church, 60 n101
mules (as legacies), 226
Mumby, church, 165 n165

N. de B., grantee of a pension from Bishop Langton of Coventry and Lichfield, 252
Neasham Priory, 120–1
Neubald, prebend of, 256
Neville, Ralph (bishop of Chichester [1224–44]), 171, 175, 218, 225 n76
Newent Priory, 113
Newport. *See* Saint John in Newport
Newton on Trent, church, 180 n50
Nicholas, brewer of Bishop Suffield of Norwich, 261
Nicholas, chamberlain of Bishop Giffard of Worcester, 262
Nicholas, *janitor* of Archbishop Winchelsey of Canterbury, 233

Nicholas, page of Bishop Suffield of Norwich, 261
Nicholas IV. *See taxatio* of Nicholas IV
Nicholas de Appletree, 115, 147, 180 n49
Nicholas de Blaston, 252
Nicholas Castelle, 253
Nicholas de Chilbauton, 58–9, 246
Nicholas Elys. *See* Durand, son of Nicholas Elys
Nicholas de Evesham, 198
Nicholas de Geneville, 93–4
Nicholas de Hodenet, 262
Nicholas de Knovile, 161
Nicholas de Oxford, 226
Nicholas de Reigate, 87 n33, 112
Nicholas de Romsey, 26
Nicholas de Saint Victor, 106
Nicholas Syre, 262
Nicholas Tessun, 198
Nonnington, prebend of, 87 n33
Norfolk, archdeacon of. *See* Ralph de Blonvilla
Normanby, church, 76
Northampton, archdeacon of, 147. *See also* Stephen de Sutton; Thomas de Sutton
Northampton,
　Saint Andrew's, church, 71 n166
　Saint Andrew's Priory, 56
　Saint James's Abbey, 198
　Saint John's Hospital, 178–80
Northamptonshire eyre, 101 n120
North Newbald, prebend of, 92
North Somercotes, Saint Mary's, church, 162 n154
Northmoor, church, 173
Norton,
　chapel of, 173
　church, 54
Norwich,
　bishops of, 46, 48, 108, 119–20, 125, 129, 137, 170, 188. *See also* Gray, John; Pandulph; Raleigh, William; Suffield, Walter; Walton, Simon
　officialis of, 205, 217
　diocese of, 62 n111, 69 n147, 119 n41
Noseley, 111
notaries, 6, 89–90, 102 n122, 108, 144, 149, 175 n29, 180 n49, 186–7, 207 n118, 208 n118, 211, 227
nuntii. *See* messengers
Nympsfield, church, 61

O. de Grandisson, 256
Oakley, church, 145
oaths, 28–30, 33, 44–5, 49, 90, 110, 111 n2, 129, 147–58, 165 n166, 166, 186, 241, 244, 253
Ockendon, church, 39
officiales (bishop's), 6, 129, 212, 217.
　See also Adam de Hailes; Alan de Beccles; Andrew de Kilkenny; Bernard of Champagne; Blund, Richard; Bronscombe, Walter; Canterbury, archbishop of; Cantilupe, Thomas; Cantilupe, Walter; Carlisle, bishop of; Exeter, bishop of; Coventry and Lichfield, bishop of; Durham, bishop of; Exeter, bishop of; Giffard, Godfrey; Giffard, Walter; Hereford, bishop of; Lexington, Henry de; Lincoln, bishop of; Gravesend, Richard, bishop of Lincoln; Grosseteste, Robert; John de Alvechurch; Luke de Bré; Merton, Walter; Pecham, John; Peter de Auxon; Ralph de Kyme; Richard de Newport; Robert de Gloucester; Robert de Hastings; Robert de Wyse; Sutton, Oliver; Thomas de Freckenham; Warham, Ranulph; Winchester, bishop of; Worcester, bishop of; York, archbishop of
officiales sede vacante. *See* Hereford; Llandaff; London; Pecham, John; Rochester; Salisbury; Winchester
offertories, 226
Ogbourne, church, 71 n166
old age, 78–9
Oliver Chesney, 198
Oliver Sutton (the younger), 78
ordination, 24, 33, 36, 43, 71, 75, 77, 93 n69, 112 n9, 117 n31, 119, 132, 134, 143 n33, 144 n38, 151, 161, 173 n22, 180 n49, 195 n34, 196 n40, 227
Orléans, 206
Orsethe. *See* Simon, rector of Orsethe
Orton, church, 137
Osbert, prebendary of Bosham, 67
Osbert, rector of Ludford Parva, 56–7
Ospringe, dean of, 14
Otho, papal legate, 46 n23, 54–5
Ottobuono, papal legate, 37, 55, 77 n205

Oxford,
  archdeaconry of, 154 n94.
    See also Ghent, Simon; Gravesend, Richard
  Saint Ebbe's, church, 180 n50
  Saint Frideswide's Priory, 100–1
  University, chancellor of, 159 n134

Paganus, legatee of Bishop Hugh of Wells of Lincoln, 261
pages, 89, 261
Pagham, church, 73
Paignton, church, 253
Pandulph. See Masca, Pandulph
pantlers, 233
Papacy, 26, 35, 37 n78, 39, 41, 57 n82, 67–9, 73–4, 88 n33, 91, 96–7, 99–100, 102, 105 n144, 110, 115–20, 124, 134, 149, 152, 175, 179 n47, 182 n57, 198 n57, 217 n35, 221–2, 235, 247, 249, 257. See also Alexander III; Boniface VIII; cardinals; Celestine V; Clement IV; Gregory IX; Honorius III; Innocent III; Innocent IV; Nicholas IV
  papal chancellor, 255
  papal chaplains, 57, 99, 217, 251, 256
  papal exemptions/dispensations, 19, 26, 78, 116–20
  papal *hostiarius*, 217, 256
  papal letters, form of, 220–1
  papal *nepos*, 103
  papal penitentiary, 216 n27, 222
  papal provisions, 103, 105 n144, 109 n175, 152, 154, 183, 195 n35
  papal scribe, 59
  papal subdeacon, 101
  papal reservations of benefices, 67 n139, 109 n175
  reform plan for curial income, 134, 184–5
  vice–chancellor of, 257
Partney, church, 174 n25
pastoral care, 3, 5, 10–11, 240
Pecham, John (archbishop of Canterbury [1279–92]), 16, 18–19, 28, 49, 70, 76, 90, 92, 114, 117 n34, 125, 129, 137–8, 146, 149, 152–3, 156, 161, 174–6, 207, 213, 217, 219, 222, 237, 252, 257
  commissary general of, 174 n25
  officiales of, 156, 207 n118

officiales of, *sede vacante*, 156
registrar of, 207 n118
penance, 26, 114–15, 120, 137–8, 146–7, 166
penitentiaries, 156–7, 162, 163 n157.
  See also papacy, papal penitentiary
Penrith, church, 161
pensions,
  pensions from churches, 49, 61, 62 n111, 63–4, 79, 80
  pensions *de camera*, 4, 39, 44, 80–109, 136, 150, 155, 183 n66, 217, 245, 251–9
  simple versus in lieu of a benefice defined, 82
Pershore Abbey, 93 n70
Peter, archdeacon of Lincoln, 73
Peter, baker of Bishop Suffield of Norwich, 261
Peter, grantee of pension from Bishop Bronscombe of Exeter, 258
Peter, messenger of Bishop Aquablanca of Hereford, 262
Peter, prebendary of Salisbury, 38–9
Peter, son of Durand de Lincoln, 163 n157
Peter de Abingdon, 107
Peter de Auxon, 229 n94
Peter de Avebari, 237 n146
Peter of Blois, 37, 39, 187 n4, 208 n121, 221 n65
Peter Caballus, 140 n20
Peter de Chevermunt, 183
Peter de Cotintone, 261
Peter de Dalderby, 75
Peter de Grossis, 257
Peter *dictus* Haverwell, 102 n125
Peter de Langon, 60
Peter de Leicester, 19, 44, 53, 69, 139, 142, 158–9, 162, 207, 246–7
Peter de Montecute, 100, 105
Peter de Saint Maur, archdeacon of Surrey, 68
Peter de Stamford, 193
Peter de Thoresby, 26 n14, 201 n83
Peter de Vienne, 253, 258
Peterborough,
  church, 64 n123
  Abbey/abbot of, 55 n68, 64 n123, 86, 179 n49, 180 n49
Philip, Master, legatee of Bishop Wyche of Chichester, 230
Philip de Barton, 67
Philip de Fauconberg, 204 n97

Index

Philip Martel, 258
Philip de Saint Austolo, 254
Philip de Saint Helen, 201 nn79–80, 202 n87
Philip le Say, 254
Philip de Swayfield, 164
Philip de Willoughby, 106
physicians, 117 n34, 215 n26
Piccardus, legatee of Bishop Aquablanca of Hereford, 262
Piddington, church, 179 n48, 180 n50
pigs, 260
Pipewell Abbey, 38
plate (as legacies), 225, 226 n78, 228, 260. *See also* cups, ewers, spoons
Pocklington, church, 137
Poncius de Cors, 165
Pont-Audemer, Hospital of, 173
Pontesbury, portions of, 60 nn101–2
Pontoise, John of (bishop of Winchester [1282–1304]; archdeacon of Exeter), 28–9, 57, 104, 139, 142, 143 n30, 218–19, 254–5
  register of, 85 n18
Poore, Richard (bishop of Durham [1228–37]; bishop of Salisbury [1217–28]), 34, 65 n125, 120–1, 172–3, 236
Prebends, 38, 47, 98, 104. *See also* specific prebends
Premonstratensians, 50 n48
Preston, prebend of 60 n101
prisons, bishops', 14, 18, 139, 146–8, 166
probate, 76 n197, 115 n25, 124, 130 n106, 145 n41, 147 n52, 161, 181 n56, 195 n34, 196 n39, 217, 234, 236. *See also* executors
proctors, 6, 43–4, 45 n21, 77 n205, 83 n13, 87, 88 n33, 90–1, 108, 115, 117–18, 121, 126 n83, 139 n27, 142, 147 n52, 152, 155–7, 164, 179 n47, 181, 196 n38, 201 n80, 207, 216 n27, 217 n35, 229–30, 237, 245, 252, 259. *See also* lawyers
procurations, 71 n161, 99, 123–4, 133
professions of obedience (suffragan to metropolitan), 149
protection by bishops, 114–15
psalters. *See* books
pugilarii, 87, 88 n33, 94
punishment, 3, 5, 10, 44, 70, 136–66, 187, 212, 224, 239–41, 244–7, 249
Pytchley, church, 77, 179 n49

Quarrington, church, 195 n35
queen of England, 91 n53, 92–3, 94 n73, 99 n101, 109, 232, 254, 256
Quivil, Peter (bishop of Exeter [1280–91]), 90–2, 102 n125, 148 n61, 150, 253–4, 258

R., plaintiff against bishop of Wells, 82
R. de Arundel, 63 n116
R. de Bremertone, 258
Raleigh, William (bishop of Norwich [1239–43], bishop of Winchester [1244–50]), 204, 206
Ralph, clerk among the valets of Bishop Swinfield of Hereford, 89
Ralph, doorman of the chamber of Bishop Suffield of Norwich, 261
Ralph, marshal of Bishop Wyche of Chichester, 260
Ralph de Geyton, 163
Ralph de Hengham, 73, 256
Ralph de Kyme, 246
Ralph de Malling, 73
Ralph de Salop, 76 n200
Ralph de Waraville, 193
Ralph de Watervile, 93 n69, 252
Ralph le Weyte, 233
Ramsbury. *See* Robert, vicar of Ramsbury
Ramsey Abbey, 60–1, 96, 100, 104, 109, 143 n33, 176
Ranulph de Rye, 53
Ranulph de Warham. *See* Warham, Ranulph
Rationes dictandae of Bologna, 221
Ravendale Priory, 181
Raymond Hispanus, 257
Reading Abbey, 172
rectories, rectors, 31–3, 35–8, 47, 50, 121. *See also* individual churches and rectors
Reginald, carter of Bishop Hugh of Wells of Lincoln, 261
Reginald de Brandon, 108
Reginald de Cusaunce, 63
Reginald de Saint Albans, 217 n35
Reginald de Treilly, 261
registers,
  bishops', 8–9, 84–5, 112–13, 116, 150–3, 155–7, 173, 176, 190–1, 211, 215
  of the Court of Arches, 143

registers (cont.)
   monastic, 85–6, 106
   papal, 26, 115, 176
registrar, bishops', 6, 77, 151, 164, 207 n118
Remigius de Pocklington, 78, 113 n17, 198
reward (general topic, not instances), 3–4, 111, 239–44, 248–9
Richard, carter of Bishop Suffield of Norwich, 261
Richard, clerk and almoner of Archbishop Winchelsey of Canterbury, 230
Richard, cobbler of Bishop Suffield of Norwich, 262
Richard, marshal of Archbishop Winchelsey of Canterbury, 233
Richard, marshal of Bishop Hugh of Wells of Lincoln, 261
Richard, marshal of Bishop Gravesend of London, 260
Richard, son of Richard de Lat, 255
Richard, tailor of Bishop Aquablanca of Hereford, 262
Richard, vicar of Peterborough, 64 n123
Richard I of England, 172
Richard de Bello, 126
   boy of, 126
Richard de Bromholm, 194, 199
Richard de Dale, 112
Richard de Douai, 29, 218
Richard Filliol, 260
Richard de Fingest, 198
Richard de Fremyngham, 254
Richard de Gloucester, 175
Richard Gravesend, *nepos* of Bishop Richard Gravesend of London, 226 n78, 232 n116
Richard de Grosherst, 233
Richard de Gryndeham, 253
Richard de Hertford, 87 n33
Richard de Horton, 195
Richard de Ispania, 261
Richard de Lat. See Richard, son of Richard de Lat
Richard de Linwood, 192
Richard de Ludlow, 145
Richard de Mepham, 67
Richard de Merton, 111
Richard de Newport, 225
Richard de Oxford, 192 n25
Richard de Palgrave, 164
Richard Paz, 164 n160

Richard de Persouere de Ludlow, 145
Richard de Pocklington, 179, 198
Richard de Puddlestone, 88 nn33–4, 89 n35, 152
Richard de Rothwell, 195, 200
Richard de la Sole, 175 n29
Richard de Sottwell, 150, 226
Richard de Tirington, 28
Richard de Totnes, 186–7
Richard de Tubervile, 107 n160
Richard de Wansford, 64 n123
Richard Wyche. See Wyche, Richard
Richard de Wisbech, 198
Richard de Wolvy, 252
Richard de Wyndesor, 192 n25
Richmond, archdeacon/archdeaconry of, 137. See also Honorius, Master
Rigaud, Eudes (archbishop of Rouen [1248–75]), 176 n33
rings, 227, 229
Ripple, church, 228
Robert, baker of Bishop Wyche of Chichester, 260
Robert, brewer of Bishop Giffard of Worcester, 262
Robert, clerk of the chapel of Bishop Swinfield of Hereford, 89
Robert, farrier of Bishop Aquablanca of Hereford, 262–3
Robert, vicar of Ramsbury, 226 n83
Robert, vicar of Saint Albans, Spridlington, 163 n157
Robert Avenal, 201 n83, 236
Robert de Balliol, 212 n7
Robert de Benningworth, 56–7
Robert Bernard, 164 n159
Robert de Blonvilla, 73
Robert de Bolsover, 193
Robert de Bremertone, 258
Robert de Burton, 163
Robert de Cadney, 198
Robert de Chafford, 163 n157
Robert de Cilahurst, 230 n102
Robert de Crowhurst, 230
Robert Deynte, 263
Robert de Driffield, 201 n82
Robert de Dunholm, 179 n47
Robert de Essex, 188 n8
Robert de Farleye, 225
Robert de Gloucester, 88 n33, 237 n145. See also Robert de Wyse
Robert de Gravele, 193

Robert de Gray, 256
Robert de Grendon, 115
Robert Haget, 117
Robert Harlond, 263
Robert de Hastings, 230
Robert de Iernumue, 226 n83
Robert de Kibworth, 164 n161, 179
Robert de Kirmington, 181
Robert de Lacy, 13, 18, 20
Robert de Lafford, 216
Robert de Littlebury, 108
Robert de Marisco, 194
Robert de Pratellis, 164
Robert de Redeswell, 226
Robert de Ros, 256
Robert de Ruddeby, 207 n116
Robert de Saint Agatha, 193, 198, 236
Robert de Saint Meldred, 201 n79
Robert de Sanford, 233
Robert de Scarborough, 44, 63, 70, 142
Robert de Sidesterne, 117 n34
Robert de Sixil, 180 n49
Robert de Swillington, 164
Robert Tailor, 262
Robert de Warsop, 179 n47
Robert de Wiche, 139
Robert de Wyche. *See* Robert de Gloucester
Robert de Worcester, 55–6
Robert de Wyse, 16–19, 146, 226, 237
Robert of York, 177
robes. *See* clothing
Roches, Peter des (bishop of Winchester [1205–38]), 172, 204
Rochester, 235 n130
    bishops of, 203. *See also* Merton, Walter
    officiales sede vacante, 156
    priory of, 66 n133
Rodes, Robert E., 240
Rodington, church, 55 n69
Roger, bishop of Worcester (1164–79), 206
Roger, carter at Hoxne of Bishop Suffield of Norwich, 261
Roger, former keeper of the park of Bishop Aquablanca of Hereford, 262
Roger, *hostiarius* of Bishop Gravesend of London, 233
Roger, marshal of Bishop Hugh of Wells of Lincoln, 261
Roger, son of Adam, nepos of Brother William, papal *hostiarius*, 255
Roger, son of William, legatee of Bishop Hugh of Wells of Lincoln, 261

Roger de Auckland, 201 n81
Roger Bacon, 192
Roger de Beaufoy, 71 n165
Roger de Bello Campo, 254
Roger Blund, 198
Roger de Bristol, 197
Roger de Bohun, 197
Roger de Burwardescot. *See* Roger de Buscot
Roger de Buscot, 198
Roger Caperon, 87
Roger de Dartford, 164 n160
Roger le Estrange, 254
Roger de Fretwell, 113 n17
Roger de Fuldon, 162 n154
Roger de Hertford, 65–6
Roger de Martival. *See* Martival, Roger
Roger of Noyers, 35
Roger of the pantry of Bishop Gravesend of London, 260
Roger Pincerna, 118, 204 n101
Roger de Raveningham, 229
Roger de Rothwell, 55 n68
Roger Rufus, 164 n160
Roger le Rus. *See* Roger Rufus
Roger de Seaton, 201 n81, 236
Roger de Sevenake, 88 n33
Roger de Sixil, 162, 180 n49, 200
Roger Strik, 260
rolls of institutions. *See* registers, bishops'
Rome. *See* papacy
Romeyn, John (archbishop of York [1286–96]), 18–20, 39, 44, 63, 70, 92, 115, 137, 142, 146, 213 n15, 216, 256
Ross, 139
    church, 60 n101, 126 n85
Ross-on-Wye, church, 87 n33, 113, 121
Rouen, archbishops of, 41 n4, 206. *See also* Rigaud, Eudes
Rowing, church, 172
royal government. *See* courts (secular); law (Common law); king of England; king of France
Rubinettus, butler of Bishop Aquablanca of Hereford, 262
Rudby, church, 110
rural deans, 6, 35, 37 n86, 122, 129–30, 219–20, 247. *See also* Guildford; Holland; Ospringe; Weobbley

Saint Alban's Abbey, 99
Saint Albans, Spridlington, 163 n157

Saint Asaph,
  archdeacons of. *See* Griffin, archdeacon of Saint Asaph
  bishops of. *See* Anian II
Saint Bartholomew's Priory, London, 17 n21
Saint Cutherbert's, church, 96
Saint David's,
  bishops of. *See* Carew, Richard de; Wallensis, Thomas
  diocese of, 16
Saint Decuman's, church, 51
Saint Ebbe's, Oxford, church, 180 n50
Saint Elizabeth, chapel of, 66
Saint Eustace's, church, 257
Saint Frideswide's Priory. *See* Oxford, Saint Frideswide's Priory
Saint Fromund's Priory, Séez, 164, 181
Saint Giles' Hospital, 261
Saint Guthlac's Priory, 62
Saint Hugh of Avalon. *See* Avalon, Saint Hugh of
Saint John, Northampton, Hospital of. *See* Northampton, Hospital of Saint John
Saint John in Jerusalem, Hospital of, 108, 171
Saint John in Newport, church, 146
Saint Katherine's Priory, Lincoln. *See* Lincoln, Saint Katherine's Priory
Saint Mary de Gloria, Anagni, monastery of, 101
Saint Mary's and All Saints, prebend in college of Warwick Saint Mary's, 123
Saint Mary's, North Somercotes, church, 162 n154
Saint Mary's in Porticu, church, 257
Saint Merryn, church, 258
Saint Neot's Priory, 180 n49
Saint Nicholas's Abbey, Angers. *See* Angers
Saint Paul, 114
Saint Peter, 114
Saint Peter's, Stamford. *See* Stamford, Saint Peter's
Saint Thomas's Hospital, Southwark, 18
Salisbury, 235 n130
  bishops of, 52–4, 68, 88 n33, 111, 137 n3, 183, 204. *See also* Bingham, Robert; Bohun, Jocelin de; Bridport, Giles; Ghent, Simon; Longespee, Nicholas; Martival, Roger; Poore, Richard; Wickhampton, Robert; Wyle, Walter de la
  dean and chapter of, 172
  prebends in cathedral of, 183
  treasurer of, his vicar, 226 n83
  vicars choral of, 226 n83
  diocese of, 71, 156, 172, 198
  officiales sede vacante, 156
Saint Martin's, Salisbury, church, 52
Salop, archdeacons/archdeaconry of, 122. *See also* Adam de Fileby; James de Aquablanca; John de Swinfield
Saltmarsh, William de (bishop of Llandaff [1186–91]), 48 n37
Salvagius de Florence, 253
Sandwich, Henry de (bishop of London [1263–73]), 238
Sarsden, church, 180 n50
Saunderton, church, 175
Savoy, Boniface of (archbishop of Canterbury [1245–70]), 17, 228–9, 232, 253
  officialis of, 229 n94
  vicar-general of, 229 n94
Savoy, count of, 255
Sayers, Jane E., 221
Scot the naked, legatee of Bishop Suffield of Norwich, 262
scullions, 233
seals/sealers/sealing, 6, 55, 130–4, 186–7, 189, 213
secular lords (not individuals), 98, 200, 207, 223 n72, 238 n154, 247–9
Séez, Saint Fromund's Priory, 164
Semman of the kitchen of Bishop Suffield of Norwich, 261
seneschals, 7, 88 n33, 114, 126, 175, 212, 231
sequestrator, 6, 157, 163, 164 n164. *See also* Sutton, Oliver
sergeants at law, 83 n13
Shaftsbury Abbey, 175
Sheehan, M. M., 160
Shelford Priory, 165
Sherburn, church, 178
Sherington, 111
Shrewsbury, prior of, 108
Shropshire, archdeaconry of, 60 n101
Shropshire Eyre, 34
Sibbertoft, church, 174
Silvester, Master, clerk of Roger, Bishop of Worcester and of Bishop Baldwin of Forde, 206

Simon (little), legatee of Bishop Suffield of Norwich, 261
Simon, rector of Ailby. *See* Simon de Luda
Simon, rector of Orsethe, 226 n78
Simon, smith of Bishop Suffield of Norwich, 261
Simon de Ardern, 113 n17
Simon Constable, 113 n17
Simon Langton, 122
Simon de Luda, 76, 195, 197
Simon Sauage, 262
Simon de Schelving, 126
Simon de Senliz, 218
Simon de Tarring, 230
simony, 4, 27–30, 38, 43, 57, 66, 130, 177 n39, 244
Sion, dean of. *See* Peter de Vienne
skinners, 262
Slipton, church, 180 n50
Smith, David M., 59–60, 175, 192
smiths, 255, 261
Snarford, church, 171 n11
Sotby, church, 163 n157
Souldern, church, 180 n50
South Creake, church, 59
South Stoke, church 180 n50
Southwell, church, 56
Spencer, Andrew, 243–4
spirituality, 10, 239–40
spoons, 229
Spridlington, Saint Albans, church, 163 n157
Stafford, archdeacon of, 123
Saint Mary's Binewerk, Stamford, 55
Stamford, Saint Peter's, church, 181
Stanton, 122 n62
Staunton, church, 180 n50
Stapleford, church, 179 n46, 180 n50
Stephen, *nuntius* of Bishop Suffield of Norwich, 261
Stephen Ambrois, 230
Stephen of the buttery of Archbishop Winchelsey of Canterbury, 233
Stephen de Castello, 192
Stephen de Chichester, 197
Stephen de Doene, 55
Stephen the goldsmith, Master, 255
Stephen de Gravesend, 164 n164
Stephen de Monte Luelli, 229 n94
Stephen de Montgomery, 146
Stephen de Suchie, 252

Stephen de Sutton, 115
Stephen de Thanet, 88 n33, 126
Steppingley, church, 61
stewards, 7, 44, 53, 69, 106 n152, 124, 142, 156, 164 n160, 189, 205, 218, 228 n90, 236–7, 246–7. *See also* Peter de Leicester; seneschals
Stichill, Robert (bishop of Durham [1261–74]), 201, 236
stipends, 26, 34 n60, 46, 80, 89, 96, 99 n101, 132, 137 n3, 184
Stone, church, 143
Stow, archdeacon/archdeaconry of, 114 n25, 153 n93, 180 n49. *See also* Durand de Lincoln; William, son of Fulk; Willliam de Ockham; William de Sausthorpe
Stow Park, 198
Studley, Prioress of, 193 n29
Sturminster Marshall, church, 173
Sudbury, archdeacon of, 118 n37
Suffield, Walter (bishop of Norwich [1245–57]), 37, 188, 229, 231–2, 236, 261–2
Suffolk, archdeacon of. *See* Roger Pincerna
suffragan bishops (without sees in England), 91
Sulby Abbey, 174
summoners, 89 n36
Surrey, archdeacons/archdeaconry of, 68, 73, 118, 124
Sutton, church, 75
Sutton, Oliver (bishop of Lincoln [1280–99]), 37, 56–8, 70–1, 76–7, 93, 111–15, 131 n112, 143–7, 153 n95, 154, 156–7, 160–5, 175, 179, 180 n49, 181, 190, 194–7, 199–200, 202, 218–19, 234, 254
officialis of, 112, 157, 179 n49, 195 n34, 200
registrar of. *See* John de Schalby
sequestrator of, 163, 164 n164
Swinfield, Richard (bishop of Hereford [1283–1317], clerk of Bishop Cantilupe of Hereford), 9, 29, 87–9, 90 n48, 93–4, 99 n101, 111–13, 121–2, 126, 138–9, 145–6, 152, 165, 175, 216, 237, 259
household roll of, 87–9
officialis of, 88 n33

tailors, 233, 262
Taunton, archdeacon of. *See* Peter de Avebari, Philip de Saint Quentin
Tarvin, church, 252
Tawstock, church, 139
taxatio of Nicholas IV, 30–1, 35, 100
taxation, 110, 115
Tewkesbury Abbey, 97–8, 112, 158, 162, 246–7
Teynham, church, 114
Theddlethorpe, church, 162
Theobald, archbishop of Canterbury (1139–61), 129
Theobald de Bar, 73, 254–5
Theobald de Kent, 197–8
Theydon Mount, 179 n47
Thomas, baker of Archbishop Winchelsey of Canterbury, 233
Thomas, baker of Bishop Aquablanca of Hereford, 263
Thomas, carter of Bishop Hugh of Wells of Lincoln, 261
Thomas, marshal of Bishop Hugh of Wells of Lincoln, 261
Thomas, *seccus* of Bishop Aquablanca of Hereford, 262
Thomas, watchman of Bishop Giffard of Worcester, 262
Thomas de Ashby, 113 n17, 192, 198
Thomas de Birland, 112, 115
Thomas de Bitton, 100, 251
Thomas de Blakesly, 108
Thomas de Brugge, 87, 94
Thomas de Cantebrigg, 103
Thomas de Cobham, 106, 230
Thomas de la Dane, 88 n33, 126
Thomas de Fiskerton, 192
Thomas de Freckenham, 203 n92, 237
Thomas Gaylhun, 173
Thomas de Gentham, 43–4
Thomas de Grimestone, 212 n7
Thomas de Hertford, 237
Thomas de Kirkeswold, 161
Thomas de Levesham, 201 nn82–3, 202, 236
Thomas de Luda (dictus Malherb), 76, 162
Thomas de Perariis, 165
Thomas de Porres de Maidestane, 58 n83
Thomas de Port, 57 n83
Thomas de Port de Maydenstan. *See* Thomas de Porres de Maidestane

Thomas de Rumesi, 118
Thomas de Standon, 75
Thomas Stede, 64
Thomas de Sutton, 58, 63–4, 143
Thomas de Windsor, 99, 252
Thomas de Wycheford, 227
Thornbury, church, 158, 246–7
Thornholm Priory, 162, 200
Thorpenhow, 17
Thoward, legatee of Bishop Suffield of Norwich, 261
Threxton, church, 63 n114
Tillington, church, 112
Tilmanstone, church, 171
Titchfield Abbey, 172
Totnes,
  archdeacon of. *See* Thomas de Hertford
  church, 62 n113
Tretire, church, 60 n101
Trot, legatee of Bishop Suffield of Norwich, 262
trust between bishops and clerks, 95, 140–1, 244–7
Twynham Priory, 61 n105
Twyning, church, 139

vestments, 121, 227
vicarages/vicars, 26, 32–4, 37, 47–51, 62 n111, 68, 99 n101, 119–20, 152 n85, 170–3, 199. *See also* individual churches and vicars
vicars–general, bishops', 76, 155, 171, 179 n46, 199, 226, 229 n94, 230, 237 n145. *See also* vicegerens
vicars choral, 26, 49
vice–archdeacon, 6
vicegerens, bishops', 194. *See also* vicars–general
Vincent, Nicholas, 189

W. de Saint Quentin, 122
W. de Smalebrok, 251
Wakke, legatee of Bishop Suffield of Norwich, 261
Walens, cook of Bishop Hugh of Wells of Lincoln, 261
Wales
  custom of, 48 n37
  prince of, 92
Wales, Thomas of. *See* Wallensis, Thomas
Walgrave, church, 58

Wallensis, Thomas (bishop of Saint David's [1248–55]), 237 n149
Walter, carpenter of Bishop Longespee of Salisbury, 260
Walter, *hostiarius* of Bishop Hugh of Wells of Lincoln, 261
Walter, Hubert (archbishop of Canterbury [1193–1205]), 66 n135, 69, 205, 207, 236, 245
Walter, page of Bishop Aquablanca of Hereford, 263
Walter, vicar of Appleby, 162
Walter, vicar of Totnes, 62 n113
Walter de Bauntone, 253
Walter de Berton, 228
Walter le Boteler, 20
Walter Burdon, 152
Walter de Campeden, 230
Walter de Clipston, 252
Walter de Eylesbury, 171
Walter de Fotheringhay, 181
Walter de Gray, 255
Walter Gray, 260
Walter of Guisborough, 17
Walter Hervey, 52 n52, 111 n2
Walter Lithfot of the Buttery of Bishop Gravesend of London, 260
Walter de Loddiswell, 186–7
Walter de London, 226 n78
Walter de Luda, 162
Walter de Malling, 162, 195–6
Walter de Merrow. *See* William de Merrow
Walter de Merton. *See* Merton, Walter
Walter de Norton, 71
Walter de Rudmarley, 237
Walter de Selby, 201 nn79–80, 202 n87
Walter de Somercote, 203 n92
Walter de Thorp, 161
Walter de Vienne, 117–18
Walter de Wooton, 112, 115
Walter de Wyke, 260
Walter de Wylburham, 258
Walton, Simon (bishop of Norwich [1258–66]), 205, 207 n116
officialis of, 205
Walton-on-Trent, 76 n200
Ward de Hansingham, 262
wardship, 125
Warham, Ranulph (bishop of Chichester [1218–22], *officialis* of the bishop of Norwich), 204–5
Warin de Boys, 259

Warpsgrove, church, 178
Warsop, church, 147 n52
Warwick Saint Mary's, college of, 123
watchmen, 233, 261–2
Waverley, abbot of, 212
Weedon Pinkney, church, 71 n166
Welbeck Abbey, 50 n48
Wellington, prebend of, 87 n33, 138
Wells,
    archdeaconry of, 122
    cathedral/dean and chapter of, 49, 82 n9, 84 n15, 92, 149
    chancellorship of, 100
    precentorship of, 251
Wells, Hugh of (bishop of Lincoln [1209–35]), 31 n42, 174–5, 179, 183, 191–2, 196–8, 201, 228–9, 231, 261
Weobbley, dean of, 175 n29
Weseham, Roger (bishop of Coventry and Lichfield [1245–56]), 121 n56
West Alvington, church, 172
West Kerle, church, 255
Westbury, church, 60 n101, 145, 246 n26
Westcott Barton, church, 180 n50
Wetheral
    church, 48
    priory of, 48
Wheathampstead, 196 n41
Wherwell Abbey, 54 n67, 85 n18
Whitbourne, church, 60 n101
Whitfield, 180 n50
Whitney, church, 175 n29
Whixley, church, 63
Wickhampton, Robert (bishop of Salisbury [1274–84]), 121 n56
Wickwane, William (archbishop of York [1279–85], chancellor of York), 44, 93, 212, 216, 256
Willard, former cook of Bishop Wyche of Chichester, 260
Willekin, legatee of Bishop Aquablanca of Hereford, 262
William, barber of Bishop Gravesend of London, 260
William, brewer of Bishop Suffield of Norwich, 261
William, clerk of Bishop Aquablanca of Hereford, 227
William, Duke of Normandy, 41 n4
Willliam, *hostiarius* of Bishop Aquablanca of Hereford, 263

William, *nuntius* of Bishop Suffield of
    Norwich, 261
William, *nuntius* of Bishop Wyche of
    Chichester, 260
William, page of Bishop Suffield of
    Norwich, 261
William (Brother), papal *hostiarius*, 255
William, rector of Bramber, 230 n102
William, rector of Gatintone and clerk of
    Queen Eleanor, 256
William, servant at Buckden of Bishop
    Hugh of Wells of Lincoln, 261
William, servant at Leicester of Bishop
    Hugh of Wells of Lincoln, 261
William, scribe of Hugh of Wells, bishop of
    Lincoln, 228
William, skinner of Bishop Suffield of
    Norwich, 262
William, son of Fulk, archdeacon of Stow,
    192
William, tailor of Archbishop Winchelsey
    of Canterbury, 233
William de Abingdon, 226
William de Anlauby, 196 n40
William le Archer, 14 n5
William de Aysterby, 162
William de Bereford, 257
William de Biggleswade, 173–4
William de Blockley, 201 n79
William Blund de Lincoln, 174
William de Bolington, 256
William de Bosco, 164 n164
William de Bramber, 230
William de Brampton, 179 n48
William de Braybrok, 226
William de Brumpton, 179 n48
William of the bushels, legatee of Bishop
    Aquablanca of Hereford, 262
William de Cardene. *See* William de
    Sardinia
William Cauchais de Tinghurst, 261
William de Corneria, 174 n25
William de Croy, 56 n71
William de Cryk, 55
William de Estiniaco, 154, 157, 165
William fitzWalter, 73
William de Fotheringhay, 257
William de Foceston, 229
William de la Gare, 76, 165, 179 n46
William de Hancot, 253
William Howard, 257

William de Humfrayville, 54 n67
Willliam de Insula, 252
William de Kempsey, 230
William de Lanham, 120 n55
William de Langworth, 160–3
William de la Leye, 107
William de Lorey, 93
William de Luda, 76 n197
William de Luda, rector of Ailby.
    See Simon de Luda
William Lupus, 72, 261
Willliam Lyndwood, 28, 129–30
William Marsh, 226 n78
William de Merrow, 201 nn80–1, 202
William de Montfort, 237
William de Mortimer, 88 n33, 126 n82
William de Morton, 88 n33, 175
William de Newark, 77, 179 n46
William de Noyers, 100–1
William de Ockham, 117
William de Otteringham, 90–1
William de Passele, 230
William de Packenham, 229, 231
William Pikeril, 158–9, 162, 165, 207, 247
William de Plaiz, 38
William de Pocklington, 194 n33
William de la Pommery, 179
William de Rotherfield, 121 n56
William de Rothwell, 145
William le Rus de Bristol, 251
William de Saham, 92, 256
William de Saint Edmund, 203 n92
William de Saint Quentin, 107
William de Sardinia, 114, 161
William de Sausthorpe, 181
William de Schelving, 230
William Segin de Got, 57–8, 142
William de Selsey, 230
William de Southwell, 113 n17, 194, 198
William de Stow, 259
William de Swayfield, 175
William de Thornton, 196
William de Tunring, 261
William de Wells, 179
William de Whitwell, 229, 231
William de Winchecombe, 193
William de Wlchurch, 107 n160
William de Wodeford, 261
William de Wychingham, 229
wills of bishops, 126–7, 129, 210–11,
    224–38, 260–3

Wiltshire, archdeacon of, 150.
    See also Richard de Sottwell; Roger
    de Buscot
Wiltshire Eyre, 34
Winchcombe Abbey, 139
Winchelsey, Robert (archbishop of
    Canterbury [1294-1313]), 13-15,
    18, 20, 29, 34 n60, 43-4, 60-1, 73,
    78, 85, 92-3, 102, 104, 111, 127,
    130, 132-3, 143, 150, 159 n136,
    176, 208, 211-12, 215, 217 n35,
    222 n69, 230-4, 252, 257, 260
  vicar-general of, 230
Winchester,
  bishop of, 15, 18, 28, 32, 54 n67,
    65-7, 74, 91, 118-19, 172, 207.
    See also Exeter John de; Lusignan,
    Aymer de; Pontoise, John of;
    Raleigh, William; Roches, Peter des
  officialis of, 54 n67, 67, 111
  officiales sede vacante, 156
  pipe rolls of, 105-6, 204
  register of, 85
  diocese of, 51 n48, 55-6, 119 n41, 124
  officiales sede vacante, 156
Wing, church, 180 n49
Winwick, church, 195 n36, 199
Withington, church, 140 n20
Wittenham, church, 226 n80
Woburn, church, 196 n39
Wolford, church, 171
Wonston, church, 57-8
Woodeaton, church, 180 n50
Woolpit, church, 212, 217
Wootten Wawen, vicar of, 35
Worcester, bishops of, 19, 29, 46, 64, 73,
    93 n70, 111, 119 nn41-2, 120-1,
    123, 140 n20, 149, 174, 176,
    203. See also Blois, William of;
    Cantilupe, Walter; Forde, Baldwin
    of; Giffard, Godfrey; Gray, Walter;
    Roger, bishop of Worcester
  diocese of, 119 n41, 158 n51, 205
  prior/priory of, 64, 89 n36, 99, 134, 205,
    246 n26
    annals of priory of, 72, 246 n26
  Saint Peter's, Worcester, church, 93 n70
Worfield, church, 76 n200

Wormsley, prior, 139 n27
Worthen, church, 60 n101
Wotton, church, 55-6
Wyche, Richard (bishop of Chichester
    [1245-53]; chancellor of archbishop
    of Canterbury), 128-9, 206, 229-
    30, 232, 233 n17, 234, 236, 260
  officialis of, 230
Wyke, church, 111 n2
Wyle, Walter de la (bishop of Salisbury
    [1263-71]), 235
Wyndelaboys, legatee of Bishop Suffield of
    Norwich, 261

Yarmouth, 129
Yarnscombe, church, 136-7
Yarnton, church, 180 n50
York, 20
  archbishops of, 5, 13, 15, 17, 19, 28
    n21, 30, 44, 46, 48, 69, 110, 117,
    119 nn41-2, 121 n56, 124, 148,
    207 n118, 211. See also Geoffrey
    (Plantagenet); Giffard, Walter; Gray,
    Walter; Romeyn, John; Wickwane,
    William
  chancellor of, 118 n34
  Court of, 90, 252
  officialis of archbishop of, 18
  archdeacons of. See Aymo, archdeacon
    of York
  archdiocese of, 44, 73, 91 n52,
    119 n41
  chapter of, 36 n76, 121 n56, 211, 256
  canon of, 103
  chancellor of, 213, 215-16
  dean of, 44
  prebend in, 256. See also individual
    prebends
  treasurer of. See William de
    Rotherfield
  dean of Christianity of, 212
  hospital of Saint Peter's of, 212
  Saint Mary's Abbey, 61,
    69 n147
York, Robert of (bishop of Ely [1215-19,
    elect only]), 177
Yvo of the buttery of Archbishop
    Winchelsey of Canterbury, 233